Epistemic Modality

Epistemic Modality

EDITED BY
Andy Egan and Brian Weatherson

OXFORD
UNIVERSITY PRESS

OXFORD
UNIVERSITY PRESS

Great Clarendon Street, Oxford OX2 6DP

Oxford University Press is a department of the University of Oxford.
It furthers the University's objective of excellence in research, scholarship,
and education by publishing worldwide in

Oxford New York

Auckland Cape Town Dar es Salaam Hong Kong Karachi
Kuala Lumpur Madrid Melbourne Mexico City Nairobi
New Delhi Shanghai Taipei Toronto

With offices in

Argentina Austria Brazil Chile Czech Republic France Greece
Guatemala Hungary Italy Japan Poland Portugal Singapore
South Korea Switzerland Thailand Turkey Ukraine Vietnam

Oxford is a registered trade mark of Oxford University Press
in the UK and in certain other countries

Published in the United States
by Oxford University Press Inc., New York

© The several contributors 2011

The moral rights of the authors have been asserted
Database right Oxford University Press (maker)

First published 2011

British Library Cataloguing in Publication Data
Data available

Library of Congress Cataloging in Publication Data

Data available

Typeset by SPI Publisher Services, Pondicherry, India
Printed in Great Britain by
MPG Books Group, Bodmin and King's Lynn

ISBN 978–0–19–959159–6 (Hbk)
ISBN 978–0–19–959158–9 (Pbk)

Contents

Notes on Contributors

KENT BACH Department of Philosophy, San Francisco State University.

DAVID CHALMERS Research School of Social Sciences, Australian National University and Department of Philosophy, New York University.

ANDY EGAN Department of Philosophy, Rutgers University and Arché Philosophical Research Centre, University of St Andrews.

KAI VON FINTEL Department of Linguistics and Philosophy, Massachusetts Institute of Technology.

ANTHONY S. GILLIES Department of Philosophy, Rutgers University.

FRANK JACKSON Research School of Social Sciences, Australian National University and Department of Philosophy, Princeton University.

JOHN MACFARLANE Department of Philosophy, University of California, Berkeley.

JONATHAN SCHAFFER Philosophy Programme, Australian National University; Department of Philosophy, Rutgers University; and Arché Philosophical Research Centre, University of St Andrews.

ROBERT STALNAKER Department of Linguistics and Philosophy, Massachusetts Institute of Technology.

ERIC SWANSON Department of Philosophy, University of Michigan.

BRIAN WEATHERSON Department of Philosophy, Rutgers University and Arché Philosophical Research Centre, University of St Andrews.

STEPHEN YABLO Department of Linguistics and Philosophy, Massachusetts Institute of Technology.

SETH YALCIN Department of Philosophy, University of California, Berkeley.

Introduction: Epistemic Modals and Epistemic Modality

Brian Weatherson and Andy Egan

1. Epistemic Possibility and Other Types of Possibility

There is a lot that we don't know. That means that there are a lot of possibilities that are, epistemically speaking, open. For instance, we don't know whether it rained in Seattle yesterday. So, for us at least, there is an epistemic possibility where it rained in Seattle yesterday, and one where it did not. It's tempting to give a very simple analysis of epistemic possibility:

- A possibility is an epistemic possibility if we do not know that it does not obtain.

But this is problematic for a few reasons. One issue, one that we'll come back to, concerns the first two words. The analysis appears to quantify over possibilities. But what are they? As we said, that will become a large issue pretty soon, so let's set it aside for now. A more immediate problem is that it isn't clear what it is to have *de re* attitudes towards possibilities, such that we know a particular possibility does or doesn't obtain. Let's try rephrasing our analysis so that it avoids this complication.

- A possibility is an epistemic possibility if for every p such that p is true in that possibility, we do not know that p is false.

If we identify *possibilities* with metaphysical possibilities, this seems to rule out too much. Let p be any contingent claim whose truth value we don't know. We do know, since it follows from the meaning of *actually*, that p iff *actually* p is true. But that biconditional isn't true in any world where p's truth value differs from its actual truth value. So the only epistemic possibilities are ones where p's truth value is the same as it actually is. But p was arbitrary in this argument, so the only epistemic possibilities are ones where *every* proposition has the same truth value as it actually does. This seems to leave us with too few epistemic possibilities!

A natural solution is to drop the equation of *possibilities* here with metaphysical possibilities. We've motivated this by using a proposition that is easy to know to be true, though it isn't true in many metaphysical possibilities. There are many problems from the other direction; that is, there are many cases where we want to say that there is a certain kind of epistemic possibility, even though there is no matching metaphysical possibility. We'll go through five such examples.

First, there are necessary a posteriori claims that arise from the nature of natural kinds. The standard example here is *Water is atomic.* That couldn't be true; necessarily, anything atomic is not water. But until relatively recently, it was an epistemic possibility.

Second, there are claims arising from true, and hence metaphysically necessary, identity and non-identity statements. A simple example here is *Hesperus is not Phosphorus.* This could not be true; by necessity, these celestial bodies are identical. But it was an epistemic possibility.

Third, there are claims about location. It isn't quite clear what proposition one expresses by saying *It's five o'clock*, but, plausibly, the speaker is saying of a particular time that that very time is five o'clock. It's plausible that if that's true, it's true as a matter of necessity. (Could this very time have occurred earlier or later? It doesn't seem like it could have.) So a false claim about what time it is will be necessarily false. But often there will be a lot of epistemic possibilities concerning what time it is.

Temporal location raises further matters beyond the necessary a posteriori. We want there to be epistemic possibilities in which it is four o'clock, five o'clock, and so on. But it isn't altogether clear whether claims like that can be true in metaphysical possibilities. If we identify a metaphysical possibility with a possible world, then it isn't clear what would make it the case that it is four o'clock in a possible world. (What time is it in this possible world?) This might suggest there are different *kinds* of facts at a metaphysical possibility as at an epistemic possibility.

Fourth, there are issues about mathematics. Actually, there are two kinds of puzzle cases here. One concerns propositions that are logical consequences of our mathematical beliefs, but which we haven't figured out yet. Twenty years ago, it certainly seemed to be an epistemic possibility that the equation $a^n + b^n = c^n$ had positive integer solutions with $n > 2$. Now we know that there are no such solutions. Moreover, if mathematics is necessarily true, then there isn't even a metaphysical possibility in which there are such solutions. So we shouldn't think that there was some metaphysical possibility that twenty years ago we hadn't ruled out. Rather, we were just unsure what metaphysical possibilities there are.

Finally, there are issues about logic. (Some views on the nature of logic and mathematics will deny that our fourth and fifth categories are different.) Getting the metaphysics of taste right is hard. One option that we think at least can't be ruled out is that intuitionist logic is the correct logic of taste talk. That is, when it comes to taste, we don't even know that it's true that everything either is or is not tasty. But that doesn't mean we're committed to the existence of a possibility where it isn't true that everything is tasty or not tasty; if such a state isn't actual, it probably isn't possible. The liar paradox is even harder than the metaphysics of taste. Anything should be on the table, even the dialethist view that the Liar is both true and false. That is, the Liar might be true and false. In saying that, we certainly don't mean to commit to the existence of some possibility where the Liar is true and false. We're pretty sure (but not quite certain!) that no such possibility exists.

The last two cases might be dealt with by being more careful about what an epistemic possibility is. There are quite simple cases in which we want to resist the identification of epistemic possibilities with what we don't *know* to be the case. For discussion of several such cases, see Hacking (1967), Teller (1972), and DeRose (1991). If we could very easily come to know that p does not obtain, perhaps because p is clearly ruled out by things we do know, then intuitively it isn't the case that p is epistemically possible. If we know that if q then not p, and we know q, then p is not possible, even if we haven't put conditional and antecedent together to conclude that p is false. So we need to put some constraints on the epistemically possible beyond what we know to be false. Perhaps those constraints will go so far as to rule out *anything* inconsistent with what we know. In that case, it wasn't possible all along that Fermat's Last Theorem was false. And, assuming the non-classical approaches to taste and alethic paradoxes are incorrect, those approaches aren't even possibly correct. We're not endorsing this position, just noting that it is a way to rescue the idea that all epistemic possibilities are metaphysical possibilities.

The papers in this volume that most directly address these issues are by Frank Jackson, David Chalmers, and Robert Stalnaker. Jackson argues against the view that accounting for epistemic possibilities requires us to think that there is a kind of possibility, conceptual possibility, that is broader than metaphysical possibility. He briefly reviews the reasons some people have had for taking this position, including those we've just discussed, and some of the reasons he rejected in *From Metaphysics to Ethics*. But he adds some new arguments as well against this position, what he calls the 'two space' view of possibility. One argument says that if there is a possibility of any kind where water is not H_2O, then being water and being H_2O must be different properties by Leibniz's Law. But then we have an implausible necessary connection between distinct properties. Another argument turns on the difficulty of identifying the *water* in these supposed conceptual possibilities that are not metaphysically possible.

David Chalmers discusses what kind of thing epistemic possibilities, or as he calls them, 'scenarios', might be. He discusses the strengths, weaknesses, and intricacies of two proposals: what he calls the 'metaphysical' and 'epistemic' constructions. The metaphysical construction is fairly familiar: it takes epistemic possibilities to be centered possible worlds. The epistemic construction takes epistemic possibilities to be maximally possible sentences of a specially constructed language. The metaphysical construction requires several assumptions before it matches up with the intuitive notion of epistemic possibility, while the epistemic construction requires a primitive notion of epistemic possibility. But both constructions seem to illuminate the elusive notion of an epistemic possibility. Chalmers ends with a discussion of several applications of his constructions in semantics, in formal epistemology, and in moral psychology.

Another place where one finds an important role for a distinctively epistemic (or at least doxastic) sort of possibility is in theorizing about indicative conditionals. In Robert Stalnaker's contribution, he examines two types of accounts of indicative conditionals, which differ in where they locate the conditionality. One view analyzes assertions of indicative conditionals as a special sort of *conditional assertion*, and another analyzes them as an ordinary assertion of a special sort of *conditional proposition*. Stalnaker argues that the two views are not so different as we might initially have thought.

2.   Three Approaches to Epistemic Modals

Even when we settle the issue of what epistemic possibilities are, we are left with many issues about how to talk about them. Speakers will often say that something is (epistemically) possible, or that it might be true. (It's plausible that claims that *p* must be true, or that *p* is probable, are closely related to these, but we'll stick to claims about (epistemic) possibility at least for this introduction.) It's plausible to think that a proposition isn't possible or impossible *simpliciter*, it's rather that it is possible or impossible relative to some person, some group, some evidence, or some information. Yet statements of epistemic possibility in plain English do not make any explicit reference to such a person, group, evidence set, or information state. One of the key issues confronting a semanticist attempting to theorize about epistemic modals is what to do about this lack of a reference. We'll look at three quite different approaches for dealing with this lack: contextualist, relativist, and expressivist.

2.1. Contextualism

Consider a particular utterance, call it *u*, made by speaker *s*, of the form *a might be F*, where the *might* here is intuitively understood as being epistemic in character. To a first approximation, the sentence is saying *a*'s being *F* is consistent with, or not ruled out by, a certain body of knowledge. But whose body of knowledge? Not God's, presumably, for then *a might be F* would be true iff *a is F* is true, and that's implausible. The contextualist answer is that the relevant body of knowledge is supplied by context.

When discussing the ways in which context fills in content, some writers will start with the pronoun *I* as an example. And to some extent it's a useful example. The sentence *I am a fool* doesn't have truth-conditional content outside of a context of utterance. But any utterance of that sentence does express something truth conditional. Which truth-conditional sentence it expresses is dependent on facts about the context of its use. In fact, it is dependent on just one fact, namely who utters it. So when Andy utters *I am a fool* he expresses the proposition that Andy is a fool. And when Brian utters *I am a fool* he expresses the proposition that Brian is a fool.

So far *I* is a useful example of a context-sensitive expression. But in many ways it is an unusual example of context-sensitivity, and focussing too much on it can lead to an overly simplistic view of how context-sensitive terms work. In particular, *I* has three properties that are unusual for a context-sensitive expression.

- Its content in a context is computable from the context by a simple algorithm—namely *the content is the speaker*.
- Its content does not depend on any properties of the intended audience of the utterance.
- It behaves exactly the same way in embedded and unembedded contexts.

Some terms have none of these properties. Consider, for example, *we*.

There isn't any obvious algorithm for computing the content of a particular use of *we*. The content may depend on the intentions of the speaker. It may depend on which people have been talked about. In sentences of the form *We are F*, different values of *F* might constrain what values can be rationally assigned to *we*. And when that is so, the interpretation of *we* will (usually) be constrained to those groups.

Perhaps most notably, it depends a lot on the audience. If S is talking to H, and says *We should grab some lunch*, the content is that *S and H should grab some lunch*. And that's the content because H is the intended audience of the utterance. Intended audiences can change quickly. If Andy says *We will finish the paper this afternoon, then we will go for a walk*, talking to Brian when he utters the first conjunct, and Fido when he utters the second, the content is that Andy and Brian will finish the paper this afternoon, then Andy and Fido will go for a walk.

That *we* has neither of the first two properties is uncontroversial. What is perhaps a little more controversial is that it does not have the third either. When *we* is in an unembedded context it (usually) behaves like a free (plural) variable. Under certain embeddings, it can behave like a bound variable. Barbara Partee and Phillipe Schlenker offer the following examples.

(1) John often comes over for Sunday brunch. Whenever someone else comes over too, we (all) end up playing trios. (Partee, 1989)
(2) Each of my colleagues is so difficult that at some point or other we've had an argument. (Schlenker, 2003)

In neither case does *we* contribute a group consisting of the speaker plus some salient individuals. Indeed, in neither case does it so much as contribute a group, since it is (or at least behaves like) a bound variable. There's nothing in the contextualist story about *we* that prevents this.

It's worthwhile reviewing these facts about *we*, because on the most plausible contextualist stories about *might*, it too has these three properties. The contextualist theory we have in mind says that the content of *u* is *For all that group X could know using methods M, a is F*. The group *X* will usually consist of the speaker and some salient others, perhaps including the intended audience. The salient methods might include little more than easy deduction from what is currently known, or may include some wider kinds of investigation. (See DeRose (1991) for arguments that the relevant methods include more than deduction, and that they are contextually variable.)

Now it isn't part of the contextualist theory that there is an easy method for determining who is in *X*, or what methods are in M. So in that respect it is like *we*. But, just as the group denoted by *we* typically includes the intended audience of the utterance, the group *X* will typically include the intended audience of *u*. And the methods M will typically include any method that can be easily carried out. This can be used to explain some phenomena about disagreement. So if Andy says, to Brian, *a might be F*, and Brian knows that *a* is not *F* (or can easily deduce this from what he knows), Brian can disagree with what Andy says. That is, he can disagree with the proposition that it is consistent with what members of the conversation know that *a* is *F*. And, the contextualist says, that's just what Andy did say. If Brian presents Andy with his grounds for disagreement, Andy might well retract what he said. Since arguments about disagreeing with utterances like *u* have been prominent in the literature, it is worth noting that the contextualist theory can explain at least some facts about disagreement.

Nor is it part of the contextualist theory that *might* behaves exactly the same way in embedded and unembedded contexts. Indeed, like *we*, *might* can behave like a bound variable. On the most natural reading of *Every pedestrian fears that they might be being watched*, there is no single group *X* such that every pedestrian fears that for all *X* (could easily) know, that pedestrian is being watched. Rather, every pedestrian fears that for all they themselves know, they are being watched. The naturalness of this reading is no embarrassment to the contextualist theory, since it is a commonplace that terms that usually get their values from context can also, in the right setting, behave like bound variables.

Indeed, thinking about these parallels between context-sensitive expressions and epistemic modals seems to provide some support for contextualism. In his contribution to the volume, Jonathan Schaffer argues that various features of the way epistemic modals behave in larger sentences support the idea that an evaluator place must be realized in the syntax. For instance, consider the natural interpretation of "Anytime you are going for a walk, if it might rain, you should bring an umbrella." We interpret that as saying that whenever you go for a walk, you should bring an umbrella if your evidence *at that time* is consistent with rain. Schaffer interprets that as evidence that there is hidden syntactic structure in epistemic modals, and argues that the contextualist offers the best account of how the hidden structure gets its semantic values.

So the contextualist has a lot of explanatory resources, and a lot of flexibility in their theory, which are both clear virtues. But there are some limits to the flexibility. There are some things that the contextualist, at least as we're using the term 'contextualist', is committed to. In particular, the contextualist is committed to the content of a particular speech act (or at least of a particular assertion) being absolute, not assessor-relative. And they're committed to the truth value of those contents being the same relative to any assessor. Let's give those two commitments names.

(C) The semantic content of an assertion is the same relative to any assessors.

(T) The truth value of the semantic content of an assertion is the same relative to any assessors.

The first of these rules out the possibility that the semantic content of an assertion differs with respect to different groups. The second rules out the possibility that semantic contents have assessor relative truth values. Modern relativists have proposed theories that dispense with these dogmas, and we'll investigate those in the next section, after going over some of the motivations for relativism.

2.2. Relativism

In many fields, relativism is motivated by instances of "faultless disagreement", and epistemic modals are not left out of this trend. Here is the kind of case that we used in Egan, Hawthorne, and Weatherson 2005 to motivate relativism.

Consider the following kind of case. Holmes and Watson are using a primitive bug to listen in on Moriarty's discussions with his underlings as he struggles to avoid Holmes's plan to trap him. Moriarty says to his assistant

(24) Holmes might have gone to Paris to search for me.

Holmes and Watson are sitting in Baker Street listening to this. Watson, rather inexplicably, says "That's right" on hearing Moriarty uttering (24). Holmes is quite perplexed. Surely Watson knows that he is sitting right here, in Baker Street, which is definitely not in Paris. (Egan, Hawthorne, and Weatherson, 2005: 146–7)

Here we have Watson somewhat surprisingly *agreeing* with Moriarty. In some sense, it seems wrong for him to have done so. He should have disagreed. Well, imagine that he did, by saying "That's not right." The quick argument for relativism is that the contextualist cannot make sense of this. Whatever group's knowledge Moriarty intended to be talking about when he spoke, it presumably didn't include Holmes and Watson; it just included him and his intended audience, i.e. the underlings. And it's true that for all *they* know, Holmes is in Paris. So the content of Moriarty's utterance is true. But it seems that Watson can properly disagree with it (and can't properly agree with it). That, we thought, was a problem.

There are three kinds of response to this argument on behalf of the contextualist that we think look promising. All of these responses are discussed in von Fintel and Gillies (2008). We might look harder at the denotation of the "that" in Watson's reply, we might think again about what the relevant group is, and we might look at other cases where the contextualist story is more promising, as a way of motivating the first two responses. Let's look at these in turn.

Above we said that Watson *disagreed* with Moriarty by saying "That's not right." But that's potentially reading too much into the data. What seems correct is that Watson can say "That's not right." But that's only to disagree with Moriarty *if* the "that" denotes what Moriarty said. And that might not be true. It's possible that it picks out, say, the embedded proposition that Holmes has gone to Paris. And it's fine for Watson to disagree with that.

Even if Watson is disagreeing with the semantic content of Moriarty's utterance, it might be that he's doing so properly, because what Moriarty said is false. That might be the case because it might be that, in virtue of hearing the utterance, Watson became part of the relevant group X. Typically speaker intentions, particularly singular speaker intentions, are not the final word in determining the content of a context-sensitive expression. If Brian points over his shoulder, thinking a nice glass of shiraz is behind him, and says *That is tasty*, while in fact what he is pointing at is a vile confection of Vegemite-infused Chardonnay, he's said something false. The simplest thing to say about a case like this is that Brian intended the denotation of "That" to be the thing he was pointing at, whatever it is. Similarly, Moriarty might have intended the relevant group X to be whoever heard the utterance at that time, even if he didn't know Watson was in that group. (Or it might be that, whatever Moriarty's intentions, the semantic rules and conventions for "might" in English determine that the relevant group includes everybody who heard the utterance at the time.)

This second response would seem somewhat ad hoc were it not for a class of examples von Fintel and Gillies describe concerning assessors from radically different contexts. Typically the anti-contextualist commentary on cases like these suggests that any hearer who knows that a is not F can disagree with u. But that doesn't seem to be in general true.

Or consider the case of Detective Parker. He has been going over some old transcripts from Al Capone's court case in the 1920s—Capone is being asked about where some money is in relation to a particular safe:

(20) a. Capone: The loot might be in the safe.
     b. Parker: ??Al was wrong/What Al said is false. The safe was cracked by Geraldo in the 80s and there was nothing inside. (2008: 86)

The knowledge of at least *some* hearers, such as Detective Parker, does not seem to count for assessing the correctness of Capone's speech. A contextualist might suggest that's because contemporaneous hearers are in the relevant group, and later reviewers are not.

So there are definitely some contextualism-friendly lines of response available to the argument for relativism from disagreement. But interestingly, some of these contextualist responses do not work as well as a response to a similar argument from *agreement*. Imagine that Andy, after doing some reading on the publicly available evidence, correctly concludes that it doesn't rule out Prince Albert Victor. He doesn't think this is very likely, but thinks it is possible. Andy hears someone on TV talking about the

Ripper who says "Prince Albert Victor might have been Jack the Ripper", and Andy says "That's true." Intuitively Andy is right to agree with the TV presenter, but this is a little hard to explain on the contextualist theory.

Note that here we can't say that Andy is agreeing because he is agreeing with the embedded proposition, namely that Prince Albert Victor was the Ripper. That's because he *doesn't* agree with that; he thinks it is an open but unlikely possibility.

Nor does it particularly matter that Andy, as one of the people watching the TV show, is part of the relevant group X. All that would show is that if Andy knew Prince Albert Victor wasn't the Ripper, the presenter's assertion is false. But unless Andy *is* the group X, the fact that Andy's knowledge, or even what is available to Andy, does not rule out the Prince does not mean Andy should agree with the statement. For all Andy knows, someone else watching, perhaps even someone else the presenter intends to include in her audience, has evidence exculpating the Prince. If that's right, then he does not know that the proposition the contextualist says the speaker asserted is true. But yet he seems justified in agreeing with the presenter. This seems like a real problem for contextualism.

A quite different objection to contextualism comes from metasemantic considerations. The most casual reflection on the intuitive content of utterances like u suggests there is staggeringly little rhyme or reason to which group X or method M might be relevant. The argument here isn't that the contextualist's *semantic* proposal is mistaken in some way. Rather, the argument is that the accompanying *metasemantic* theory, i.e. the theory of how semantic values get fixed, is intolerably complicated. Slightly more formally, we can argue as follows.

1. If contextualism is true, the metasemantic theory of how a particular use of "might" gets its semantic value is hideously complicated.
2. Metasemantic theories about how context-sensitive terms get their values on particular occasions are never hideously complicated.
3. So, contextualism is false.

The problem with this argument, as Michael Glanzberg (2007) has argued, is that premise 2 seems to be false. There are examples of uncontroversially context-sensitive terms, like "that", for which the accompanying metasemantic theory is, by any standard, hideously complicated. So the prospects of getting to relativism from metasemantic complexity are not, we think, promising.

But there is a different metasemantic motivation for relativism that we think is a little more promising. Compare the difference between (1) and (2).

(1) Those guys are in trouble, but they don't know that they are.
(2) ??Those guys are in trouble, but they might not be.

Something has gone wrong in (2). This suggests that (2) can't be used to express (1). That is, there's no good interpretation of (2) where those guys are the group X. This is a little surprising, since we've made the guys pretty salient. Cases like this have motivated what we called the *Speaker Inclusion Constraint* (hereafter SIC) in

"Epistemic Modals in Context." That is, in unembedded uses of "might" the group X always includes the speaker. Now the explanation of the problem with (2) is that for the speaker to assert the first clause, she must know that the guys are in trouble, but if that's the case, and she's in group X, then the second clause is false.

Now a generalization like this doesn't look like it should be grounded in the *meaning* (in some sense of "meaning") of "might." For comparison, it seems to be part of the meaning of "we" that it is a first-person plural pronoun. It isn't just a meta-semantic generalization that the speaker is always one of the group denoted by "we." By analogy, it is part of the meaning of "might" that the speaker is always part of the group X.

Further, when the meaning of a context-sensitive expression constrains its value, those constraints still hold when the term is used as a bound variable. For instance, it is part of the meaning of "she" that it denotes a female individual. If Smith is male, then the semantic content of *She is happy* can't be that Smith is happy. Similarly, when "she" is behaving like a bound variable, the only values it can take are female individuals. So we can't use *Every student fears she will fail the test* to quantify over some students some of whom are male. And there's no interpretation of *Every class hopes we will win* where it means that every class hopes that that class will win. Even when under a quantifier and an attitude-ascribing verb, "we" must still pick out a group that includes the speaker. The natural generalization is that constraints on context supplied by meaning do not get overridden by other parts of the sentence.

The problem for contextualists about "might" is that it doesn't behave as you'd expect given these generalizations. In particular, the SIC doesn't hold when "might" is in certain embeddings. So there is a reading of *Every student fears they might have failed* where it means that every student fears that, for all *they* know, they failed. The knowledge of the speaker isn't relevant here. Indeed, even if the speaker knows that many students did not fail, this sentence can be properly uttered. This suggests the following argument.

1. If contextualism is true, then the explanation of the SIC is that it is part of the meaning of "might" that the relevant group X includes the speaker.
2. If it is part of the meaning of "might" that the relevant group X includes the speaker, then this must be true for all uses of "might", included embedded uses.
3. When "might" is used inside the scope of an attitude ascription, the relevant group need not include the speaker.
4. So, contextualism is not true.

Premise 1 would be false if the metasemantics was allowed to be systematic enough to explain why the SIC holds even though it is not part of the meaning. Premise 2 would be false if we allowed "might" to have a systematically different meaning inside and outside the scope of attitude ascriptions. And premise 3 would be false if any attitude ascriptions that are made are, contrary to intuition, tacitly about the speaker's knowledge. Since none of these seems particularly plausible, there does seem to be a problem for contextualism here.

In their contribution to this volume, Kai von Fintel and Thony Gillies reject one of the presuppositions of the argument we've just presented. Classical contextualism, what they call 'the canon', says that context picks out a particular group, and an utterance of "It might be that *p*" is true iff that group's information is consistent with *p*. That's what we've taken as the stalking horse in this section, and von Fintel and Gillies are certainly right that it is the canonical version of contextualism. Von Fintel and Gillies agree that the broad outline of this contextualist story is correct. But they deny that context picks out a determinate group, or a determinate body of information. Rather, uttering an epistemic modal will "put into play" a number of propositions of the form "For all group *G* knows, *p*." This ambiguity, or perhaps better indeterminacy, is crucial they argue to the pragmatic role that epistemic modals play. And once we are sensitive to it, they claim, we see that contextualism has more explanatory resources than we'd previously assumed, and so the motivation for relativism fades away.

In summary, there are four motivations for relativism that have been floated in the literature. These are:

- Intuitions about disagreement;
- Intuitions about agreement;
- Arguments from metasemantic complexity; and
- Arguments from semantic change in attitude ascriptions.

As noted, the third argument doesn't seem very compelling, and it is a fairly open question whether the first works. But the second and fourth do look like good enough arguments to motivate alternatives.

2.3. Two Kinds of Relativism

We said above that contextualism is characterized by two theses, repeated here for convenience.

(C) The semantic content of an assertion is the same relative to any assessors.

(T) The truth value of the semantic content of an assertion is the same relative to any assessors.

So there are two ways to be a relativist, deny (C) and deny (T). One might deny both, but we'll leave that option out of our survey.

What we call *content relativism* denies (C). The picture is that contextualists were right to posit a variable X in the structure of an epistemic modal claim. But the contextualists were wrong to think that X gets its value from the context of utterance. Rather, the value of X is fixed in part by the context of assessment. In the simplest (plausible) theory, X is the speaker and the assessor. So if Smith asserts that Jones might be happy, the content of that assertion, relative to Andy, is that for all Smith and Andy know, Jones is happy, while relative to Brian its content is that for all Smith and Brian know, Jones is happy.

The primary motivation for content relativism is that it keeps quite a bit of the contextualist picture, while allowing enough flexibility to explain the phenomena that troubled contextualism. So for the content relativist, contents are exactly the same kinds of propositions as the contextualist thinks they are. So we don't need to tell a new kind of story about what it is for a content to be true, to be accepted, etc. Further, because we keep the variable X, we can explain the 'bound variable' readings of epistemic modals discussed in the first section.

A worry about content relativism is that the 'metasemantic' argument against contextualism might equally well tell against it. The worry there was that the constraints on X seemed to depend, in an unhappy way, on where in the sentence it appeared. The content relativist has a move available here. She can say that as a rule, whenever there's a variable like X attached to a term, and that term is in an attitude ascription, then the variable is bound to the subject of the ascription. This might be an interesting generalization. For instance, if she is a content relativist about both epistemic modals and predicates of personal taste, she has a single explanation for why both types of terms behave differently inside and outside attitude ascriptions.

There are two interesting "near cousins" of content relativism. One is a kind of content pluralism. We might hold (a) that an assertion's content is not relative to an assessor, but (b) some assertions have many contents. So if s says *a might be F*, and this is assessed by many hearers, s asserts *For all s and h know, a is F*, for each h who hears and assesses the speech. Now when a hearer h_1 does this, she'll probably focus on one particular content of s's assertion, namely that *For all s and h_1 know, a is F*. But the content pluralist accepts (while the content relativist denies) that even relative to h_1, s's assertion also had the content *For all s and h_2 know, a is F*, where h_2 is a distinct assessor.

Another near cousin is the view, defended in this volume by Kent Bach, that the semantic content of an epistemic modal is typically not a complete proposition. In the case just described, it might be that the semantic content of what s says is *For all_knows, a is F*, and that's not a proposition. Now a given hearer, h, might take s to have communicated to them that *For all s and h know, a is F*, but that's not because that's the semantic content of what s says. It's not the absolute content (à la contextualism), the content relative to h (à la content relativism) or one of the contents (à la content pluralism).

It's a very big question how we should discriminate between these theories. Some readers may even worry that there is no substantive differences between the theories, they are in some sense saying the same thing in different words. One big task for future research is to clearly state the competing theories in the vicinity of here, and find arguments that discriminate between them.

A quite different kind of relativism denies (T). This view says that the content itself of an assertion can be true for some assessors, and false for others. Such a view is not unknown in recent philosophy. In the 1970s and 1980s (and to a lesser extent in subsequent years) there was a debate between temporalists and eternalists about propositions. The temporalists thought that a tensed proposition, i.e. the content of a tensed assertion, could be true at one time and false at another. The eternalists denied this, either taking truth to be invariant across times, or in some cases denying that it even made sense to talk about truth being relative to something, e.g. a time.

Contemporary forms of truth relativism generalize the temporalist picture. The temporalists thought that propositions are true or false relative to a world-time pair. Modern relativists think that propositions are true or false relative to a world-assessor pair, or what loosely following Quine (1969) we might call a *centered world*. (Quine used this to pick out any world-place-time triple, but since most times and places don't have assessors at them, world-assessor pairs, or even world-assessor-time triples, are more restricted.) For example, as a first pass at a truth-relativism about predicates of personal taste, one might propose that the proposition expressed by a typical utterance of "beer is tasty" will be true at any centered world where the person at the center of the world likes the taste of beer.

The truth relativist has an easy explanation of the data that motivated the rejection of contextualism. Recall two puzzles for the contextualist about terms like "tasty": that it is so easy to agree with claims about what's tasty, and that reports of the form *X thinks that beer is tasty* are always about X's attitude towards beer, not about X's beliefs about how the speaker finds beer. On the first puzzle, note that if to agree with an assertion is to agree with its propositional content, and that content is true at the center of your world iff you find beer tasty, then to agree with an assertion that beer is tasty, you don't have to launch an inquiry into the sincerity of the speaker, you just have to check whether you like beer. If you're in a world full in insincere speakers, and abundant beer, that's relatively easy.

On the second puzzle, if propositional attitude ascriptions report the subject's attitude towards a proposition, and if a proposition is a set of centered worlds, then the subject's attitude towards "Beer is tasty" should be given by their attitude towards whether that proposition is true in their centered world. That is, it should be given by their attitude towards beer. And that's just what we find.

The extension of all this to epistemic modals is more or less straightforward. The simplest truth relativist theory says that an utterance of the form *a might be F* is true iff, for all the assessor at the center of the world knows, *a* is *F*. As Richard Dietz (2008) has pointed out, this won't do as it stands. If the speaker knows *a* is not *F*, then their utterance seems like it should be false relative to everyone. (Conversely, a speaker who knows *a* is *F* speaks truly, relative to any assessor, when they say *a must be F*.) If we're convinced of this, the solution is a mild complication of the theory. The utterance is both somewhat context-sensitive, and somewhat relative. So *s*'s utterance of *a might be F* is true at a centered world iff for all *s* plus the person at the center of the world know, *a* is *F*. We might want to add more complications (is it knowledge that matters or available information, for example?) but that's one candidate truth relativist theory.

There are three worries we might have about truth relativism. One is a very big picture worry that the very notion of truth being relative is misguided. This is a theme of Herman Cappelen and John Hawthorne's *Relativism and Monadic Truth*. Another is that it overgenerates "explanations." We can't explain cases like the Capone/Parker example. And a third is that, by making propositions so different from what we thought they were, we'll have to redo a lot of philosophy of language that presupposed propositions have the same truth value for everyone. In particular, we'll have to rethink what an assertion is. (That challenge is addressed—in different ways—in recent work by John MacFarlane and by Andy Egan.)

The strongest defence of relativism in this volume comes from John MacFarlane. His work on tense (MacFarlane, 2003), and on knowledge attributions (MacFarlane, 2005a), and on the broader philosophical status of relativism and other rivals to classical contextualism (MacFarlane, 2005b 2009), have been immensely influential in the contemporary debates. Here he develops a *relativistic* semantics for epistemic modals, along the lines of the proposals he has offered elsewhere for tense and knowledge attributions. He argues that many phenomena, several of which we've discussed in this introduction, raise trouble for contextualism and promote relativism. These phenomena include third-party assessments, retraction, and disagreement. He argues that only the relativist can explain the troublemaking phenomena.

2.4. Expressivism

So far we've looked at two of our three major approaches to epistemic modals. The contextualist says that which proposition is asserted by an epistemic modal depends crucially on the context of utterance. The relativist says that the contextualist is ignoring the importance of the context of assessment. The content relativist says that they are ignoring the way in which the context of assessment partially determines what is said. The truth relativist says that they are ignoring the way in which propositions uttered have different truth values at different contexts of assessment.

The expressivist thinks that there is a common assumption behind all of these theories, and it is a mistaken assumption. The assumption is that when we're in the business of putting forward epistemic modals, we're in the business of *asserting* things that have *truth values*. The expressivist rejects that assumption. They say that when we say *a might be F*, we're not asserting that we are uncertain about whether *a* is *F*, we're expressing that uncertainty directly. The contextualists and relativists think that in making these utterances, we're expressing a second-order belief, i.e. a belief about our own knowledge, or lack thereof. The expressivists think we're expressing a much simpler mental state: uncertainty.

One way to motivate expressivism is to start with the anti-contextualist arguments, and then argue that relativism is not an acceptable way out. So we might, for instance, start with the argument from agreement. The expressivist notes that there are many ways to agree with a statement. If Smith says "Let's have Chinese for dinner", and

Jones agrees, there need not be any proposition that Smith asserted that Jones is agreeing to. We're happy to call all sorts of meetings of minds agreements. So the agreement phenomena that the contextualist can't explain, the expressivist can explain. When Smith says "Brown might be a spy", and Jones agrees, there isn't necessarily any proposition they both accept. Rather, their agreement consists in having a common mental state, namely uncertainty about whether Brown is a spy.

The expressivist may then run out any number of arguments against relativism. For instance, they might argue (against content relativism) that it is a requirement of a speech act being an assertion that it have a determinate content. And they might argue, perhaps motivated by theoretical considerations about the role of assertions in conversation, that contents which vary in truth value among hearers couldn't be contents of assertions. If true, that would rule out truth relativism. We're moved, perhaps by elimination as much as anything, to expressivism.

There are more direct arguments for expressivism as well. Isaac Levi (1996: 55) motivated a view on which epistemic modals don't have truth values by thinking about learning. Imagine someone previously thought that Brown might be a spy, perhaps on quite good grounds, then they learn that he is not a spy. If that's all they learned, then it seems odd to say that there's something that they previously knew, that now they don't know. It seems learning shouldn't destroy knowledge. That's what happens in standard models for belief revision (which were one of Levi's primary concerns) and it is independently plausible. But if epistemic modals express propositions, and those are true or false, then there is a proposition that the person did know and now doesn't know, namely that Brown might be a spy.

There are clearly a few possible responses to this argument. For one thing, we could make the epistemic modal claims explicitly tensed. Both before and after the learning experience, the subject knew that Brown might, at t_1, have been a spy, but didn't know that Brown might, at t_2, have been a spy. (Indeed, they learned that that was false.) Or, and this is more in keeping with the spirit of this introduction, we might spell out the epistemic modal claim. Before and after the learning experience, the subject knew that it was consistent with everything the subject knew prior to the learning experience that Brown was a spy. So there's no information lost.

The problem with this move is that it seems to make epistemic modals overly complex. Intuitively, it is possible for a child to grasp a modal, and for the most natural interpretation of that modal to be epistemic, without the child having the capacity to form second-order thoughts. (This point is one that Seth Yalcin uses in his argument for a kind of expressivism in this volume.) This question seems like it would be good to test empirically, though we don't know of any existing evidence that settles the question. Introspectively, it does seem that one can think that the cat might be in the garden without thinking about one's own epistemic or doxastic states as such. Those kinds of introspections might tell in favour of an approach which identifies epistemic modality with a distinct kind of relation to content, rather than a distinct kind of content.

Following important work by Gibbard (1990), there is a natural way to formal-ize an expressivist theory of epistemic modality. Identify a "context" with a set of propositions. Sentences, whether epistemic modals or simple sentences, are satisfied or unsatisfied relative to world-context pairs, where a world and a context make a pair iff every proposition in the context is true at that world. Then an epistemic modal, say *Brown might be a spy*, is satisfied by such a pair iff *Brown is a spy* is consistent with everything in the context. A simple sentence, like *White is a spy* is satisfied by such a pair iff *White is a spy* is true at the world. The pairing becomes useful when consid-ering, say, conjunctions. A conjunction is satisfied iff both conjuncts are satisfied. So *White is a spy and Brown might be* is satisfied by a world-context pair iff White is a spy at the world, and Brown's being a spy is consistent with the context.

So far this looks a lot like relativism. A world-context pair is just like a centered world, with the context being what's known by the person at the center of the world. If we apply the formalism to real-life cases, perhaps taking the contexts to be genuine contexts in the sense of Stalnaker (1978), the two formalisms might look very close indeed.

But there is, or at least we hope there is, a substantive philosophical difference between them. The expressivist has a restricted sense of what it is to make an assertion, and of what it is for an expression to be an expression of a truth. The expressivist most insistently does not identify satisfaction with truth. The only sentences that are true or false are sentences that are satisfied by a world-context pair $w-c_1$ iff they are satisfied by every other pair starting with the same world. The expression of such a sentence, and perhaps only of such a sentence, constitutes an assertion. Otherwise it constitutes some other speech act.

And this is no mere difference in how to use the words 'truth', 'assertion', and so on. Nor is it even just a difference about truth and assertion and so on. It hopefully makes a difference to what predictions we make about the way epistemic modals embed, especially how they embed in propositional attitude ascriptions. We used that fact to argue against expressivism in "Epistemic Modals in Context", since we thought there were in some cases *more* examples of successful embedding of epistemic modals, especially in conditionals, than the expressivist would predict. On the other hand Seth Yalcin uses facts about embedding to argue, in his paper in this volume, in favour of expressivism. He argues that on a non-expressivist view, we should be able to *suppose* that *p* is true but might not be true, and that can't be supposed.

This argument is part of the argument by elimination that Yalcin posits against what he calls 'descriptivism' about epistemic modals in this contribution to the volume. He uses 'descriptivism' to pick out a broad category of theories about epistemic modals that includes both contextualism and relativism. He argues against all descriptivist views, and in favour of what he calls 'expressivism'. He says that when someone utters an epistemic modal, they do not describe their own knowledge (or the knowledge of someone else), rather they express their own mental state. Some of Yalcin's arguments for expressivism are related to arguments against contextualism; in particular he thinks like we do that there isn't a viable form of contextualism. But he also thinks that there are problems for relativism, such as the difficulty in supposing Moore paradoxical propositions. He also notes that it is a puzzle for descriptivists to make sense of belief ascriptions involving epistemic modals. On a descriptivist model, a sentence like "X believes that it might be that p" reports the existence of a second-order belief state. But Yalcin notes there are reasons to doubt that is right. He develops in detail an expressivist model that avoids what he takes to be shortcomings of descriptivist approaches.

The two papers we haven't discussed so far, those by Eric Swanson and Stephen Yablo, are both related to this expressivist family of theories, though their positive proposals head off in distinctive directions.

Eric Swanson's contribution locates epistemic modals within a broader category, which he calls "the language of subjective uncertainty." He also emphasizes the diversity of epistemic modal locutions, and draws attention to the risks involved in focusing too closely on just a few examples. In the literature so far, "might" and "must" have tended to get the lion's share of the attention, while other sorts of epistemic modality—including the more explicitly quantitative sorts ("four to one against that", "there's a 55% chance that", etc.)—have gone mostly unnoticed. Swanson argues that attending to other instances of the language of subjective uncertainty serves to undermine many of the standard proposals about epistemic "might" and "must", and motivates a *probabilistic* semantics.

Somewhat relatedly, Stephen Yablo develops a theory about epistemic modals where their primary function is not to state facts about the world, but to update the conversational score. Theories of this kind are quite familiar from the dynamic semantics tradition, but Yablo notes that the existing dynamic theories of epistemic modals are quite implausible. One of the challenges a dynamic approach to epistemic modals faces is to say how we should update a context (or a belief state) with *It might be that p* when the context previously was incompatible with *p*. Yablo adopts some suggestions from David Lewis's "A Puzzle about Permission" (Lewis, 1979) to try and solve this puzzle.

References

Cappelen, Herman, and Hawthorne, John (2009). *Relativism and Monadic Truth* (Oxford: Oxford University Press).

DeRose, Keith (1991). "Epistemic Possibilities", *Philosophical Review* 100: 581–605.

Dietz, Richard (2008). "Epistemic Modals and Correct Disagreement", in Manuel García-Carpintero and Max Kölbel (eds.), *Relative Truth* (Oxford: Oxford University Press), 239–64.

Egan, Andy (2007). "Epistemic Modals, Relativism and Assertion", *Philosophical Studies* 133: 1–22.

——Hawthorne, John, and Weatherson, Brian (2005). "Epistemic Modals in Context", in Gerhard Preyer and George Peter (eds.), *Contextualism in Philosophy: Knowledge, Meaning, and Truth* (Oxford: Oxford University Press), 131–68.

Gibbard, Allan (1990). *Wise Choices, Apt Feelings: A Theory of Normative Judgment* (Cambridge Mass.: Harvard University Press).

Glanzberg, Michael (2007). "Context, Content, and Relativism", *Philosophical Studies* 136: 1–29.

Hacking, Ian (1967). "Possibilities", *Philosophical Review* 76: 343–68.

Levi, Isaac (1996). *For the Sake of the Argument: Ramsey Test Conditionals, Inductive Inference and Nonmonotonic Reasoning* (Cambridge: Cambridge University Press).

Lewis, David (1979). "A problem about permission", repr. in Lewis, *Papers in Ethics and Social Philosophy* (Cambridge: Cambridge University Press), 20–33.

MacFarlane, John (2003). "Future Contingents and Relative Truth", *Philosophical Quarterly* 53: 321–36.

—— (2005a). "The Assessment Sensitivity of Knowledge Attributions", *Oxford Studies in Epistemology* 1: 197–233.

—— (2005b). "Making Sense of Relative Truth", *Proceedings of the Aristotelian Society* 105: 321–39.

—— (2009). "Nonindexical Contextualism", *Synthese* 166: 231–50.

Partee, Barbara H. (1989). "Binding Implicit Variables in Quantified Contexts", in Caroline Wiltshire, Randolph Graczyk, and Bradley Music (eds.), *Papers from the Twenty-fifth Regional Meeting of the Chicago Linguistic Society* (Chicago: Chicago Linguistic Society), 342–56.

Quine, Willard van Orman (1969). "Propostional Objects", in his *Ontological Relativity and Other Essays* (New York: Columbia University Press), 139–60.

Schlenker, Philippe (2003). "Indexicality, Logophoricity, and Plural Pronouns", in Jacqueline Lecarme (ed.), *Research in Afroasiatic Grammar II* (Selected Papers from the Fifth Conference on Afroasiatic Languages, Paris, 2000) (Amsterdam: John Benjamins), 409–28.

Stalnaker, Robert (1978). "Assertion", in Peter Cole (ed.), *Pragmatics: Syntax and Semantics 9* (New York: Academic Press), 315–32.

Teller, Paul (1972). "Epistemic Possibility", *Philosophia* 2: 303–20.

von Fintel, Kai, and Gillies, Anthony (2008). "CIA Leaks", *Philosophical Review* 117: 77–98.

1

Perspectives on Possibilities: Contextualism, Relativism, or What?

Kent Bach

There are many kinds of possibility: logical, metaphysical, nomological, physical, biological, technological, political—and epistemic. The focus here will be on epistemic possibilities and mainly on how we talk about them.[1]

Epistemic possibilities typically arise whenever we ask a *wh*-question, such as "Where is it?" or "Whodunit?". They arise, for example, when one searches for misplaced glasses or when a detective tries to solve a murder case. Ideally, the different answers that come to mind exhaust the relevant epistemic possibilities. They also arise when, in contemplating a course of action, we consider the risks involved. That's why people carry an umbrella, buy auto insurance, or get a colonoscopy. Finally, they arise in connection with knowledge claims. We think we know something (or are tempted to draw a certain conclusion or to assert something), but then a counterpossibility occurs to us and we think again. Or someone else claims to know something and we object by way of raising a counterpossibility, something that if it obtained would directly contradict the claim in question or at least weigh against it.

Epistemic possibilities are relative, not absolute. They are relative to bodies of information, or *perspectives*. This perspective relativity gives rise to some interesting puzzles, about the language of epistemic possibility as well as epistemic possibility itself.[2] Our

I am grateful to an anonymous OUP referee and to the not so anonymous editors for their valuable comments. Thanks also to audiences at the universities of California at Davis, California at Santa Cruz, Chicago, Edinburgh, London (Institute of Philosophy), St Andrews, Sheffield, and Wisconsin-Milwaukee, where many of the ideas in this paper were presented.

[1] Note that this is not the sort of epistemic possibility that philosophers contrast with metaphysical possibility when they discuss identity statements. In that special, technical sense, something is epistemically possible, for example that Hesperus is distinct from Phosphorus, if its negation is not knowable *a priori*.

[2] Perhaps not just epistemic possibility but other sorts of possibility are relative too. If so, then what distinguishes the different sorts is what the possibility is relative to. For example, whereas epistemic possibilities are relative to bodies of information, nomological possibilities are relative to sets of states of affairs

main question will be how to handle this relativity, especially in connection with sentences that do not make this relativity explicit. Compare these two sentences:

(1) Richard Branson might go to the moon by 2015.

(2) As far as Elton John knows, Richard Branson might go to the moon by 2015.

Let's call (1), which mentions no perspective, a *bare* EP sentence, in contrast to the *relativized* (2), which contains the phrase 'so far as Elton John knows'.[3] There are various other constructions that can be used to relativize an EP sentence, such as 'given what Elton John knows', 'relative to the information available to Elton John', and simply 'for Elton John'. Obviously, bare EP sentences lack something that relativized ones have—a mention of a perspective. This suggests to me that because epistemic possibility is perspective-relative, the semantic contents of bare EP sentences lack something as well.

The recent debate on their semantics has overlooked relativized EP sentences. Its almost exclusive focus on bare EP sentences, hence failure to compare them to their relativized counterparts, has confined the debate to a forced choice between two needlessly elaborate views, *Contextualism* and *Relativism,* which both impute dubious semantic roles to context. Implicitly accepting the grammar-school dictum that every sentence expresses a complete thought, proponents of both views take for granted that bare EP sentences semantically express propositions.[4] Rather than defend this assumption, they rely on intuitions about truth values of utterances of such sentences. And, because these truth values seem to vary (even with all the facts fixed) depending on the context in which the utterance is made or considered, contextualists and relativists both reject *Propositional Invariantism* and maintain instead that bare EP sentences are context-sensitive. They disagree on just how: contextualists think that their semantic contents shift, and relativists think that their contents, though fixed, can still shift in truth value.

I will propose a simple, alternative view, one that has been overlooked because it abandons the assumption that bare EP sentences express propositions in the first place. According to *Radical Invariantism,* as I call it, bare EP sentences are not context-sensitive in either of the ways claimed by contextualists and relativists. Rather, these sentences are *propositionally incomplete:* their invariant semantic contents are not full-fledged propositions but merely *propositional radicals,* which lack a constituent needed

---

and scientific laws. Accordingly, it might be argued that modal terms are not systematically ambiguous but semantically neutral as between different sorts of modality. What a given use is relativized to would determine which sort of modality is involved.

[3] Interestingly, replacing this phrase with 'for all Elton John knows' makes 'might' redundant. Even with 'will' in place of 'might', the sentence 'For all Elton John knows, Richard Branson will go to the moon by 2015' expresses epistemic possibility.

[4] From now on, I will usually use 'express' rather than 'semantically express' when talking about sentences (as opposed to speakers). I think 'semantically express' is redundant in that case, but I will occasionally use it anyway, just for emphasis. I call what a sentence expresses its *semantic content,* but note that sentences containing indexicals can have different semantic contents (express different things) in different contexts.

for being true or false. By distinguishing propositional incompleteness from context sensitivity, Radical Invariantism does not have to resort to semantic bells and whistles, as both Contextualism and Relativism do. It does not need to lavish special powers on context or introduce propositions with special semantic properties.

Radical Invariantism agrees with Contextualism that there are only classical EP propositions, ones that are absolutely true or absolutely false, but it denies that bare EP sentences manage to express them, even in context. And it agrees with Relativism that bare EP sentences do not express different EP propositions in different contexts, but only because it denies that they express propositions at all. What relativists think of as relative propositions are really, depending on whether we are considering objects of thought or semantic contents of bare EP sentences, either underspecified classical propositions or propositional radicals. Radical Invariantism says that bare EP sentences leave a certain semantic slack.

It is a separate question how speakers who use and encounter these sentences manage to pick up the slack. Although Contextualism and Relativism both offer insights about the statements we make in using the language of epistemic possibility, accounting for the contents of such statements and our evaluations of them as true or false is a job that goes well beyond accounting for the semantics of the sentences themselves.[5] The intuitions about truth values on which contextualists and relativists base their semantics of bare EP sentences are responsive not to the semantic contents of these sentences but to the propositions we have in mind or those that come to mind when we use or hear these sentences. Epistemic possibilities are perspective-relative, but bare EP sentences do not mention or otherwise advert to perspectives, not even implicitly. So, I claim, these sentences lack truth values, even relative to contexts. Even so, what a speaker means when using a bare EP sentence can and generally does involve a perspective, one that he could have mentioned explicitly if he had needed to, by using a relativized rather than a bare EP sentence. This suggests that there is nothing special about the semantic contents of bare EP sentences but something lacking in them.

In the first three sections, I will distinguish propositions about epistemic possibilities from epistemic possibilities themselves, contrast different conceptions of the relativity of epistemic possibility, and make some observations about the language of epistemic possibility. In the next three sections, I clarify the differences between the three approaches to be discussed, illustrate the basic kinds of problem cases that have motivated Contextualism and Relativism, and then present some less familiar problem cases. I will explain how, and how well, each approach handles each case. In the next two sections I will identify some general difficulties first for Relativism and then for Contextualism, ones that go beyond their trouble handling specific cases. Finally, I will identify and respond to the best objections to Radical Invariantism that I can think of.

---

[5] Putting an excessive burden on the semantics leads inevitably to great complications, as illustrated by the ingenious and highly sophisticated theories recently developed by Tamina Stephenson (2007) and by Seth Yalcin (2007).

1. Epistemic Possibilities and EP Propositions

Just as a chair cannot be comfortable without being comfortable for someone, so a state of affairs cannot be epistemically possible without being epistemically possible for someone.[6] Being epistemically possible is a relation, and being epistemically possible for someone is a relational property of a state of affairs, just as being comfortable to someone is a relational property of a piece of furniture or an article of clothing. We might say that a state of affairs is epistemically possible for someone at a time if it is not ruled out by the information available to that person at that time.[7] A person's current body of information, or perspective, determines which states of affairs are epistemically possible for him at the time. So we can think of a state of affairs as possible either relative to a person at a time or relative to a perspective. In some cases the relevant perspective is not a particular person's but that of a group.

Importantly, something can be epistemically possible for someone at a time even if the person does not believe that it is (you can mistakenly believe that your knowledge rules out something that it does not). And a person can believe that something is epistemically possible for them even if it is not (you can overlook a relevant part of what you know). *Being* epistemically possible *for* someone is distinct from *seeming* epistemically possible *to* someone.

An epistemic possibility is one thing; an epistemic possibility proposition is another. Epistemic possibilities are states of affairs, not propositions. States of affairs either obtain or do not obtain, and some states of affairs, whether or not they do obtain, are epistemically possible—relative to a perspective. Different propositions can ascribe possibility to the same state of affairs, but relative to different perspectives. A state of affairs can be possible relative to one perspective while not being possible relative to another. So, for example, if you don't know that my cat is gray, that my cat is black would be possible for you but not for me. And if you saw my cat, that my cat is black would go from being possible to not being possible for you.

This case suggests that when one goes from accepting to rejecting an epistemic possibility, typically one does so relative to a different perspective. When Hillary Clinton no longer deemed it possible that there were WMDs in Iraq in 2003, she judged this relative to the information she had later, not relative to the more limited information she had earlier. Indeed, she could still believe that this was possible relative to the information she had earlier. In general, however, as information accumulates it is of little interest to us what was formerly possible, that is, possible relative to the information we formerly had. Normally what matters is what is possible relative to the information we have now, which tends to be greater than what we had before. When focusing on what is possible relative to our current information, we generally

---

[6] As I am using 'state of affairs', some states of affairs obtain, and some do not.

[7] There are different ways of construing this, as we will see in Section 2.

do not make this relativity explicit, not just in talking about the possibility but even in thinking about it.

This last observation points to one obvious difference between using a bare EP sentence such as (1) rather than a relativized one like (2):

(1) Richard Branson might go to the moon by 2015.

(2) As far as Elton John knows, Richard Branson might go to the moon by 2015.

Common to both sentences is what we might call the *core proposition,* here the proposition that Richard Branson will go to the moon by 2015. It represents the state of affairs of Branson going to the moon by 2015, whose possibility both (1) and (2) can be used to assert. But whereas (2) can be used only to assert this possibility relative to Elton John's perspective, (1) can be used to assert it relative to anyone's perspective. Normally, but as we will see not always, this is (or includes) the speaker's perspective. That and related facts about sentences like (1) has led some to suggest that context somehow "determines" or "provides" the relevant relativization.

This suggestion is supported by the thought that a sentence like (1), or an utterance of it, can be true relative to one perspective and false relative to another. For example, so this thought goes, (1) could be true relative to what John knows now and false relative to what he knows in 2014 when, let's suppose, Branson announces that he has abandoned his lunar ambitions. It could even be false right now, relative to Branson's perspective, say if he has long since given up on ever going to the moon. Does this mean that (1) semantically expresses different propositions (in these different contexts), each true or false absolutely, or just a single proposition, but one that can be true or false from different perspectives? Or does it fall short of expressing any proposition at all?

Whatever the answer to that, different speakers can use (1) to express their belief that Richard Branson might go to the moon by 2015. This does not settle the question whether, even if they differ in perspective, they count as expressing belief in the same EP proposition. So let us distinguish *believing an epistemic possibility proposition* from *accepting an epistemic possibility*. We can say that one accepts a certain epistemic possibility if, relative to one's perspective at the time, one believes that the state of affairs in question is epistemically possible. This allows that one can go from accepting to rejecting a certain epistemic possibility without going from believing to disbelieving some one epistemic possibility proposition. By the same token, it allows that two people can in some sense disagree about a certain epistemic possibility even if there is no particular epistemic possibility proposition that one believes and the other disbelieves.

2. The Perspective Relativity of Epistemic Possibilities

In everyday conversation we raise, examine, dispute, and ultimately accept or reject epistemic possibilities. The same thing happens in more formal situations, such as investigations, trials, and debates. Some possibilities are left open—they're "live" possibilities—and some are eliminated or closed. Some are summarily dismissed, some are just overlooked, and some are looked into. Epistemic possibilities come in degrees—we describe them variously as likely, strong, good, significant, realistic, reasonable, moderate, slight, insignificant, remote, idle, and far-fetched. It is not obvious that these reduce to degrees of probability, subjective or otherwise.

These simple observations raise many interesting epistemological questions, both descriptive and normative, but I will not be addressing such questions. Trying to pin down what epistemic possibilities are is hard enough. I have loosely described an epistemic possibility as a state of affairs that is compatible with available information, but what counts as information, to whom must it be available, what counts as being available, and what counts as being compatible with the information? A little reflection suggests that these questions do not have clear, determinate answers.

First of all, what counts as information? Must be it knowledge, or can it be something weaker, such as evidence or even just a set of (firm) beliefs? We do not have to answer. Instead, we can distinguish *evidential* and *doxastic* possibility from strictly *epistemic* possibility.[8] When people use terms like 'maybe', 'might', 'perhaps', and 'possibly', they probably do not have any such distinction in mind.[9] Even so, for the sake of discussion let's assume that the relevant kind of body of information is a body of knowledge and pretend that when people use such terms what they have in mind literally is *epistemic* possibility. Although I will not try to justify this, much (but not all) of what I'll say about how we talk about epistemic possibility will apply just as well to evidential and to doxastic possibility, insofar as we ordinarily distinguish these.[10]

Assuming the relevant sort of information is knowledge, we can say that to be (epistemically) possible a state of affairs must be compatible with a certain body of knowledge. But whose body of knowledge? One's own, someone else's, a group's, a discipline's, all of humanity's? It seems to me that these are all perfectly good answers. Epistemic possibility is relative. We can pick any body of knowledge—individual, collective, past, present, or future, or even hypothetical, and say that a given state of affairs is compatible with it, hence epistemically possible relative to it. In particular,

---

[8]   The distinction between evidential and epistemic possibility obviously presupposes that evidence is not limited to knowledge. This conflicts with Tim Willliamson's well-known but controversial "E = K" doctrine (2000: ch. 9).

[9]   I suspect that this may explain, at least in part, the variability and shiftiness of people's intuitions about the truth values of statements made using bare EP sentences.

[10]   One point made earlier applies to all three: something can be possible (epistemically, evidentially, or doxastically, as the case may be) for you even if you do not believe that it is (with doxastic possibility this is true only up to a point, for if a person believes that something is not doxastically possible for him, then it is not—by virtue of that very belief). You could be mistaken about what your knowledge (evidence, belief set) is or about what it rules out. Similarly, something could fail to be epistemically (evidentially, doxastically) possible for you even if you think it is. What you know (what evidence you have, what you believe) might exclude more than you think it does. So something can *be* impossible *for* you even if it *seems* possible *to* you, and vice versa.

a given state of affairs can be possible relative to (that is, compatible with) what I know but not relative to what you know. Something that is possible relative to what I know today might not be possible relative to what I know tomorrow. Something could be possible relative to what you and I know but not relative to what an expert knows. For an omniscient being nothing is merely epistemically possible: the only epistemic possibilities there are are those that actually obtain. Since we are far from omniscient, there is much that is epistemically possible for each of us that does not in fact obtain. However, if we consider collective bodies of knowledge, information considered pooled even if not actually shared (available to everyone in a group even if it is not fully possessed by anyone), there will be things that are epistemically possible for us individually that are not epistemically possible for us collectively.

Then there is the question of what counts as having information and what counts as its being available. Must it be accessible to memory? Is it enough, even if we do not possess it, that the information at least be readily available, say after a little googling? Does it even have to be *readily* available?[11] As I see it, there is no determinate answer to these questions, and there doesn't need to be. Since epistemic possibility is perspective-relative, that is, relative to a body of information, the real question in any given case is which body of information is the relevant one (relevance is itself a relative matter).

Finally, what counts as being compatible with a body of knowledge? Being logically consistent with what is known? That seems much too weak, since it would lead to an odd kind of skepticism, according to which, even though we know a lot, our knowledge rules out far fewer possibilities than we think. Less demanding conceptions of ruling out do not require logical incompatibility—ruling out (closing off, eliminating) a possibility can be construed in various ways, and in various degrees. One interesting question, which I will not take up, is whether, in the case of two people with the same relevant knowledge, something can be epistemically possible for one but not for the other (because of different inferential powers or propensities?).

There are many interesting epistemological issues lurking behind the questions just raised, and I am not going to address them here, much less try to settle them. I will just continue to say that epistemic possibilities, whatever they are exactly and whatever their relationship is to what is known, are relative to perspectives or, equivalently, to persons or groups with particular perspectives. A state of affairs is epistemically possible for a person (or a group) if it is compatible with their perspective, with the information available to them. Something can be epistemically possible relative to one perspective and not to another, and nothing is epistemically possible except relative to a perspective. In this respect, being epistemically possible is like being obvious, being surprising, and being puzzling: nothing can be obvious, surprising, or puzzling *simpliciter*.

---

[11] Questions of these sorts are discussed in Hacking (1967), Teller (1972), DeRose (1991), and Egan, Hawthorne, and Weatherson (2005).

3. Perspectives and Bare Epistemic Possibility Sentences

Various expressions can be used to express epistemic possibility, such as the modals 'might', 'could', and 'may' and the adverbs 'possibly', 'perhaps', and 'maybe'.[12] We can also use locutions like 'it is possible that', 'for all I know', and 'there's a chance that'.[13] Most of our examples will use 'might'. Even though epistemic possibilities are relative to perspectives, in asserting a possibility we generally do not need to make the perspective explicit, usually because it is our own. Generally we can (and do) use bare, unqualified EP sentences instead. But sometimes we have to make explicit what the relevant perspective is and use a sentence like one of these:

(3) As far as Jack knows, Jill might still be on the hill.
(4) According to Jill's preliminary diagnosis, Jack might have a concussion.
(5) Given the information currently available to the local authorities, the fire might have been caused by lightning.

Making the perspective explicit is necessary whenever it would not otherwise be evident to our audience what perspective is the relevant one. In assertively uttering sentences like (3)–(5) we do not commit ourselves one way or the other about the relevant possibility, that is, from our own perspective. We are asserting the possibility relative to another perspective. For example, an arsonist might utter (5) knowing full well that the core proposition is false.

When we do not make the perspective explicit, typically our own perspective is the relevant one, as in a likely utterance of (6).

(6) The front door might be unlocked.

However, our own perspective can and often does incorporate our audience's, insofar as we take for granted that their knowledge does not rule out the possibility in question. Sometimes the relevant perspective is that of a uniquely salient group of which we are a member or to which we defer, but some stage setting may be necessary for this to be understood, as in the following examples.

(7) The fire might be the result of arson.
(8) String theory might never be verified.

Suppose that the chief of the local fire department utters (7). He would intend, and could reasonably expect, to be taken as speaking from the department's perspective. And if I, having no expertise on string theory, were the speaker of (8), I could well be deferring to the perspective of the physics profession. At any rate, typical uses of bare

---

[12] 'Perhaps' and 'maybe' are special cases (for this reason I will not discuss them in this paper). For one thing, not only can they be used to express epistemic possibility, they can also be used to indicate that one is suggesting the core proposition—or just guessing. They are then being used as *utterance modifiers*, to comment on the act the utterance rather than to modify its content. For a discussion of utterance modifiers and a taxonomy of them, see Bach (1999: 356–60).

[13] This use of 'There's a chance that' does not imply that epistemic possibility is reducible to probability. This idiomatic use does not mean 1 chance in 10, 1 in 1,000, 1 in 1,000,000, or anything of the sort. And surely being epistemically possible is not just having a (subjective) probability greater than zero.

EP sentences are, we might say, *egocentric* or at least *ego-inclusive*, depending on whether the relevant perspective is strictly one's own or incorporates a larger perspective to which one as it were subscribes. This could be a perspective one is presumed to share with one's audience or it could be the perspective of a uniquely salient larger group to whose authority on the matter one defers.

In special circumstances bare EP sentences can be used to assert that something is epistemically possible from a perspective disjoint from one's own. This is clearest when they are embedded in attitude attributions or are used to explain actions:

(9) Anne thinks that Andy might be in Anchorage.

(10) Ben called Betty because she might have Bertha's phone number.

In (9) the relevant perspective is Anne's, not the speaker's, since it is her attitude that is being reported. In (10) the relevant perspective is Ben's, because it is his action that is being explained. But when there is no such indication, as with (6) above, speakers are likely to be taking their own perspectives. The situation with 'might' is roughly analogous to that with such terms as 'nearby' and 'fun'. If I uttered (11) or (12), for example, normally I would be speaking from my own point of view.

(11) There is a gym nearby.

(12) Working out on an elliptical trainer will be fun.

In some situations, however, someone else's perspective would be understood. If the person were speaking to his sister on the phone, he would be telling her that a gym is near her, not him. And if he hated exercise, presumably he would be suggesting that working out on an elliptical trainer will be fun for her, not him.

4. Contextualism, Relativism, or What?

The relativity of epistemic possibility has led to the widespread impression that there must be something context-sensitive about bare EP sentences, presumably having to do with perspective. The debate has concerned just what shifts with context. Contextualists hold that a bare EP sentence, though not mentioning any perspective, semantically expresses a *perspective-involving* proposition and, indeed, that it can express different perspective-involving EP propositions in different contexts of use.[14] Relativists deny this and see a different sort of context sensitivity. They claim that a bare EP sentence expresses the same proposition (modulo any irrelevant indexicality) regardless of context. However, this is not a classical proposition, one that is true or false absolutely, independently of context. It is not the sort of proposition that is true or false depending simply on whether or not the world is as it says. Rather,

---

[14] I am using 'perspective-involving' on the model of 'object-involving' as commonly used in discussions of singular thought. On my preferred, Russellian conception of propositions as structured (with objects, properties, and relations as constituents), perspectives are constituents of perspective-involving EP propositions.

the truth value of this one proposition can shift with the context. This non-classical proposition does not contain a perspective—it is *perspectivally neutral*—but is true or false relative to a perspective.[15]

Contextualists and relativists both reject Propositional Invariantism, the view that a bare EP sentence expresses a classical proposition independently of context. It does not deny that epistemic possibility is relative, but it does deny that this relativity is variable. On its most natural construal, Propositional Invariantism says that a state of affairs is epistemically possible just in case its obtaining is not ruled out by *any* body of knowledge.[16] The obvious trouble with this view is that it renders false any bare EP sentence whose core state of affairs is known by anyone not to obtain. Suppose, for example, that the whereabouts of Freddie the Fugitive is known only to Freddie. Then, according to Propositional Invariantism, the proposition that Freddie the Fugitive might be in Philly is absolutely false if Freddie is somewhere else. A detective hot on his trail who assertively utters, "Freddie the Fugitive might be in Philly", speaks falsely, no matter how strong his evidence. This does not seem plausible.

Recognizing this fatal problem with Propositional Invariantism, contextualists and relativists agree that there must be something context-sensitive about bare EP sentences. Although they disagree on what varies with context, they both take for granted that bare EP sentences do express propositions. I have never seen any defense of this assumption.[17] In fact, I think there is good reason to reject this assumption. Compare (1) and (2) again.

(1) Richard Branson might go to the moon by 2015.

(2) As far as Elton John knows, Richard Branson might go to the moon by 2015.

(2) mentions a perspective; (1) does not. (2) is true just in case the state of affairs in question, that Richard Branson goes to the moon by 2015, is possible so far as

---

[15] There is a further question, on which Relativists disagree, as to whether this evaluation is tied to the context of use or, more liberally, to a context of assessment, which may be remote from the context of use. John MacFarlane (this volume) takes this liberal view, for which he reserves the term 'Relativism'. He calls the more restrictive view 'Non-indexical Contextualism'.

[16] This version of Propositional Invariantism, which Egan, Hawthorne, and Weatherson call "universalism" (2005: 144), is not the only possible one. On the opposite extreme is the version which says that a state of affairs is epistemically possible just in case there is some body of knowledge that does not rule it out. This version implausibly makes any state of affairs epistemically possible. Intermediate versions of Propositional Invariantism are possible too, but any choice among them seems arbitrary.

[17] Contextualism was motivated by the obvious inadequacy of (Propositional) Invariantism, and Relativism, more recently, by Contextualism's inability to handle certain cases. For example, Egan, Hawthorne, and Weatherson (2005), although they forthrightly acknowledge that Relativism is not without problems of its own, proceed by arguing against "invariantist solutions", which they assume without argument to be propositional, and "contextualist solutions." (Lasersohn (2005), in his defense of a kind of relativism about unrelativized sentences containing predicates of personal taste, proceeds in part by arguing against propositional invariantist and contextualist views.) MacFarlane's case for Relativism also depends on this line of argument. He does consider "non-truth-conditional approaches", but only those that treat epistemic modals as "force modifiers" (this volume, p.157).

Elton John knows now. But epistemic possibilities are relative to perspectives. That is, a state of affairs can be epistemically possible relative to one perspective not epistemically possible relative to another. This suggests that (1), by failing to mention a perspective, falls short of expressing a proposition. It is not that a bare EP sentence is context-sensitive, either as to which proposition it expresses (Contextualism) or as to the truth value of the one proposition it does express (Relativism). Rather, it has a context-independent *non*-propositional content. Its content does not add up to a proposition, and is neither true nor false. On this view, *radical* rather than *propositional* invariantism, bare EP sentences are *propositionally incomplete:* their invariant semantic contents are not propositions but merely *propositional radicals.* These notions are straightforward if you think in terms of (structured) propositions rather than truth conditions. Since structured propositions are made up of building blocks assembled in a particular way, it makes sense to suppose that with some (in fact many) sentences this assemblage, put together compositionally from the sentence's constituents according to its syntactic structure, might fail to comprise a proposition (numerous examples are presented in Bach 1994). Even though it comprises the entire semantic content of the sentence, this propositional radical lacks at least one constituent needed to be true or false and to be the content of a thought or a statement.

Although bare EP sentences semantically do not express full-fledged propositions, hence are not capable of being true or false, they are perfectly capable of being used to assert propositions and of being taken as so used. In that case, the speaker implicitly adverts to the perspective with respect to which the relevant possibility is to be considered. But bare EP sentences, unlike relativized ones, do not themselves express propositions. From the radical invariantist standpoint, both contextualists and relativists commit the *Proposition Fallacy:* they assume that if a sentence, with all of its constituents being used literally, can be used to convey a proposition, the sentence itself must express one. Contextualists also commit the *Context Sensitivity Fallacy:* they conflate propositional incompleteness with context sensitivity.[18] They implicitly assume that if, while using all of the constituents of a given sentence literally, speakers in uttering that sentence can mean different things in different contexts, there must be something context-sensitive about the sentence.

Radical Invariantism has something in common with Contextualism and something else in common with Relativism. It agrees with Contextualism on what epistemic possibility propositions there are, and it agrees with Relativism that the

---

[18] This fallacy underlies not just contextualism about bare EP sentences but other sorts of contextualism as well, including the extreme view that virtually all sentences are context-sensitive. Such views require assigning an unduly extensive role to context. Cappelen and Lepore (2005) and I (Bach 2005) have both argued that its semantic role should be limited to determining semantic values of clearly indexical expressions. Cappelen and Lepore, however, fail to distinguish between context sensitivity and propositional incompleteness (Bach 2006). In assuming that sentences must semantically express propositions, they escape the Context Sensitivity Fallacy, but still get trapped by the Proposition Fallacy. The alternative to their Propositional Minimalism is what I call Radical Minimalism, which allows for sentences with invariant but propositionally incomplete semantic contents.

semantic contents of bare EP sentences are not context-sensitive. It shares the contextualist view that the only EP propositions there are involve perspectives, the ones that can be expressed independently of context by relativized EP sentences, but it rejects the contextualist claim that these propositions are expressed, relative to context, by bare EP sentences. For it denies that bare EP sentences express propositions at all. Radical Invariantism agrees with Relativism that bare EP sentences do not express perspective-involving EP propositions and that their semantic contents are invariant, but it rejects the Relativist assumption that these contents must be propositions.

Radical Invariantism aims to capture these elements of truth in Contextualism and Relativism. Otherwise, it treats the so-called context sensitivity of bare EP sentences as a pragmatic phenomenon, not a semantic one. From a pragmatic point of view, the question is not how context fixes semantic content or its evaluation for truth or falsity but, rather, how contextual information can enable speakers to use bare EP sentences to convey propositions that these sentences do not fully express. This is not always feasible, however, and sometimes speakers, anticipating incomprehension or misunderstanding, use relativized EP sentences.

It will immediately be objected that the radical invariantist claim about bare EP sentences is obvious but irrelevant: of course bare EP *sentences* do not express propositions—*utterances* of them do—and the puzzle is about utterances, not the sentences themselves. Moreover, so the objection goes, not sentences but utterances are the primary linguistic items that have propositional or truth-conditional contents, and it is the business of semantics to give a systematic account of the truth conditions of what utterances express. This idea is reflected in commonly used phrases like 'the proposition expressed by an utterance', 'the truth-conditional content of an utterance', and the simple 'utterance truth'.

In my view, these phrases are highly misleading, and the project of utterance semantics is misguided. For reasons that I can only hint at here, *linguistic* semantics concerns sentences, not utterances.[19] Yes, if some sentences do not have truth conditional contents, even relative to contexts of use, then it cannot be the job of semantics to account for their truth conditions.[20] However, it is a mistake to infer from this that semantics must therefore be concerned with the nearest things that do have truth conditions, namely utterances. Considered as distinct from sentences, utterances do not express anything—speakers do. If by 'utterance' we mean an act of uttering a sentence rather than the uttered sentence, there is nothing for the content of an utterance to consist in other than what the speaker means. It is an illusion to suppose that utterances, being speech *acts,* are *linguistic* entities over and above sentences. Their contents are what speakers mean in performing them. Moreover, there is nothing in between sentences

---

[19] The following reservations about utterance semantics are spelled out more fully in Bach (2005: 22–5)

[20] The qualification 'relative to contexts of use' allows for the case of sentences containing indexicals to have truth-conditional but context-relative semantic contents.

and intentions (in uttering sentences) that are also capable of having contents.[21] So, I conclude, to be semantic theses Contextualism and Relativism must be construed as concerning the semantic contents of bare EP sentences.

One preliminary point in favor of Radical Invariantism is that although terms like 'might' and 'possible' apply not just to epistemic possibility but also to other kinds, such as logical, metaphysical, nomological, physical, biological, technological, and legal possibility, this does not make these terms semantically ambiguous. That is, the fact that there are various sorts of possibility does not show that 'possibility'—or 'might' or 'possible'—has various meanings. This fact strongly suggests that perspective relativity is not built into the semantics of these terms. Sentences containing such terms can just as well be relativized to, for example, physical laws or legal codes.[22]

Whether or not this point counts for much, the more pressing question is how well the different views—Contextualism, Relativism, and Radical Invariantism—handle a wide range of cases. I will compare them on this score in the next two sections, where we will first take up some basic examples and then some trickier cases.

5. Shifting Perspectives: Basic Examples

Contextualism and Relativism are each motivated by intuitions about the truth values of ostensibly conflicting possibility claims made or considered in various situations. Three basic types of case have been discussed in the literature. In the first case, one person asserts a certain possibility and is overheard by someone else who knows that this possibility doesn't obtain. The second is a case of direct disagreement between two people about a certain possibility. In the third case, a person accepts a certain possibility and then changes his mind about it. In each case there is a tendency to think that there are two conflicting claims and yet that they are both correct. The puzzle is to explain how this can be—or to explain it away. In this section I will present illustrations of each case, sketch contextualist, relativist, and radical invariantist accounts of the variable role of perspective in each case, and identify certain difficulties and complications for each.[23] I won't hide my preference for Radical Invariantism.

The first two examples involve two people who, with different bodies of knowledge, take different perspectives on the same possibility. This situation raises the question of what is going on when one believes that something is possible and the other believes that it is not. Do they really disagree? Or, since they are considering

---

[21] It won't help to invoke sentence tokens, as if these have autonomous semantic properties. In my view, token semantics is, well, token semantics.

[22] The adverbs 'maybe' and 'perhaps' are exceptions, being used only for epistemic possibility.

[23] Some of the problems I mention with contextualist treatments of particular examples are similar to those pointed out by Egan, Hawthorne, and Weatherson (2005: 135–44) and by MacFarlane (this volume). And some of the problems I mention with relativist treatments of particular examples are similar to those pointed out by Wright (2007) or by von Fintel and Gillies (2008). So, many of the following observations are not original with me. Space does not permit pinpointing the similarities and differences. Several of the examples in the next section are new, so far as I know.

it from different perspectives, are they not really considering the same proposition? Keep in mind that although two clearly distinct perspectives figure in these examples, there are also common cases in which the two perspectives are relevantly similar (or in effect merged), in which case the disagreement clearly is genuine. This is the situation when, for example, two people engaged in an inquiry share all relevant information (or treat it as shared). In that case, clearly they can genuinely disagree on whether this information leaves open or excludes a given possibility. For instance, two radiologists with the same knowledge and expertise can disagree on whether a certain shadow they both see on an X-ray might be the image of a tumor.[24] However, in the next two cases there is a definite difference in perspective, and this difference contributes to the "disagreement." I use scare quotes because part of what is at issue here is whether the disagreement is genuine, that is, whether there is some one proposition that the two parties are disagreeing about.

5.1. "Disagreement" I: Eavesdropping

I am looking for my keys and, after not finding them in the usual places, I wonder if, when letting myself in while holding several large packages, I dropped them outside the front door on the sidewalk. So I mutter something like this:

(13) The keys might be out on the sidewalk.

My wife, who has just come home and entered the house very quietly, overhears me. Still holding my keys, after removing them from the front door and using them to let herself in, she thinks to herself that what I said was wrong—my keys are in her hand and they were in the front door, not on the sidewalk. She has not yet said anything, much less shown me the keys.

There is a bit of a puzzle here. I was right to think my keys might be out on the sidewalk, and my wife was right to think that they couldn't be. But how can we both have been right? One answer is that we believed two different things and that each of us was right in what we respectively believed. What I believed was a proposition that involved my perspective, and what she disbelieved was a proposition that involved hers. This view of the situation, which Contextualism and Radical Invariantism share, seems to imply that there was no genuine disagreement, since there was no proposition that we disagreed about. Even though I made no reference to my perspective when I muttered (13), the proposition I had in mind was that, as far as I knew (or relative to my perspective), my keys might be out on the sidewalk. But this is not the proposition that my wife rejected when she overheard me. When she heard me mutter (13), she was in a different context, and grasped a different proposition, that relative to *her*

---

[24] I suppose it could be argued that in a case like this the two people's perspectives cannot be relevantly similar, much less identical in all relevant respects. The idea here would be that if there is a difference in attitude about the possibility in question, there *must* be a relevant difference in perspective, even if the parties haven't pinned down what it is. But it could be that one of them is just wrong about what their shared information rules out.

perspective my keys might be out on the sidewalk. This proposition was false, since it conflicted with her knowledge that she was holding my keys.

The relativist would reject this take on the situation, for it implausibly implies that my wife misunderstood what I said. For if she did understand it, and it was a proposition that involved a perspective (mine), she would have agreed that from my perspective my keys might be out on the sidewalk. But that is not how she took my utterance. When she heard it, she considered this possibility relative to her perspective, not mine. Even so, the relativist would insist that my wife and I were considering the same proposition, as fully expressed by (13). This is the proposition that my keys might be out on the sidewalk, period. Since I believed it and she disbelieved it, we disagreed. However, we were both right, since we considered it from different perspectives. It was true relative to (or from) my perspective and false relative to hers. So this is a case of what relativists, following Max Kölbel (2003), call "faultless disagreement." But, as many have wondered, how could this be a case of *genuine* disagreement, even if it *is* about the same proposition?

Radical Invariantism denies (13) expresses any proposition. Like Relativism, it holds that (13) expresses the same thing independently of who is considering it or from what perspective, but it denies that this semantic content amounts to a proposition of any kind. On the other hand, Radical Invariantism agrees with Contextualism that perspectives enter into the propositions speakers have in mind when using or hearing sentences like (13). Radical Invariantism is thus forced to concede that the proposition that my wife entertained upon hearing me mutter (13) is not the one that I had in mind when I muttered it. So she and I do not disagree. Rather, we are taking opposite stances toward different propositions, just as the Contextualist says.

Is this a fatal objection to Radical Invariantism (and to Contextualism)? Not quite. Both views can at least pay lip service to Relativism in the following way. Even though my wife and I did not disagree about any (relevant) proposition, we do "disagree" about the relevant possibility. I accept it and she rejects it, relative to our respective perspectives. I thought that the state of affairs of my keys being out on the sidewalk was possible (relative to my perspective), while she thought that it was not possible (relative to hers). This "disagreement" is not genuine—it is not about any one proposition—but it can seem genuine because no perspective is mentioned. That makes it seem as though my wife and I disagree about some one thing. It explains why I would look for them out on the sidewalk and she would not.

5.2. "Disagreement" II: Disputing

In the previous case there was no communication between the two parties. But what happens if they do communicate and, indeed, get into a dispute about the possibility in question? Again I have misplaced my keys, and I have started looking for them. Aware of my predicament, my wife joins the search. Getting frustrated I say, "The keys might be out on the sidewalk" (13). My wife disputes what I say, remarking that she distinctly remembers me coming in and dropping them on the kitchen table.

I don't remember that and tell her I'm going outside to look for them. Eventually they turn up in a bag of groceries on the floor near the kitchen table.

It seems that relative to what I knew but not relative to what my wife knew, my keys might have been out on the sidewalk. So, were we both right? If so, were we right about the same thing, a perspectivally neutral proposition that was true relative to my perspective but false relative to hers, or about different things, two distinct perspective-involving propositions? Contextualism and Radical Invariantism say the latter, but they disagree on whether those perspective-involving propositions are semantically expressed by (13). Contextualism says they are, one relative to my context and one relative to my wife's. Radical Invariantism denies that they are semantically expressed at all. As before, it agrees with Relativism that (13) expresses the same thing independently of who is considering it or from what perspective, but again, since no perspective is mentioned, it denies that this thing is a proposition.

One difficulty with the above contextualist treatment of this example is that there is only one context. In the *Eavesdropping* case it is plausible to suppose that the context in which my wife heard me utter (13) was different from the context in which I uttered it, although how plausible this suggestion is obviously depends on how the operative notion of context is fleshed out. Here, clearly, the context in which my wife hears my utterance is the same as the context in which I make it—presumably, according to Contextualism, the relevant sort of context is the context of utterance—but our perspectives differ.[25]

This is one consideration that motivates the relativist view that in *Disputing* my wife and I are entertaining the very same proposition, albeit a perspectivally neutral proposition. Relative to our respective perspectives, from which I correctly believe it and she correctly disbelieves it, it is true for me and false for her. John MacFarlane (this volume) characterizes such a proposition as true or false relative to a "context of assessment", but it is important to note that what matters is not the assessing but the perspective, the relevant body of knowledge.[26] But then, as we saw with *Eavesdropping*, it's not clear that my wife and I genuinely disagree.

Can Radical Invariantism avoid the problems of these other views? It agrees with Relativism that a bare EP sentence like (13) has a fixed semantic content but it denies that this proposition adds up to a proposition. It agrees with Contextualism that the only epistemic possibility propositions to be had are perspective involving and, although it denies that (13) semantically expresses any such proposition, it agrees that what I believe and what my wife rejects are perspective-involving propositions, but

[25]   However, there is an alternative version of Contextualism, due to Brian Weatherson (2009), according to which what he calls the "context of evaluation" can fix semantic content. Although he calls this view "Indexical Relativism" (he applies it to the case of open indicative conditionals), it is clearly not Relativism of the sort we have been discussing. Applying such a view to bare EP sentences would make for a difference between my wife's context and mine and for a corresponding difference between the perspective-involving propositions we believe. But then, on this view, we would not be disagreeing.

[26]   As pointed out earlier, judging that a state of affairs is epistemically possible is neither necessary nor sufficient for its being epistemically possible.

not the same ones. Even though there is no one proposition that she and I disagree about, we "disagree" (in the way explained earlier) about the possibility that my keys are out on the sidewalk.

As before, it seems that the fact that the perspectives are not made explicit creates the illusion that my wife and I are disagreeing about the same proposition. For consider what happens if we make the perspectives explicit (for precision the times could be made explicit too):

(14) Relative to KB's perspective, the keys might be out on the sidewalk.

(15) Relative to CB's perspective, the keys might be out on the sidewalk.

Clearly (14) can be true while (15) is false. Of course, if I knew what my wife knows, that I dropped the keys on the kitchen table, then I would deny that my keys might be out on the sidewalk, but in that case my perspective would have changed. I would not only reject (15) but also an updated version of (14).

An alternative explanation of what is going on in this example is that initially my wife and I were genuinely disagreeing about a single perspective-involving proposition, that relative to KB and CB's joint perspective, the keys might be out on the sidewalk. Of course she and I were not explicitly thinking about this proposition in these terms. Nonetheless, as Radical Invariantism has it, that was the proposition we were both considering. It is only after we recognized that our perspectives diverged and I retreated into mine and she maintained hers that we came to entertain different perspective-involving propositions. But at least, even after this realization, we were at least "disagreeing" about the same possibility.

5.3. Changing your mind

We often go from accepting to rejecting a possibility—we consider it, accept it, but then look into it further and eliminate it. For example, early in a murder investigation a detective is disposed to utter (16) but later, after confirming the butler's alibi, he's ready to take it back and to go with its negation (17) instead.[27]

(16) The butler could have done it.

(17) The butler couldn't have done it.

He might even say, "I was wrong—the butler couldn't have done it." On the other hand, even though the detective has changed his mind about whether the butler could have done it, it seems that he was right to think what he did originally, and not merely in the sense that his earlier belief was justified—his earlier belief was true. But what he came to believe later, after he changed his mind, seems to be true too. This raises the question of what he believed before and what he believed later.

The contextualist take on this is that even though sentence (17) is the negative version of (16), they do not express contradictory propositions. (16) and (17) are

---

[27] In these examples I use 'could' rather than 'might' because negating 'might' requires the cumbersome 'it might not be the case that'—'might not' is obviously too weak.

sensitive to their respective contexts of utterance, specifically to the contextually relevant perspective of the detective. Relative to those contexts, they express these propositions:

> (18) Relative to the detective's perspective at t_1, the butler could have done it.
>
> (19) Relative to the detective's perspective at t_2, the butler couldn't have done it.[28]

Obviously (19) does not contradict (18), even though there is a sense in which the detective has changed his mind about the possibility that the butler did it. First he accepted this possibility, but later he rejected it. However, he has not gone from believing a proposition to disbelieving it (or believing its negation), for what he later disbelieves is a different proposition. The same epistemic possibility is involved, but not the same epistemic possibility proposition. (Radical Invariantism agrees with Contextualism about what the detective believes, but it denies that (16) and (17) manage to express these propositions, even relative to the respective contexts in which the detective utters them.)

The contextualist view explains the intuition that the detective, though right to change his mind, was right before (and not merely justified in what he believed then). His earlier belief was true (that, relative to what he knew then, the butler could have done it), and his later belief was true too (that, relative to his more informed body of knowledge, the butler could not have done it). However, since the detective does not disbelieve the EP proposition he believed earlier, he hasn't really changed his mind about the original proposition. He still believes it, but it is no longer the EP proposition of interest and is no longer under consideration.

Relativism takes (16) and (17) at face value, and maintains that each sentence fully expresses what the detective believes at the time. So what he believes later is, just as appearances suggest, the negation of what he believed earlier, and in this respect he really has changed his mind. But this does not mean that the detective was first mistaken and later correct. Rather, these seemingly contradictory propositions are both true, but only relative to the relevant perspectives, not absolutely. The detective's belief that the butler could have done it was true relative to his earlier perspective, and his later belief, that the butler could not have done it, was true too, relative to his later perspective.

Part of the puzzle about a case like *Changing Your Mind* is that when the detective rules out the butler it seems that if he thought to himself, "I was wrong", we would tend to think he was right in so thinking. But this is not what any of our three theories predicts, at least not straightforwardly (only Propositional Invariantism

---

[28] To express these propositions in a fully explicit way (and exploiting the context sensitivity of 'now', the detective could have used (i) at t_1 and (ii) at t_2:

> (i) Relative to my perspective now [= t_1], the butler could have done it.
> (ii) Relative to my perspective now [= t_2], the butler couldn't have done it.

straightforwardly predicts this, but that view is highly implausible). So how should they characterize the detective's situation, even if not straightforwardly?

Contextualism has to attribute a certain error to him. It says that in now judging himself previously mistaken, he is mistaken about what he previously believed. He is correct insofar as the proposition now expressed by the sentence he used previously is false, but that is not the proposition it expressed on the previous occasion. He mistakes the positive version of what he believes now (that, relative to his current perspective, the butler could have done it) for what he believed before (that, relative to his earlier perspective, the butler could have done it). The fact that the perspective is not made explicit in how the detective would put what he previously believed and now disbelieves helps explain the error. This fact also explains *our* error in thinking that he changed his mind (went from believing to disbelieving a certain proposition). It may seem implausible to suppose that the detective—or we—are mistaken about what he previously believed, but in defense of Contextualism it can at least be said that he is right about the status of the relevant possibility (the butler's having done it), both earlier *and* later. Earlier he correctly believed that such a possibility was compatible with his then current body of information, and later he correctly believed that it was incompatible with his now current body of information. Moreover, whether he (or we) realize it or not, he still believes that this possibility is compatible with his earlier body of information—he hasn't changed his mind about that. He is just no longer concerned with that proposition, with what was possible for him when he was less informed.

Relativism views the detective's situation very differently. It claims that (16) expresses the same (non-classical, perspectivally neutral) proposition later as it did earlier, and that this is the proposition the detective first accepts and later rejects, from his different perspectives. So he is now rejecting the right proposition, and he is right to reject it. And, in thinking he was wrong earlier, he is right about which proposition he is now rejecting. However, there is still a problem here for Relativism. In thinking he was wrong earlier, he does not believe that he was wrong earlier to believe that proposition from his perspective now, since he wasn't in that perspective then. On the other hand, if he thought he was mistaken in believing that proposition from his earlier perspective, he'd be wrong about that! After all, according to Relativism, at the later time he is constrained to evaluate that proposition as false. Of course, he can readily evaluate as true the classical, perspective-involving proposition that relative to his earlier perspective the butler could have done it. However, this is not the perspectivally neutral proposition the relativist needs. So it seems that Relativism is hard put to capture, *in relativist terms,* what it is that the detective rightly thinks he was wrong about.

Relativism seem to render the consideration of a relative proposition context-bound. In the case of the detective, it seems to reckon him no longer able to occupy the cognitive position he was in earlier. He can now think what he thought then but only from his current perspective. In general, it seems impossible to entertain a relative proposition from a perspective other than the perspective one occupies. Relativism seems to lead to a certain *perspectival solipsism:* one can consider EP propositions only from one's current perspective, not from one's earlier perspectives, much less from anyone else's, past or present. There is an obvious way out of this predicament, of course, but that requires considering classical, perspective-involving EP propositions. So it doesn't really deal with the problem of considering relativist, perspectivally neutral propositions from perspectives other than the perspective one is in. Not only that, it raises the question of whether there is any reason to suppose that what one believes from one's current perspective isn't a classical proposition after all, one that involves that perspective.

Radical Invariantism relies on the distinction between the propositional radicals expressed by bare EP sentences and the classical perspective-involving propositions they are used to convey. However, invoking this distinction alone is not enough to address the "I was wrong" problem. Radical Invariantism agrees with Contextualism that the detective initially believes one such proposition and later disbelieves another. The problem, as we saw with Contextualism, is that although in a way he is right to say that he was wrong, in another way he is not. The solution is to say that he is right insofar as he could not use (16) to assert what he now believes but that he is wrong if he thinks that he no longer believes what he believed before. In fact, he still does—he just can no longer use (16) to assert it—and it is no longer of interest anyway.

Is this enough to explain why he is right to say he was wrong before, or at least why we feel some inclination to think so? It seems that we also need an explanation of why he is confused about what he was wrong about. Surely he was not mistaken earlier because he accepted a possibility that would be excluded by his later perspective. Yet that seems to be why he now thinks he was wrong then and why it is natural to describe him as having changed his mind. It is not just that he would no longer assertively utter a sentence he was prepared to use then.

What is going on here, I think, is that we are generally not interested in what is possible relative to other perspectives so much as in what is possible relative to what we know now. During the course of an inquiry about a given matter, we update, usually narrowing, the range of open possibilities whenever some get eliminated.[29] Moreover, our real interest is in what is the case, not what might be the case. When we go from accepting to rejecting a possibility and concede that we were wrong before, our attention is misdirected from the proposition we previously believed to the one that we now reject, a proposition that we can now convey with the same sentence.

I concede, then, that Radical Invariantism is committed to a kind of error theory here. The detective *is* confused about what he was wrong about, though right about which sentence it is that he would no longer use. But he is right about more than

---

[29] This updating is not necessarily a monotonic process, since new evidence can reopen possibilities that were previously ruled out.

that. He is also right about the epistemic possibility that he previously accepted. Now that he has ruled it out, presumably correctly, it is no longer the open possibility that it was. But since earlier it was open, in that respect he is wrong to think now that he was wrong then.

5.4. New evidence, same possibility

The case of *Changing Your Mind* should not divert our attention from an even simpler case, one that tends to be overlooked in the literature on epistemic possibility. This is the case of *not* changing one's mind even as one's body of information expands. Consider what goes on when a person who accepts a certain possibility at one stage of an inquiry, after looking further into the matter, continues to accept that possibility. The matter might be the possibility itself, or it might be some other question, the answer to which either confirms or rules out this possibility. Either way, the person goes from accepting the possibility given his initial information to accepting the same possibility after acquiring additional information.

Suppose the possibility is that the butler could have done it, as in (16). And suppose that the detective thinks at one time that the butler could have done it and then, after further investigation, continues to think that the butler could have done it.[30] It should be obvious what the different views say about this case and what the problem is for each. Although Contextualism and Radical Invariantism differ as to whether sentence (16), as used on either occasion, manages to express a (perspective-involving) proposition, they agree that in using it on those two occasions the detective would be asserting two different things, each involving his perspective at the time. After he gathers additional evidence, he believes something he didn't believe before. He may continue to believe what he believed before (that, relative to his earlier perspective, the butler could have done it), but this is not the belief he expresses in making the later assertion. According to the Relativist, on the other hand, the detective believes the same thing all along, that the butler could have done it, but this non-classical proposition is first true relative to his earlier perspective and later true relative to his later perspective.

Relativism captures the natural intuition that the detective continues to believe the same thing, but it is hard put to explain just how the detective can rightly say that he was right all along (just as in *Changing Your Mind* it is hard put to explain how the detective can rightly say that he was wrong earlier). To be sure, he continues to believe the same thing, but he does so from a different perspective. Again, Relativism is faced with the problem of perspectival solipsism—it cannot readily explain how one can consider a given perspectivally neutral EP proposition from different perspectives.

---

[30] Notice that I don't say "continues to believe that" because I do not want to assume that he continues to believe the same thing. In this regard, I am not assuming that the 'that'-clause of a true belief attribution must fully specify something that the subject believes. In my view, identical 'that'-clauses of two different true belief attributions can partially specify two different beliefs. See Bach (1997).

Whenever another perspective is involved, Relativism seems forced to change the subject to perspective-involving propositions. And this raises the question whether perspectivally neutral propositions are needed after all.

Perhaps that is not as serious a problem as that facing Contextualism and Radical Invariantism, which have the detective believing two different things, one before and another after gathering additional evidence. Indeed, both these views seem to make it difficult to verify an EP proposition. For as soon as one gathers additional evidence for a given epistemic possibility, one ends up verifying a new perspective-involving proposition. Just as Contextualism and Radical Invariantism seem to have trouble explaining how in *Changing Your Mind* the detective could have rightly thought that he was wrong earlier, in this case they seem to have trouble explaining how he could rightly think that he has verified what he previously thought.

The solution, as before, is to distinguish accepting or rejecting an epistemic possibility from believing or disbelieving an epistemic possibility proposition. When the detective verifies the possibility that the butler did it, he is gathering additional evidence that supports the proposition that this state of affairs obtains. A new EP proposition is verified, but it is the same possibility that remains open, now relative to his updated knowledge base. As before, what is important is not what is possible relative to what perspective but what is possible relative to what one knows now.

6. Further, Trickier Examples

So far we have considered uses of bare EP sentences where the speaker's perspective figures in. As we will now see, there are other cases in which it does not. And in some of those cases not even the perspective of the person considering the utterance figures in.[31]

6.1. *Suggesting a possibility*

Sometimes one mentions a possibility not because it is open relative to one's own information but because it is open relative to the audience's, as when a parent or a teacher suggests a possibility to a child or a student. In such cases it is the audience's perspective, not one's own, that comes into play. For example, suppose you have hidden a ball from your child. Your child has looked in various places, but has not thought to look in certain other places. So you mention a possibility:

(20)   The ball might be under a cushion on the sofa.

You know that it is actually in the empty vase on the coffee table. But in uttering (20) you don't mean that as far as *you* know the ball might be under a cushion. Even so, what you mean is true. For what you mean is that as far as the child knows the ball

---

[31] I am using 'figure in' in a neutral way, to finesse the difference between being a constituent of a perspective-involving proposition and being the perspective relative to which or from which a perspectivally neutral proposition is evaluated.

might be under a cushion. Or, as the relativist has it, what you mean is that the ball might be under a cushion, a relative proposition which, though not true relative to your perspective, is true relative to the child's.

Something similar happens when a teacher asks a student a question about an overlooked possibility. Suppose you are teaching chess and your student is trying to find the best move in a certain position. The student proposes what is in fact the best move and gives some analysis to back it up, but he has overlooked a plausible but unsound sacrificial reply. So you say "What about the knight sac on e6?" or, less colloquially,

(21) Sacrificing the knight on e6 might be good for White.

Since you see the refutation of that move, you don't mean that as far as *you* know the knight sac might be good. Rather, you mean that as far as the student knows the knight sac might be good. Here the relativist would say that what you suggested is that the knight sac might be good, which though not true relative to your perspective, is true relative to the student's.

In these two examples, it seems that what the speaker means is true, even though the mentioned states of affairs are not possible relative to his perspective. So the relevant perspective cannot be the speaker's. If it were, then, given the speaker's evident authority on the subject matter, the hearer could infer that the core propositions are true (that the ball *is* under a cushion or that the knight sac *is* good), which obviously is not intended. In these cases, clearly the hearer's perspective is the relevant one.

These cases pose a problem for both Contextualism and Relativism. Whether what the speaker means is a proposition involving the hearer's perspective, as Contextualism has it, or is a perspectivally neutral proposition, as on Relativism, these views need to explain how, as a matter of *semantic* fact, it is specifically the hearer's perspective that figures in and why it is neither the speaker's nor an arbitrary eavesdropper's. For there is nothing special about the sentences: (20) and (21) could both be used, in a different situation, to make statements in which the speaker's perspective figures in. The speaker could be the one looking for the ball or wondering if the knight sac is good. The difference in situation affects what the speaker could reasonably intend and plausibly be taken to mean, not the semantic content of the uttered sentence. This factor favors Radical Invariantism.

6.2. Asking about a possibility

This case poses a little puzzle. Often when we are curious or concerned about something, we naturally ask someone who is more informed about it than we are. Even if they are not in a position to resolve the issue, we can still ask them about the possibilities. For example, a bout of chronic coughing might lead you to consult a pulmonary specialist. At some point in the course of the examination, unnerved by the doctor's silence you come out and ask.

(22) Is it possible that I have lung cancer?

Here's the little puzzle. If you are asking about this possibility, presumably it is not ruled out by the information you already have. So it is possible for you that you have lung cancer. But, then, why are you asking the question? It seems that you are asking a question to which you already know the answer! This is not like the case of the teacher asking a question to mention a possibility to a student, where the teacher's own information already rules out that possibility. You ask the doctor not because you want to see if she knows the answer but because you yourself want to know it. But it seems that you already do. So why ask?

There must be a simple solution to this little puzzle, having something to do with the fact that you do not know the answer relative to the superior information available to the person you are asking. Obviously, the pulmonary specialist, with her expertise and the information she gains by examining you, is in a much better epistemic position than you to assess your medical condition. Although you know that further tests would be needed to determine if you actually do have lung cancer, you are confident that the examination is providing her with information that could definitively rule out that possibility.

Radical Invariantism, when augmented with simple pragmatic considerations, seems best able to give a straightforward account of what is going on in this case. The patient is asking the doctor whether it is possible, relative to the doctor's body of information, that the patient has lung cancer. Contextualism and Relativism might try to explain the irrelevance of the speaker's perspective on the grounds that the speaker knows less than the hearer.[32] However, this is not a necessary condition for asking a question about a possibility. Here is a case in which the speaker knows more. A lawyer challenges a witness's testimony by asking, "Isn't it possible that you saw the defendant's twin brother, not the defendant himself?" Even though the questioner knows *more* (the lawyer knows perfectly well that her client, not his twin brother, was at the scene of the crime), the perspective that figures in here is that of the person being asked, not the questioner's.

6.3. *Attitude reports*

When we ascribe beliefs or other attitudes about possibilities to other people and use bare EP sentences in the 'that'-clause of the ascription, normally the relevant perspective is that of the person we're talking about, as in (23).

(23) Ed thinks that Earl might have a chainsaw.

The ascribee's perspective figures in here, not the ascriber's or the audience's. Indeed, it seems that this is the only perspective that figures in, even if the focus of the

---

[32] Another suggestion is that it is the interrogative form of a sentence used to ask a question that explains why the hearer's perspective figures in. However, this explanation can't be right, since one can ask a question with declarative sentences, of forms like 'I wonder who ...' or 'I would like to know what ...'. But if the explanation is based not on the form of the sentence but on the speech act being performed in uttering it, then clearly it is a pragmatic explanation.

conversation is on someone else's perspective. So, for example, suppose that we are discussing why Ed stopped his violent son Ted from going to his reclusive neighbor Earl's house. We couldn't use (23) to indicate that Ed, who knows that Earl doesn't have a chainsaw, thinks that as far as Ted knows, Earl might have a chainsaw.

There seems to be no room for shifting perspectives in this case. Contextualism says that it is the context of utterance that determines which perspective gets included in the proposition expressed by (23). However, the perspective can only be Ed's—whose it is can't vary with the context. I suppose a contextualist could reply that when the bare EP sentence is embedded in the 'that'-clause of an attitude ascription, the relevant fact about the context is that the attitude is being ascribed to a certain person, so that it is this person's perspective that figures in. But this linguistic fact is relevant only because of its pragmatic relevance. It is something that a speaker can reasonably expect a reasonable hearer to regard as the relevant perspective. Radical Invariantism can exploit this fact, because it does not require the semantics of bare EP sentences to account for the relevant perspective. Rather, as a matter of pragmatic fact, the conversationally relevant perspective is the uniquely salient one, in this case the ascribee's. It is made salient by the fact that the incompletely specified attitude content is the ascribee's. So it is the one that a speaker can reasonably expect a reasonable hearer to regard as the relevant one. This suggests that if some other perspective were the relevant one, it would have to be mentioned, as in the relativized (24):

(24) Ed thinks that as far as Ted knows Earl might have a chainsaw.

Here the content of the ascribed belief is explicitly a perspective-involving proposition.

The relativist will insist that both Contextualism and Radical Invariantism mischaracterize the content of the belief ascribed by a speaker of (23). Because (23) mentions no perspective, no perspective is included in its content. That is, the speaker is reporting that what Ed thinks is merely the bare EP proposition that Earl might have a chainsaw. But this poses a problem for Relativism. Consider that for Ed's belief to be true, the proposition that Earl might have a chainsaw must be true relative to Ed's perspective. However, Relativism does not discriminate among perspectives. One way for that proposition to be true is for it to be true relative to Fred's perspective, which it could be even if it is not true relative to Ed's. So suppose Ed says to Fred, "Earl might have a chainsaw", and then it dawns on Ed that Earl does not own any large tools and that it's his brother Burl who does. Ed knew this all along, despite his momentary memory lapse. So Ed was mistaken in thinking that Earl might have a chainsaw, as he immediately realized. Yet what if Fred believes that Earl owns many large tools? From Fred's perspective it is true that Earl might have a chainsaw. So from Fred's perspective Ed correctly said that. But what Ed said was false, as Ed is the first to admit. Relativism seems unable to limit the relevant evaluation of what Ed said to Ed's perspective.

6.4. Factive attitude reports

When the attitude verb is factive, it is even more difficult for Relativism to account for why only the ascribee's perspective is relevant. Consider this example.

(25) Ed realizes that Earl might own a chainsaw.

The reporter's use of a factive verb ('realizes') indicates his agreement with the ascribee about the epistemic possibility proposition in question and his endorsement of the ascribee's belief. But change the case slightly and things are different. Put it in the past tense and suppose that the reporter knows full well that the core proposition is false. Let's say that Fred is talking about why antisocial Ed called on his neighbors last year. He knows that Earl has never owned a chainsaw, but remembers that Ed was looking to borrow various things from various people. Ed's limited information about who owned what enabled him to narrow down the possibilities somewhat. Knowing that a chainsaw was one of the things Ed wanted to borrow, Fred utters (26), in order to explain why Ed went to Earl's house.

(26) Ed realized that Earl might have owned a chainsaw.

Fred seems to be speaking truly here. But suppose Fred knows that Ed doesn't own a chainsaw. Then Fred doesn't believe (relative to his own perspective) that Earl might have owned a chainsaw. In asserting that Ed realizes that Earl might have owned one, he endorses the proposition that Earl might have owned a chainsaw, but relative to Ed's perspective, not his own. The problem for Relativism is to account for the irrelevance of Fred's perspective, from which what Ed realizes is false. After all, Fred is sincerely and truly asserting that Ed realizes that Earl might have owned a chainsaw (a perspectivally neutral proposition, according to Relativism), even though Fred himself disbelieves it. The relativist needs a way for the reporter's perspective to stay out of the picture so that the reporter can endorse this perspectivally neutral proposition from the agent's perspective (as opposed to endorsing the perspective-involving proposition that has the agent's perspective as a constituent).

6.5. Action explanation

Even without being embedded, a bare EP sentence can be used to explain an action. For example, a visitor asks my wife why I briefly went outside, and she replies with (27),

(27) He might have left the keys in the front door.

What matters here is my perspective, not hers. Having just come in through the front door, she might know full well that the keys can't be there. So her perspective doesn't matter. Indeed, she could have gone further and replied with the factive (28).

(28) He realized that he might have left the keys in the front door.

As we just saw, this doesn't commit her to believing that from her perspective I might have left the keys in the front door.

It might be objected regarding (27), where the bare EP sentence is not embedded, that there is no commitment to the relevant perspective-involving proposition; my wife is committed only to the fact that I *thought* that I might have left the keys in the front door. However, this objection, if valid, would show too much. We frequently explain people's actions in terms of facts they are aware of. For example, my wife could explain why I shut off the stove by saying, "The water was boiling." She does not have to hedge her explanation by saying, "He thought the water was boiling." Of course, if the whistling I heard were not that of the tea kettle, then this explanation would be incorrect. But it doesn't follow that it is actually incorrect. What's more, to shift to the attitude attributing form is to shift from a reasons explanation to a causal explanation. My reason for turning off the stove was that the water was boiling, not that I thought it was boiling.

6.6. Temporal modification

It seems that temporal modifiers that occur in bare EP sentences with 'might' and 'possible' generally take narrow scope even when they occur outside the EP term. Consider (29), for example:

(29) Yesterday Barry might have been in New York.

An utterance of (29) would seem to concern where Barry might have been the previous day, not whether on that day it was possible that he was there. It is more plausibly read as saying that Barry might have been in New York yesterday. However, the situation is less clear with (30), which contains two tense markers.

(30) Yesterday it was possible that Barry was in New York.

The preferred reading of (30) seems to be that it was possible yesterday (even if not today) that Barry was in New York (presumably yesterday but perhaps at some earlier time). Indeed, it does not seem that (30) has a reading according to which it is now possible that Barry was in New York yesterday. For that we need (31), which has 'is' in place of the first 'was' in (30):

(31) It is possible that Barry was in New York yesterday.

Even so, I am not suggesting that the preferred reading of (30) is all that good. That is because (30) does not indicate the relevant perspective. The relativized (32) does:

(32) Yesterday, given what we knew then, it was possible that Barry was in New York.

This point is clearer in cases where the state of affairs in question is atemporal, as here:

(33) Twenty years ago it was possible that Fermat's Last Theorem was false.

In this case, the temporal modification cannot plausibly be taken to bear on the time at which Fermat's Last Theorem was false. Indeed, even someone who thinks that a mathematical claim can change truth value over time would need to use (34), not (33), to mean that Fermat's Last Theorem might have been false twenty years earlier.

(34) It is possible that Fermat's Last Theorem was false twenty years ago.

So it seems that with their two tense markers temporally modified 'it was possible' sentences, such as (30) and (33), concern the time of the perspective, not the time of the state of affairs, whereas temporally modified single clause 'might' sentences, such as (30), concern the time of the state of affairs.

These brief observations are provisional. The subject of temporally modified bare EP sentences is much too complicated to discuss here in detail. Unfortunately, the in-depth investigations I am familiar with, notably Condoravdi (2002) and von Fintel and Iatridou (2003), do not specifically discuss the place of perspective or address the contrast between bare and relativized EP sentences. For now I can only speculate that wherever there is a puzzle involving tense or temporal modification in bare EP sentences, the puzzle probably arises because despite there being an indication of the time of the relevant perspective there is no indication of whose perspective it is. This just goes to show that if you wish to assert that something was possible relative to a certain perspective at a certain time, you need to indicate, as in (32), the perspective as well as the time.

7. General Problems for Relativism

Contextualism and Relativism are subject to problems that go beyond their difficulties at handling particular cases. These concern their underlying assumptions and the philosophical motivations behind them. I will discuss problems with Relativism first, because of its appeal to non-classical perspectivally neutral propositions. In the next section I will turn to some basic problems for Contextualism.

Relativists rarely mention, much less discuss, relativized EP sentences and their semantic contents. Even so, I think it is safe to assume that relativists do not deny that these sentences semantically express perspective-involving EP propositions, classical propositions true or false independently of the context in which they are conveyed or considered. What relativists claim is that there are perspectivally neutral EP propositions as well, that these are non-classical, relative propositions, and that bare EP sentences express them. This view gives rise to several problems. One concerns the relativist conception of propositions in general, and several are specific to the relativist account of bare EP sentences. I will touch only briefly on the general worry about the relativist's propositions, since it is not specific to the semantics of bare EP sentences. A question specific to them is whether, in order to make sense of our uses of bare EP sentences and of the semantic contents of the sentences themselves, there is any need to invoke perspectivally neutral propositions in the first place.

The relativist's non-classical propositions are supposed to be true or false relative to or from a perspective, so that such a proposition could be true from one perspective and false from another. The following example suggests a problem with that.[33] Suppose that the (putative) proposition in question is that Central Park might be larger than Golden Gate Park. Suppose Rudy figures that since New York is so much bigger than San Francisco, its most famous park could well be bigger too. Meanwhile, I know for a fact that Golden Gate Park is more than 20% larger in area than Central Park. Now the relativist view is that there is one proposition, that Central Park might be larger than Golden Gate Park, which is true relative to Rudy's perspective and false relative to mine. But what is such a proposition? Offhand it would seem that a proposition corresponds to a possible or conceivable way the world is. That is, the proposition is true just in case the world is as the proposition says it is. This view of propositions is not preserved on the relativist conception. If it were, the world could be one way from Rudy's perspective and another way relative to mine.[34] Of course the world could *seem* different from our respective perspectives, but obviously that is not the relativist's point. Nor is it that being possible from Rudy's perspective is compatible with not being possible from mine. These are two different relational properties that a state of affairs (such as Central Park being larger than Golden Gate Park) could have, as ascribed by different perspective-involving EP propositions. The relativist claim is that one and the same proposition (that Central Park might be larger than Golden Gate Park) could be true relative to Rudy's perspective and false relative to mine.[35]

From the standpoint of Radical Invariantism, the propositions posited by Relativism amount to no more than propositional radicals, if considered as the semantic contents of bare EP sentences, or partially specified classical propositions, if considered as contents of thoughts about epistemic possibilities. I think it is fair to regard this as the default hypothesis about them. To show that this hypothesis is inadequate, the relativist needs to show that perspectivally neutral EP propositions play an indispensable role in our talk about epistemic possibility. For example, he needs to argue that people can disagree and change their minds about epistemic possibilities in a way that attributing classical propositional contents to our attitudes cannot make sense of.

---

[33] There is also at least a terminological problem with the relativist notion of assessment sensitivity. MacFarlane describes epistemic modal terms (and expressions of certain other types, such as predicates of personal taste) as "assessment-sensitive", but this is misleading. For it is not the assessment but the context of assessment to which the truth of a relative EP proposition is supposed to be relative. What matters is not whether the agent assesses this proposition as true or false but that the agent possesses a certain body of knowledge (information, evidence) relative to which this proposition is true or false. MacFarlane seems to use 'true at a context of assessment' interchangeably with 'true as assessed from a context of assessment' (this volume: 168 n.24), but, so far as I can tell, the assessing itself plays no role in his account.

[34] Worth noting here is what Michael Glanzberg (2009) calls "the easy road to relativism", the argument that since truth is relative to a world anyway, there is no principled roadblock to extending its relativization to other parameters, such as perspectives. Glanzberg argues that, contrary to popular opinion, relativization of truth to worlds plays no essential role in semantic theory and plays merely a heuristic role in meta-theory.

[35] This and related problems are brought out more fully by Crispin Wright (2008). Wright and also Paul Boghossian (2006), in the course of discussing various sorts of relativism, register their doubts as to whether truth relativism in a given area can amount to anything more than property relativism in that area.

Because they have restricted their attention to bare EP sentences, it has not occurred to relativists to do this.

The burden on the relativist is to show that what he regards as the truth of a perspectivally neutral EP proposition relative to a given perspective amounts to something other than the truth of a classical EP proposition that involves that perspective. To show this it is not enough to point out that two people who both think that possibly *p*, their different perspectives notwithstanding, must have something in common. For that does not show that they believe the same thing. It shows only that they believe something of the same sort and to that extent have a belief property in common. Surely it does not follow from the fact that two people love their mother that they love the same person. Even so, they share the property of loving their (respective) mothers. Similarly, the mere fact that two people could use the same bare EP sentence to convey their respective beliefs does not show, even if the sentence has invariant semantic content, that they believe the same thing. Even if they share the property of accepting the same epistemic possibility, it does not follow that they believe the same EP proposition.

Another challenge for Relativism is show that its account of bare EP sentences coheres with the semantics of relativized EP sentences, which express perspective-involving EP propositions. Such a proposition says that a certain state of affairs is possible relative to a certain perspective. So if a bare EP sentence expresses all but a perspective, the simple (perhaps naïve) conclusion to draw is that it falls short of expressing a full-fledged EP proposition—it seems to lack an essential ingredient. To rebut this simple conclusion the relativist needs to explain how and why the semantic content of a bare EP sentence amounts to anything more than an underspecified content of any corresponding relativized EP sentence. And it must explain this in such a way that expressions like 'might' and 'possible' have the same meanings regardless of which sort of sentence they occur in.

Finally, there is our earlier worry that Relativism seems to lead to a certain *perspectival solipsism:* one can consider a perspectivally neutral EP proposition only from one's current perspective, not from an earlier perspective, much less from anyone else's, past or present. To consider an EP proposition relative to an earlier or another's perspective is just to consider a relativized EP proposition involving that perspective—one can't consider a perspectivally neutral EP proposition (if there is such a thing) from any but one's current perspective. All this makes one wonder whether what one believes from one's current perspective isn't just a classical EP proposition involving that perspective.

8. General Problems for Contextualism

Contextualism and Radical Invariantism agree that all EP propositions involve perspectives, propositions that are absolutely true or false and are expressed (invariantly) by relativized EP sentences (given that any and all indexical, including time, references are fixed). But Contextualism maintains that they can also be expressed by *bare*

EP sentences, though which such proposition a given bare EP sentence expresses depends on the context in which it is used. The semantic content of a given bare EP sentence as used in a given context involves a perspective, which is somehow provided or otherwise determined by that context. The question is whether there is any good reason to suppose this.

From the standpoint of Radical Invariantism, it is gratuitous to attribute complete propositional contents, however variable, to bare EP sentences just on the basis of intuitions of truth or falsity. That just takes for granted that these intuitions pertain to the sentences themselves.[36] The mere fact that we can convey propositions when we use them and grasp propositions when we hear them does not show that they semantically express those propositions. The semantically more modest position, that of Radical Invariantism, is that there is nothing variable or shifty in the semantic content of a bare EP sentence. What is variable is how the sentence can be used or how an utterance of it can be taken, with its semantically invariant but propositionally incomplete content completed by the addition of a perspective, thereby turning a propositional radical into a proposition. Rather than appeal to supposedly semantic intuitions, proponents of Contextualism need to provide some linguistic basis for claiming that bare EP sentences contain variables that get assigned values by certain features of the context of utterance (or else are quantified over by being in the scope of some suitable quantifier phrase). Lacking evidence for this supposition, we should adopt the default hypothesis that there are no such variables.

Contextualism must also confront what I'll call the uniqueness problem. That is, it needs to be formulated in a way that works for the variety of ways in which bare EP sentences can be used, as illustrated in Sections 5 and 6. The relevant perspective generally includes the speaker's, but in many cases it extends beyond that, beyond even the joint perspective of the speaker and hearer. In order to come up with a unitary account, the contextualist can try to extend the reach of the relevant group but, as John MacFarlane points out, "there is no way to keep the group from expanding indefinitely" (this volume: 161).[37] Besides, as some of our examples illustrated, the perspective that figures into the proposition allegedly expressed by the bare EP sentence sometimes does not include the speaker's. The relevant one might be the hearer's

---

[36] I discuss the error of putting too much credence in seemingly semantic intuitions, e.g. by mistaking pragmatic regularities for matters of semantic fact, in Bach (2002) and (2005: 29–33).

[37] As MacFarlane explains, "The problem is that once we let data about third-party assessments and retraction motivate an expansion of the contextually relevant group to include more than just the speaker, there is no way to stop this machine. The same kind of arguments that motivate expanding the relevant group of knowers to include [the eavesdropper] would motivate expanding the relevant group of knowers to include anybody who will ever consider the claim" (this volume: 151). "There [does not] seem to be any stable position that balances these two competing desiderata. If we focus on uptake (third-party assessments, retractions, and disagreement), we are led to expand the relevant body of knowledge, seemingly without end. But if we focus on production, we are led to contract it (on pain of making ordinary, apparently reasonable assertions unwarranted). We are led to a kind of paradox: although the truth of a claim made using epistemic modals must depend somehow on what is known—that is what makes it 'epistemic'—it does not seem to depend on any particular body of knowledge" (155).

perspective, a group perspective that includes the hearer's but not the speaker's, or some third party's or separate group's perspective. And it won't do for the contextualist to offer an *ad hoc* story about which perspective counts as the relevant one in a given case. Nor can the contextualist just summarily claim that in each case the context somehow "determines" which perspective is the relevant one. Which one it is must be a determinate function of some specified contextual parameter. And it would be facile to try to solve the uniqueness problem by claiming that the operative parameter is appropriateness, salience, or the like. That would be a flimsy attempt to sweep a semantic problem under the pragmatic rug.

Invoking the speaker's intention does not help here.[38] That would effectively concede that context plays merely a pragmatic role, not a semantic one. For once we invoke the speaker's intention, we can no longer claim that context itself determines which perspective is the relevant one.[39] For context here plays only an evidential role. It comprises the mutually salient contextual information that the audience is to use to ascertain the speaker's communicative intention, partly on the basis that they are so intended. Context in this sense does not determine, in the (metaphysical) sense of constituting, what the speaker means. An unreasonable speaker could mean something that his audience is unable to identify, and nothing in the context (or in the meaning of the bare EP sentence he uses) prevents him from meaning that. When communication succeeds, the speaker must utter a sentence whose utterance makes evident what he means. In that case, context combines with what he says *and the fact that he says it* (this is what makes its role pragmatic) to provide the audience with the basis for determining, in the (epistemological) sense of ascertaining, not constituting, what the speaker means. Whereas context bears on what the speaker can reasonably mean (this comes to the same thing as what his audience can plausibly take him to mean), the speaker's communicative intention determines what he does mean.

So any version of Contextualism worthy of the name must explain how context literally determines the relevant perspective involved in the proposition allegedly expressed by a bare EP sentence in a given context. From the standpoint of Radical Invariantism, this problem arises only because of the Context Sensitivity and the Proposition Fallacies, which combine to lead contextualists to think that if a sentence doesn't semantically express a proposition independently of context, it must do so in a way that depends on context. Fortunately, you don't have to be a contextualist to accept the view that all EP propositions involve perspectives and are true or false absolutely. To accept this you do not have to suppose that bare EP sentences manage (in some context-sensitive way) to semantically express such propositions.

---

[38]   The points in this paragraph about speakers' intentions and context are defended more fully in Bach (2005: 36–9).

[39]   It is important to note that the speaker's communicative intention is not itself part of the context. For if context is to play the explanatory role claimed of it, it must be something that is the same for the speaker as it is for his audience, and obviously the role of the speaker's intention is not the same for both.

9. Radical Invariantism: Objections and Replies

As noted earlier, Contextualism was motivated by the obvious inadequacy of Propositional Invariantism, and Relativism in turn by the shortcomings of Contextualism. Radical Invariantism is partly motivated by the shortcomings of both, but also by their insights. It agrees with Contextualism about what EP propositions there are and it agrees with Relativism that the semantic contents of bare EP sentences do not vary. I take Radical Invariantism to be the default position on the semantics of bare EP sentences, but that doesn't mean it isn't subject to objections. I will take up the best ones I can think of. The first charges that Radical Invariantism is nothing more than a version of Contextualism, and the others allege that Radical Invariantism implies something false about the claims we make and thoughts we express when we use bare EP sentences.

9.1. Radical Invariantism is just a version of Contextualism

People often complain to me that Radical Invariantism is just a version of Contextualism (and fraught with the same problems). After all, it agrees that EP propositions involve perspectives, that the meaning of a bare EP sentence underdetermines which such proposition a speaker means in using the sentence literally, and that in some sense context fills in the gap. But, I say, there the resemblance ends. For one thing, the sense in which context fills in the gap is radically different. Radical Invariantism rejects the contextualist claim that context literally determines which perspective figures into the relevant EP proposition. What proposition this is can vary from context to context, but this doesn't mean that the context determines which one. And, as explained in the previous section, invoking either salience or the speaker's intention is tantamount to conceding that context plays not a semantic but merely an evidential, pragmatic role. It provides the hearer with evidence regarding what EP proposition the speaker means, but it does not fix the EP proposition that is supposed to be expressed semantically.

Another source for this objection is the idea, discussed at the end of Section 4, that what is at issue is the semantic content of *utterances* of bare EP sentences, not that of the sentences themselves. To that I can only repeat what I said then. The term 'utterance' can refer either to a sentence that is uttered or to an act of uttering a sentence. Here it doesn't apply to sentences. But if it applies to acts of uttering sentences, this won't help. Utterances are speech acts, the subject matter of pragmatics, not semantics.

9.2. Radical Invariantism gets the phenomenology wrong

It might be objected on phenomenological grounds that, despite arguments to the contrary but in accordance with appearances, bare EP sentences really do express propositions. This objection is based on the observation that when we entertain, accept, or reject a possibility, we do not *seem* to do so relative to a perspective. The perspective does not strike us as getting into the content of the attitude we have toward the possibility. Accordingly, when as speakers we utter a bare EP sentence, we straightforwardly say what we mean, and what we mean is a perspectivally neutral proposition. We do not have the sense that we are speaking elliptically, omitting reference to our perspective, in the way we would if we uttered "I haven't have lunch" and meant that we haven't yet had lunch that day. In the latter case, we would immediately acknowledge, if asked, that this is what we meant. This difference leaves open the question of what it is for a perspectivally neutral proposition to be true, but that is where Relativism comes in (assuming Propositional Invariantism is a non-starter). Relativism is an answer to that question, but the objection itself does not assume Relativism.

The short answer to this objection is that appearances can be deceiving, in particular about the structure of propositions about epistemic possibilities. Consider other cases, involving predicates like 'offensive', 'scary', and 'obvious'. People can use them in simple sentences to say things and express attitudes that they take to be absolute, not relational. However, it does not follow that the relevant facts are absolute rather than relational. If they are relational, as presumably they are, then it is plausible that these facts are captured only by perspective-involving propositions (in a broad sense of 'perspective').

I suppose that one could concede this reply, so far as it goes, but argue that even though there are no bare epistemic possibility facts (because of the perspective relativity of epistemic possibility), people can still have beliefs and make claims about epistemic possibilities that are not relativized. This would be analogous to the suggestion that people believe things and make claims about motion or weight without realizing that motion and weight are relative (to frame of reference and gravitational field, respectively). However, implementing this suggestion would require adopting a strong error theory about people's ordinary epistemic possibility beliefs and claims. Such a theory seems relatively plausible regarding beliefs and claims about motion and weight, but it is much less plausible regarding beliefs and claims about offensiveness, scariness, or obviousness—or epistemic possibility, whose relativity seems, well, obvious.[40]

9.3. Radical Invariantism mischaracterizes the mental representation of EP propositions

This objection is similar to the previous one, but it concerns the representation of EP propositions, not the phenomenology of believing or asserting them. The objection, quite simply, is that when we assertively utter bare EP sentences or have beliefs that dispose us to utter them, we do not mentally represent perspectives. Not only does the bare EP sentence that a speaker utters not represent a perspective, neither does the speaker or his mental state.

---

[40] Boghossian (2006) and Wright (2008) insightfully examine this and related issues that arise from different versions of theses that certain ostensibly monadic properties are actually relational.

This contention provides the basis for an indirect argument against Radical Invariantism. Assume that when a speaker assertively utters a sentence, what he asserts is a proposition and, since assertion is the expression of belief, the content of the belief he expresses is that proposition. But Radical Invariantism denies that bare EP sentences express propositions. So it implies that the belief a speaker expresses when using a bare EP sentence has a content that includes more than the semantic content of the sentence, namely a perspective, typically the speaker's (could this objection plausibly apply to any other case?). But there is no mental representation of a perspective in this case. So the proposition that a speaker asserts and presumably believes when uttering a bare EP sentence does not include a perspective.

I grant that this would be a compelling argument against Radical Invariantism if indeed speakers who use bare EP sentences do not represent perspectives. But I do not concede that. A perspective can be represented without being explicitly represented. Here is an analogy. Considering a possibility relative to one's current body of information is like seeing an object as being at a certain distance and direction. Just as you do not have to represent your location and orientation to see (or judge) an object as being roughly twenty feet away and off to your right, so you do not have to represent your current body of information in order to judge that some possibility is compatible with it. As with polar coordinates, the center is built into the system of representation and does not itself have to be represented. Whether you deem a possibility as live or far-fetched, you do so from your current perspective, that is, relative to your current view of things. To represent something as from your point of view does not require representing your point of view. It just requires occupying that point of view.[41]

In this connection it is plausible to suppose that by default we represent epistemic possibilities from our own current cognitive perspective. Epistemic possibilities are, we might say, *default-egocentric*. That is, we consider them from our own current perspective unless we are prompted to consider them from a different perspective. It is only when some other perspective comes into play that we explicitly consider the possibility relative to a perspective (we can't view it *from* that perspective since we do not occupy that perspective). Only when the relevant perspective is different from our own current one does the perspective have to be represented. When considering or even temporarily adopting a different perspective, we must represent a possibility as relative to that perspective. So, for example, if you believe that your grandfather thought it possible that the world was created in 4004 BC, you take it that he thought this relative to the body of information he had. The situation is analogous to believing that a certain object in another person's field of vision is at a certain distance and direction from them.

---

[41] This observation ties in with views about thought that invoke notions like belief *de se*, essential indexicals, or centered possible worlds.

9.4. Radical Invariantism "overgenerates"

The worry here is that by keeping perspectives out of the semantics of bare EP sentences, Radical Invariantism imposes no constraint on what speakers can mean in uttering such sentences. It allows that a speaker could utter 'I might be a spy', knowing full well that he is not a spy, but mean that from Dick Cheney's perspective the speaker might be a spy.

It is true that Radical Invariantism, as a thesis about the semantics of bare EP sentences, imposes no such constraint. That is the job of a pragmatic account of how such sentences can reasonably be used or plausibly be understood to convey more than they express semantically. Such an account begins with the observation that there is a general, rational constraint on speakers' communicative intentions, namely that they be recognizable by the intended audience. A speaker cannot utter a sentence and rationally mean anything he pleases. He must mean something that he can reasonably expect to be taken as meaning. In the case of bare EP sentences, there must be a unique candidate that the audience can identify as the relevant perspective. Otherwise, there would be no determinate way of taking the utterance, in which case the speaker would need to make the relevant perspective explicit. As we saw in discussing various cases, the uses of an unembedded bare EP sentence often involves the joint perspective of the interlocutors, not a third party's. There has to be some evident reason for the hearer to suppose that the relevant perspective is one that does not include the speaker's and it needs to be evident whose perspective that is. We saw cases, namely *Suggesting a Possibility* and *Asking about a Possibility,* where the relevant perspective is the hearer's. And, as we saw with cases in which a third party's attitude is being reported or action is being explained, normally it is that person's perspective that comes into play. In such cases the focus is not on the possibility itself but on the person's attitude or action.

In my view there is no semantic account to be had of how perspectives enter into the uses of bare EP sentences, in either of the ways suggested by contextualists and relativists. There is also no need for such an account. In denying that perspectives enter into the semantic contents of these sentences I am not denying the need for a pragmatic account of the ways in which speakers can reasonably intend and expect utterances of bare EP sentences to be taken and the ways in which such utterances can reasonably be taken (see the Appendix for some general conjectures in this regard). This is a matter of accounting for which perspective comes into play in a given case even though it is not mentioned. In some cases no unique perspective comes into play, and interlocutors talk past each other. In those cases, as well as those in which the intended perspective is not the one that would be uniquely salient if none were mentioned, the speaker needs to make explicit what the intended perspective is. From a pragmatic point of view, the problem posed by bare EP sentences is not to account for how extralinguistic facts combine with sentence meaning to determine what perspective figures in to an utterance of the sentence. Rather, the challenge is explain under what circumstances a speaker does not need to use a relativized EP sentence to communicate what the relevant perspective is. In some cases, a wary speaker will use a bare EP sentence to leave himself some wiggle room as to what the relevant perspective is. He could be poised either to embrace the perspective of the audience (or perhaps an outside source of information) or to retreat to his own perspective. So, it turns out that the semantics of bare EP sentences is not all that interesting. Much more interesting are the uses to which we put them, as illustrated by the examples we have discussed.

10. The Bottom Line

It is agreed on all sides that a state of affairs is or is not epistemically possible only relative to a perspective, a body of information. Epistemic possibility sentences that mention perspectives (or persons with perspectives) semantically express propositions that include perspectives (or persons) as constituents. These are classical proposititions, absolutely true or false (orthogonal issues of vagueness aside). The semantic puzzle about epistemic possibility arises with sentences that do not mention perspectives. Solving it requires recognizing a couple of distinctions. First, we need to distinguish the semantic question of what bare EP sentences express from the metaphysical question of what EP propositions there are to be expressed. That leaves open whether the semantic contents of bare EP sentences add up to propositions. We also need to distinguish this semantic question from the pragmatic question of what propositions speakers can use such sentences to convey (and how hearers understand these uses).

Contextualism holds that a given bare EP sentence expresses perspective-involving EP propositions, different ones in different contexts. Relativism holds that such a sentence expresses (irrelevant indexicality aside) a single, perspectivally neutral proposition independently of context, but that this non-classical proposition can be true or false from, or relative to, different contexts. Both views have trouble handling certain cases, but they face more general difficulties as well. Partly as the result of focusing on bare EP sentences and neglecting their relativized counterparts, both contextualists and relativists have overlooked the possibility that bare EP sentences, like a great many other sentences, simply fall short of fully expressing propositions. These theorists have not asked themselves if their seemingly semantic intuitions are responsive not to the truth values of the sentences themselves but rather to how speakers use and understand uses of these sentences. That takes us beyond semantics into the realm of pragmatics.

Radical Invariantism, considered strictly as a view about the semantics of bare EP sentences, agrees with Contextualism about what propositions there are for EP sentences to express but denies that bare EP sentences (as opposed to relativized) are fit to express them. It claims that bare EP sentences express propositional radicals, not full-fledged propositions. Radical Invariantism agrees with Relativism that bare EP sentences are not inherently context-sensitive, but it denies that their invariant semantic contents are fully propositional. From the radical invariantist point of view, contextualists mistake propositional incompleteness for context sensitivity and relativists mistake propositional radicals for propositions. The blind spot induced by the Proposition Fallacy sustains the false hope of formulating some sort of context-sensitive truth-conditional semantics for these sentences. However, it is not a semantic but a metaphysical fact that epistemic possibility is perspective-relative. This is a fact not about 'is possible' but about being epistemically possible, that it is a relation, not a property.[42] Neither contextualists nor relativists have given us any reason to expect this fact to be reflected in the semantics of EP sentences that do not mention perspectives.

Since speakers must use bare EP sentences to convey propositions, at least when they mean something determinate, what they mean must involve a perspective. The relevant perspective is not determined by context, at least not in any legitimate sense of 'determine' or 'context', but by what speakers can reasonably mean (and what hearers can plausibly take them to mean) in uttering these sentences. The problem is not to give a semantic account of the propositional contents of bare EP sentences but to explain pragmatically how we can use or understand uses of them to convey a proposition involving a certain perspective. Usually the perspective is or includes the speaker's, but not always, especially when the bare EP sentence is embedded. In some cases, in order to forestall misunderstanding or incomprehension, we need to make the relevant perspective explicit and must use a relativized epistemic possibility sentence. But we generally know when using a bare epistemic possibility sentence will do, in which case we do not bother mentioning the relevant perspective. Just what this ability involves is something for us as theorists to figure out, but as speakers we have already mastered it pretty well.

Appendix: Possibilities and Pragmatics

Here is a series of observations about the pragmatics of utterances of bare EP sentences. To avoid being tendentious I frame them in as theory-neutral a way as possible. So, for example, when I speak of asserting a possibility, I leave open whether or not the asserted proposition involves a perspective. Space does not permit explaining, illustrating, or justifying these observations in any detail, but they mostly apply basic platitudes in pragmatics to the special case of utterances about epistemic possibilities.

---

[42] Similarly, it is a metaphysical fact that tastiness, offensiveness, boringness, and amusingness are perspective-relative. This is not a semantic fact about 'is tasty', 'is offensive', 'is boring', or 'is amusing'. Rather, it is a metaphysical fact about the things they semantically express, that these things are relations, not properties. Predictably enough, I develop a radical invariantist account of unrelativized sentences containing so-called predicates of personal taste in a companion piece called "Relatively Speaking."

- When you use a bare EP sentence assertively, ordinarily you do not assert a mere or idle possibility. If it is worth mentioning, presumably you take it to be a more serious possibility than that and intend it to be taken as such.
- In asserting that $\Diamond p$('$\Diamond$' means 'it is epistemically possible that'), sometimes you are not so much committing yourself to its being true as refraining from committing yourself to the falsity of its core proposition p.
- Often the point of asserting that $\Diamond p$ is not to inform your audience that $\Diamond p$ or to get them to believe it but, rather, to call it to their attention or, if it is obvious that they already believe that $\Diamond p$, to remind them of it.
- When you assert a possibility, you often do something more than just assert it. Depending on the circumstances, you might be suggesting that it is worth looking into, challenging a claim (a knowledge claim, say), or even advising somebody not to do something because of the risk associated with the possibility.
- You can utter an unembedded bare EP sentence without asserting that $\Diamond p$. You could instead be suggesting that p or even just guessing that p, especially if you use 'perhaps' or 'maybe' rather than 'might' or 'possibly'. In that case, you would be using the term not as a content modifier but as an utterance modifier, to indicate something about what you are doing in uttering the rest of the sentence.
- When you assert that $\Diamond p$, normally you leave open that $\Diamond \sim p$ as well. For if you were foreclosing that possibility, you would be prepared to deny that $\sim p$, hence to assert that p, in which case it would be misleading to assert the weaker $\Diamond p$. Similarly, if you were considering an exhaustive list of possible answers to a *wh*-question and ruled out all but A, you would not merely say that A is a very strong possibility. You would conclude (by elimination) is that the answer *must* be A.
- When you sincerely assert that $\Diamond p$, often you do not expect your audience's knowledge and beliefs to exclude that possibility. In that case, you implicitly assume that if you knew what they know and believed what they believe, you could still coherently believe and assert that $\Diamond p$. So your assertion implicitly incorporates their perspective into your own. You intend the possibility that p to be compatible with your joint perspective.
- On some occasions, however, your audience believes something that if true would rule out the possibility in question. In that case, your assertion that $\Diamond p$, which leaves open that $\Diamond \sim p$ (as observed above), cannot coherently incorporate their perspective.
- In some cases of using an unembedded bare EP sentence, the fact that a state of affairs is compatible with one's *current* perspective is not at issue. Suppose you say, for example, "I have no idea whether $\Diamond p$", and go on to say you are going to look into the matter or proceed to ask your audience whether $\Diamond p$. Obviously it is already possible for you that p. However, that does not keep you from inquiring into it, since what you are interested in is whether $\Diamond p$ from a more informed perspective.
- When you use a relativized EP sentence rather than a bare one, not only do you make explicit what the relevant perspective is but also, by explicitly mentioning it, you make it the focus. Typically what is then at issue is not whether the mentioned state of affairs is possible—you and your audience may think it is not—but something else, such as what the person with that perspective hoped for or feared or perhaps why the person

did a certain thing. Or the point of the assertion may be to call attention to the person's overlooking or disregarding a certain possibility.

- Not mentioning a perspective is a way of keeping the question of the possibility in focus and, moreover, of hedging the question as to whose/which perspective is at issue. This allows for retreating from a joint perspective or distancing yourself from your earlier perspective. In this way you can avoid being overly committed without being too guarded. It allows for either deferring to your interlocutor or sticking to your guns, depending on whether or not you are prepared to let your own perspective be trumped.

References

Bach, Kent (1994). "Conversational Impliciture", *Mind & Language* 9: 124–62.

—— (1997). "Do Belief Reports Report Beliefs?", *Pacific Philosophical Quarterly* 78: 215–41.

—— (1999). "The Myth of Conventional Implicature", *Linguistics and Philosophy* 22: 327–66.

—— (2002). "Seemingly Semantic Intuitions", in J. Keim Campbell, M. O'Rourke, and D. Shier (eds.), *Meaning and Truth* (New York: Seven Bridges Press), 21–33.

—— (2005). "Context *ex Machina*", in Z. Szabó (ed.), *Semantics vs. Pragmatics* (Oxford: Oxford University Press), 15–44.

—— (2006). "The Excluded Middle: Semantic Minimalism without Minimal Propositions", *Philosophy and Phenomenological Research* 73: 435–42.

Boghossian, Paul (2006). "What is Relativism?", in P. Greenough and M. Lynch (eds.), *Truth and Realism* (Oxford: Oxford University Press), 13–37.

Cappelen, Herman, and Lepore, Ernie (2005). *Insensitive Semantics* (Oxford: Blackwell).

Condoravdi, Cleo (2002). "Temporal Interpretation of Modals", in D. Beaver, S. Kaufmann, B. Clark, and L. Casillas (eds.), *The Construction of Meaning* (Stanford: CSLI Publications), 59–88.

DeRose, Keith (1991). "Epistemic Possibilities", *Philosophical Review* 100: 581–605.

Egan, Andy, Hawthorne, John, and Weatherson, Brian (2005). "Epistemic Modals in Context", in G. Preyer and G. Peter (eds.), *Contextualism in Philosophy* (Oxford: Oxford University Press), 131–69.

von Fintel, Kai, and Gillies, Anthony S. (2008). "CIA Leaks", *Philosophical Review* 117: 77–98.

von Fintel, Kai, and Iatridou, Sabine (2003). "Epistemic Containment", *Linguistic Inquiry* 34: 173–98.

Glanzberg, Michael (2009). "Semantics and Truth Relative to a World", *Synthese* 166: 281–307.

Hacking, Ian (1967). "Possibility", *Philosophical Review* 76: 143–68.

Kölbel, Max (2003). "Faultless Disagreement", *Proceedings of the Aristotelian Society* 104: 53–73.

Lasersohn, Peter (2005). "Context Dependence, Disagreement, and Predicates of Personal Taste", *Linguistics and Philosophy* 28: 643–86.

MacFarlane, John (this volume). "Epistemic Modals are Assessment-Sensitive ", ch.5.

Stephenson, Tamina (2007). "Judge Dependence, Epistemic Modals, and Predicates of Personal Taste", *Linguistics and Philosophy* 30: 487–525.

Teller, Paul (1972). "Epistemic Possibility", *Philosophia* 2: 303–20.

Weatherson, Brian (2009). "Conditionals and Indexical Relativism", *Synthese* 166: 333–57.

Williamson, Timothy (2000). *Knowledge and Its Limits* (Oxford: Oxford University Press).

Wright, Crispin (2007). "New Age Relativism and Epistemic Possibility: The Question of Evidence", *Philosophical Issues* 17. *The Metaphysics of Epistemology*: 262–83.

——(2008). "Relativism about Truth Itself: Haphazard Thoughts about the Very Idea", in M. García-Carpintero and M. Kölbel (eds.), *Relative Truth* (Oxford: Oxford University Press) 157–85.

Yalcin, Seth (2007). "Epistemic Modality", *Mind* 116: 983–1026.

2

The Nature of Epistemic Space

David J. Chalmers

1. Ways Things Might Be

There are many ways things might be, for all I know. For all I know, it might be that there is life on Jupiter, and it might be that there is not. It might be that Australia will win the next Ashes series, and it might be that they will not. It might be that my great-grandfather was my great-grandmother's second cousin, and it might be that he was not. It might be that brass is a compound, and it might be that it is not.

There are even more ways things might be, for all I know with certainty. It might be that there are three chairs in this room, and it might be that there are not. It might be that water is H_2O, and it might be that it is not. It might be that my father was born in Egypt, and it might be that he was not. It might be that I have a body, and it might be that I do not.

We normally say that it is *epistemically possible* for a subject that *p*, when it might be that *p* for all the subject knows. So it is epistemically possible for me that there is life on Jupiter, or that brass is a compound. One can define various different standards of epistemic possibility, corresponding to various different standards for knowledge. For example, one might say that it is *epistemically possible in the Cartesian sense* (for a subject) that *p* when it might be that *p*, for all a subject knows with certainty. So in the Cartesian sense, it is epistemically possible for me that water is not H_2O, and it is epistemically possible for me that I do not have a body.

A natural way to think about epistemic possibility is as follows. When it is epistemically possible (for a subject) that *p*, there is an epistemically possible *scenario* (for that subject) in which *p*. A scenario is a maximally specific way things might be: a sort of epistemically possible world, in a loose and intuitive sense. On this picture,

Thanks to the many audiences to which I have presented versions of this paper: at the 2001 Central APA, the 2003 Modality workshop at St Andrews, the 2003 Northwest Philosophy conference, the 2004 Aspects of Knowing conference at UNSW, the 2006 Epistemic Modality conference at ANU, and at talks at the Institut Jean Nicod, Leeds, Melbourne, Nebraska, Oxford, Sheffield, Texas, UCLA, and Vermont. Thanks also to Jens Christian Bjerring, Berit Brogaard, Kit Fine, Gregg Rosenberg, Wolfgang Schwarz, Brian Weatherson, and Bruno Whittle for comments on earlier versions of this paper.

corresponding to the epistemic possibility that Australia will win the next Ashes series are various epistemically possible scenarios in which they win in all sorts of different ways. And corresponding to the Cartesian epistemic possibility that I have no body are various scenarios in which I am disembodied, each epistemically possible by the Cartesian standard: e.g. scenarios in which I am a brain in a vat, or in which I am a disembodied Cartesian mind.

To fill out this picture, we might imagine that there is an overarching space of scenarios. These scenarios constitute *epistemic space*. If a subject did not know anything, all scenarios would be epistemically possible for the subject. When a subject knows something, some scenarios are excluded. Every piece of substantive knowledge corresponds to a division in epistemic space: some scenarios are excluded out as epistemically impossible for the subject, while others are left open. More specifically, it is natural to hold that for a given *p*, there may be scenarios in which *p* is the case, and scenarios in which *p* is not the case. Then when a subject knows that *p*, scenarios in which *p* is not the case are excluded, while others are left open. The scenarios that are epistemically possible for a subject are those that are not excluded by any knowledge of the subject.

One can naturally suppose that the space of scenarios is equally divided by *belief*, and perhaps that the division by belief underlies the division by knowledge. Every substantive belief, whether or not it qualifies as knowledge, corresponds to a division in the space of scenarios. When a subject believes that *p*, we might say that some scenarios (in particular, scenarios in which ¬*p*) are ruled out as *doxastically impossible*, while others are left open. A scenario is doxastically possible for a subject if and only if it is not doxastically ruled out by any of the subject's beliefs. When a belief qualifies as knowledge, the scenarios ruled out as doxastically impossible are also ruled out as epistemically impossible.

A picture of this sort is often present in philosophical discussions of knowledge and belief. Within epistemology, it is common to think of knowledge in terms of the "elimination of possibilities", with some sort of underlying space of possibilities presumed. In discussions of skepticism, for example, the fact that certain skeptical scenarios are not eliminated is used as evidence that certain knowledge claims are not true. In epistemic logic and the theory of belief revision, it is common to model epistemic possibility using epistemic relations to an underlying space of possible worlds. The same goes for the theory of subjective probability: a subject's credences are usually taken to be distributed over a space of epistemically possible worlds.

It is surprisingly difficult, however, to make the intuitive picture precise. What sort of possibilities are we dealing with here? In particular, what is a scenario? And what is the relationship between scenarios and items of knowledge and belief?

It is natural to think of scenarios as possible worlds, and to think of a scenario in which *p* as a world in which *p*. But it is immediately clear that this will not work, at least on the most common contemporary understanding of possible worlds. There are subjects for whom it is epistemically possible that Hesperus is not Phosphorus; but on the usual understanding, there is no possible world in which Hesperus is not Phosphorus. It is epistemically possible for me that my great-grandparents were cousins and it is epistemically possible that they were not; but on the usual understanding, my great-grandparents are cousins either in all worlds in which they exist or in none. In the Cartesian sense, it is epistemically possible for me that water is not H_2O, but on the usual understanding (assuming that water really is H_2O), there are no possible worlds in which water is not H_2O. So if we are to maintain that it is epistemically possible that p iff there is an epistemically possible scenario in which p, we cannot identify a scenario in which p with a possible world in which p, at least on the usual understanding.

Some might react to this by denying the intuitions about what is epistemically possible (e.g. holding that it is never epistemically possible that Hesperus is not Phosphorus), and some might react by denying the coherence of the picture connecting epistemic possibility to epistemically possible scenarios. Both reactions would be premature: the first loses touch with the phenomenon we are trying to analyze, and the second assumes that possible worlds as currently understood are the only available tool.

Instead, we should try to understand epistemic possibility on its own terms. We are not dealing here with counterfactual space: the space of ways things might have been. Here, we are dealing with epistemic space: the space of ways things might be. This epistemic space calls for its own epistemic tools of analysis. Where the analysis of counterfactual space invokes possible worlds as maximally specific ways things might have been, the analysis of epistemic space should invoke scenarios as maximally specific ways things might be. The two notions are quite distinct, although they have a deep underlying relationship.

In this paper, I will try to make sense of epistemic space. I will explore different ways of making sense of scenarios, and of their relationship to thought and language. I will discuss some issues that arise, and I will outline some applications to the analysis of the content of thought and the meaning of language.

2. Principles of Epistemic Space

On the picture suggested above, we might say that the notion of *strict epistemic possibility*—ways things might be, for all we know—is undergirded by a notion of *deep epistemic possibility*—ways things might be, prior to what anyone knows. Unlike strict epistemic possibility, deep epistemic possibility does not depend on a particular state of knowledge, and is not obviously relative to a subject. Whereas it is strictly epistemically possible (for a subject) that p when there is some epistemically possible scenario (for that subject) in which p, it is deeply epistemically possible that p when there is some deeply epistemically possible scenario in which p. Since all scenarios are deeply epistemically possible on this picture, we can put this more simply: it is deeply epistemically possible that p when there is some scenario in which p.

The notion of deep epistemic possibility can be understood in different ways for different purposes. One might adopt a conception on which every proposition is deeply epistemically possible. One might also adopt a conception on which every proposition that is not logically contradictory is deeply epistemically possible, or on which every proposition that is not ruled out a priori is deeply epistemically possible. In this paper, I will mainly work with the latter understanding, which I flesh out in the next section. But first I will lay out some background structure that is largely independent of the notion of deep epistemic possibility that we adopt.

What are the objects of epistemic possibility? So far I have spoken as if they are propositions. I think that this view is ultimately correct, but the contested nature of propositions raises difficulties. For reasons given above, we want to hold that it can be epistemically possible for a subject that Hesperus is not Phosphorus, even if it is not epistemically possible that Hesperus is not Hesperus. On the popular Russellian conception of propositions, however, the proposition that Hesperus is not Hesperus is identical to the proposition that Hesperus is not Phosphorus. If so, and if propositions are the objects of epistemic possibility, it will be hard to obtain the result above. We could simply assume a Fregean view of propositions according to which these propositions are distinct, but the viability of such a view is contested. Furthermore, one aim of the present treatment is to use epistemic space to help make sense of a Fregean conception of propositions. If so, one cannot simply presuppose such a conception.

The alternative is to adopt an approach on which the entities that are assessed for epistemic possibility are linguistic items, such as sentences (or utterances), or mental items, such as thoughts (or beliefs or items of knowledge). Here I will work with sentences, but the framework is naturally extendible to thoughts. The sentences in question are restricted to assertive sentences, at least initially. To accommodate contextual variability in the use of sentences between subjects and occasions, these sentences should be individuated as sentence tokens (or as sentences in contexts) rather than sentence types. I will take it that every assertive sentence token expresses a thought, and that every thought is expressed by a possible sentence token, so there is a natural correspondence between sentence tokens and thoughts. Below, reference to sentences without further explanation should be taken as invoking reference to sentence tokens.

The key to the picture is a relation of *verification* between scenarios and sentences. Any sentence divides the space of scenarios into those scenarios that *verify* the sentence and those that *falsify* the sentence. More formally, we can say that there is a relation *ver* between scenarios and sentences, such that $ver(w, s)$ can take on the same range of truth values (e.g. true, false, and indeterminate) that sentences can take on. We can say that w verifies s when $ver(w, s)$ is true, and that w falsifies s when $ver(w, s)$ is false. When w verifies s, we can say that s is true at w. When w falsifies s, we can say that s is false at w. In some cases, it may be that s is indeterminate at w, or perhaps that s has some other truth value at w.

There is also a relation of actualization between scenarios and sentence tokens. This is needed to capture the idea that for any utterance, one scenario is singled out as the scenario of utterance. A scenario w is actualized at sentence token s when w is the scenario of utterance for s. This scenario corresponds intuitively to the way things really are (relative to the subject) when the expression is uttered.

As discussed above, we also have a basic notion of *deep epistemic possibility* (here abbreviated as simply "epistemic possibility") that applies to sentence tokens.

Scenarios, sentences, verification, actualization, and epistemic possibility should obey at least the following principles. In these principles, quantification over sentences is to be understood as quantification over possible (not just actual) assertive sentence tokens.

> *Plenitude*: For all sentences s, s is epistemically possible iff there exists a scenario w such that w verifies s.
>
> *Actualization*: For all sentences s and scenarios w, if w is actualized at s, then the truth value of s is $ver(w, s)$.
>
> *Compositionality*: When a complex sentence s is composed from simpler sentences s_i and truth-functional connectives, $ver(w, s)$ is determined by $ver(w, s_i)$ in the corresponding truth-functional way. For example, $ver(w, \neg s) = \neg ver(w, s)$, and $ver(w, s\&t) = ver(w, s)\&ver(w, t)$.

Plenitude and Actualization are basic principles of the framework that it would be hard to deny. There might be versions of the framework that deny Compositionality (perhaps to model non-ideal reasoners who accept s and t while denying $s\&t$, for example), but I will largely presuppose this principle in what follows.

The following three principles also have some attractions, although they are not obviously compulsory. For the purposes of the second and third principles below, let us say that scenarios w_1 and w_2 are *equivalent* iff for all possible sentences s, $ver(w_1, s) = ver(w_2, s)$.

> *Uniqueness*: For any sentence s, if scenarios w_1 and w_2 are actualized at s, then $w_1 = w_2$.
>
> *Parsimony*: If scenarios w_1 and w_2 are equivalent, then $w_1 = w_2$.
>
> *Specification*: For every scenario w, there is some sentence d such that w verifies d and such that if any scenario w' verifies d, then w' is equivalent to w.

Uniqueness says that there is a unique scenario of utterance for every sentence. This makes sense given the picture of scenarios outlined earlier, although one can also imagine a very fine-grained conception of epistemic space on which more than one scenario could be actualized simultaneously. Parsimony says, in effect, that there are no more scenarios than there need to be to differentiate their application to possible sentences. Specification says, in effect, that for each scenario there exists a *specification* that singles it out up to equivalence (and which singles it out uniquely, if Parsimony is true). Specification will require infinite sentences, raising issues that I discuss later in the paper. The framework will still deliver acceptable results if some or all of these principles are false, but these principles make it better behaved in certain respects.

Given this framework, we can say that the *epistemic intension* of a sentence *s* is a function from scenarios to truth values mapping a scenario *w* to *ver(w, s)*. The epistemic intension of a sentence corresponds to the way it divides epistemic space.

3. Epistemic Necessity and Apriority

Before proceeding, we need to say more about what deep epistemic possibility involves. There are various different ways that this notion can be understood, and these understandings may each be useful for different purposes.

On a maximally liberal conception, any sentence at all is deeply epistemically possible. One can motivate this by observing that there are subjects that do not know anything at all, and for such subjects any sentence is strictly epistemically possible. If strict epistemic possibility entails deep epistemic possibility, then every sentence is deeply epistemically possible.

On this picture, there will be scenarios verifying arbitrary sentences, including all sorts of logical contradictions. This leads naturally to a picture on which the space of scenarios is something akin to the power set of the set of sentences: to any set of possible sentences, there corresponds a scenario, and vice versa. This picture might be useful for some purposes—say, for making sense of the epistemic states of extremely non-ideal thinkers. However, for many purposes it is useful to have a space of scenarios with a less trivial structure. For example, the maximally liberal picture will be of little use when it comes to analyzing meaning and content. On this picture, the epistemic intension of any sentence *s* will be true in precisely those scenarios corresponding to sets of sentences that include *s*. It follows that non-trivial relations among the meanings of sentences will never be reflected in their epistemic intensions.

A more useful notion of deep epistemic possibility will involve some imposition of a rational idealization, for example to rule out scenarios on which logical contradictions are true. We might say that the corresponding notion of deep epistemic necessity should capture some sort of rational *must*: a statement is deeply epistemically necessary when in some sense, it rationally must be true. Such a notion can be understood in various ways, but for our purposes there is an obvious candidate.

We can say that *s* is deeply epistemically necessary when *s* is *a priori*: that is, when *s* expresses actual or potential a priori knowledge. More precisely, *s* is a priori when it expresses a thought that can be justified independently of experience, yielding a priori knowledge. I have discussed this conception of apriority at length elsewhere (Chalmers 2004), but I will recap the essentials here.

On this picture, a thought is a sort of token mental state: in particular, a thought is an occurrent propositional attitude with a mind-to-world direction of fit. So occurrent beliefs are thoughts, as are mere entertainings. Like beliefs, thoughts are assessible for truth. Thoughts can come to be *accepted*, yielding beliefs, and thoughts can come to be *justified*, often yielding knowledge. We can then say that a thought is a priori when it can be justified independently of experience, yielding a priori knowledge.

The relation of expression is such that every assertive utterance expresses a thought.[1] Typical assertive utterances express occurrent beliefs, and even when they do not, perhaps because the utterance is insincere or speculative, they plausibly express thoughts whose associated credence falls short of what is required for belief. The expression relation should be understood as one that preserves truth value and truth conditions: it is guaranteed that when an utterance expresses a thought, the utterance is true if and only if the thought is true.

The expression relation allows us to move back and forth between thoughts and sentence tokens. We can predicate apriority, deep epistemic necessity, and deep epistemic possibility of both thoughts and sentence tokens in the obvious way. For example, a sentence s is deeply epistemically possible when the thought that s expresses cannot be ruled out a priori.[2]

This idealized notion of apriority abstracts away from contingent cognitive limitations. If there is any possible mental life that starts from a thought and leads to an a priori justified acceptance of that thought, the thought is a priori.[3] So if a hypothesis can be known to be false only by a great amount of a priori reasoning, it is nevertheless deeply epistemically impossible. For example, 'There are integers $a, b, c, n > 2$ such that $a^n + b^n = c^n$' is deeply epistemically impossible. As a result, this idealization

---

[1] What of apparently assertive utterances that do not express thoughts, such as some utterances by actors, sleeptalkers, distracted individuals, and so on? One might reasonably say that these utterances are not assertions at all. In any case, the current framework does not directly apply to them, as one cannot use their association with thoughts to assess apriority and define epistemic intensions. However, if one develops the framework for paradigmatic assertive utterances, one might be able to apply it to these atypical utterances indirectly, perhaps in virtue of relations that hold between these utterances and (actual or possible) paradigmatic assertions.

[2] A small complication is required to handled cases of indeterminacy. If it is a priori that s is indeterminate, then the negation of s will also be indeterminate. If we assume that indeterminate sentences cannot be known a priori, it follows that this negation is not epistemically necessary, and that s will count as deeply epistemically possible by the definition above. But this seems the wrong result. To handle this we can say that s is deeply epistemically possible when $\neg det(s)$ is not epistemically necessary: that is, when the thought that s expresses cannot be ruled false or indeterminate a priori. (Or in the framework below, s is deeply epistemically possible when a negation of a determination of a thought that s expresses is not epistemically necessary, where determination is a mental analog of the determinacy operator.)

[3] An issue arises if one thinks there may be a posteriori necessities limiting the space of possible mental lives. For example, if it is necessary that no mental life can involve more than 10^{100} steps, then a mathematical statement whose proof requires this many steps will not be deemed a priori by the current definition. For reasons discussed in the next section, I do not think that there are a posteriori necessities of this sort. If one holds that there are such necessities, it is probably best not to define apriority in modal terms.

is best suited for modeling the knowledge and belief of idealized reasoners that may be empirically ignorant, but that can engage in arbitrary a priori reasoning.

There are other, less idealized ways to understand deep epistemic necessity. It may well be that there is a spectrum of notions ranging from this highly idealized notion to the maximally liberal notion discussed earlier. At the end of this article, I will discuss notions that relax the idealization. For present purposes, however, the idealized notion is the best-behaved and the easiest to work with.

When apriority is understood as above, it is clear that typical tokens of sentences such as 'Hesperus is Phosphorus' are not a priori. The thoughts expressed by these tokens are such that there is no possible mental life that starts from that thought and leads to an a priori justified acceptance of that thought. It may be that there is some *other* a priori justifiable thought (say, one expressed by saying 'Hesperus is Hesperus') that involves a relation to the same Russellian proposition as the first thought, but because these two thoughts are not themselves connectable a priori, the apriority of one does not entail the apriority of the other.

Apriority here is associated with sentence tokens rather than sentence types, to accommodate possible differences in use among fully competent speakers on different occasions. For example, in one context 'If someone is bald, they have no hair' may express a priori knowledge, while in another context it may not. Likewise, one speaker might use the names 'Bill' and 'William' of a particular individual interchangeably, so that 'Bill is William' expresses a priori knowledge, while another speaker who has acquired the two names through different routes might not. (For more on these cases, see Chalmers 2002a).

When an expression (e.g., 'bald', 'Bill') supports potential differences in apriority among fully competent users in this way, I will say that it is epistemically variant (or just variant); if not, it is epistemically invariant (or just invariant). For the special case of a sentence composed of invariant expressions, we can associate apriority with a sentence type, not just with sentence tokens: such a sentence type is a priori if some possible token of the type is a priori.

Some further structure will be useful for the constructions that follow. I also assume that the thoughts of a given thinker can stand in relations of negation, conjunction, and disjunction to each other: so one thought can be formed by another by an operation of negation, or from another two thoughts by operations of conjunction or disjunction. We can then say that one thought *implies* another when a disjunction of the latter with a negation of the former is a priori. When s and t are epistemically invariant sentence types, we can say that s implies t when $\neg s \lor t$ is a priori. In addition, when s is an epistemically invariant sentence type and t is a thought, we can say that s implies t when some possible thought expressed by a token of s implies t. When s is an epistemically invariant sentence type and t is a sentence token, s implies t when s implies the thought expressed by t. As defined here, implication is a sort of epistemic necessitation, akin to a priori entailment.

4. Scenarios as Centered Worlds

The most natural way to think of scenarios, at least initially, is as possible worlds. In a way this is trivial—scenarios are defined as possible (in some sense) ways things might be (in some sense). But the notion of possibility invoked here differs from the notion of possibility that is usually associated with possible worlds: it is a sort of epistemic possibility, whereas possible worlds are usually understood to be associated with a sort of "metaphysical" possibility. Still, the question arises as to whether possible worlds understood in the latter sense might serve to help us model the space of scenarios, at least indirectly. That is: can we use the space of metaphysically possible worlds to construct a space of scenarios, and to make the case for a verification relation between scenarios (so understood) and thoughts?

I think we might. The intuitive idea is simple: to every possible world w, there corresponds a very specific (deep) epistemic possibility: the epistemic possibility that w is actual. So we might start by suggesting that scenarios *are* worlds. We could then say that a world w verifies a sentence token s when d implies s, where d is a canonical specification of w.[4] We could likewise say that w is actualized at s when w is the world in which s is uttered.

I will say more about canonical specifications shortly. For now I will note as above that they are best taken as sentence types, rather than tokens, in an epistemically invariant language. It is desirable that canonical specifications be *epistemically complete*, in that they leave no matters epistemically open. More precisely, we can say that d is epistemically complete iff for all sentences s, if d is epistemically compatible with s, then d implies s.

This is an attractive picture, but it runs into immediate problems. These problems lead to various clarifications to and modifications of the picture above. There are four main sources of problems: indexicality, rigidity, strong necessities, and parsimony.

4.1. Indexicality

The first problem arises from the indexical phenomena involving expressions such as 'I', 'here', and 'now'. Let d be a full non-indexical specification of an "objective" world w. Let s be an indexical claim, such as 'I am a philosopher' or 'It is raining here now' or 'Today is Friday'. Then in each case, it may be that utterances of both $d\&s$ and $d\&\neg s$ are epistemically possible. So both $d\&s$ and $d\&\neg s$ are verified by a scenario. These scenarios must be distinct, as no scenario verifies both s and $\neg s$. But there will plausibly be only one world (objectively understood) in which d is the case. And even if there is more than one objectively indistinguishable d-world, it is hard to make out

---

[4] If we have only two truth values, we can say that w falsifies s when d does not imply s. If there are more than two truth values, these can be handled in a manner parallel to that discussed under the epistemic construction in the next section.

a distinction between those that verify 'I am a philosopher' and those that do not.[5] So it appears that if scenarios are construed as objective possible worlds, they will not satisfy Plenitude.

The natural solution is to identify scenarios with centered worlds: ordered sequences of worlds along with (optionally) individuals and times. The move to centered worlds requires that an "objective" specification d of a possible world w be supplemented by certain indexical claims that characterize the location of the center. This can be done as follows. Let us say that such a predicate ϕ *identifies* an individual x in w when ϕ is true of x in w and is true of no other entity in w. A canonical specification of a centered world w' will then take the form d & 'I am ϕ_1' & 'now is ϕ_2', where d is a canonical specification of the uncentered world w, ϕ_1 identifies the individual at the center, and ϕ_2 identifies the time at the center.

It is useful to stipulate that the marking of centered elements in a centered world is optional. This way, we can accommodate the (arguable but plausible) aposteriority of claims such as 'Thinkers exist' and 'The universe is temporal'. If we allow centered worlds without marked subjects or times, then there will be subjectless scenarios and timeless scenarios to falsify these claims. There can even be an empty scenario to verify 'Nothing exists', which is arguably a deep epistemic possibility. (Here I assume that 'I exist' is a posteriori, being justified by experience. If someone holds that 'I exist' is a priori, then they can require that centered worlds contain marked subjects.)

It may also be that we sometimes need additional optional marked information at the center of a world. This need arises in Austin's (1990) case of a demonstrative thought t to the effect that *that spot is red*, in a subject with a symmetrical visual field involving experience as of two red spots. Here, a full objective-plus-indexical specification of the world and of the subject's location within it (including a description of the spots, the subject's experience, and the connections between them) may not settle the truth value of t. For example, the specification may tell the subject that a red spot is causing one spot-experience, and that a blue spot is causing another, without telling the subject which spot-experience is *this* spot-experience. To handle cases of this sort, one needs to allow one or more marked experiences at the center of a world: in effect, there will be a marked experience corresponding to each perceptual demonstrative involved in a thought. A canonical specification of the world will then involve certain phenomenal demonstratives ('This experience is ϕ', where ϕ identifies the relevant marked experience), where this phenomenal demonstrative is linked to the perceptual demonstrative in such a way that the canonical specification allows one to determine the truth value of the thought.

In a few cases involving completely symmetrical worlds, there may be no identifying predicates available: that is, there may be no predicate (or at least no neutral

---

[5] Just possibly, one could retain Plenitude for uncentered worlds by allowing that individuals and times have very few essential properties, and that there are distinct but qualitatively indistinguishable worlds where I coincide with arbitrary individuals, where now coincides with arbitrary times, and so on.

predicate, in the sense discussed below) that is true of only the individual (or the time, or one of the experiences) at the center. In that case, one can invoke a maximally specific predicate instead: a predicate ϕ_1 such that for all (neutral) ϕ_2 true of the individual, ϕ entails 'everything that is ϕ_1 is ϕ_2'. Here, two centered worlds that differ only in symmetrical placement of the center will yield the same canonical specification. This phenomenon will be discussed more under the heading of parsimony, below.

4.2. Rigidity

The second problem has also already been discussed. 'Hesperus is not Phosphorus' is epistemically possible for some subjects. But on the usual understanding of possible worlds (following Kripke 1980), 'Hesperus' and 'Phosphorus' are *rigid designators*, picking out the same object (Venus) in all possible worlds. If so, then there is no possible world *satisfying* 'Hesperus is not Phosphorus', where satisfaction is the standard sort of post-Kripkean evaluation of sentences in worlds. Something similar applies to 'water is not H_2O', 'my greatgrandparents were cousins', and so on. Adding centers to the possible worlds does not help with this. So if scenarios are centered worlds, and if verification is the same as satisfaction, then Plenitude is false.

To avoid this problem, we must deny that a world verifies a statement when it satisfies that statement. It may be that no centered world satisfies 'Hesperus is not Phosphorus', but some centered world may still verify 'Hesperus is not Phosphorus'. This conclusion is already forced on us by considering a claim such as 'I am a philosopher'. If w is a centered world in which David Chalmers is a mathematician and George Bush is a philosopher, centered on Bush, then this world satisfies 'I am not a philosopher'. But according to the definition above, this world will verify 'I am a philosopher'.

The key difference is that satisfaction is tied to metaphysical necessitation, where verification is tied to epistemic necessitation. To a first approximation, w satisfies s if a canonical specification of w metaphysically necessitates s, while w verifies s if a canonical specification of w epistemically necessitates s. The definition of verification above already appeals to epistemic necessitation, so the problem is automatically avoided.

An important residual issue, however, concerns the nature of the expressions used in a canonical specification of scenarios. To specify a scenario, we choose sentences that are true of it. But scenarios are centered worlds, should these be sentences that the world *verifies*, or sentences that the world *satisfies*? If we choose the first, there is a danger of circularity: verification of a sentence by a world will be defined in terms of canonical specifications, which will be defined in terms of verification. If we choose the second option, there is a danger of incoherence. The framework requires that not all centered worlds verify 'Hesperus is Phosphorus', even though all worlds satisfy 'Hesperus is Phosphorus'. But if a canonical specification can include any sentence that a world satisfies, including 'Hesperus is Phosphorus', then all worlds will verify 'Hesperus is Phosphorus', which is the wrong result.

The solution is to restrict canonical specifications to *neutral* expressions (plus index-icals to specify the location of the center). Intuitively, a neutral expression is one that behaves the same with respect to both verification and satisfaction. We cannot sim-ply *define* a neutral expression in this way, for fear of circularity, but nevertheless we have a good grasp on the notion. For example, 'water' and 'Hesperus' are not neu-tral; but 'and', 'philosopher', 'friend', 'consciousness', and 'cause' plausibly are. To a first approximation, an expression is neutral if it is not "Twin-Earthable": that is, if one cannot devise a Twin-Earth case where a twin of a fully competent user of the expression uses their counterpart expression with a different meaning. There is more to say about the notion of neutrality than this (see Chalmers 2004), but this gloss will suffice for present purposes.

For this framework to yield fully adequate canonical specifications of worlds, it is required that there be epistemically complete specifications of arbitrary worlds involv-ing only neutral terms and indexicals. If we assume that there is no problem with epistemically complete specifications that allow non-neutral terms, we can derive this claim from the thesis that every non-neutral sentence that is epistemically possible is implied by some epistemically possible sentence involving only neutral expressions and indexicals.

4.3. Strong necessities

We have seen that the existence of a posteriori necessities such as 'water is H_2O' poses no deep problem for the picture of scenarios as centered worlds, as long as we distinguish verification from satisfaction. When n is a standard a posteriori necessity, it is plausible that although all worlds satisfy n, some centered world verifies $\neg n$. When this is the case, we can say that n is a *weak a posteriori necessity*. In these cases, we have a centered world verifying the relevant deep epistemic possibilities as Plenitude requires.

By contrast, a *strong a posteriori necessity* (or just a *strong necessity*) is an a posteriori necessity that is verified by all centered worlds. Strong necessities provide a more serious threat to Plenitude. Let us say that Metaphysical Plenitude is the thesis that for all sentences s, s is epistemically possible iff there exists a centered world that verifies s. If n is a strong necessity, then $\neg n$ is a counterexample to Metaphysical Plenitude. But on the assumption that scenarios are centered worlds, then Metaphysical Plenitude is equivalent to Plenitude. So if there are strong necessities, and if scenarios are centered worlds, then Plenitude is false.

For an example, consider a theist view on which 'An omniscient being exists' is necessary, but is not a priori. On such a view, this sentence (s) is plausibly a strong necessity. This follows from the claims that (i) s is a posteriori, (ii) every world satisfies s (as it is necessary), and (iii) a centered world verifies s iff the corresponding world satisfies the sentence (as there are no relevant two-dimensional phenomena here). On this view, although it is deeply epistemically possible that there are no omniscient beings, there are no centered worlds that correspond to this epistemic possibility. In effect, there are not enough centered worlds to go round.

Some other potential strong necessities are provided by the following philosophical views:

(i) A particularly strong "strong laws" view on which the fundamental laws and properties instantiated in our world are the fundamental laws and properties of every possible world. Let us say the view also holds (plausibly) that fundamental laws are a posteriori. On this view, a denial of the law of gravity (say) will be deeply epistemically possible, but there will be no possible world satisfying this denial, and there will also be no possible world verifying the denial.

(ii) A materialist view on which truths Q about consciousness are necessitated by the conjunction P of physical truths, but on which Q is not a priori derivable from P. Here, a psychophysical conditional $P\&\neg Q$ will be epistemically possible. It is not hard to show that if there is even a possible world verifying this conditional (as in the Kripkean cases), problems for materialism ensue. So some materialists deny that even a verifying world exists. If so, the conditional 'If P, then Q' is a strong necessity.

(iii) A view on which there are mathematical claims m—perhaps the Continuum Hypothesis?—that are true and are necessary, but are not knowable a priori by any possible being. On such a view, it seems that m will be a strong necessity: $\neg m$ will be epistemically possible, but verified by no possible world.

Other such views could be developed: e.g. one on which moral claims can be true and necessitated by natural truths, without being a priori derivable from natural truths; or a similar view about vague claims. In each of these cases, the distinction between verification and satisfaction does not seem to help. If the views in question are correct, there are simply not enough possible worlds to verify all epistemically possible thoughts and statements.

The simplest response to this problem, and the response that I think is correct, is to deny that there are any strong necessities. Each of the views listed above is at least controversial. In some cases, proponents claim support from the Kripkean cases, but these cases give no reason to believe in this much stronger phenomenon. In fact, one can argue in reverse: the fact that the link between epistemic possibility and verification by possible worlds is so strong elsewhere gives reason to believe that these claims are incorrect. One can also argue that there are deeper problems with these views. I have argued for these claims elsewhere (e.g. Chalmers 2002c), and will not repeat those arguments here.

It is at least clear that these views provide no *clear* reason to reject the model of scenarios as centered worlds, since in no case is the view in question clearly true. Still, the existence of these views entails that the claim that scenarios can be modeled by centered worlds will be at least as controversial as the denial of the views. And it would be desirable to give an account of scenarios that even holders of these views could accept. If so, that provides at least some reason to look at other models of scenarios.

4.4. Parsimony

So far, we have examined reasons for thinking that there are *not enough* possible worlds to act as scenarios. But there are also reasons for thinking that there are *too many* possible worlds to act as scenarios. That is, while the problems above are mostly problems for Plenitude, one can also raise problems for Parsimony. In particular, it seems that there exist groups of centered worlds such that any possible sentence is equally verified or falsified by any world in the group. If so, it seems that each world in the group corresponds to the same scenario.

One way this can happen is with symmetrical worlds. Say that a world is mirror-symmetrical, and consider centered worlds w_1 and w_2 centered on corresponding subjects on each side, at the same time. Then as defined above, a canonical specifications of w_1 and w_2 will be exactly the same. Furthermore, this seems to mirror intuitions about the case. Intuitively, there is no sentence s such that s is verified by w_1 but not by w_2. The main candidates for such a sentence are of the form 'I am ϕ', but centering works in such a way that both worlds will verify these claims equally.

The same goes for a world with a cyclic Nietzschean eternal recurrence of indistinguishable cycles, extending indefinitely into the past and the future. If we take a group of centered worlds w_i centered on corresponding subjects and times in different cycles, then it seems that for any t, if one world w_i verifies t, then all worlds w_i verify t. In these cases, it seems that the different centered worlds all correspond to the same epistemic possibility, violating Parsimony.

Parsimony might also be violated if possible worlds can contain inconceivable features. Say that there are two possible worlds w_1 and w_2 that are otherwise indistinguishable, except that at a certain point they contain different features ϕ_1 and ϕ_2. And say that ϕ_1 and ϕ_2 are inconceivable, in the sense that there is no possible neutral concept picking out ϕ_1 or ϕ_2. Then it may be that any neutral claim true of w_1 will also be true of w_2, so that canonical specifications of these worlds will be identical. If so, there is no sentence s that is verified by w_1 but not w_2.

Finally, suppose that (as some believe) there are qualitatively indistinguishable possible worlds. Take two identical twins Bill and Bob in the actual world. Some argue that there can be qualitatively indistinguishable worlds w_1 and w_2 such that only Bill exists in w_1 and only Bob exists in w_2. If so, it will plausibly still be the case that w_1 and w_2 verify all the same sentences.

The last two cases arise from possible ways in which the space of metaphysical possibilities may be more fine-grained than the space of epistemic possibilities. These two rest on controversial presuppositions that might be denied. But the first two, which arise from ways in which the space of *centered* metaphysical possibilities is more fine-grained than the space of epistemic possibilities, are relatively uncontroversial. So it seems that the space of centered worlds and the verification relation, as understood above, do not satisfy Parsimony.

One could respond in different ways. One might simply jettison Parsimony, holding that it is an inessential principle. Certainly, it seems less essential than Plenitude. One might also modify the picture slightly, by identifying scenarios with equivalence classes of centered worlds, where the worlds in groups such as the above will all fall into the same equivalence class. Either response will still allow a serviceable construction. Still, both responses suggest that there is at least a mild mismatch between scenarios and centered possible worlds.

What is the upshot of the four obstacles to identifying scenarios with possible worlds that we have discussed? The obstacles due to indexicality and rigidity can be overcome relatively easily, by invoking centered worlds and distinguishing verification from satisfaction. The obstacle due to strong necessities can be denied, and the obstacle due to parsimony can be dealt with as above.

Still, the last two obstacles suggest that while centered worlds may do a good job of modeling scenarios, the match is not perfect. The existence of philosophical views on which there are strong necessities suggests that even if these views are misguided, an analysis of scenarios as centered worlds will be at least mildly controversial. Because it makes a substantive (if plausible) claim about the relationship between possible worlds and epistemic possibility, this analysis goes beyond a surface analysis of epistemic possibility itself. The problems with parsimony also suggest a slight conceptual mismatch between the notions. So while centered worlds may provide a very useful way of thinking about scenarios, it is also useful to look at other ways.

5. The Epistemic Construction of Scenarios

The obstacles in the previous section all have a common source. They arise because we are taking a class of entities—the possible worlds—developed in the service of a *different* notion of possibility (metaphysical possibility, or what might have been the case), and adapting it to help analyze the notion of epistemic possibility (what might be the case). It is inevitable that this adaptation will lead to certain complications. An alternative strategy suggests itself. Instead of adapting a different modal space, we might construct the space of scenarios directly, by a construction grounded in epistemic notions. In particular, we might take (deep) epistemic possibility as basic, and proceed from there. In this way, we can give an account of epistemic space in its own right.

A further motivation for this sort of construction is that it might generalize to the case of non-idealized epistemic possibilities. There is little hope that a construction in terms of centered worlds will generalize in this way. For example, a complex mathematical truth M is true in all centered worlds, so centered worlds cannot model the (non-ideal) epistemic possibilities in which the sentence in question is false. But if we adopt a non-idealized notion of deep epistemic possibility as primitive, then it is at least reasonable to hope that a version of the construction below might model the non-ideal epistemic possibilities in question. I will proceed by assuming an idealized notion here, but later I will discuss the generalization to the non-ideal case.

The natural way to proceed is to identify scenarios with constructions out of sentences. We already have a notion of epistemic possibility that applies to these entities, and this notion can be exploited to construct scenarios directly. These sentences will need to be sentence types of an ideal language, since it is unlikely that any existing language will have sufficient expressive power to specify all scenarios.

The ideal language must have certain properties. First, it must allow infinite sentences, in order to specify scenarios with infinite extent. I will discuss the precise nature of these infinite sentences later on, in Section 9. Second, the ideal language should be restricted to epistemically invariant expressions. This ensures that we can associate epistemic properties with sentence types, not just with sentence tokens: when s is epistemically invariant, then if some possible competent utterance of s is epistemically necessary, all possible competent utterances of s are epistemically necessary. It also ensures that we can appeal to implication relations between sentences in the ideal language and sentence tokens in a non-ideal language, as defined earlier.

It is arguable that most terms of a natural language such as English are not invariant. It is plausible that most ordinary proper names are not invariant, so they should be excluded from the ideal language, though arguably some descriptive names can be allowed. Something similar applies to most natural kind terms, but here there will often be an invariant term in the vicinity. In the case of theoretical terms, for example, these might be used by different speakers with somewhat different theoretical reference-fixers, but we can stipulate an invariant term in the vicinity with a fixed theoretical reference-fixer. Something similar applies to most context-dependent terms. For most context-dependent terms as used in a context, there will be a possible term that is not context-dependent in this way. For example, if 'know' is context-dependent because of variation in standards, there will be possible terms such as 'know$_{high}$' and 'know$_{low}$' that are not context-dependent in this way.

Applying this process to a natural language such as English will plausibly leave a residue of many invariant terms. Certainly 'I' and 'now' are invariant (at least if precisified somewhat to remove certain sources of variation with speakers' intentions), as will be cleaned-up versions of many mental and physical terms, causal and dispositional terms, as well as logical and mathematical terms and so on. So there does not seem to be a problem with the idea of an ideal language consisting only of invariant expressions.

Finally, the ideal language must have a sufficiently broad lexicon. For now, we might as well stipulate that for *any* possible invariant simple expression e, the ideal language contains a synonym of that expression: that is, an expression e' such that any competent utterance of '$e \equiv e'$' is epistemically necessary.

We can say, much as before, that a sentence d of our ideal language L is epistemically complete when (i) d is epistemically possible, and (ii) there is no sentence s of L such that both $d\&s$ and $d\&\neg s$ are epistemically possible. When d is epistemically complete, it is in effect as specific as any epistemically possible sentence in the language can be. As before, let us say that d is *compatible* with s when $d\&s$ is epistemically possible, and d *implies* s when $d\&\neg s$ is epistemically impossible. Then if d is epistemically incomplete, it leaves questions open: there will be s such that d is compatible with s but d does not imply s. If d is epistemically complete, d leaves no questions open: if d is compatible with s, d implies s.

We can now identify scenarios with equivalence classes of epistemically complete sentences in L, where d_1 is equivalent to d_2 iff d_1 implies d_2 and d_2 implies d_1. It is plausible, though not completely trivial, that L contains epistemically complete sentences. For example, as long as there are maximal classes of mutually compatible finite sentences of L (classes such that the conjunction of every sentence in the class is epistemically possible, but the conjunction of these sentences with any sentence outside the class is not), then the conjunction of the sentences in such a class will be epistemically complete. It is not completely trivial that such maximal classes exist, but I sketch an argument for the existence of the needed epistemically complete sentences below.

If s is a sentence of an arbitrary language, we can say that a scenario w verifies a sentence s ($ver(w, s)$ is true) when d epistemically necessitates s, for some sentence d in the equivalence class of w. We can say that w falsifies s ($ver(w, s)$ is false) iff d epistemically necessitates the negation of s. If we have an "indeterminate" truth value, we can say that $ver(w, s)$ is indeterminate when d epistemically necessitates $indet(s)$. If there are any further truth values v, something similar applies: $ver(w, s) = v$ when d epistemically necessitates $O(s)$, where O is an operator such that $O(s)$ is true iff s has truth value v.[6]

The Plenitude thesis now requires the following:

> *Epistemic Plenitude*: For all sentence tokens s, if s is epistemically possible, then some epistemically complete sentence of L implies s.

This thesis is entailed by the conjunction of the following two theses:

> (E1) For all sentence tokens s, if s is epistemically possible, then some epistemically possible sentence of L implies s.

> (E2) For all sentences s of L, if s is epistemically possible, then some epistemically complete sentence of L implies s.

---

[6] In the case where s is a sentence token, this should be understood as the claim that d implies a negation of the thought expressed by s. Something similar applies to the other truth values: for example, $ver(w, s)$ is indeterminate iff d implies an indetermination of the thought expressed by s, where indetermination is understood as a mental analog of the indeterminacy operator.

The first thesis requires, in effect, that every sentence token s is implied by some invariant sentence. We could rephrase the second thesis by saying that any epistemically incomplete sentence s of L is *completable*: this requires officially that s is implied by some epistemically complete sentence in L, which comes to the claim that s can be expanded into an epistemically complete sentence by adding further conjuncts. Neither claim is trivial, but both are plausible (subject to a complication regarding (E1) that I will discuss). I will not try to prove these principles here, but I will make a prima facie case for them.

A case for (E2) runs as follows.[7] First, we can note that if s is *true*, s is plausibly completable. The world itself is determinate, making all sentences of L true or false (setting aside borderline cases of vague sentences, and the like, whose impact on this sort of argument is discussed in Section 9). Conjoining all true sentences of L, if it were possible, would yield an epistemically complete sentence that implies s. Such a conjunction is probably impossible (perhaps because this sentence would have to be one of its conjuncts), but it remains plausible that some conjunction of sufficiently many atomic sentences of L is epistemically complete and implies s. All this depends on the details of the language L, but assuming a suitable language, this reasoning is plausibly a priori. That is, for any epistemically possible s, it is a priori that if s is true, s is completable. It follows that if s is epistemically possible, it is not a priori that s is uncompletable. Furthermore, the uncompletability of s seems to be the sort of thing that is knowable a priori if it is knowable at all. So unless the uncompletability of s is wholly unknowable (even given ideal reasoning), s is completable.

This is not a rigorous proof of (E2), but it gives (E2) some prima facie support. Under certain assumptions (discussed in Section 9 of this paper), unknowability can be excluded entirely, strengthening the support. But even without these assumptions, the hypothesis that some s are uncompletable but not knowably uncompletable is not especially attractive. At least, if the rest of the reasoning is correct, we can know that we will never be able to discover a counterexample to (E2).

As for (E1): to a first approximation, (E1) is plausible because the ideal language (L) should be able to capture more fine-grained possibilities than any given sentence token in natural language. If s is a token of an invariant expression, (L) will contain a synonymous sentence, so there is no problem here. And plausibly, when s is a token of a variant sentence, there will be some invariant expression that matches its content on any given occasion of use. The most likely exceptions here are indexicals. 'I' and 'now' are no problem as they are invariant, but a complication arises because of the case of demonstratives discussed earlier.

The picture so far suggests a common space of scenarios for all speakers. This picture has to be qualified slightly to handle the case of demonstratives. We have

---

[7] This argument is loosely inspired by an argument given by Cresswell (2006) for a modal principle analogous to (E2). Cresswell attributes this sort of argument to Aristotle. Cresswell also has a useful discussion of the conditions under which modal principles such as (E2) are true, focusing on other varieties of modality, but suggesting that such principles are especially plausible where epistemic possibility is concerned.

seen already that to handle these cases, canonical specifications of scenarios sometimes need to include phenomenal demonstratives that are specific to subjects. One might regard these demonstratives as terms of the ideal language, albeit unusual terms in that any one of them can be used by a single speaker. Perhaps better, one can say that for a given subject at a given time, the language L^* for the specification of scenarios may involve one or more such demonstratives in addition to the common language L. Understood this way, then thesis (E1) will be false of L^*, due to cases where s contains a relevant demonstrative, but both (E1) and (E2) will be true of L.

This yields a small modification of the original picture, with a subject-and-time-relative space of scenarios (or alternatively, a common space such that some elements of the space can be related only to specific subjects). However, to analyze sentences that do not contain relevant demonstratives or expressions that depend on them, then the common space of scenarios characterizable in the common language L will suffice. And even for subjects using relevant demonstratives, one can still map scenarios from one subject to another, up to isomorphism.

(It is also worth noting that if principle (E1) above is more radically false, because many epistemically variant sentence tokens are not implied by invariant sentences, then one could still engage in a version of the current construction by allowing arbitrary possible epistemically variant sentence tokens into canonical specifications of scenarios. This would yield a construction that satisfies Plenitude, at cost of having the space of scenarios be entirely subject-relative, without a useful notion of isomorphism between scenarios of different subjects.)

It is easy to see that this construction will satisfy Compositionality, as the principle follows from the analogous principle about implication. The construction will also satisfy Parsimony: if two sentences of L imply the same sentence tokens, then they will imply each other (at least assuming that the sentences can be uttered), so they will be members of the same equivalence class. The language is also designed so that it satisfies Specification.

As for Actualization and Uniqueness: it is not obvious how to define the relation of actualization between scenarios and sentence tokens. To do this we need to define a corresponding relation of actualization between epistemically complete sentences d and sentence tokens. It is tempting to say: such a sentence d is actualized at s iff, were the subject uttering s to utter d, the utterance of d would be true. But this cannot work, for the obvious reason that uttering d would change the world in which s is uttered. An alternative definition appeals to the notion of a canonical specification of a centered world from the previous section. For a sentence token s, let w be a centered world centered on the speaker and the time of utterance (and any experiences associated with demonstratives, if necessary), and let d' be a canonical specification of w: that is, an epistemically complete sentence including neutral terms and indexicals that is true of w. Then d is actualized at s iff d implies d'. It would be nice to have a definition that does not appeal to the notion of neutrality, or to the thesis that there are epistemically complete neutral/indexical specifications, as this notion and the associated thesis are otherwise unnecessary for the epistemic construction. But the nature of such a definition is currently an open question. For now, I will take it that we have a reasonably good intuitive grip on the notion, and the definition just given is also available. So I will assume a relation of actualization between scenarios and sentence tokens henceforth.

An important residual issue concerns the question of how small the ideal language can be while still satisfying Plenitude. If the language needs a term for every invariant expression, then the resulting semantic values at least for invariant sentences will be fairly uninteresting: they may simply be implied by all sentences of the ideal language that contain the original sentence as a conjunct. However, if the language only needs a relatively limited class of invariant expressions, then the structure will be much more interesting. I have argued elsewhere that a relatively small vocabulary suffices at least for the purposes of specifying scenarios that correspond to the actual world: see, for example, Chalmers and Jackson (2001). An extension of this reasoning suggests that a reasonably limited (if larger) vocabulary suffices to specify any scenario. Such a vocabulary will serve as a sort of basis for epistemic space. I will not investigate the character of such a basis here, but I discuss the issue at length in forthcoming work.[8]

Although we have constructed scenarios out of sentences here, other constructions are quite possible. One can even take the linguistic construction and convert it into another sort of construction. For example, if there is an epistemically complete invariant language including just neutral terms and indexicals, then each neutral term will have some object, property, or relation as its extension. We can then convert the neutral part of any epistemically complete specification into an abstract object that is a complex of the relevant objects, properties, and relations. This abstract object can be seen as a sort of "quasi-world", akin to a possible world except that the relevant state of affairs may or may not be metaphysically possible. One could then see scenarios as centered quasi-worlds. This has the advantage of moving epistemically constructed scenarios out of the realm of language and into the realm of being.

6. Epistemically Constructed Scenarios and Metaphysically Possible Worlds

We might call the constructions of scenarios in the last two sections the metaphysical and the epistemic construction respectively.[9] How are these two constructions

---

[8] For some related discussion in published work, see the discussion of scrutability principles in Chalmers (2002c and 2004), as well as the discussion of PQTI (involving physical, phenomenal, and indexical vocabulary along with a "that's all" clause) as a specification of the actual world in Chalmers and Jackson (2001).

[9] The metaphysical and epistemic constructions correspond roughly to the "one-space" and "two-space" views of modality discussed by Jackson (this volume: Ch. 4). Like Jackson, I think that the one-space model is adequate, but unlike Jackson, I think that the two-space model is coherent and useful for various

of scenarios related to each other? Assuming both are coherent and that the relevant assumptions (not including Metaphysical Plenitude) are satisfied, there will be epistemically complete canonical specifications for each centered world and each epistemically constructed scenario. We can then say that a centered world and an epistemically constructed scenario *correspond* if their specifications imply one another. It will now certainly be true that for every centered world, there is a corresponding epistemically constructed scenario. *If* Metaphysical Plenitude is true (as I think it is), then for every epistemically constructed scenario, there will be a corresponding centered world (possibly more than one, due to failures of parsimony). If Metaphysical Plenitude is false, on the other hand, there will be epistemically constructed scenarios with no corresponding centered world.

If Metaphysical Plenitude is false, this will pose a serious obstacle to the metaphysical construction, but not to the epistemic constuction. Even on the theist views discussed earlier that deny Metaphysical Plenitude, for example, there will be scenarios verifying 'There is no omniscient being'. Even on the relevant mathematical view, there will be scenarios verifying the negation of the Continuum Hypothesis. Even on the relevant views on laws, there will be scenarios verifying the negation of laws. Even on relevant views on the mind–body problem, there will be scenarios verifying the claim that there are zombies. It is just that on these views, there will be no metaphysically possible world corresponding to these scenarios.

Apart from questions involving Metaphysical Plenitude, the constructions differ mostly in requiring somewhat different assumptions. The metaphysical construction requires notions of epistemic and metaphysical necessity and a notion of neutrality, along with the thesis that every sentence is implied by some invariant neutral/indexical sentence. The epistemic construction requires only the notion of epistemic necessity and of invariance (both of which are also required by the metaphysical construction), along with the thesis that every sentence is implied by some invariant sentence. These assumptions are significantly weaker, which is another reason for preferring the epistemic construction if one is aiming for maximal generality.

Even on the epistemic construction of scenarios, there are many interesting interactions between epistemically possible scenarios and metaphysically possible worlds. One such interaction concerns epistemic possibilities concerning what is metaphysically possible. For example, one might hold that it is epistemically possible that Metaphysical Plenitude is true, and epistemically possible that it is false. One might even hold that it is epistemically possible that there is only one metaphysically possible world. If these views are correct, then there will be scenarios at which Metaphysical Plenitude is true, scenarios at which Metaphysical Plenitude is false, and scenarios at which 'There is only one possible world' is true.

---

purposes. Jackson's central arguments against the two-space model depend, in effect, on the assumption that individuals can be re-identified across scenarios. I argue in Section 8 that this assumption should be rejected.

These cases are naturally modeled in a two-dimensional way, by supposing that every scenario is associated with a modal space of putatively metaphysically possible worlds. (These putative worlds might themselves be modeled linguistically, or in some other way.) On the view just described, some scenarios will be associated with a space involving just one putative world (one that presumably corresponds to the scenario itself), while others will be associated with a space that has a putative world for every scenario.

If one accepts (as I do) that Metaphysical Plenitude is both true and a priori, then the structure will be simpler than this. In particular, every scenario will be associated with a space of putative worlds such that there is a putative world for every scenario. This raises the possibility that we can use the same set of possible worlds to model the space of putative worlds associated with every scenario, as on certain versions of two-dimensional semantics.[10] But in any case, the epistemic construction of scenarios gives us the tools to model a wide range of views about metaphysical modality.

7. Subsentential Epistemic Intensions

So far I have defined the evaluation of expressions in scenarios only for sentences. For many purposes it is useful to define this sort of evaluation for arbitrary expressions that have an extension, such as singular terms, general terms, kind terms, and predicates. I will take it that we have already decided on independent grounds what sort of extensions these expressions should have: e.g. individuals, classes, kinds, and properties. We then want to define an epistemic intension for any such expression, mapping scenarios to extensions within those scenarios.

Formally, we need a function ext from scenarios and these expressions to extensions, such that $ext(w, e)$ (the extension of e in w) is an entity of the appropriate sort. The epistemic intension of an expression e is a mapping from scenarios w to extensions $ext(w, e)$. We can stipulate that when e is a sentence, $ext(w, e) = ver(w, e)$. This function should obey a principle analogous to Compositionality: insofar as the extension of a complex expression e depends on the extension of its parts, the extension of e in a scenario w depends on the extension of its parts in w in the same way. And it should obey a principle analogous to Actualization: if w is actualized at e, the extension of e should correspond to $ext(w, e)$.

The details depend to some extent on whether we take the metaphysical or the epistemic approach to scenarios. The difference is that centered worlds already come populated with individuals and the like, or at least we are familiar with how to regard them as so populated. By contrast, epistemically constructed scenarios as outlined so far do not come populated with individuals, or at least we are less familiar with how to regard them as so populated.

---

[10] This issue is discussed at more length in Chalmers 2004, section 3.10.

If we take the metaphysical approach to scenarios: let w be a centered world with canonical specification d, and let t be a singular term. Let us say that ϕ is an identifying predicate relative to d iff d implies 'Exactly one individual has ϕ'. Then for most referring singular terms t, there will be some neutral identifying predicate ϕ such that d implies 't has ϕ'. In such cases, let us say that the extension of ϕ in w is the individual that satisfies ϕ in w. We can then say that $ext(t, e)$ is the extension of ϕ in w.

In some symmetrical worlds, for some terms t there may be no such neutral identifying predicate ϕ. In many such cases, there will be an identifying predicate ϕ' involving neutral terms and indexicals. In this case, one can replace the indexicals in ϕ' by singular terms (which need not be neutral) picking out the entities at the center of the world, yielding an expression ϕ''. We can then say that $ext(w, t)$ is the extension of ϕ'' in w. If there is no such neutral/indexical identifying predicate ϕ', then $ext(w, t)$ is null.

One can do the same for general terms (assuming these have extensions). If g is a general term, one can appeal to a neutral (and possibly indexical) predicate ϕ such that d implies '$\forall x(x$ is a g iff $\phi(x))$', holding that $ext(w, g)$ is the extension of ϕ in w (or of a de-indexicalized version thereof): that is, the class of individuals in w that satisfy ϕ. Kind terms and property terms are treated just as singular terms are (although here, of course, the denotation will be kinds and properties respectively). For predicates h, we appeal to neutral (and possibly indexical) predicates ϕ such that d implies '$\forall x(h(x)$ iff $\phi(x))$'. This method can be extended to arbitrary expressions (and different proposals for their extensions), delivering epistemic intensions for all such expressions.

If we take the epistemic view of scenarios, then we need to populate scenarios with individuals and the like. If we simply admit scenarios as a basic sort of abstract object with certain properties, one could simply stipulate that they contain individuals that can serve as the extensions of relevant expressions—much as many of those who introduce possible worlds simply stipulate something similar. But it is useful to go through an explicit construction.

Let w be a scenario with canonical specification d. Let us say that a denoting term is a singular term or a definite description. Then we can say that two denoting terms t_1 and t_2 are equivalent under w if d implies 't_1 is t_2'. Then we can identify every equivalence class of denoting terms under w with an individual in w, and hold that for a singular term t, $ext(w, t)$ is the individual corresponding to t's equivalence class in w. As for general terms: for a general term g, $ext(w, g)$ is that class of individuals whose corresponding equivalence class includes a denoting term t such that d implies 't is a g'. One can do something similar for predicates and kind terms: the details will depend on the precise view one takes of properties and kinds and their relation to individuals, so I will not go into them here.

There is one worry: what if a scenario requires that there are individuals that are not denoted by any denoting term? In particular, what if the truth of certain existentially quantified claims in a scenario requires individuals that are not the referent of any denoting term? For example, there may be a predicate ϕ such that d implies '$\exists x\phi(x)$', and d does not imply any claim of the form '$\phi(t)$', where t is a denoting term. Because d is epistemically complete, it will at least tell us exactly how many individuals have ϕ, whether some individuals with ϕ also have ψ and some do not, and so on. Of course if it tells us that some individuals with ϕ have ψ and some do not, then we can move to the conjunctive predicates $\phi\&\psi$ and $\phi\&\neg\psi$. Repeating this process, it is not hard to see that this sort of case requires predicates ϕ (perhaps an infinitely conjunctive predicate) such that d implies that there exists more than one individual with ϕ, and such that for all predicates ψ, d implies that these individuals are indistinguishable with respect to ψ. In this case, the individuals will be indistinguishable even in our idealized language, perhaps because of deep symmetries in the scenario.

In such a case, if d implies that there are n individuals with ϕ, one can arbitrarily construct n individuals, perhaps as ordered pairs $(\phi', 1) \ldots (\phi', n)$, where ϕ' is the equivalence class containing ϕ. We can then stipulate that all these individuals fall under the extension of ϕ. Likewise, all these individuals fall under the extension of ψ for all predicates such that d implies 'everything that is ϕ is ψ'', and fall under the extension of general terms g such that d implies 'everything that is ϕ is a g', and so on.

One can populate a scenario with kinds by applying the same treatment as above to kind terms. One can populate it with properties, relations, and other entities in a similar manner. In this way, we can populate a scenario with entities that are needed to serve as the extensions of expressions, and we can specify the extensions of all relevant expressions at arbitrary scenarios.

As in the case of possible worlds, the entities we have used to construct individuals in scenarios are not themselves concrete objects, but they serve as proxies for concrete objects that exist if the scenarios are actualized (or that would exist if the worlds were actual). Where the objects in the actual world are concerned, one can treat the relevant abstract objects (classes of descriptions and the like) as proxies for the corresponding actual object, thereby yielding a version of the principle of Actualization. Of course once one has engaged in this sort of construction, one need not usually bother with the details again. Just as in the case of possible worlds, it is reasonable thereafter to speak of a scenario as containing individuals and the like, and to speak about terms as picking out various individuals in a scenario, quite independently of the details of the construction.

Compositionality is ensured by the details of the construction. For an identity statement (e.g. '$t_1 = t_2$'), compositionality will be ensured by the equivalence class construction. For a predication (e.g. 't is a g', or $\phi(t)$) this will be ensured by the appropriate construction of extensions for general terms (as above) or predicates. The machinations two paragraphs above ensure that existential quantification will work straightforwardly, and universal quantification is guaranteed to work (if d implies $\forall x \phi(x)$, then every individual constructed above will have ϕ). Logical compositionality is guaranteed at the sentential level (if d implies both s and t, d will imply $s\&t$, and so on). Something similar applies to any construction involving compositionality of extensions. So for any such construction, the epistemic intension of a complex expression will be a compositional function of the epistemic intension of its parts.

8. Trans-Scenario Identity

One of the most hotly contested issues concerning possible worlds concerns whether there is transworld identity: can the same individual be identified across two different worlds? In the domain of epistemic space, an analogous issue arises: the question of *trans-scenario identity*. Can we say that an individual in one scenario is the same individual as that in another scenario?

In many cases, it seems that the answer is no. Consider the actualized scenario (for me now), in which 'Hesperus is Phosphorus' is true. Relative to this scenario, 'Hesperus' and 'Phosphorus' pick out an individual x. In another scenario w, 'Hesperus is Phosphorus' is false. Relative to this scenario, 'Hesperus' picks out one individual, and 'Phosphorus' picks out another. Can one say that both of these individuals are x, or that just one of them is? Neither answer seems attractive. So it seems that one cannot say that in any given scenario, x is identical to the referent of 'Hesperus', or that in any given scenario, x is identical to the referent of 'Phosphorus'.

Is there any other way to ground trans-scenario identity? Of course if scenarios are understood as possible worlds, we could appeal to transworld identity. To avoid entangling the epistemic and metaphysical modalities here, however, I will first work with the epistemic construction of scenarios, and will later consider the metaphysical construction.

A natural way to ground trans-scenario identity would be to isolate a *canonical designator n* for any individual x in a scenario, and say that in any scenario, x is the referent of n with respect to that scenario. The trouble is that at least for the objects designated by most ordinary singular terms, there does not seem to be any obvious choice of a canonical designator. For example, in the case of Venus, the designators 'Venus', 'Hesperus', 'Phosphorus', and many others will all give different results. The same goes for tables, people, countries, and so on.

In some cases involving abstract objects, there do seem to be canonical designators. For example, as Ackermann (1978) has discussed, numerals seem to function as canonical designators for numbers. These canonical designators can be used to ground claims of trans-scenario identity. Assuming that '2' designates the number two in the actual world, then it will designate an entity in many or all scenarios (depending on one's view of the apriority of the existence of numbers), and we can stipulate that these entities are identical with each other. One could do the latter either by modeling trans-scenario identity between individuals with a relevant relation, or, if it is important that individuals in scenarios literally be identical to each other, one can modify the previous construction of individuals. To do the latter, one could identify individuals with classes of individuals (as previously constructed) in different scenarios that are picked out by a canonical designator. Or in cases where the designator picks out an object in the actual world (as might be the case for '2'), one could identify individuals in a scenario with the actual object itself, invoking a "present in" relation between individuals and scenarios, and invoking claims about the predicates that an individual falls under relative to a scenario.

What is the relevant difference between '2' and 'Hesperus', and between two and Hesperus? Intuitively, the difference is that '2' is *epistemically rigid*—that is, it picks out the same object in all scenarios—while 'Hesperus' is not. Of course this intuitive characterization presupposes a notion of trans-scenario identity (just as Kripke's notion of rigid designation presupposes a notion of transworld identity), so it cannot be used to provide an independent grounding for trans-scenario identity, but it at least helps give a sense of what is going on. One might try to characterize epistemically rigid expressions in other terms. One useful suggestion is that an epistemically rigid expression is one such that one can know what it refers to a priori. This definition inherits the imprecision of the notion of knowing what an expression refers to, but there is at least an intuitive sense in which one can plausibly know a priori what '2' refers to (or better, what object two is), while one cannot know a priori what 'Hesperus' refers to (or better, what object Hesperus is).

When an expression is epistemically rigid, it will usually also be rigid in the Kripkean sense (subjunctively or metaphysically rigid). In such a case, and when the term is rigid *de jure* rather than merely *de facto*, we can say that the expression is *super-rigid* (a term due to Martine Nida-Rümelin). Any super-rigid term is neutral, but not every neutral term is super-rigid. For example, a general term such as 'philosopher' is arguably neutral without being epistemically rigid, subjunctively rigid, or super-rigid (it picks out different classes in different worlds). On the other hand, if 'philosopher' is neutral, the nearby property term 'the property of being a philosopher' will be both neutral and super-rigid. For any neutral term, one can find a super-rigid property term in the vicinity in this way.

Many properties have super-rigid canonical designators. For example, I have argued elsewhere that our central phenomenal concepts designate phenomenal properties super-rigidly. Something similar may apply to many mental properties, many causal and dispositional properties, and so on. However, when properties are constitutively tied to external objects (e.g. the property of being taller than Fred) or kinds (e.g. the property of containing water), then if there are no super-rigid designators for those objects and kinds, then there will plausibly be no super-rigid designators for the corresponding properties.

It seems plausible that while there are super-rigid designators for many abstract objects and many properties, there are no super-rigid designators for concrete objects. At least, such designators are extremely hard to find. One might suggest that if an object x has an essential identifying property ϕ—that is, a property ϕ such that necessarily something is x iff it has ϕ—then one can use a super-rigid designator for this property to construct a super-rigid designator for ϕ. But the most plausible candidates for such essential identifying properties (such as the property of being descended from a particular sperm and egg) will themselves be object- or kind-involving, so that there will be no obvious canonical designators for them, or at best there will be a regress of designators.

Likewise, the property terms discussed above that are candidates for super-rigid designation do not seem to obviously yield candidates for essential identifying properties. *Perhaps* one could argue that one's ontology should admit an object x such that necessarily, an object is x iff it is the biggest object in the universe, or iff it is the only individual with phenomenal property ϕ, or iff it is the first philosopher in the world. If so, then one could allow canonical designators and trans-scenario identity for objects of this sort. But these are at best objects of a very unusual sort.

One might think that one can at least refer super-rigidly to oneself. In this case, there is at least a canonical designator: the first-person pronoun. But this designator does not obviously support super-rigid reference. On the centered worlds model of scenarios, 'I' picks out many different individuals in different centered worlds. And on the epistemic construction, the individual at the center can have almost any range of properties (and need not even exist). Perhaps one could hold that at the center of any scenario there is always a common individual, EGO. But this would be a very odd sort of object—even odder than those discussed before, in that there seems to be no subject-independent fact of the matter about who is EGO in a world. Given the absence of a clear definition of epistemic rigidity, these facts do not conclusively establish that 'I' is not epistemically rigid, but they at least give good reason to doubt it. Something similar applies to 'now', and to demonstratives for token experiences (although terms for *properties* of experiences may be epistemically rigid, as discussed above).

If one wants to hold that reference to oneself is epistemically rigid, the best way to do so would be to hold that different individuals are related to their own subject-relative spaces of scenarios, such that each scenario in a subject's epistemic space has that subject at the center. This model might fit well with a Russell-style account that allows direct reference to the self as well as to properties and sense-data. But this model is at odds with our previous construction of scenarios, requiring significant modifications to both the epistemic and the metaphysical constructions. More importantly, this model makes cross-subject identification of scenarios impossible, and likewise makes it impossible for two subjects to share epistemic intensions. If extended to times and experiences, as parity would suggest, then the model would have even less generalizability across occasions. Finally, there is arguably an underlying epistemic difference between reference to numbers and properties, on the one hand, and reference to oneself on the other: merely possessing a concept of the former seems to put one in a position to know the nature of the referent a priori, whereas possessing a concept of the latter does not.

Still, it should be acknowledged that the choice between these models turns on delicate questions about the explanatory role one needs epistemic space to play, about just what is involved in epistemic rigidity, and about just what is involved in first-person reference. A pluralistic picture giving a role to both models is not out of the question. Nevertheless, I am tentatively inclined to favor a model on which epistemically rigid reference to oneself is impossible.

In the absence of canonical designators, is there any other way to pin down trans-scenario identity between ordinary objects? One might try to use *de re* claims such as it is a priori of Venus that it is such-and-such. The trouble is that no such claims seem clearly to be true, except perhaps for trivial claims involving self-identity and the like. Perhaps there is a loose sense in which it is a priori of Venus that it is visible in the evening (if it exists) in virtue of the fact that it is a priori that Hesperus is visible in the evening (if it exists). But in this sense, all or almost all of Venus's properties will be a priori of it (for example, where ϕ is such a property, one can stipulate a partially descriptive name 'ϕ-Venus' such that it is a priori that if ϕ-Venus exists, ϕ-Venus is Venus and ϕ-Venus is ϕ). So one does not get to any interesting sort of trans-scenario identity this way.

One might try an analog to Kripke's method of asking, of an object such as Venus, whether if such-and-such a world obtained, then *it* would have been visible in the morning. Here, we could ask of Venus whether, if such-and-such a scenario obtains, then *it* is visible in the morning. But there seems to be no good way to answer this question. Consider a scenario verifying 'Hesperus is not Phosphorus', in which separate objects are visible in the morning and evening. If this scenario obtains, is Venus visible in the morning? There seems to be no way to say. Perhaps, following the analogy with Kripke, one could simply stipulate that the scenario in question is one in which *Venus* (that very object) is visible in the morning and not the evening. But such a stipulation will lead to serious problems, on the current model.

Consider the question: in a scenario stipulated to be such that the object has ϕ, can 'Hesperus has ϕ' be false? If no, then presumably by parity the scenario must also verify 'Phosphorus is ϕ', 'Venus is ϕ', and so on. So any such scenario will verify 'Hesperus is Phosphorus', 'Hesperus is Venus', and so on for any pair of names of the object. This entails that the object can exist only in a tiny fraction of scenarios, and arguably only in the actual scenario, since it is arguable that for any non-actual scenario, there is some pair of names a and b for Venus such that 'a is b' is false in that scenario (appealing to names such as 'ϕ-Venus' for appropriate ϕ, for example). If the answer to the question is yes, so that 'Hesperus has ϕ' can be false of such a scenario, then presumably the same goes for 'Phosphorus is ϕ', 'Venus is ϕ', 'that object is ϕ' (for any demonstrative way of picking it out), and so on. But now, the behavior of the object across scenarios will float free of any of our ways of talking or thinking about it, so that there are aspects of scenarios that float free of their role in verifying sentences and beliefs. Perhaps such aspects are not incoherent, but they seem to have no explanatory role to play in the current framework.

This is not to say that talk of *de re* epistemic possibilities is incoherent. It seems intuitively reasonable to say of the cup on my desk that I know that it is brown, while

I do not know when it was made. So it is intuitive to say that there are epistemic possibilities open to me in which that very cup was made on such-and-such a date, or on such-and-such a date. But if we are to model epistemic possibilities of this sort in such a way that they stand in a verification relation to our sentences and beliefs, then either we need to say that an epistemic possibility in which x is ϕ verifies 'n is ϕ' for any name n of the object, or we will be led to say that whether x is ϕ in a scenario can float free of whether the scenario verifies 'n is ϕ' for any name n of the object. Both models are coherent, but neither is useful for our current purpose.

When the first model is fleshed out, it will almost certainly be a model on which all true identities involving proper names (such as 'Hesperus is Phosphorus') are true in all scenarios, undermining one of the main explanatory aims of the current project. When the second model is fleshed out, it will naturally lead to a model on which the object-involving aspects of a scenario are largely independent of the role they play in verifying sentences and thoughts, which will render them largely useless in the explanatory structure of the current project. Still, there may be other projects for which these models are useful. The first model in particular may play a useful role in illuminating aspects of *de re* thought, and our epistemic relations to Russellian contents (see Soames (2004) for a treatment of epistemic possibility that resembles the first model here). One can reasonably be a pluralist about epistemic space.

Returning to the preferred model I have outlined: it seems clear that this model supports trans-scenario identity only for certain abstract objects, and not for ordinary concrete objects. We might think of this as a "qualitative" conception of epistemic space. There are objects in scenarios, and they have properties, but only the properties are re-identifiable across scenarios (and here only some of them), and not the objects (except for abstract objects). For the purposes for which we are using this model, a notion of trans-scenario identity for concrete objects has no role to play. Of course, for nearby scenarios in which familiar identities ('Hesperus is Phosphorus') and so on are true, there is not much harm in talking of these scenarios as scenarios in which the object in question has various properties. But strictly speaking, this *de re* talk should always be cashed out by *de dicto* locutions, speaking of scenarios in which Hesperus has various properties (or to be maximally explicit, scenarios verifying 'Hesperus has ϕ'), and so on.

The last point brings out a terminological nicety: if a scenario verifies 'Hesperus is ϕ', is it reasonable to call it a scenario in which Hesperus is ϕ? I do not see why not, as long as one is careful. In particular, in describing scenarios in this way, one cannot freely substitute terms that are coreferential in our world. So a scenario in which Hesperus is ϕ need not be a scenario in which Phosphorus is ϕ. That is to say that talk of "a scenario in which..." creates an opaque context. There may also be some subject-relativity: if we use the terms somewhat differently, it could be that what you and I count as "a scenario in which Hesperus is ϕ" may differ. But as long as one is alert to these phenomena, then there is no objection to using this convenient way of speaking.

The discussion above all presupposes the epistemic construction of scenarios. What about the metaphysical construction? Here, one might think that there will be a notion of trans-scenario identity that derives from the notion of transworld identity. It is arguable that object-involving metaphysical possibilities are *relatively* unproblematic: names function as canonical designators for objects in modal contexts, *de re* modal claims are reasonably well-behaved (at least if we allow that statues are distinct from the lumps that constitute them), and so on. If so, and if scenarios are constructed from such possibilities, then it may seem that transworld identity yields trans-scenario identity.

We have already seen that things are not as simple, however. The discussion of parsimony earlier suggests that the distinctly object-involving aspects of centered worlds are largely irrelevant to the way they function as scenarios. For example, qualitatively identical centered worlds involving distinct objects will verify all the same sentences, so they can naturally be seen as corresponding to a single scenario. And where transworld identity between concrete objects is present, it need not correspond to anything interesting at the epistemic level (in effect, it yields only a version of the "second model" discussed above). For example, if we stipulate a centered world where Aristotle died in childbirth while someone else wrote the books that have come down to us under the name of 'Aristotle', then where *verification* of our sentences and beliefs is concerned, the latter is more relevant than the former.

All this suggests that even if one believes in transworld identity, it is best to set it aside in considering the role that centered worlds play when functioning as scenarios. Or perhaps even better, for this purpose one can invoke a purely qualitative construction of centered worlds out of properties, so that the worlds in question do not support a natural relation of transworld identity between objects. As with epistemic space, one can be a pluralist about the construction of modal space, depending on one's purposes. For the role that modal space is needed to play here, a qualitative construction seems best.

The discussion above tends toward a conclusion suggested by Burgess (1997): that insofar as Quine's critique of quantified modal logic was concerned with *epistemic* modalities, it was not far from the mark. Burgess argues plausibly that Quine is concerned with modalities such as analyticity and apriority. Where these modal notions are concerned, many of the points above mirrors Quine's: different designators for an object yield different results in these modal contexts, and there are no canonical designators, so there is no way to derive *de re* quantified modal claims from *de dicto* modal claims, and there is no clear way to make sense of *de re* modal claims of this sort independently. Kripke responds to Quine, in effect, by invoking a different sort of modality, the subjunctive modality, to which Quine's arguments do not apply. As with Kripke's response to Frege, there is room for a split verdict: Kripke is right about subjunctive modality, while Quine is right about epistemic modality.

9. Infinitary Scenarios

Some tricky issues arise from the fact that scenarios can have infinite extent, and that we have used an infinitary language to characterize scenarios.[11] There are questions about the exact size of the space of scenarios, closely related to problems that Kaplan (1995) raises concerning the size of the space of possible worlds. More basically, there is the question of the choice of infinitary language. What sort of infinitary constructions should be allowed: infinite conjunctions, infinite disjunctions, infinite sequences of quantifiers? Furthermore: how infinite are infinitary conjunctions (and so on) allowed to be? A countable number of conjuncts? Uncountable? As many conjuncts as an arbitrary infinite cardinal from set theory?

There are reasons to believe that one should allow scenarios corresponding to arbitrarily large conjunctions. One way to see this is to note that for any cardinal κ, it seems to be epistemically possible that there are at least κ independent atomic entities in the universe, such that each entity can have or fail to have a simple property ϕ. This suggests that there are at least 2^{κ} scenarios, such that each scenario can be described using a conjunction of κ conjuncts.[12] If κ is an infinite cardinal, and if we stipulate that each conjunct must have length less than κ, then this scenario will not be describable using a conjunction of fewer than κ statements. So our ideal language should allow infinitary conjunctions with size corresponding to arbitrary cardinals, and some scenarios will require arbitrarily large conjunctions for their specification.

These issues are closely related to Kaplan's paradox concerning possible worlds, which we can put as follows. The following three claims are all prima facie plausible but are inconsistent:

(i)   There are at least as many propositions as sets of worlds.
(ii) There are at least as many worlds as propositions.
(iii) There are more sets of worlds than worlds.

Claim (i) can be understood as stipulative if we take propositions as sets of worlds (it is also plausible on many other understandings of propositions). Claim (ii) is intuitively justified by mapping any proposition to a world in which that proposition is uniquely asserted (or in which it is uniquely entertained). Claim (iii) seems to follow from Cantor's theorem, which suggests that the set of all worlds, like any set, has more subsets than members. Prima facie, this situation suggests that there is no good candidate to be the cardinality of the set of all worlds, and that there may be no such set.

---

[11] I am grateful to Bruno Whittle for pressing Kaplan-style worries about the space of scenarios in the case of epistemic space, and to Kit Fine and Wolfgang Schwarz for very helpful discussion. Whittle (2009) presses these worries in depth, responding in part to an earlier version of this paper in which these issues were not discussed.

[12] Strictly speaking, where epistemic possibility as opposed to metaphysical possibility is concerned, symmetries within the scenarios and the absence of trans-scenario identity might yield many fewer than 2^{κ} different scenarios: when κ is infinite, it might yield only $g(\kappa)$ different scenarios, where $g(\kappa)$ is the number of cardinals less than κ. But even this is enough to make the key point that for every κ there must be at least 2^{κ} scenarios, as for every κ there is some cardinal μ such that $g(\mu) > 2^{\kappa}$.

Kaplan's paradox arises at least as strongly when worlds and propositions are replaced by scenarios and intensions. If anything, the situation is worse. Lewis (1986) responds to Kaplan's problem by holding that there are propositions that are not asserted or entertained in any possible world. One might likewise hold that there are intensions (sets or classes of scenarios) that are not uniquely asserted or entertained in any scenario. But it is far from clear that the unique assertion or entertaining of any given intension can be ruled out a priori. Prima facie, any scenario can be specified by an infinitary conjunction, and any set of scenarios can be specified using an infinite disjunction of such conjunctions. There is no obvious a priori obstacle to the entertaining of such a conjunction or disjunction by an infinite being.

(Kaplan also gives a constructive version of the paradox which does not turn directly on considerations about cardinality. To simplify, he constructs a proposition p consisting of those worlds w in which the set of worlds determined by the unique proposition asserted at w does not include w. Then if v is a world in which p is uniquely asserted, the set of worlds determined by p cannot include or exclude v, leading to contradiction. Whittle (2009) develops a version of the constructive paradox for the framework of epistemically possible scenarios. I focus on the non-constructive version of the paradox here because, like Anderson (2009), I take the constructive version of Kaplan's paradox to be a version of the liar paradox that does not have much especially to do with possible worlds.[13] To support this point, it is worth noting that Kripke (forthcoming) gives a version of the constructive paradox with times in place of worlds.)

Lewis's official reasons for denying that every proposition can be entertained rest on his functionalism, which he takes to be a priori, so one might think these reasons also apply to epistemic possibility. But his argument rests also on the unargued claim that there is some cardinal upper bound on the number of functional roles. And once we allow arbitrarily complex infinitary beings, it is easy to generate arbitrarily many functional roles. Given κ states (each corresponding to a thought, for example), one

---

[13] To see this, note that the key proposition p will be expressed at v by a liar sentence such as "The unique proposition asserted at this world is false." As such, the status of p should be handled by whatever mechanism best handles the liar paradox. Whittle makes a case (by invoking a somewhat more complex construction) that where epistemically possible scenarios are concerned, the move of holding that the problem sentence does not express a proposition is more difficult than in the case of metaphysically possible worlds. This may be right, but I take it that this move is a highly problematic treatment of liar sentences in any case, for reasons tied to compositionality. Other more promising strategies for handling the liar paradox appear to apply to the current case as well as they apply in the original liar case. For example, if one holds that the liar sentence has a nonstandard truth value, we can say that the problem sentence above will have an intension mapping v to this nonstandard truth value. Of course there are many unresolved issues concerning the liar paradox (including especially problems arising from strengthened liar sentences), but these issues are problems for everyone.

The constructive and non-constructive paradox are not unrelated: the former can be generated from arguments for the latter, by applying the standard diagonal proof of Cantor's theorem to the mapping that generates thesis (ii) of the non-constructive paradox. Nevertheless, one should distinguish the issue generated by the truth of Cantor's theorem (which has no particular connection to the liar paradox) from the issue generated by its standard proof. Thanks to Bruno Whittle for discussion here.

can straightforwardly define 2^κ functional roles in terms of those states (each corresponding to a conjunction of some of the original thoughts, for example). Likewise, a belief involving any real number can be functionally defined in terms of beliefs involving rational numbers (using comparisons to smaller and larger rationals); a belief involving any set of real numbers can be functionally defined in terms of beliefs about real numbers (using judgments about whether the real number in question is in the set in question); and so on. So there do not seem to be clear a priori limitations here. If one is prepared to accept strong necessities, one might accept brute limitations on the complexity of worlds and on the complexity of possible thinkers. But this strategy will not help where epistemic possibility is concerned.[14]

Another response to the paradox, suggested by Kaplan himself, is to ramify the space of propositions and the corresponding space of worlds. Level-0 propositions concern only extensional matters, and level-0 worlds are (or correspond to) maximal level-0 propositions. Level-1 propositions concern extensional matters and level-0 propositions, and level-1 worlds are (or correspond to) maximal level-1 propositions. And so on. Then there is a level-n proposition for every set of level-n worlds, and there is a level-$n+1$ world (but not a level-n world) for every level-n proposition, so paradox is avoided (though there remains an issue concerning propositions and worlds "simpliciter", analogous to an issue I discuss below).

Kaplan's response might in principle be applied to epistemic space, but there are reasons for concern. One worry is that it is arguable that all truths about propositions are epistemically necessitated by level-0 truths, and likewise when truths are replaced by epistemically possible sentences: if so, the level-n scenarios will simply correspond to the level-0 scenarios for all n. Another worry is that Kaplan's treatment disallows assigning semantic values uniformly to all sentences of natural language. Some sentences, such as 'All propositions are true', cannot be assigned a semantic value at all, and for any n, one can generate sentences that can only be assigned semantic values for levels greater than n: 'All level-n propositions are true', for example.

Furthermore, both Kaplan's and Lewis's responses turn on considerations specific to Kaplan's paradox and to issues about entertaining or referring to propositions. But I am inclined to think that the source of the worry is not as specific as this. The case at the start involving κ atomic entities appears to have much the same moral as Kaplan's paradox: it suggests that for any κ, there are more than κ scenarios (or worlds), so that there are too many worlds to form a set. And this case has nothing especially to do with entertaining or referring to propositions. I draw the moral that the source of both worries is that the worlds are broadly analogous to the sets. Any space of scenarios (like the space of sets) is in some sense indefinitely extensible. Ever more complex spaces of scenarios, of larger and larger cardinalities, can be generated, so that the scenarios as a whole (like the sets as a whole) cannot be collected into a set. This

---

[14]   In *Counterfactuals*, Lewis suggests that the cardinality of the space of worlds might be beth$_2$, for reasons tied to the character of spacetime. But it is hard to see why our spacetime should restrict the space of worlds.

suggests that we might use the same sort of tools used to understand the set-theoretic paradoxes to understand this situation.

At this point it is natural to respond to Kaplan's paradox by denying (iii): just as there are no more sets of sets than sets, there are no more sets of worlds than worlds. (Cantor's theorem does not apply when the entities in question do not form a set.) I think that this is the correct response, although it raises important issues about how intensions (or propositions) are then to be understood, and about how epistemic space can work if its members do not form a set.

In what follows, I will develop two strategies for responding to the paradox. The first strategy involves a stratified picture of the scenarios, with different spaces of scenarios corresponding to different cardinalities. On this view, each space forms a set, and the corresponding intensions can be understood in set-theoretic terms. The second strategy involves understanding intensions in non-set-theoretic terms, for example in terms of defining formulae. I think the second strategy runs deeper than the first and is also less technical and more general, so one could in principle skip straight to the second strategy. Still, I think that the first strategy helps to illuminate the situation by fleshing out a stratified structure among scenarios that is at least somewhat analogous to the stratified structure among sets.

9.1. The stratified construction of scenarios

Let us assume an infinitary language L. I will assume that L has a countable lexicon, consisting at least of the sort of expressions that make up a basis for epistemic space as discussed earlier, and perhaps of expressions corresponding to arbitrary invariant expressions in possible natural languages spoken by finite speakers.[15] Various rules concerning infinitary constructions are possible, but I will assume that the language at least allows infinitary disjunctions and conjunctions of arbitrary length. We might also allow infinite sequences of quantifiers, as is familiar from infinitary logic. There is no obvious obstacle to the claim that thoughts corresponding to sentences of L could be entertained by sufficiently infinitary beings, so I will assume that sentences of L can be assessed for epistemic possibility and necessity as before.

For any infinite cardinal κ, let us say that a κ-sentence is a sentence of length less than κ. Then there will be at most $f(\kappa)$ κ-sentences, where $f(\kappa)$ is the sum of ω^α for all cardinalities $\alpha < \kappa$. (If the Generalized Continuum Hypothesis is true, $f(\kappa) = \kappa$ for all κ.) We can then say a κ-conjunction is a conjunction of at most $f(\kappa)$ κ-sentences. A κ-complete sentence is an epistemically possible κ-conjunction d such that for all

---

[15] One might worry that the choice of language will make the space of scenarios language-relative. If the lexicon is restricted to an epistemic basis, one can argue that imposing certain further constraints (e.g. requiring that the members of the basis are conceptually primitive in a certain sense) will remove any language-relativity from the resulting space of scenarios (although there remains the problem discussed under (E1*) below). If we allow the lexicon to include expressions corresponding to arbitrary invariant natural language expressions (plus the relevant indexicals), then as long as such expressions form a basis for epistemic space, the problem is removed. If there is not a countably infinite basis here, then an alternative model will allow a larger basic lexicon, or perhaps a lexicon whose size varies with κ.

κ-sentences s, $d\&s$ and $d\&\neg s$ are not both epistemically possible. We can then identify a κ-scenario with an equivalence class of κ-complete sentences, each of which will then be a specification of that scenario.

An important special case is the class of ω-scenarios, where ω is the cardinality of the integers. An ω-sentence is a finite sentence. There will be ω $(= f(\omega))$ ω-sentences. An ω-conjunction will be a conjunction of at most a countably infinite number of finite sentences. An ω-scenario will be an equivalence class of ω-complete conjunctions of this sort.

We can then say that κ-Plenitude is the claim that all sentence tokens (in a human natural language such as English) are verified by some κ-scenario. As with Epistemic Plenitude earlier, κ-Plenitude will follow from versions of principles (E1) and (E2).

(E1$\star$), the analog of (E1), holds that any epistemically possible sentence token in such a language is implied by some member of $L(\kappa)$, the class of κ-conjunctions. Given that these sentence tokens are all finite, the fact that $L(\kappa)$ is restricted to κ-conjunctions does not raise any obvious reasons for concern for the argument given earlier. The restriction to a countable lexicon raises a potential concern, given that the previous argument for (E1) turned on the language having a synonym for arbitrary invariant expressions in natural language. Using that argument here requires the thesis that there is only a countable number of synonymy classes of possible invariant lexical expressions in natural language. This thesis is highly plausible in light of the fact that natural language speakers are finite beings.[16] If the thesis is denied, though, then one will need to appeal to a more limited countable basis, or perhaps better, one will need to expand the lexicon accordingly.[17]

The argument for (E2$\star$), the analog of (E2), requires more work.[18] (E2$\star$) holds that any epistemically possible κ-conjunction is κ-completable: that is, is implied by some κ-complete sentence. One can argue for this roughly as I argued for (E2) earlier. If s is true, then s is κ-completable: s is implied by the conjunction of all true κ-sentences, and this conjunction is κ-complete (at least given that all κ-sentences are true or false, or given weaker assumptions discussed below). This reasoning is a priori, so it is a priori that if s is true, s is κ-completable. It follows that if s is epistemically possible, it is epistemically possible that s is κ-completable. That is, one cannot establish a priori that s is κ-uncompletable. Given that uncompletability of s is knowable a priori if it is knowable at all, it follows that unless this uncompletability is wholly unknowable (even given ideal reasoning), s is κ-completable. Unknowability can be excluded given

---

[16] More specifically: for each such synonymy class there will be at least one corresponding cognitive state (that of a speaker using an expression in the class), and for finite beings it is plausible that there are only a countable number of relevantly distinct cognitive states. The second claim is particularly clear if one holds that natural language speakers can be modeled computationally.

[17] One might think that one could simply invoke a lexicon consisting of a countable basis for epistemic space. But a residual issue is that although we know that any epistemically possible natural-language sentence S is implied by an epistemically possible sentence in this lexicon, we do not know that any such sentence S is implied by a κ-conjunction in this lexicon.

[18] The next three paragraphs can be skipped by those not interested in the technicalities.

certain assumptions about apriority, and even without these assumptions it seems a much less plausible option. So depending on whether these assumptions are granted, we have either a demonstration or a prima facie case for (E2★). I will give a concrete illustration of this case for completeness in the mathematical case described below.

This argument makes assumptions at two points: to make the case for κ-completability and to make the case against unknowability. At the first point, it suffices to assume that the basic vocabulary in $L(\kappa)$ is not vague, so that every κ-sentence is either true or false. Certain weaker assumptions also suffice. One sufficient assumption is the claim that the vocabulary includes an "indeterminately" operator *indet* such that when s is neither true nor false, $indet(s)$ is true. Then as long as the connection between determinacy and epistemic possibility behaves as described earlier, $indet(s)\&s$ and $indet(s)\&\neg s$ will not be epistemically possible, and a conjunction of κ-sentences including $indet(s)$ sentences will be epistemically complete. One could also assume a multiplicity of such operators for various intermediate truth values in borderline cases. Or one could assume that there is a precise subset of the vocabulary such that sentences using this subset determine the truth value of all vague sentences.

At the second point, making the case against unknowability, certain assumptions about apriority suffice. These assumptions are most easily formulated using an apriority operator A. The first assumption is an S5 principle for apriority: (A1) if $\neg As$, then $A\neg As$. The second is a conjunctive closure principle (for arbitrary infinite conjunctions): (A2) if As for all s in a set S, then At where t is a conjunction of all members of S. These assumptions are not plausible for an unidealized notion of apriority, but they are reasonably attractive for a sufficiently idealized notion. Given these assumptions (along with other very plausible assumptions), one can establish (A3): if s is κ-uncompletable, it is a priori that s is κ-uncompletable. Given (A3), the argument above establishes (E2★). The argument from (A1) and (A2) to (A3) is in a footnote.[19]

Given (E1★) and (E2★), κ-Plenitude follows. One can likewise make a case for κ-analogs of Actualization, Compositionality, Uniqueness, Parsimony, and Specification,

---

[19] Let us say that Kd holds when d is κ-complete, i.e. when for all κ-sentences s, $A\neg(d\&s)$ or $A\neg(d\&\neg s)$. Suppose that s is κ-uncompletable: that is, there is no d such that Kd and $A(d \supset s)$. Principle (A1) then implies $A(\neg A(d_1 \supset s)\&\neg A(d_2 \supset s)\&\ldots)$, where d_1, d_2, and so on are all the κ-complete sentences. Now, *if* it is a priori that $d_1, d_2, \ldots$ include all the κ-conjunctions, it follows that it is a priori that s is κ-uncompletable, as required. The antecedent of this conditional follows from two theses: (A4) given a list of all the κ-conjunctions, it is a priori that these are all the κ-conjunctions, and (A5) given a κ-conjunction d, it is apriori whether d is κ-complete (that is, either AKd or $A\neg Kd$). (A4) is a very plausible assumption. To make the case for (A5), first suppose that Kd. Then there will be a subset T' of the set T of κ-sentences such that $A\neg(d\&s)$ for all $s \in T'$, and such that $A\neg(d\&\neg s)$ for all s in T'', the complement of T' in T. It follows from (A2) that the conjunction of all sentences $\neg(d\&s)$ (for s in T') and $\neg(d\&\neg s)$ (for all s in T'') is itself a priori. Combined with the very plausible assumption (A6) that it is a priori that these d are all the κ-sentences, it follows that Kd is a priori. So if Kd, then AKd. Similarly but more straightforwardly, by appealing to principle (A1), we can establish that if $\neg Kd$, then $A\neg Kd$. So (A5) is true. Putting all this together, assumptions (A1), (A2), and (A6) establish (A5), and these together with (A4) establish (A3).

where the sentences in question are restricted to natural language sentences or κ-sentences, and where the scenarios in question are restricted to κ-scenarios.

One might think that κ-scenarios could not satisfy κ-Plenitude for reasons given earlier: it is epistemically possible that there be μ atomic entities, where $\mu > f(\kappa)$, so there will be at least 2^{μ} μ-scenarios requiring specifications of length μ. That is, the space of μ-scenarios will be more plenitudinous than the space of κ-scenarios, so κ-Plenitude will be false of the latter. But here, the sentences that are not verified by any κ-scenarios are too large to be κ-conjunctions, so (E2$\star$) is not violated, and are too large to be sentences of natural language, so κ-Plenitude is not violated.

Of course the space of κ-scenarios does not exhaust epistemic space. In $L(\kappa)$, most of the 2^{μ} epistemic possibilities above cannot be fully specified. For many κ-scenarios w, a specification of w will be verified by specifications of multiple μ-scenarios, so that specifications of κ-scenarios are not epistemically complete in an absolute sense. But they do not need to be epistemically complete in such a sense for our purposes. For these purposes, κ-completeness suffices.

We can illustrate the situation (and also illustrate the case for (E2$\star$)) by considering the space $\mathbb{R}^{\mathbb{R}}$ of functions from real numbers to real numbers, and by considering ω-sentences and ω-conjunctions characterizing such functions in mathematical language.[20] For example "$\forall x(F(x) = x)$" specifies one such function. Many such functions can be specified uniquely with a ω-conjunction: for example, any continuous function can be specified by specifying its values on the rational numbers (using a series of successive approximations for each value) and by specifying that it is continuous. Not all such functions are uniquely specifiable by an ω-conjunction, though, as there are c^c members of $\mathbb{R}^{\mathbb{R}}$ (where c is the cardinality of the real numbers) but only c ω-conjunctions. Still, for any such function f, we can take $D(f)$ to be the conjunction of all ω-sentences satisfied by f. Then $D(f)$ will be ω-complete. The ω-scenarios here correspond to equivalence classes of functions, where two functions are equivalent if there is no finite sentence that is true of one but not the other. Some ω-scenarios will correspond to a single function, and some will correspond to many functions that cannot be distinguished using finite sentences or infinite conjunctions thereof, although of course they might be distinguished using other infinite sentences.[21] Any epistemically possible ω-sentence will be satisfied by some function and will be verified by the corresponding ω-scenario, as (E2$\star$) requires.

In fact, for our main explanatory purposes, which involve the epistemic possibility of sentence tokens in English, all of which are finite, it will probably suffice to invoke the space of ω-scenarios, and ω-intensions defined over this space. Of course this

---

[20] Thanks to Brian Weatherson for suggesting this case as an illustration.

[21] For example, any two members of $\mathbb{R}^{\mathbb{R}}$ can be distinguished by specifying an ordered pair of real values that belongs to the first but not the second. This cannot be achieved in general by using countable conjunctions of finite sentences, but it could be achieved using other infinite sentences, such as quantified countable conjunctions.

space will collapse certain scenarios that would otherwise have been held distinct, and it will not make maximally fine-grained distinctions between possible thoughts, but the distinctions it does not capture will be distinctions that we cannot express or even entertain. Unlike a ramified type-theoretic construction, this construction will have no problem handling sentences about propositions, and no problem handling sentences describing arbitrarily large universes, as long as the sentences themselves are finite: if a sentence like this is epistemically possible, it will be true at some ω-scenario. So for the purpose of assigning semantic values to English sentences, and contents to the thoughts of finite thinkers, the space of ω-scenarios may well suffice.

It is perhaps desirable that we have scenarios rich enough to fully specify the actual world. This requires the empirical claim that there is a true ω-conjunction fully specifying the actual world (one that is epistemically complete, not just ω-complete). This thesis appears to be reasonably plausible: at least, contemporary physics seems to invoke only separable spaces (spaces with a dense countable subset) and continuous functions between these spaces, and these entities can be specified with ω-conjunctions.[22] Of course if the actual world cannot be described in this way, we can move to a larger cardinality, but otherwise the space of ω-scenarios will be rich enough for our purposes.[23]

That said, once we move beyond natural-language semantics, the stratified approach does not give us everything that we might ask for. For a start, it can happen that infinite sentences with non-vague vocabulary nevertheless have indeterminate truth values at some κ-scenarios. More importantly, there will be many infinite sentences that are epistemically possible, but whose ω-intension is not true at any ω-scenario. (A sentence specifying a particular uncomputable function in $\mathbb{R}^{\mathbb{R}}$ may have no truth value at the corresponding ω-scenario, while being false at all the others.) So a version of ω-Plenitude that applies to all possible sentences will be false. The same goes for other κ-Plenitude theses. So it is worth examining whether we can recover something closer to the original picture with scenarios, intensions, and a plenitude thesis that applies to all possible sentences. I will approach this matter by first considering how the framework will deal with Kaplan's paradox.

Recall that Kaplan's paradox turns on the claims that (i) there is a proposition for every set of worlds, (ii) there is a world for every proposition, and (iii) there are more

---

[22] Thanks to Marcus Hutter for discussion here.

[23] One tricky issue is that specifying the actual world plausibly requires some sort of "that's-all" clause, saying roughly that the world does not contain anything beyond what is specified or implied by the rest of the description. As usually construed, this "that's-all" sentence will be infinite (at least if the world is infinite), and so will not be an ω-sentence. For the actual world, we can avoid the problem by making the case that there are finite sentences that can do the work of the that's-all clause. But an issue like this arises with other scenarios, and there may be some for which a scenario that can otherwise be specified using an ω-conjunction requires a longer that's-all clause. One could simply deny that these scenarios are ω-scenarios, but alternatively one could modify the definition of an ω-scenario (and a κ-scenario more generally) to allow a single longer that's-all clause to be included.

sets of worlds than worlds. If we replace worlds here by κ-scenarios, and propositions by κ-intensions (sets of κ-scenarios, or better, functions from κ-scenarios to truth values), the prima facie case for (ii) is removed. For most κ-intensions, there will be no κ-scenario in which that intension is entertained, as specifying such a scenario would require more than a κ-conjunction.

Now, one could stipulate that a scenario (*simpliciter*) is an entity that is a κ-scenario for some cardinal κ. Or perhaps better, we can remove coarse-grained κ-scenarios by requiring that a scenario is a *complete* κ-scenario, one specified by a κ-conjunction s that is not just κ-complete but epistemically complete (there is no sentence T, even of length longer than κ, such that $s\&t$ and $s\&\neg t$ are both epistemically possible). To attempt to generate the paradox, we might also stipulate that an intension (*simpliciter*) is an entity that is a κ-intension for some cardinal κ. These stipulations have the slightly awkward consequences that not every κ-scenario is a scenario *simpliciter* and that intensions *simpliciter* are not defined over scenarios *simpliciter*, but we can at least assess the elements of Kaplan's paradox where they are concerned.

Under these stipulations, (ii) will plausibly be true: for every κ-intension, there is an epistemically possible μ-scenario (for some $\mu > \kappa$) that verifies a sentence saying that someone is entertaining that intension. It is tempting to say that (i) is false, on the grounds that there can be sets of scenarios with unbounded cardinality, which will not correspond to κ-intensions for any cardinality κ. But this is not quite right. Just as there are no sets of sets with unbounded cardinality (for any sets of sets, the cardinality of their union will serve as an upper bound), there are no sets of scenarios with unbounded cardinality. For any set of scenarios, there will be a corresponding set of cardinals (for each scenario, this will be the least cardinal κ such that the scenario is a κ-scenario), with upper bound μ. Then this set of scenarios will correspond to a μ-intension. So (i) will be true, also.

Instead, the right thing to say is that where scenarios are concerned, (iii) is false. Just as there are not more sets of sets than sets, there are not more sets of scenarios than scenarios. Given that there is no sets of all sets, the sets do not have a cardinality, and one cannot form a power set, so Cantor's theorem does not get off the ground. Likewise, if there is no set of all scenarios, then Cantor's theorem does not get off the ground. We can take the moral of Kaplan's paradox to be that there is no cardinal upper bound on the size of a scenario, so that there are too many scenarios to form a set.

It is tempting at this point to appeal to proper classes, holding that there is at least a *class* of all scenarios, and that there will be more classes of scenarios than scenarios. But as in other domains, the appeal to classes does not change anything fundamental. If we understand classes as analogous to sets (just larger), we could go on to define ultra-intensions (classes of scenarios, or functions from scenarios to truth values) and ultra-scenarios (scenarios constructed using proper-class size conjunctions), and will find ourselves in the same situation. If the paradox is cast in terms of ultra-intensions, ordinary scenarios, and classes, (ii) will be false; if it is cast in terms of ultra-intensions, ultra-scenarios, and classes, (iii) will be false; if it is cast in terms of ultra-intensions, ultra-scenarios, and a more general notion of collection, (i) will be false. We could iterate further to metaclasses and so on, but nothing will change. Even if we try to cast the paradox in terms of a general notion of collection and a corresponding general notion of scenario (assuming these notions are coherent), we will encounter the same issues that we encountered with sets: just as there is no collection of all collections, there is no collection of all scenarios (in this putatively general sense), and so on. It is more straightforward to set aside proper classes, holding (with Boolos 1998, Shapiro 2003, and others) that all collections are sets, and drawing the morals that one would have to draw at the level of collections in any case at the level of sets.

At this point in the set-theoretic case, various theorists hold either (a) that although we can quantify in an absolutely unrestricted way over sets (or collections), there is no set (or collection) corresponding to the domain of quantification here (e.g. Boolos 1998, Cartwright 1994), (b) that we cannot quantify in an absolutely unrestricted way over sets (or collections), and can instead quantify over them in various restricted but indefinitely extensible ways (e.g. Dummett 1993, Fine 2008), or (c) that we do not have a single notion of set (or collection), but instead have an indefinitely extensible hierarchy of notions of set-like entities. All of these options are available in the case of scenarios. The third option is perhaps the least popular in the set-theoretic case, and I will set it aside in the case of scenarios. But analogs of options (a) and (b) are both open here, and I will not try to choose between them.[24]

A consequence of there being no set (collection) of all scenarios is that some problems arise with the use of intensions. In particular, all intensions as understood so far will be κ-intensions for some κ. Any set of scenarios *simpliciter* is a set of κ-scenarios for some κ, so if intensions are understood as sets of scenarios *simpliciter*, any intension will be a set of κ-scenarios. On the standard understanding, if such an intension were to be evaluated at a μ-scenario for $\mu > \kappa$ (where this μ-scenario is not itself a κ-scenario), its value would be false there, as the μ-scenario is not included in the intension. This has the odd consequence that if we attempt to understand these intensions as intensions that can be evaluated at arbitrary scenarios, all intensions will be false at all sufficiently large scenarios, and there will be no sensible way of negating intensions. On the other hand, if we understand intensions as functions from scenarios to truth values, where functions are understood in the usual way as sets of ordered pairs, then κ-intensions will not be defined at μ-scenarios, and no intension will have a truth value at all scenarios. Nevertheless, there is something intuitive about the idea

---

[24] If we take option (b), the many sentences in this paper at which I appear to quantify over all scenarios need to be reinterpreted. Most such sentences in earlier sections are still coherent if understood as quantifying over κ-scenarios, for some κ. This will not work for some sentences in this section (e.g. those concerning the impossibility of quantifying over all scenarios), for reasons familiar from the set-theoretic case, but I think that these claims can be reinterpreted by more complex means, for example using the dialectical strategy suggested by Fine (2008).

of an intension that is true at all scenarios, or one that is true at a scenario if it contains particles, and so on.

9.2. The non-set-theoretic understanding of intensions

We have seen that there are too many scenarios to form a set, and that this raises problems with the understanding of intensions as sets of scenarios. It also raises problems with the understanding of intensions as functions from scenarios to truth values, where functions are understood as sets of ordered pairs. At this point, an alternative strategy understands intensions as functions. This is familiar from the set-theoretic case, in which the axiom of replacement in effect understands functions in terms of formulae that define them. Given any set, such a formula returns another set. Even though there is no set of ordered pairs to yield a set-theoretic entity that counts as a function in the official sense, one can still see such formulae as determining mappings from sets to sets in an intuitive sense. For example, there is certainly a mapping that maps any set S to the set S^* that contains S as its only member.

Something similar applies in the case of intensions. On the current picture, one can certainly evaluate any sentence at any κ-scenario, yielding a truth value. So one can evaluate any sentence at any scenario (simpliciter), yielding a truth value. This is in effect to say that we have a coherent understanding of the notion of verification of a sentence s by an arbitrary scenario w, which we can represent as usual with the locution $ver(w, s)$. Of course ver does not correspond to a set of ordered pairs (or ordered triples), but it is still a mapping from ordered pairs to truth values in the intuitive sense. Likewise, we can understand the mapping ver_s which maps an arbitrary scenario w to $ver(w, s)$. Again, this mapping cannot be represented as a set of ordered pairs, but it is still a well-defined mapping, just as the mappings from sets to sets defined by formulae of set theory are well-defined mappings. We can think of this mapping as the intension of s.

Of course functions in this sense cannot be identified with set-theoretic objects. But for most purposes, the absence of such an object does not matter. As long we have given sense to the notion of verification of a sentence by an arbitrary scenario, this is all we need for the core aspects of the current framework. In particular, the notion of verification (along with the notions of epistemic possibility, scenarios, sentences, and actualization) is all we need in order to satisfy the core principles of epistemic space. It is possible that functions so understood can be modeled using the tools of non-standard versions of set theory, such as Fine's (2005) theory of classes and Linnebo's (2008) theory of properties, on which the relevant entities are individuated by defining formulae rather than by members. But all that matters for our purposes is that talk of functions in this sense is coherent.

Does this intuitive notion of a mapping give rise to Kaplan's paradox once again? One might think that there will be a mapping for every class of scenarios, whether or not that class forms a set: for example, the mapping that maps all scenarios to "true" will correspond to the class of all scenarios. And one might think that there will be a possible thinker for every such mapping. But the first claim is false. The intuitive notion of function invoked in the axiom of replacement does not yield a function for every class of sets (even though there is a function in this sense, corresponding to a predicate, that maps every set to true), but just a function for every formula. Likewise, the notion of mapping used here does not yield a function for every class of scenarios, but just one for every sentence. It may be that there is a sentence for every set of scenarios, but there is no reason to think that there is a sentence for every class of scenarios, at least in any sense in which there are more classes than sets. As before, it is probably best to avoid talk of classes here, except in an intuitive sense in which classes can be glossed in terms of predicates, analogous to the intuitive sense in which functions can be glossed in terms of formulae. Once we do this, it is clear that there is no reason to think that there are more classes than sets, and the threat of paradox dissolves.

It is even possible to introduce a special sort of abstract object corresponding to these intensions. Of course these abstract objects cannot be sets of ordered pairs. But we might think of an intension formally as an abstract object which when combined with an arbitrary scenario yields a truth value (or an extension). Then every sentence will yield an intension in this formal sense. One might leave the further nature of intensions unspecified, perhaps invoking an analog of Bealer's (1982) algebraic conception of propositions, according to which propositions are characterized by how they behave under various logical operations but are metaphysically simple. Or one might develop a theory of these non-set-theoretic objects, perhaps along the lines of Fine's theory of classes or Linnebo's theory of properties, on which these entities, individuated by defining formulae, are adjoined to the standard set-theoretic ontology. Importantly, on any of these approaches, there is no reason to believe that there are more intensions than scenarios. This understanding will satisfy all the central principles of epistemic space, and is consistent with elements (i) and (ii) of Kaplan's paradox, along with the falsity of (iii). This is perhaps the closest we can come to recapturing the original framework of sentences, scenarios, and intensions.

What about Kaplan's original paradox, applied not to scenarios but to metaphysically possible worlds? Of course if Metaphysical Plenitude is true, what I say here about scenarios will also apply to metaphysically possible worlds. Even if Metaphysical Plenitude is false, the same framework might apply. As long as there are no restrictions on how many atomic entities could exist, or on what propositions could be believed, then a standard space of possible worlds will generate Kaplan's paradox. One might initially adopt a stratified construction along the lines above. We will have κ-worlds for various κ, corresponding to equivalence classes of κ-conjunctions that are κ-complete (in a sense defined in terms of metaphysical possibility), using an appropriate lexicon (perhaps including expressions for fundamental properties along with logical expressions and the like). For many or most applications of possible-worlds semantics, taking worlds to be κ-worlds for an appropriate κ should suffice, and taking intensions to be κ-intensions, should suffice.[25]

For a broader framework of worlds and intensions simpliciter, we can understand a world as an entity that is a complete κ-world for some κ. Of course there will be no set of all worlds, and no functions in the set-theoretic sense mapping arbitrary worlds to truth values. But we can still evaluate sentences at arbitrary worlds, yielding truth values, and corresponding to this sort of evaluation, one will have intensions in the intuitive sense above. Worlds and intensions of this sort can arguably fill most of the explanatory purposes to which possible worlds have been put.

10. Non-Ideal Epistemic Space

The notion of (deep) epistemic possibility that we have been dealing with is an idealized one: if s is a priori, then $\neg s$ is not epistemically possible, even when s is far from obvious, and even when no one in the world knows that s. But in the ordinary sense of epistemic possibility, $\neg s$ is often epistemically possible even when s is knowable a priori. It is natural to wonder if there is a less idealized notion of deep epistemic possibility that might be useful in modeling less idealized sorts of reasoners.[26]

To develop such a conception, we must start with a *non-ideal* notion of deep epistemic possibility. Instead of saying that s is epistemically possible when $\neg s$ cannot be ruled out a priori, we might say that s is epistemically possible when $\neg s$ cannot be ruled out *through reasoning of a certain sort*. Equivalently, we can say that s is epistemically necessary when s can be established through reasoning of a certain sort. Here, there are various options.

For example, we might hold that it is (non-ideally) epistemically necessary that s when:

(i) it is obvious a priori that $\neg p$;

(ii) s can be known through such-and-such amount of a priori reasoning;

(iii) s can be proved through logical reasoning alone;

(iv) s can be proved in n steps of logical reasoning;

(v) s can be established through non-moral a priori reasoning;

(vi) s is cognitively insignificant.

Given a notion of non-ideal epistemic possibility, we can attempt to set up a corresponding *non-ideal* epistemic space, made up of *non-ideal* scenarios. The principles governing this space will be much as before. The key principle, once again, will

---

[25] It is arguable that κ-worlds are less apt for applications of possible worlds in metaphysics than for applications in semantics. I am inclined to think that possible worlds play a less essential role in metaphysical explanation than in semantic explanation: usually the relevant work can be done by the notions of possibility and necessity instead. But if necessary, the broader framework is available.

[26] Jens Christian Bjerring's ANU Ph.D. thesis (2010) is devoted to the analysis of non-ideal versions of epistemic possibility and epistemic space. I am indebted to Bjerring in what follows. For some related ideas, see Hintikka (1975), Rantala (1975), and Jago (2006).

be Plenitude: there is a scenario verifying s iff s is epistemically possible. Because many more sentences will be epistemically possible for non-ideal notions of epistemic possibility, it follows that there will be many more corresponding non-ideal scenarios.

It seems reasonable that the Actualization principle should hold on this model, but there is some question about whether Compositionality should be endorsed. For example, one may wish to allow non-ideal scenarios that verify s and t, without verifying $s\&t$. More generally, if a strong version of Compositionality holds, it is likely that if a scenario verifies some statements, it will verify all logical consequences of those statements. This will be undesirable in modeling many forms of non-ideal reasoning. If so, we may wish to do without Compositionality, or restrict it in some fashion.

The process of constructing scenarios will be more complex where non-ideal epistemic possibility is concerned. It is clear that taking scenarios to be centered worlds will lead to a failure of Plenitude: for example, a priori falsehoods are likely to be verified by no centered world. On the epistemic construction, we may need to avoid appealing to epistemically complete sentences, as these sentences are so long that they may have no interesting non-ideal epistemic properties. Instead, it may be best to appeal to *classes* of sentences: perhaps classes such that no sentence in the class is epistemically impossible, or perhaps classes such that no conjunction of sentences in the class is epistemically impossible.[27]

One could define what it is for a class c to verify a sentence s in a variety of ways: perhaps if c includes s, or perhaps if some conjunction of $\neg s$ with a subset of c is epistemically impossible, or perhaps if there is a reasoning process of the relevant sort that takes us from a subset of c to s. We can say that one class verifies another class if it verifies every sentence in that class. We can say that a class is maximal if it is verified by no class that it does not verify. There will be difficulties in setting up equivalence relations on maximal classes, due to failures of transitivity in implication, but this problem might be dealt with in a variety of ways. It seems that this sort of approach at least holds some promise.

If we can set up a non-ideal epistemic space corresponding to a non-ideal notion of epistemic possibility, we will then have a corresponding non-ideal epistemic intension. We can say that the non-ideal epistemic intension of a sentence is the sentence's intension over non-ideal scenarios, according to whether those scenarios verify the sentence. Then for any two sentences s_1 and s_2 such that it is epistemically possible

---

[27] As Bjerring establishes, both options here have problems. On the first option, the absence of any joint consistency constraints causes the resulting scenarios to behave in an extremely unconstrained way. On the second option, the joint consistency constraints have the consequences that sentences that can be ruled out only through very long chains of the relevant sort of reasoning will be excluded from all scenarios, even if they are epistemically possible. Perhaps the biggest open problem in the study of non-ideal epistemic space is that of finding a construction of non-ideal scenarios that avoids the Scylla of "anything goes" and the Charybdis of logical omniscience.

that s_1 holds without s_2 and vice versa, s_1 and s_2 will have different non-ideal intensions.

When this way of thinking is applied to different notions of epistemic possibility, it will yield various different applications. For example, if we are concerned with Frege's notion of cognitive significance, we can say that t is epistemically possible when $\neg t$ is cognitively significant (perhaps this will be whenever $\neg t$ is non-trivial), and we can set up a corresponding non-ideal epistemic space. This will yield a variety of non-ideal intension that, although unstructured, is as fine-grained as a Fregean sense.

It is likely that there is no canonical notion of non-ideal epistemic possibility. If so, there will be no canonical notion of non-ideal content. Instead, we might have a spectrum of notions of deep epistemic possibility, from the ideal to the non-ideal, perhaps ending at the notion on which anything is epistemically possible and on which contents are trivial. There will be a corresponding spectrum of epistemic spaces. Every sentence might then be associated with a spectrum of epistemic intensions, each of which is an intension across scenarios within a given epistemic space. For different purposes, different intensions from within this spectrum may be relevant. Between these intensions and these epistemic spaces, there will be enough material to do significant explanatory work in many different epistemic domains.

11. Applications

I will end by briefly spelling out some applications of the notion of epistemic space.[28]

First, there are applications to the analysis of meaning and content. In many ways, epistemic intensions behave like a broadly Fregean sort of meaning. For example, two singular terms a and b have the same epistemic intension iff '$a = b$' is epistemically necessary. This is quite reminiscent of the Fregean thesis that a and b have the same sense iff '$a = b$' is cognitively insignificant. For example, tokens of 'Hesperus is Phosphorus' are not epistemically necessary, and correspondingly the tokens of 'Hesperus' and 'Phosphorus' are associated with different epistemic intensions.

The main difference between epistemic intensions and Fregean senses arises from the fact that at least on the idealized version of epistemic necessity, epistemic necessity does not imply cognitive insignificance (though the reverse implication plausibly holds). For example, '$7+3 = 10$' is epistemically necessary but cognitively significant, so '$7+3$' and '10' will have the same epistemic intension where they have different Fregean senses. Still, epistemic intensions can serve here as at least a coarse-grained sort of Fregean sense.

The current framework can be extended in order to provide finer-grained senses. One way to extend the framework is to invoke structured epistemic intensions, so

---

[28] For more on some of these applications, see my (2002a) (Fregean sense), (2002b) (narrow content), (forthcoming a) (probability), and (forthcoming b) (Fregean sense and attitude ascriptions).

that complex expressions are associated with complexes constituted from the epi-stemic intensions of their parts. Then '7+3' is associated with a structured epistemic intension quite different from that of '10', and so on. Another way to proceed is to start with a non-idealized notion of deep epistemic necessity. For example, if one adopts understanding (vi) above, on which deep epistemic necessity is understood as cognitive insignificance, then if we can make sense of a corresponding nonideal epistemic space, we can expect that a and b will have the same non-ideal epistemic intension if $a = b$ is cognitively insignificant, just as the Fregean framework requires.

One can also apply this framework to the contents of thought, yielding a variety of content such that different modes of presentation of the same referent—*Hesperus* and *Phosphorus*, say—are associated with different contents. This sort of content will plaus-ibly behave like a sort of cognitive content, not constitutively tied to reference. And under certain plausible assumptions, it will behave like a sort of narrow content, so that the contents of a subject's thoughts do not constitutively depend on the character of a subject's environment.

The idealized sort of epistemic space can also be applied to the analysis of subjective probability, providing a candidate for the space of entities over which the subjective probabilities of an idealized agent are distributed. It is also not out of the question that one might be able to use a non-ideal epistemic space to model the entities over which the subjective probabilities of a non-ideal agent are distributed.

Non-ideal epistemic spaces may also be useful in analyzing various specific domains, such as the moral domain. We may think that the connection between the non-moral and the moral is ultimately a priori, or we may think that moral beliefs are ultimately not truth-evaluable, but as long as the connection and the non-truth-evaluability is not obvious, there will be an interesting hypothesis space to investigate. To do this, we can invoke a notion of deep epistemic possibility along the lines of notion (v) above: it is epistemically possible that p when p cannot be ruled out through non-moral a priori reasoning. This will plausible yield a space of "moral scenarios" which is much like the space of ideal scenarios, except that it may have an additional dimension of variation in the way that it associates moral claims with non-moral claims. These moral scenarios (which are reminiscent of the "factual-normative" worlds of Gibbard (1990)) may have some use in analyzing moral thought and discourse without presupposing substantive moral views.

Finally, epistemic space may be useful in giving an account of the semantics of various ordinary language constructions. Elsewhere, I have discussed how intensions of the sort discussed here may be useful in analyzing attitude ascriptions and indicative conditionals. Closer to home, they may have some use in understanding ascriptions of epistemic possibility in the ordinary sense, and in understanding about what might or might not be the case, for all one knows.

For the ordinary notion of strict epistemic possibility, it is plausible that p is epi-stemically possible when one could not *easily* come to know that $\neg p$ given what one already knows. The corresponding notion of deep epistemic possibility is something like the following: it is deeply epistemically possible that p when $\neg p$ is not easily knowable a priori. From this notion, we will be able to set up a corresponding non-ideal epistemic space. For this space, we can then say that p is strictly epistemically possible for a subject iff there is a p-scenario that is not excluded by any item of that subject's knowledge.

We can apply this framework to utterances involving epistemic modals, such as 'It might be the case that s'. According to a natural view, such an utterance is true iff there is a scenario that verifies s and that is epistemically possible for the speaker. This view involves a contextualist treatment of epistemic modals, where the standards of epistemic possibility are set by the context of utterance. If one instead adopts a relativist treatment of epistemic modals, where the standards of epistemic possibility are set by a context of assessment, one can instead say that 'It might be the case that s' is true (at a context of assessment) iff there is a scenario that verifies s and that is epistemically possible for the subject in the context of assessment. Other treatments of epistemic modals (such as those on which sentences containing epistemic modals are not assessible for truth, but merely for acceptability), can also be combined with the present framework. In this way, we can use the framework of epistemic space to help shed light on the ordinary claims about epistemic possibility with which this paper began.

References

Ackermann, F. (1978). "De re propositional attitudes toward integers", *Southwestern Journal of Philosophy* 9: 145–53.

Anderson, C. A. (2009). "The lesson of Kaplan's paradox about possible world semantics", in J. Almog and P. Leonardi (eds.), *The Philosophy of David Kaplan* (Oxford: Oxford University Press).

Austin, D. F. (1990). *What's the Meaning of "This"?* (Ithaca, NY: Cornell University Press).

Bealer, G. (1982). *Quality and Concept* (Oxford: Oxford University Press).

—— (1996). "A priori knowledge and the scope of philosophy", *Philosophical Studies* 81: 121–42.

Bjerring, J. C. (2010). *Non-Ideal Epistemic Spaces*, Ph.D. thesis, Australian National University.

Boolos, G. (1998). *Logic, Logic, and Logic* (Cambridge, Mass.: Harvard University Press).

Burgess, J. (1997). "Quinus ab omni naevo vindicatus", *Canadian Journal of Philosophy*, supp. 23: 25–66.

Cartwright, R. L. (1994). "Speaking of everything", *Noûs* 28: 1–20.

Chalmers, D. J. (2002a). "On sense and intension", *Philosophical Perspectives* 16: 135–82.

—— (2002b). "The components of content" (rev. version), in *Philosophy of Mind: Classical and Contemporary Readings* (Oxford: Oxford University Press).

—— (2002c). "Does conceivability entail possibility?", in T. Gendler and J. Hawthorne (eds.), *Conceivability and Possibility* (Oxford: Oxford University Press).

—— (2004). "Epistemic two-dimensional semantics", *Philosophical Studies* 118: 153–226.

—— (forthcoming a.) "Frege's puzzle and the objects of credence", http://consc.net/papers/credence.pdf.

Chalmers, D. J. (forthcoming b). "Propositions and attitude ascriptions: A Fregean account", *Noûs*. http://consc.net/papers/propositions.pdf.

—— and Jackson, F. (2001). "Conceptual analysis and reductive explanation", *Philosophical Review* 110: 315–60.

Cresswell, M. (2006). "From modal discourse to possible worlds", *Studia Logica* 82: 307–27.

Dummett, M. (1993). "What is mathematics about?", in *The Seas of Language* (Oxford: Oxford University Press).

Fine, K. (2005). "Class and membership", *Journal of Philosophy*, 102: 545–72.

—— (2008). "Relatively unrestricted quantification", in G. Uzquiano and A. Rayo (eds.), *Absolute Generality* (Oxford: Oxford University Press).

Gibbard, A. (1990). *Wise Choices, Apt Feelings: A Theory of Normative Judgement* (Oxford: Oxford University Press).

Hintikka, J. (1975). "Impossible possible worlds vindicated", *Journal of Philosophical Logic* 4: 475–84.

Jago, M. (2006). "Imagine the possibilities: Information without overload", *Logique et Analyse* 49: 345–71.

Kaplan, D. (1995). "A problem in possible-world semantics", in W. Sinnott-Armstrong, D. Raffman, and N. Asher (eds.), *Modality, Morality and Belief: Essays in Honor of Ruth Barcan Marcus* (Cambridge: Cambridge University Press).

Kripke, S. A. (1980). *Naming and Necessity* (Cambridge, Mass.: Harvard University Press).

—— (forthcoming). "A puzzle about time and thought", in *Collected Papers, vol. 1.* (Oxford: Oxford University Press).

Lewis, D. (1986). *On the Plurality of Worlds* (Oxford: Blackwell).

Linnebo, O. (2008). "Sets, properties, and unrestricted quantification", in G. Uzquiano and A. Rayo (eds.), *Absolute Generality* (Oxford: Oxford University Press).

Rantala, V. (1975). "Urn models", *Journal of Philosophical Logic* 4: 455–74.

Shapiro, S. (2003). "All sets great and small: And I do mean ALL", *Philosophical Perspectives* 17: 467–90.

Soames, S. (2004). *Reference and Description: The Case Against Two-Dimensionalism* (Princeton: Princeton University Press).

Whittle, B. (2009). "Epistemically possible worlds and propositions", *Noûs* 43: 265–85.

3

'Might' Made Right

Kai von Fintel and Anthony S. Gillies

1. Introduction

The simplest story about modals—*might, must, possibly, necessary, have to, can, ought to, presumably, likelier,* and the rest—is also the canon: modals are context-dependent quantifiers over a domain of possibilities. Different flavors of modality correspond to quantification over different domains of possibilities. Logical modalities quantify over all the possibilities there are, physical modalities over possibilities compatible with the laws of physics, deontic modalities over possibilities compatible with what ought to be. And epistemic modals—and in particular epistemic *might* and *must*, the stars of the show here—quantify over possibilities compatible with *what is known*.

But fixing a flavor of modality need not always fix what the modal says since context can still figure prominently in determining the domain. That seems right for epistemic modals: in one context it is what Holmes knows that is relevant, in another it is the information Watson has at hand that counts. The modals quantify over possibilities compatible with the information at hand—they quantify over what's not ruled out by a relevant *information state*. Just whose information state is something decided by the context.

That is the canon. It is simple and elegant but not quite right. It says that bare[1] epistemic modals quantify over the information available to a contextually relevant group. The context decides the group (and perhaps the standards by which they know) and thereby the domain the modals quantify over. But—as we will argue—in

This paper has been with us—in the form of notes, handouts, and talks—since 2003. That is a long time, and we have gotten attached to it. It has even done us the favor of reproducing a time or two, spinning off bits and pieces that grew up faster than it did (von Fintel and Gillies 2007, 2008). While we're happy to have finally got it off our to-do list, we will miss it. For comments, we would like to thank Josh Dever, Angelika Kratzer, Chris Potts, and audiences at the University of Osnabrück, at the Workshop on (In)determinacy of Meaning in Cologne at the annual meeting of the German Linguistics Society, at the University of Texas at Austin (twice), and in a mini-seminar on epistemic modals and conditionals at the University of Frankfurt. We are also indebted to an anonymous reviewer for Oxford University Press.

[1] "Bare" epistemic modals because they occur without accompanying restrictors.

perfectly ordinary conversations this story gets off track, making bare epistemic modals either too hard to reasonably assert or by making their uptake or dissent mysterious.

Of course, the canon is not the only game in town. And the kind of context-dependence embodied by it has recently gone in for some rough treatment. CIA agents—those arguing that epistemic modals only get assigned truth values relative to contexts of utterance, indices of evaluation, and (the new wrinkle) points of assessment—have been trying to incite a revolution against it.[2] (Relativism is the new black.) And that kind of story is meant to be better suited for dealing with some of the puzzling behavior of epistemic modals, including we'll assume the problem we raise here. It is not a state secret that we have our doubts about whether CIA theories hold water (see e.g. von Fintel and Gillies 2008). Still, if nothing else could solve the problem we raise for the canon, we would have to reconsider.

But, we will argue, there are other options and so we need not yet reconsider. The problem with the canon isn't that it has an impoverished set of superscripts. The problem is that it is weighed down by the fiction that there is a determinate context in which an utterance of a bare epistemic modal is issued. We will sketch a story about the pragmatics and conversational dynamics of these modals that goes a bit like this. Bare epistemic modals quantify over the information available to a contextually relevant group of investigators. That part the canon gets right. But, given a context, there are multiple ways of drawing the group boundaries. And "the context" often does not decide which of these is to be preferred. Thus, it is indeterminate just which group—just which aggregated information state—is quantified over by such bare epistemic modals. That part the canon gets wrong.

We need to be more precise about the problem we see for the canon. But first we want to sketch our preferred version of it (Section 2). Then, after raising the problem as we see it (Section 3), we will turn to exploring how a story that exploits this contextual indeterminacy can explain what needs explaining without departing from what's right about the canon and so without positing anything semantically peculiar about bare occurrences of epistemic modals (Sections 4-6).

2. The Canon

We will assume a generic logical form for modals along these lines:

(1) MODAL$(B)(\varphi)$

The interpretation of MODAL is just some quantifier Q—maybe first-order definable, maybe a fancier generalized quantifier—supplying the relevant force of the modal.[3]

---

[2] Some recent CIA agents: Egan (2007); Egan et al. (2007); MacFarlane (this volume); Stephenson (2007a,b).

[3] More generally, the interpretation of MODAL is a quantifier Q_D over domain D, the value of D being a function of context or the preceding discourse and the modal saying that Q_D of the possibilities in B are possibilities in which the prejacent is true. Putting things this way is useful for dealing with modal subordination, but since such issues aren't our focus here, we suppress D.

The first argument B—the *modal base*—determines the restriction on the domain of worlds over which the modal in question quantifies. The second argument is the *prejacent*—the sentence that the modal claim says holds in Q of the possibilities in B. Vary the quantificational force, or vary the domain of possibilities determined by B, and we get different modals.[4]

One way (the value of) B gets determined is as the denotation of restricting phrases like *in view of*.[5] Some examples:

(2) a. In view of what the laws are, cars cannot park on the Turnpike.
     b. In view of the information available to Holmes, the gardener might have done it.
     c. In view of the preferences Sally has, she has to take the early train.

The modals quantify over the possibilities compatible with the laws, the information Holmes has, and the satisfaction of Sally's preferences. And in each case the modal base is (plausibly) just the denotation of the relevant restricting *in view of* phrase that occurs earlier in the sentence.

But sometimes there is no restricting phrase; then B must be determined in some other way. Some examples:

(3) a. Sally presumably will not make it to the meeting.
     b. Alex must be hungry.
     c. Your keys might be on the desk.

These are *bare modals* since there is no restrictor explicit. The canon says that what helps determine the value of B for bare modals is "the context." Our focus here is on bare *epistemic* modals (BEMS): bare modals where the modal base B supplied by "the context" is epistemic and thus (the denotation of) B is the set of worlds compatible with the relevant information state. To repeat the rough gloss of the canon: such modals are quantifiers over possibilities compatible with the available evidence or the information at hand or the relevant information state—that is what makes them *epistemic* modals—saying that all/some/most/just the right such possibilities are possibilities in which the prejacent is true.

So *might* and *must* are quantifiers over information states, true at a context–index pair just in case the prejacent is true in some or every possibility compatible with the contextually-relevant information state. The range of possibly contextually relevant information states that determine the set of possibilities quantified over is pretty big. At one end of the spectrum lies the solipsistic reading, the reading where the BEM is used to report solely on the speaker's information state. Here is an old example from Kratzer (1986):

---

[4] This is the now canonical analysis of the logical structure of modal statements developed by Kratzer (1977, 1981, 1991).

[5] As in most of the literature, we will not attempt to spell out a compositional semantics of how such phrases get to determine the value of B. And, when this won't be too confusing and when style demands it, we'll also skate over the difference between B and its denotation (at a context–index pair) $[\![B]\!]^{c,i}$.

Suppose a man is approaching both of us. You are standing over there. I am further away. I can only see the bare outlines of the man. In view of *my* evidence, the person approaching may be Fred. You know better. In view of *your* evidence, it cannot possibly be Fred, it must be Martin. If this is so, *my* utterance of (4) and *your* utterance of (5) are both true.

(4) The person approaching might be Fred.
(5) The person approaching cannot be Fred.

Had *I* uttered (5) and *you* (4), both our utterances would have been false.

Kratzer claims that the BEMs in this example are claims about the speaker's evidence. When we consider that the first speaker may well be aware that the second speaker has a better vantage point and may thus have a better idea about who is approaching, it makes sense to assume that the first speaker is only making a claim about *her own* somewhat limited information state.

But the speaker-centric interpretation is not the only one available. If it were—as DeRose (1991) points out—it would never make any sense to say *I don't know whether it might be that p*. But it can make sense to say that. John has had a screening test that can rule out cancer but will not determine that he has it if he does. After the test has been run and the doctors have the results, Jane can say things like

(6) I don't know whether John might have cancer; only the doctors know. I'll find that out tomorrow when the results of the test are revealed.

And if the speaker-centric interpretation were the only one available, we would expect to be able to gloss (6) with a sentence in which the restricting *in view of* phrase picks out Jane's knowledge. But that isn't so:

(7) ?? I don't know whether in view of what I know John might have cancer; only the doctors know. I'll find that out tomorrow when the results of the test are revealed.

Whatever information state this *might* quantifies over, it doesn't include just Jane's knowledge.[6]

More objective readings—readings in which the modal quantifies over a modal base that goes beyond the speaker's information state—need to be available. One way of achieving greater objectivity is by allowing modal bases to provide possibilities compatible with the information that a *group* of agents has. For example, it is plausible that Jane fully intends her *might* to be, in part, about the information John's doctors have. But we may need more. Sometimes a *might*-claim seems false even if, in the context, the prejacent isn't ruled out by anything the speaker or hearer or any pooling thereof knows—for instance, if that information was there and they made some mistake in

---

[6] Another case in which we clearly don't have a purely solipsistic reading can be manufactured out of Kratzer's scenario above. The speaker who is further away might well ask the plausibly better informed person *Might the person approaching be Fred?*, which could not be exclusively about her own information state.

not seeing it and thus *should* have known better.[7] Holmes never botches an investigation. But his lesser-known cousin Schmolmes sometimes does. Reading through his interview notes, Schmolmes makes some errors in his deductions and declares

(8) Ah, the gardener might be the culprit.

Alas, the gardener not only didn't do it, but—as Schmolmes's own interview notes conclusively establish—he couldn't have. Poor Schmolmes just got confused and didn't connect all the dots. Even if his conversational partners aren't any the wiser, and so even if there is no plausible way of drawing the contextually relevant group boundaries to include anyone who knows that the gardener didn't do it, we still get the impression that Scholmes said something false.[8]

The canon as such is non-committal about how context can decide the relevant body of information that BEMs quantify over. So it is compatible with insisting that the relevant body of information represents some pooling of the information available to the relevant group of agents and it is compatible with insisting that the relevant body of information represents not merely what those agents know but what they may come to know—what is, borrowing Egan's (2007) nice phrasing, within their epistemic reach.

The basic lesson is that these amendments are not really deviations from the canon: it has plenty of room for this kind of flexibility in readings available for BEMS. The canon is thus a big tent, with lots of room for family squabbles about just how context decides to pool information and just what counts as within an agent's epistemic reach. Since our main point here is independent of how those disputes get resolved, we don't want to take sides and so we consider the canon in its most general flavor.[9]

---

[7] The point was first made by Hacking (1967) and then by Teller (1972) and then by DeRose (1991).

[8] Well, actually, the judgments here aren't uniform. As in other spots, this variability in judgments is itself something that needs to be explained by our best theory. So it is a mistake to tailor the theory—canon or otherwise—to automatically deliver the verdict that (8) is false.

[9] We do want to register one thought, though. It is hard to cash out what, in a context, counts as "within epistemic reach." Hacking says it's "practicable investigations" that count; DeRose says it's "contextually relevant" ones that do. But neither of these ways of constraining the notion seems right. For it is easy to find cases in which there is a "practicable" way of finding out the truth of the matter about φ and yet *might* φ and *might not-φ* both seem true. An example from Teller (1972):

(i) It might be a girl and it might be a boy. Should I buy blue or should I buy pink?

Doting soon-to-be grandmas say things like this—and thereby speak truly—even though there is a practicable test that can give them just the information they lack to help inform their buying behavior.

And saying that it is "contextually relevant" ways of coming to know seems no better. For it is easy to find cases in which there are relevant ways of coming to know that φ is false and yet *might* φ seems true. Alex is helping Billy in the search for her lost keys and says:

(ii) They might be in the car.

The keys, in fact, are not in the car. Has Alex thereby said something false? Not to our ears. Does that mean that checking the car does not count, in this context, as a "relevant way" of coming to know? No, since the point of Alex saying what she did is precisely to get Billy to check it out. Consulting Schmolmes's interview notes can count, as can ships logs (Hacking), and medical test results in a sealed envelope (DeRose). But performing a baby gender test does not, and apparently, neither does looking in the car. The project of gerrymandering epistemic reach to fit these boundaries has all the hallmarks of a project we wouldn't want to take up. So we would instead just take BEMs to quantify over the information held by a contextually relevant group of agents, and be quite egalitarian about the kinds of agents we

But we do want to insist that the pooling of information be constrained in sensible ways, and that does throw some versions of the canon out of the tent. The only context-dependence at issue for us here is the dependence of BEMs on the possibilities compatible with the information a relevant group has. So, where c is a context, we will often write G_c as the c-relevant group. And when it suits our purposes we will sometimes talk as if contexts just are the sets of agents themselves, eliminating c altogether in favor of G.

We might—as Hacking and DeRose both do—say that a BEM requires that no member of G_c know that the prejacent is false. Putting things the other way around: it is compatible with what each knows that φ. Let's let f_x be a function from indices i (worlds) to the set of indices compatible with what x knows at i. (Thus we will assume that f_x is both reflexive and euclidean.) Formally, this proposal is:

(9) $[\![might\ \varphi]\!]^{c,i} = 1$ iff $\forall x \in G_c : \exists w \in f_x(i)$ such that $[\![\varphi]\!]^{c,w} = 1$

But now we have lost the idea that a modal is a quantifier over a modal base: there is no one set of possibilities throughout which we check for some φ-worlds. That is too high a cost to pay, for it makes epistemic modals different in structure from the other modals in the language. So that is ruled out. Better to aggregate in some other way, pooling the information states of the members of G into some aggregated information state, and take BEMS to quantify over possibilities compatible with that. That would be to figure out a denotation for the modal base B in terms of what it is each $x \in G$ knows. In that case, we can simply stick with the initial modal-base skeleton that says that *might*, in a context and at an index, is an existential quantifier over the modal base $[\![B]\!]^{c,i}$. All we need is to find a good candidate for B in terms of G.

There is a spectrum of group-level modal bases—candidate values for B—that can be built from individual selection functions representing what the members of a group know.[10] But since we do not want to get involved in the family disputes about which is the right one, we will instead just insist on the following constraint:

(10) AGGREGATION:
Suppose c determines B by determining G and c' determines B' by determining G'. Then $G \subseteq G'$ implies $[\![B']\!]^{c',i} \subseteq [\![B]\!]^{c,i}$.

The more inclusive a group, the harder it is for a *might*-claim that quantifies over what it knows to be true. As an example of a story that implies (10): suppose we ignore the issue of epistemic reach (opting instead to be egalitarian about what kinds of things get to count as agents in a context), and suppose we pool information available to those in G by distributing it:

recognize: stores of information—ships logs, interview notes, and computers—can *ceteris paribus* count as "agents", but plain facts in the world—that the baby will be a girl, that it isn't raining, and that the keys aren't in the car—cannot. Exploring this feature of epistemic modals—the resistance to plain facts but sensitivity to stores of information—is a task for another occasion. We have some preliminary remarks about this feature, which makes epistemic modals related to expressions of evidentiality, in von Fintel and Gillies (2007).

[10] The classic reference for multi-agent epistemic logic is Fagin et al. (1995).

(11) Fix a c-relevant group G_c. Then $[\![B]\!]^{c,i} = \bigcap_{x \in G} f_x(i)$

Then (10) follows straightaway.[11]

So the canon is quite flexible. It captures solipsistic readings—which are almost always available—as a special case. If $G = \{\text{speaker}\}$ then what is compatible with what that group knows is just what is compatible with what she knows. And there is nothing in any of this that requires a hard-wired commitment that the speaker is always a member of the relevant group provided by context. To put it provocatively: just because s is in a context c (she's the speaker in the context of utterance after all) it does not follow that s is at all *relevant* in c and so for all the canon has said she may not be in G_c. Similarly, there's nothing that requires the members of G_c to be parties to the conversation s is having.

All of this is in the canon's favor: given the flexibility of what gets to counts as a relevant group in a context, that makes for a pretty broad spectrum of information states that can be relevant and thus for predicting flexibility at just the spots that the data demand it. It is thus tempting to think that BEMs quantify over the pooled information in a group and that the context determines what the relevant group is. So far so good. Since we like to give in to temptation, that's what we want to think. It's just that we have found a problem with the second conjunct: that *the* context *determines* what the relevant group is.

3. A Realistic Scenario

Assume that the canon is right: BEMs quantify over possibilities compatible with the pooled information of some relevant group. Given the broad range of possible meanings—all the way from solipsistic readings to ever more encompassing group readings—we would then expect that contexts are made to work hard to resolve this indeterminacy. But a look at realistic scenarios makes us suspect that contexts in fact do not bother much with resolution at all.

Alex is aiding Billy in the search for her keys:

(12) Alex: You might have left them in the car.

---

[11] Distributed knowledge is also a rather intuitive notion. Here's the comment of a 9/11 widow (heard on NPR on 4/11/2004) when the 9/11 commission report was discussed:

(i) We knew more than is being owned up to. But nobody put the pieces together.

There are other ways of "pooling" information that can plausibly lay claim to being distributed information. Here is a natural one: the information every member of the group would have after all of the members (successfully) share what they know. This notion coincides with (11) for non-modal prejacents, but diverges thereafter. Example: we know that p and that you do not know it. That is a bit of information that is distributed in our group in the sense of (11), but not something any of us will know after we all share what we know. For then you *will* know that p (and we'll know that you do). There are, of course, other group-level knowledge operators—what is common knowledge among G, what everyone in G knows, what someone in G knows, and so on—but none that are clearly as plausible as what is distributed among G for the purposes of BEMs.

From here the conversation can take one of two paths. If Billy cannot rule out the possibility raised by Alex, an appropriate response might be:

(13) Billy: You're right. Let me check.

On the other hand, if Billy *can* rule out the prejacent, we find responses such as:

(14) Billy: No, I still had them when we came into the house.[12]

This is a perfectly ordinary scenario between speaker and hearer, and there are two natural ways the dialogue could go. What reading does the BEM that they are discussing have? What resolution of the modal base does the context of their conversation supply?

For simplicity, let's consider just two candidate resolutions of the contextual parameter. Under one resolution, the relevant group has as its only member the speaker Alex. Under this speaker-centric resolution, $G = \{Alex\}$. Call the associated reading the A-reading. With respect to this disambiguation, the BEM is about Alex's evidence. The other resolution we'll consider takes both Alex and Billy to be relevant. Under this groupwise resolution $G' = \{Alex, Billy\}$. Call the associated reading the $A+B$-reading. Here the BEM is about the information that the non-trivial group of Alex and Billy has. So, which of these two candidate resolutions is the one that the context of their conversation determines to be the one giving the relevant interpretation of Alex's BEM ? We will now see that in fact neither reading can be the one that is at issue here.[13]

The speaker-centric resolution faces trouble right out of the gate. When Alex issues her BEM, both potential replies by Billy are open, one registering denial or disagreement and the other registering acceptance or uptake. But, assuming the speaker-centric resolution and thereby assuming that the dialogues traffic in the A-reading, what is it that Billy is denying or taking up?

First, take (14). What could Billy be disagreeing with by uttering this? Not the content of the A-reading: Billy has no reason to doubt that Alex's information did not rule out that the keys were in the car. Rather the "No" of Billy's answer is—plausibly—a negation of the prejacent: the keys are not in the car. Since the truth of the prejacent is ultimately what matters here, it is unsurprising that Billy would deny it directly.[14] But the reply in (13), *You're right*, is also open. What could Billy be taking up here? Again, not the content of the A-reading: Billy is in no position to comment on whether Alex's information state leaves it open that the keys are in the car. But

---

[12] Notice that it is virtually obligatory for Billy to justify the rejection of the BEM by giving the key bit of evidence that leads him to rule out the prejacent. We actually don't know exactly how to derive this obligation, even if it seems blindingly obvious.

[13] We do not even consider the possibility here that the BEM is meant under the B-reading. It is obvious that A has no business making assertions about B's information state. Later, we will resurrect the B-reading, however.

[14] The possibility that reactions to a BEM target not the modal claim but the prejacent is one that always needs to be kept in mind when using dialogues as data for the semantics of epistemic modals. At least some of the recent relativist literature is careless in this regard.

unlike the denial, targeting the prejacent here is not a plausible dodge. Whatever Billy is agreeing to, it is not that the keys *are* in the car. In fact what it *feels* like is that Billy is agreeing that it is compatible with what they *qua* group know that the keys are in the car. But that is the $A+B$-reading, not the A-reading.

And though Billy's space of responses is quite open, it is not unconstrained. One thing she definitely can't do is reply

(15) Billy: # OK, but *I* know that they're not there.

If the dialogues here trafficked in the A-reading—if the context resolved our group down to just the speaker Alex—then Billy's response in (15) should be just fine.

That would seem to leave us with the groupwise resolution of the contextual parameter and the associated $A+B$-reading. This resolution would seem to be compatible with both replies. If Billy doesn't know where the keys are, then her reply in (13) would be on the mark since in this case there would be keys-in-the-car possibilities among those compatible with what G' knows.[15] And if Billy knows they're not in the car, then since she is a member of G' her private knowledge is sufficient to guarantee that there are no such keys-in-the-car possibilities among the possibilities compatible with what G' knows. The denial in (14) is thus also on the mark.

But we've hopped out of the frying pan and into the fire. For under this resolution, it is hard to see how Alex could be in a position to assert (12) in the first place. She does not seem to be within her linguistic rights to be claiming that the group's information cannot rule out the prejacent.[16] After all, Alex does not know whether Billy has private information about the whereabouts of the keys. So if the usual norms of assertion apply in the case of epistemic modals, then—no matter whether your favorite[17] story for assertion requires justified belief or knowledge or truth of the asserted content—Alex has no business asserting the $A+B$-reading, unless she is confident that Billy has no information that goes beyond her own information. That does not seem right: in our scenario, Alex can utter the BEM without such confidence in place. (And if she did have that confidence, we wouldn't need to resort to the $A+B$-reading at all.)

Making sense of Billy's space of available replies seems to close off resolving the relevant group to just Alex and pushes us to the group reading. But making sense of Alex's assertion goes just the other way, closing off group readings as being beyond what she could reasonably assert (if the usual norms are in force at any rate). So neither

---

[15] Once we look a bit closer at this, we'll see that what we say here isn't quite true. Just because neither Alex nor Billy can rule out that the keys are in the car doesn't mean that the group of the two of them can't rule that out. We will explain later why Billy can still agree to the $A+B$-reading.

[16] As far as we know, the earlier literature on group readings of BEMS (DeRose 1991; Teller 1972) did not discuss the question of what justifies the assertion of such a reading by a speaker who does not have unusual access to the other group members' information state. Perhaps, it is not an accident that DeRose's paradigm case of an indisputable group reading is an embedded (unasserted) BEM: *I don't know whether John might have cancer*.

[17] We don't pick sides in the fight; see Williamson (1996), Weiner (2005), and Lackey (2007) for some of the contestants.

of the predicted readings is the one that the context determines as the interpretation of the BEM that Alex uttered.[18]

This is where any CIA agents who are eavesdropping on our discussion are hopping up and down impatiently. They advise that this is precisely the reason why their analyses are to be preferred: the contextualist analysis cannot make sense of the apparent observation that as far as the speaker is concerned, *the* context provides the solipsistic resolution of the context-dependency, while when the hearer comes in, *the* (*very same*) context supplies the group reading. So, why not say, they insinuate, that the way the modal is read varies with the context of *assessment*, which varies with who the assessor is: the speaker in the moment of utterance, the hearer (or the group) in the moment of reception? Well, we've already explained why not (in von Fintel and Gillies 2008). Here, we will show how the contextualist analysis can respond to the puzzle. The story we will tell will take the semantics of BEMs to be pretty much as the canon says: they are quantifiers over possibilities compatible with the information a contextually relevant group has. But we will tell a much richer story about the pragmatics of BEMs.

So, what does the BEM really mean here? Our contention is that rather than having *neither* of the solipsistic or group readings (and thus having some as of yet novel reading, perhaps such as the one promoted by the CIA agents), Alex's BEM actually has *both* readings—possibly many more, in fact—and that this kind of multiplicity of meanings is precisely what gives BEMs their peculiar properties. The context does not, in general, determine what the relevant group is. Instead, it leaves this underspecification intact, and—we will say—epistemic modals exploit this.

4. Ambiguity by Design

The canon requires contexts to do more than they in fact do: a context in which a BEM is deployed need not, it seems, fully determine a relevant group of agents. This is more feature than bug, though, generating ambiguity as if by design.[19]

Not all actual contexts of use for a natural language sentence will successfully resolve all indeterminacies and ambiguities of that sentence. That is well known. Sometimes, of course, this will cause the conversation to break down and will thus necessitate a negotiation between the participants over the interpretation of the sentence. When Bond and Leiter are looking at a group of members of parliament and Leiter suddenly shouts:

[18] A possibility we will not pursue as such here is that the contextually determined content of the BEM is in fact the $A + B$-reading, but that it is put forward by Alex not as an assertion but as a weaker kind of speech act. In our story, that is almost right: Alex does weakly put the $A + B$-reading in play but what she is in a position to assert is the A-reading. Stay tuned, we'll explain soon.

[19] Our account was partially inspired by a remark by Angelika Kratzer (p.c. to Kai von Fintel, at a UMass linguistic colloquium in December 2003). Roger Schwarzschild's talk (1999) on cases where contexts underdetermines context-dependent items was also important to us. Neither should be held responsible for what we did with their ideas.

(16) That guy is an assassin. Shoot him before he can do anything.

one presumably expects Bond to ask for a more precise reference as to which of the politicians he's supposed to take out. But other times, we proceed without full resolution of contextual ambiguities. Bond is stealthing his way through a dark corridor, his local guide in tow. A figure moves in the shadows and the guide shouts:

(17) Watch out! He's trying to shoot you.

Bond does not puzzle over the referent of that hanging anaphor; he ducks (and, amazingly, disarms the figure in one motion).[20] And yet other times, the indeterminacy is there as if by design, and this is what we claim is going on with BEMs.[21]

One more example. Billy meets Alex at a conference, and asks her:

(18) Where are you from?

That question is supposed, given a context, to partition answer-space according to how low-level in that context Billy wants his details about Alex to be. But notice that it's not really clear whether Billy wants to know where Alex is currently on sabbatical or where Alex teaches or where Alex went to graduate school or where Alex grew up. And—the point for us—Billy might not know what he wants to know. He just wants to know a bit more about Alex and will decide after she answers whether he got an answer to his question or not. He doesn't have to have the level of granularity sorted out before he asks the question. So context (or context plus Billy's intentions) need not resolve the contextual ambiguity.[22]

When a BEM is deployed, the facts about the conversation up to that point might be compatible with multiple ways of drawing the boundaries to what can plausibly count as "the relevant group." Since we are pretending that this is the only relevant contextually supplied information, that means we can think of utterances taking place against a cloud of admissible contexts—one for each resolution of the relevant group that is compatible with the facts as they are when the BEM is issued. And indeed, we will assume that there is a one–one correspondence between admissible contexts and potential resolutions of the relevant group.

It is important to realize that the proposal is not that some kind of objective context does provide a determinate resolution of the BEM and that the conversational parties are ignorant of or indifferent towards what the context is. There is no such thing as "the context", only the contexts admissible or compatible with the facts as they are. The context of the conversation really does not provide a determinate resolution and

[20] The example in (17) is due to van Deemter (1998). Idealizing, we might say that Bond is employing the strategy of diagonalization here (Stalnaker 1978): he computes the proposition that whoever the guide is referring to is trying to shoot him.

[21] It has been observed that sometimes ambiguous sentences are used purposefully to convey more than one proposition, namely in the context of jokes (Raskin 1985), poetry (Su 1994), and other less than straightforward uses of language; see Poesio (1996) for discussion. Our proposal here is that a multiplicity of meaning is also detectable in at least ostensibly more straightforward uses of language.

[22] We owe this example to Chris Potts (p.c.).

we propose to model this by saying that there is a cloud of contexts at the given point of the conversation.

There are different ways of making this intuition more precise, each way representing a different way of distributing the labor between the semantics and the pragmatics. One way is to allow the possibility that some constructions—in our case, BEMs—have as their semantic value not propositions but *sets* of propositions. And to do that we could insist that semantic values are assigned not with respect to contexts but with respect to sets of admissible contexts. With a little care this can be done in such a way that we do not have to seriously complicate the pragmatics.

But there are other options. The one we opt for here makes for a better view of some of the landmark properties of BEMs. The point for us is that there is a space of pragmatic stories that can be told that say how the contextual ambiguity of BEMs gets exploited in a way that does justice to the data about them. We tell one such story, giving some basic pragmatic principles that combine with the basic semantics for BEMs to do that work.

We begin by saying what *travels* in a conversation, or what proposition(s) the speaker of a BEM *puts into play*. When a proposition is put into play, it's available for denial and uptake. When an utterance is contextually underspecified, the propositions corresponding to the various disambiguations are put into play.

(19) TRAVEL:

Suppose the facts (linguistic and otherwise) up to t allow the groups $G_1, G_2, \ldots$ as resolutions of the contextual parameter, these resolutions delimiting the cloud C of contexts. Then an utterance of $might(B)(\varphi)$ with respect to C at t puts into play the set of propositions P such that for some $c \in C$: $[\![might(B)(\varphi)]\!]^c = P$.

This means that, as far as the semantics is concerned, there is no underspecification here: BEMs get assigned normal semantic values at (determinate) contexts. But since utterances of them take place against a cloud of such determinate contexts—since there is a set of ways compatible with the context of determining a contextual parameter—those utterances put in play a set of such semantic values. This would make our proposal here a relative of—how close we shall not guess—proposals for how the grammar deals with other types of underspecification.[23] Since multiple propositions travel following a single utterance of a BEM, there is a lot of explanatory work left for the pragmatics to do. We will look at the pragmatics of this ambiguity by design from both sides of a conversation. We will again use the simple but realistic dialogue between Alex and Billy about the whereabouts of the keys as our test case.

When Alex says *The keys might be in the car*, this BEM puts into play multiple propositions, each of which makes a claim about the information state of a group engaged in the investigation. There are arguably three such groups: the singleton groups {Alex},

---

[23] Poesio (1996), for example, gives a semantics for an underspecified language that assigns sets of standard meanings to expressions of that language.

{Billy}, and the non-trivial group {Alex, Billy}. So, there are three readings put in play: the A-, B-, and $A + B$-readings. Now, what are speaker and hearer doing with that set of propositions?

First, let's consider the speaker. She manages to put in play a set of propositions. But she does not have to be in a position to assert each one. When Alex uttered *The keys might be in the car* with its three meanings, she was not in the right position to flat out assert either the hearer-centric B-reading or the groupwise $A + B$-reading. Since those propositions are among the set of propositions she put in play, and since her utterance was appropriate, that means that she didn't have to be in a position to flat out assert each of the meanings the BEM in her mouth had.

But perhaps this relies on a mistaken theory of what the norm of assertion comes to. Perhaps, according to the right story, it turns out that when a speaker utters an underspecified sentence she must—deontic *must*, that is—be in a position to assert each of the propositions she puts in play. And perhaps someone would enjoy arguing for all that. But not us. We'll leave the norm of assertion untouched and we will say that the speaker only has to be in a position to flat out assert *one* of the propositions she puts in play; any one of them will do:

(20) ASSERT:
   Suppose an utterance of $might(B)(\varphi)$ by S puts in play the propositions $P_1, P_2, \ldots$. Then S must have been in a position to flat out assert one of the P_i's.

Our proposal is that in order for a speaker to be within her linguistic and epistemic rights when she issues a BEM against a cloud of contexts, she has to be in a position to flat out assert one of the meanings it can have, given that cloud.

Return to our little dialogue. When Alex utters the BEM, with its three meanings, there needn't be a fact of the matter as to which of the three meanings she intends to assert. But she needs to be in a position to flat out assert at least one: the A-reading, the B-reading, or the $A + B$-reading. Given the facts of the scenario, the minimal requirement is that Alex needs to be in a position to assert the A-reading. That will be the weakest reading she will stand in the appropriate relation to. In other words, given the facts of that scenario, Alex is justified in uttering the BEM iff she is justified in claiming that her evidence does not rule out the prejacent. As far as the norms of assertion go, it's as if she had uttered an explicit claim about her own evidence. But that's not what the BEM in her mouth means: it has the three meanings at once.

Things can be different in different scenarios. Part of what's right about the canon—and part of what's wrong with the CIA—is that it can be perfectly sensible to assert *might φ* even when you know that φ is false. Pascal and Mordecai are (still) playing Mastermind.[24] After some rounds where Mordecai gives Pascal hints about the solution, Pascal asks whether they might be two reds. Mordecai answers:

---

[24] We've been using this example, to make various points about epistemic modals, quite a lot lately: see e.g. von Fintel and Gillies (2007, 2008, 2010).

(21) That's right. There might be.

He can answer this way even if he knows there aren't two reds. As far as the norms of assertion go, it's as if he had uttered an explicit claim about Pascal's evidence.

Now, let's consider the hearer's side of the exchange. Since a BEM puts multiple propositions in play, we need to sort out which of these a hearer should react to, which a hearer takes as the appropriate target for uptake or denial. Again, we say that in order to take up and accept a BEM issued just prior, a hearer must be in the right relation to just one of those propositions. But now not just any one of them will do. Instead, we argue that the hearer is guided by what response to which proposition will be most informative in the conversation. When the modal is an existential like *might*, this will in fact lead to a dominance of negative replies.

(22) CONFIRM/DENY

Suppose an utterance of $might(B)(\varphi)$ by S puts in play the propositions $P_1, P_2, \ldots$. Then a hearer H can confirm (deny) the BEM if the strongest P_i that H reasonably has an opinion about is such that H thinks it is true (false).

In our dialogue, the BEM that Alex utters has the A-reading, the B-reading, and the $A + B$-reading. Alex is justified in uttering the BEM because she is in a position to flat out assert the A-reading. But just asserting the A-reading isn't what she's doing. When Alex puts the three propositions in play, the other readings, the hearer-centric reading and the strong group reading, are floated. She does not have to be in a position to assert those in order for them to be available for Billy to react to. It is as if she is conjecturing that the B-reading and the $A + B$-reading are true or asking whether they are true. Billy confirms/rejects the BEM based on those readings. Billy reasonably has an opinion on the B-reading, and especially if he can rule out the prejacent, he also reasonably has an opinion on the $A + B$-reading, namely that it is false (if he can rule out the prejacent, then so can any group to which he belongs).

One might have thought that even if Billy can rule out the prejacent based on his private information, a principle of charity should lead him to accept the BEM under the A-reading. After all, there is ambiguity one resolution of which would leave Alex having spoken truly. Instead, our principle has it that the more cooperative thing to do is to reject the BEM because it is false under the $A + B$-reading. At least, this is *ceteris paribus* the right thing to do—for instance if the goal of the conversation is to ultimately determine the truth of the prejacent or even the answer to a more general question. In our case of the misplaced keys, the ultimate goal is to find out where the keys are and the proximate goal is to figure out whether they are in the car. It is not the goal of the conversation in any important sense to find out whether the speaker's evidence or the group's evidence at the time of the conversation rules out that the keys are in the car. So, the proper thing to do—the more cooperative conversational move—is to deny the BEM under the $A+B$-reading and by entailment thus deny the prejacent.[25]

Let us look a bit closer at the case where Billy cannot rule out the prejacent on the basis of his information. Obviously, he will confirm the BEM (*You're right*). Which reading of the BEM is he reacting to? Our principle says that it is the strongest reading he reasonably has an opinion about. Which one is that? It is obvious that he reasonably has an opinion about the B-reading. What about the stronger $A+B$-reading? Can he reasonably have an opinion about that?

We have said that the group readings of BEMs make claims about the pooled knowledge of the relevant group. When Alex utters the BEM, Billy concludes that Alex is not in a position to rule out the prejacent. If Billy himself is also not able to rule out the prejacent, he might put 2 and 2 together and conclude that the group of the two of them cannot rule out the prejacent. But wait: while 2 and 2 makes 4, the group reading may actually be more like 4.5: suppose both Alex and Billy know that q and r entail $\neg p$, but just Alex knows that q and just Billy knows that r. Then p is compatible with what each knows, but not with what they know *qua* group if the pooling goes by distributed knowledge as in (26). Now even if Billy learns that p is compatible with what Alex knows, he still can't rule out this sort of thing. And so, after learning that the A-reading of a BEM $might(B)(p)$ is true, Billy does not know that the $A+B$-reading is true.

Nevertheless, we think that in many cases where B cannot rule out the prejacent, it is in fact reasonable for B to jump to the conclusion that the group reading is true—even if strictly speaking that group reading does not follow from that. That is, it tends to be a mutual expectation in a conversation that partners in it are similarly situated. That expectation is both rough and defeasible, but still ripe for being appealed to in a conversation:

> (23) DEFEASIBLE CLOSURE
>
> If H knows that φ is compatible with what x knows, for each $x \in G$, then it is reasonable for H to defeasibly infer that φ is compatible with what G knows.

This is a merely defeasible inference, since there are certainly cases where one shouldn't draw the inference: cases where the stakes are high, cases where one has reason to think that others in the group are far more informed about the prejacent than oneself and those from whom one has heard, and so on. We hypothesize that this kind of presumption is suitably conventionalized, that conversational partners naturally expect each other to draw on it, and that when the conditions are not ripe for it they expect this fact to be reasonably transparent to each other.

---

[25] Instead of justifying our principle in (22) by telling a story about cooperativity, we could also simply stipulate that a hearer confronted with a systematically ambiguous sentence whose meanings can be ordered in strength should treat the utterance as if it carried the strongest of those meanings. This would align our proposal with other work that has argued for a STRONGEST MEANING HYPOTHESIS (Dalrymple et al. 2008; Winter 2001).

If we are in a context where it is reasonable to draw the defeasible closure inference and if *B* cannot himself rule out the prejacent, then *B* upon hearing *A*'s BEM can reasonably have an opinion on the *A+B*-reading, namely that it is true. Hence, *B* can confirm the BEM on that strong reading.

Now, let us zoom out to a bird's-eye view of the BEM exchange: the BEM itself has three meanings, but Alex acts as if the solipsistic reading were the one that matters, while the hearer acts as if the hearer-centric or even the group reading were the active ones. This asymmetry is what gives BEMs their quasi-magical properties: a speaker can utter them based on just her own evidence but it serves as a probe or test or trial balloon into the hearer's evidence. When things go well and a hearer takes up a BEM, this fact becomes common ground between speaker and hearer and thus it follows that it is common belief between them that the prejacent is compatible with the information that they *qua* group have.[26]

It is easy to see why Alex might want to float those (possibly) stronger readings. If what is important is where the keys are, and not what's compatible with what who knows, then finding out the truth about those stronger readings is a pretty clear path to finding her keys. But none of that is to say that the BEM in the speaker's mouth was an assertion of that strong group reading. Take our toy example once more. If what matters goes beyond where the keys are, further moves are imaginable. If Alex and Billy are bickering already, one could encounter a dialogue like this one:

(24) A: The keys might be in the car.

B: They're not. I still had them when we came into the house. Why did you say that?

A: Look, I didn't say they *were* in the car. I said they *might be* there—and they might have been. Sheesh.

Here, Alex is sticking to her guns, defending her BEM on the basis of a weaker reading than the *A+B*-reading. Once she does this, there is no basis for a continued dispute and the only avenue open to Billy at this point is to back off.

Our story about the ambiguity-by-design of BEMs would perhaps be even more convincing if we had independent confirmation that such a story is useful beyond epistemic modals. An obvious place to look are contextual restrictions on other quantifiers:

(25) Every student was at the meeting.

It does not seem implausible to say that the precise delimitation of the contextual domain of quantification for (25) can often be indeterminate in a realistic context. We suggest that the speaker of (25) in such a context has put into play a set of propositions

---

[26] Note that because of the strength of the distributed knowledge reading of group-BEMs, it is usually not common *knowledge* that the group can't rule out the prejacent. This is why we are saying in the text that after the BEM exchange is completed, it is merely common belief (or even only common acceptance) that the group can't rule out the prejacent. But that's OK since a group can be wrong in thinking that a BEM is true.

that differ in the domain of quantification. While we can't elaborate on this suggestion here, we should point out that in such cases, it seems more often appropriate for the speaker to retreat to a weaker resolution of the domain than it does in the case of BEMS:

> (26) Sally: Every student was at the meeting.
>   George: What, even those that are on leave in Nicaragua?
>   Sally: No, what I meant was every student in residence.

In the case of BEMS, defending the BEM under the weakest, solipsistic interpretation is often—though not quite always—irrelevant (exceptions include: cases of antagonistic conversations, being on the witness stand, and playing Mastermind).

Let us end the presentation of our basic story by thinking about the conversational dynamics one more time. It might seem outlandish to claim that BEMS are typically multiply ambiguous and that this multiplicity is dealt with not as a defect but is embraced and processed quietly and without fuss. But we hope to have shown that the pragmatics of such exchanges relies on some rather intuitive principles. It should also be noted that once a hearer has confirmed or denied the BEM with all its indeterminacy, the resulting common ground is quite determinate. If B denies the BEM—and, of course, assuming the conversation does not there derail—then what's common ground is that the prejacent can be ruled out by the group, and hence that the prejacent is false. If, on the other hand, B confirms the BEM, then there are two possibilities, depending on whether the conditions are right for the principle of DEFEASIBLE CLOSURE to apply. If the standards of the conversation are too strict or there are other defeaters nearby, then there is no appeal to DEFEASIBLE CLOSURE: instead it is common ground that no member of the group can rule out the prejacent. Hence what becomes common ground is, in effect, the kind of reading of the BEM that Hacking and DeRose posit *even though that is not available as something 'might' might mean*. And if DEFEASIBLE CLOSURE *does* apply, then what is common ground between them is the distributed group reading: that their information *qua* group cannot rule out the prejacent. Again, what becomes common ground is not something any of the group members flat out asserted, but is something much stronger. That is valuable, and what exploiting ambiguity by design can buy us. There is no lingering uncertainty one would have to worry about. We hope that it has become clear that BEMS with their multiplicity of meanings are a very useful device to have in one's grammar.

5. Beyond Alex and Billy

We have been looking at a very simple but still realistic scenario involving a single speaker and a single hearer trying to ascertain the whereabouts of some keys. Somewhat realistic, but still an idealization. So we shall take our literary license and give Alex and Billy another roommate, Chuck.

All three roommates are looking for the keys. Alex again says that the keys might be in the car. In this context, possible resolutions for the BEM are the solipsistic readings (the A-,B-, and C-readings) plus the relevant group readings (the $A+B$-, $A+C$-, and $A+B+C$-readings).[27]

As before, Alex can utter the BEM because she is in a position to assert the A-reading. But at the same time, she is floating the other readings. And now, we consider the possible responses from Billy and Chuck. Our CONFIRM/DENY principle (22) says that each of them should determine their reaction to the BEM based on the strongest relevant reading about which they can reasonably have an opinion. If either Billy's or Chuck's information state rules out the prejacent, then we expect the same denial as before. And assuming the conversation does not derail, or that there is no conversational retreat like we saw in (24), then it becomes common ground between them that the keys are not in the car.

But suppose neither Billy nor Chuck has information that eliminates the possibility that the keys are in the car. We will assume that the conditions are ripe for applying DEFEASIBLE CLOSURE. (If they aren't, they confirm the BEM, and the fact that the prejacent is compatible with what each knows is common ground.) Both will then confirm the BEM. That is because each has good reason for the strongest available meaning about which he has an opinion. Billy because he believes the $A+B$-reading. and Chuck because he believes the $A+C$-reading. After both confirm the BEM (assenting, in effect, to different floated meanings of it), then it is common ground that the prejacent is compatible with Alex's information, Billy's information, and Chuck's information. All parties can then appeal to DEFEASIBLE CLOSURE once more to infer, defeasibly, the $A+B+C$-reading. And since they can expect the others to do the same, this can become common ground.

But this two-step procedure isn't always required. Sometimes conversational partners can jump straightaway to confirming the strongest group reading floated. A team of investigators has been collecting clues at the scene of the crime, when the Detective calls them all together:

(27) a. Detective: Do we think the murderer might have used an icepick and slipped out the window?
b. Investigator #1: Yes, he might have.

The investigator looks like she is answering Detective's question about what is compatible with what the whole team of investigators has been able to find out so far (he asked what *we think* about the possibility). That means she is not confirming the Detective-plus-Investigator #1-reading, but a much stronger one. And if none of her co-investigators complain, she will have done so felicitously (though she could still turn out to be mistaken). How did she do that?

---

[27] Given the set-up, it seems unlikely that Alex's utterance puts in play a $B+C$-reading. But in other scenarios it might: for example, if Alex knows full well where the keys are but her job is to test Billy and Chuck's key-sleuthing skills Billy can ask *Might the keys be in the car?* and Alex can truthfully reply *They might be.*

Answering collective queries or confirming group conjectures can be easier than you might have thought. We are at Hullabalooza when Rock Star takes the stage and asks:

(28) Rock Star: Is Springfield ready to rock?!?

The two of us are, in fact, ready to rock. But we don't know about everyone else. Plus, we are not the town spokespeople, and neither is any one person in the audience. What Rock Star wants to know is if the group is—*qua* group—ready to rock and that is something none of us could answer on our own. And he knows that. So why would he ask? Because we can *anticipate* that each of us is ready to rock, and then answer on that basis that the group is. It is excellent evidence that Springfield is ready to rock if, when he asks, we all yell *Yes!*. Excellent, but not quite conclusive: that is because, plausibly, there are group-level facts about our readiness to rock. We can all be individually ready, but not gel in the right sort of way *qua* group.

Of course, Rock Star has a hunch. He suspects that his query will be met with a raucous chorus of *Yes!* from the audience. It seems acceptable for each of us to confirm Rock Star's suspicion that Springfield is ready to rock. And it seems equally unacceptable to deny the suspicion on the grounds that we don't know the preparedness *vis-à-vis* rocking of our fellow concert goers:

(29) a. Rock Star: Is Springfield ready to rock?
     b. Crowd: ??We don't know!

Confirming such a collective query thus seems to reveal two things. First, just as in the case of BEMs, there is a reasonable expectation that we can apply something very much like DEFEASIBLE CLOSURE: if we think that each of the group is ready to rock, we may infer defeasibly that the group is itself ready to rock. Second, that the group members can *anticipate* that the base-level facts for the other group members do in fact obtain, that all the others are ready to rock.

There are three especially noteworthy features we want to point out. First, this represents a bending of normal conversational rules—it's not the norm of assertion we are living up to here when we all shout *Yes!*. But if we couldn't be relied on to bend them in this way, the rock star's question would be an infelicitous (and not just hackneyed) way to begin the show. Second, just as with BEMs, we could all get it wrong. The entire audience could (prospectively) live up to our linguistic and epistemic duties and answer *Yes!* and have it turn out that, despite our enthusiasm, we were not *qua* group ready to rock. And third, if the two of us *qua* individuals are not ready to rock, then we can conclusively and without any anticipation about the readiness of our fellow audience members answer the rock star's query with a *No*. If we aren't ready, then no group to which we belong could be ready.

Being in a conversation in which BEMs are issued is a lot like going to a rock concert. The strong group readings in our example are floated or put in play by Alex. That amounts to something like a collective conjecture and we say that the same type of conversational rules can apply for taking up such readings as apply in answering whether Springfield is ready to rock. That means that hearers can confirm a BEM and take up one of its strong group readings even if they are not in a position to flat out assert such a strong disambiguation. Denying a BEM does not involve the same bending of normal conversational rules. But neither does answering the rock star's collective query negatively: if we are not ready to rock, then it just is not true that Springfield is, and we may say so. So it is with BEMS: if the prejacent is not compatible with what a hearer knows then it is not compatible with what any group to which she belongs knows.

So we can pair DEFEASIBLE CLOSURE with another pragmatic principle, one targeted to the strong readings of BEMS that can be floated:

(30) ANTICIPATION

Suppose an utterance of $might(B)(\varphi)$ by S at i puts in play the propositions $P_1, P_2, \ldots$. And suppose that these quantify over the information available to $G_1, G_2, \ldots$ respectively. Then if $H \in G_i$ and $f_H(i) \cap [\![\varphi]\!] \neq \emptyset$, then H may infer defeasibly that $f_x(i) \cap [\![\varphi]\!] \neq \emptyset$, for each $x \in G_i$.

This is, of course, defeasible and need not be appropriately exploited in every context. All we require is that, like with DEFEASIBLE CLOSURE, it is suitably conventionalized and that conversational partners can expect each other to appeal to it when reasonably appropriate. But even if we do appeal to ANTICIPATION, we may have to retract the judgments based on it. We are inclined to answer *Yes!* when asked if Springfield is ready to rock. But if we hear booing coming from the audience, we will retract that. Similarly, if Investigator #2 pipes up with information to the contrary:

(31) a. Investigator #2: No, the window was locked from the inside.
b. Investigator #1: Oh, OK. He can't have got out that way.

This kind of retraction plays a big role in training CIA agents. No sense can be made of this, they say, unless truth values of sentences involving BEMS are sensitive to contexts and indices and points of assessment to boot. Note that when Investigator #1 retracts in this way, she retracts the strong reading floated. If the issue of the day had been what she knew and not how the culprit got away, she could stick to her guns just fine. That proposition is of little use now, but isn't and wasn't false. So there is no more reason to think this behavior of BEMS in conversation points in the direction of a radically relativized semantics than does finding out that, *contra* our expectations, Springfield is not ready to rock. It is perhaps reason for sadness, for rocking is what Springfield ought to want to do, but no reason for despair (or signing up with the CIA).

6. Eavesdroppers

The literature on readings of BEMS has established, as we mentioned earlier, that BEMS can be interpreted as making claims about evidence beyond the current awareness of speaker and hearer. Concomitantly, we will say that in particular contexts there may be many more than just a few readings for a BEM that are put in play.

The eavesdropper cases that provided much grist to the CIA mills are relevant here. Imagine that Chuck, unbeknownst to Alex and Billy, is monitoring them as they're trying to find the keys. When Alex says *They might be in the car*, Chuck says to himself (or to us who are watching this particular morality play) *She is wrong. They can't be in the car because I saw Billy come into the house with them.* What justifies Chuck's rejection of the BEM? Within the logic of our analysis, Chuck's rejection of the BEM can only be felicitous if he is part of a G that is within the relevant cloud of contexts. In other words, Chuck can felicitously reject the BEM as long as the BEM in Alex's mouth had as one of its multiple readings a reading where it was a claim about the information state of a group to which Chuck belongs.

Now, can that be? Can it be that in Alex's mouth the BEM had as one of its multiple readings a reading where it was a claim about the information state of a group to which Chuck belongs? It is by now routine to spin such scenarios in a way that makes Chuck someone who is completely unknown to Alex and Billy. So, how can Alex's BEM have a reading where its claim hinges (partly) on what Chuck knows? Simple: imagine that what makes someone part of a relevant group for a BEM is that they are engaged (in some sense) in the same investigation as the overt partners in the conversation. CIA agents complain that this makes BEMs too strong to allow any speaker to assert them. We agree. It is extremely unlikely that Alex is asserting the BEM under the reading that includes Chuck. But that is not what our story says. Alex is licensed to utter the BEM as soon as she is in a position to assert it under one relevant reading (the solipsistic one, typically). But since she utters it as a *bare* epistemic modal, she thereby puts into play multiple readings and it is one of those that Chuck rejects, which then results in the prejacent being rejected as well.

We believe there are limits to what constitutes a relevant group involved in the investigation. Here are two examples from our "CIA Leaks" that make the point. Suppose we are putting a randomly chosen card in an envelope. You catch a glimpse of the card and know that it is a black-suited face card. You say (32–a). Then, ten years later when we open the envelope—it's the Jack of Clubs—we cannot complain with (32–b):

(32) a. You: It might be the King of Spades.
      b. Us [ten years later]: ??Wrong!/What you said is false!

Or consider the case of Detective Parker. He has been going over some old transcripts from Al Capone's courtcase in the 1920s—Capone is being asked about where some money is in relation to a particular safe:

(33) a. Capone: The loot might be in the safe.
      b. Parker: ??Al was wrong/What Al said is false. The safe was cracked by
         Geraldo in the 80s and there was nothing inside.

There is just no relevant sense in which we-in-ten-years are involved in the same investigation that you-now are in. And there is no relevant sense in which the investigation that Capone and the DA were party to is now the same one taken up by Parker.

But of course there are borderline cases. If it's borderline whether a hearer H is part of a relevant group—borderline whether any group she belongs to is relevant—then we would expect the speaker's intuitions to be equivocal about attributions of falsehood or error. Since, in fact, we think there is such variability in intuitions, that makes us pretty happy.

7. Conclusion

We submit that our view of BEMs has clear advantages over other currently fashionable approaches. In particular, it involves no innovations in the semantics of epistemic modals. We make do with a standard context-dependent semantics. The new claim is that the strange properties of BEMs derive from the fact that their indeterminacy is used by design to achieve spectacular results.

References

Dalrymple, M., Kanazawa, M., Kim, Y., Mchombo, S., and Peters, S. (1998). "Reciprocal expressions and the concept of reciprocity", *Linguistics and Philosophy* 21(2): 159–210.

DeRose, K. (1991). "Epistemic possibilities", *Philosophical Review* 100(4): 581–605.

van Deemter, K. (1998). "Ambiguity and idiosyncratic interpretation", *Journal of Semantics* 15(1): 5–36.

Egan, A. (2007). "Epistemic modals, relativism, and assertion", *Philosophical Studies* 133(1): 1–22.

—— Hawthorne, J., and Weatherson, B. (2005). "Epistemic modals in context", in G. Preyer and G. Peter (eds.), *Contextualism in Philosophy: Knowledge, Meaning, and Truth* (Oxford: Oxford University Press), 131–70.

Fagin, R., Halpern, J. Y., Moses, Y., and Vardi, M. Y. (1995). *Reasoning about Knowledge* (Cambridge, Mass: MIT Press).

von Fintel, K., and Gillies, A. S. (2007). "An opinionated guide to epistemic modality", in T. S. Gendler and J. Hawthorne (eds.), *Oxford Studies in Epistemology: Volume 2* (Oxford: Oxford University Press), 32–62.

—— —— (2008). "CIA leaks", *Philosophical Review* 117(1): 77–98.

—— —— (2010). "*Must . . . stay . . . strong!*", *Natural Language Semantics* 18(4): 351–83.

Hacking, I. (1967). "Possibility", *Philosophical Review* 76(2): 143–68.

Kratzer, A. (1977). "What *must* and *can* must and can mean", *Linguistics and Philosophy* 1(3): 337–55.

—— (1981). "The notional category of modality", in H.-J. Eikmeyer and H. Rieser (eds.), *Words, Worlds, and Contexts: New Approaches in Word Semantics*, number 6 in Research in Text Theory, (Berlin: de Gruyter): 38–74.

—— (1986). "Conditionals", *Chicago Linguistics Society*, 22(2): 1–15.

—— (1991). "Modality", in A. von Stechow and D. Wunderlich (eds.), *Semantics: An International Handbook of Contemporary Research*, (Berlin: de Gruyter), 639–50.

Lackey, J. (2007). "Norms of assertion", *Noûs* 41(4): 594–626.

MacFarlane, J. (this volume). "Epistemic Modals Are Assessment-Sensitive", ch. 5.

Poesio, M. (1996). "Semantics ambiguity and perceived ambiguity", in K. van Deemter and S. Peters (eds.), *Semantic Ambiguity and Underspecification* (Stanford, CA: CSLI) 159–201.

Raskin, V. (1985). *Semantic Mechanisms of Humor* (Dordrecht: Reidel).

Schwarzschild, R. (1999). "How specific is an utterance? Comments on Glanzberg (1999)." Handout from a talk given at the conference on "Mapping the Semantics-Pragmatics Boundary: Context-Dependence", Cornell University, March 26–8, 1999.

Stalnaker, R. (1978). "Assertion", in P. Cole (ed.), *Syntax and Semantics*, Vol. ix (New York: Academic Press), 315–32.

Stephenson, T. (2007a). "Judge dependence, epistemic modals, and predicates of personal taste", *Linguistics and Philosophy* 30(4): 487–525.

——(2007b). *Towards a Theory of Subjective Meaning*, Ph.D. thesis, Massachusetts Institute of Technology.

Su, S. P. (1994). *Lexical Ambiguity in Poetry* (Studies in Language and Linguistics; London: Longman).

Teller, P. (1972). "Epistemic possibility", *Philosophia* 2(4): 302–20.

Weiner, M. (2005). "Must we know what we say?", *Philosophical Review* 114(2): 227–51.

Williamson, T. (1996). "Knowing and asserting", *Philosophical Review* 105(4): 489–523.

Winter, Y. (2001). "Plural predication and the strongest meaning hypothesis", *Journal of Semantics* 18(4): 333–65.

4

Possibilities for Representation and Credence: Two Space-ism versus One Space-ism

Frank Jackson

1.

There is a coin on the table in front of me. I can see that it lies heads up. You can't. One way I can give you the information I have but you lack is by my producing the sentence 'The coin lies heads up', or at least it is if we both understand English.

This little story highlights the compelling nature of the representational picture of language, the picture that sees language as providing putative information via the way sentences divide possibilities. There are two ways for the coin to be: heads up and tails up. The sentence 'The coin lies heads up' selects the first possibility—it represents that the first possibility obtains—and anyone who understands the sentence knows this, and this is how the sentence provides the putative information that the coin lies heads up.[1] To generalize, sentences—or at least a great many, for not all sentences represent that things are a certain way—divide the possibilities, the ways things might be, into those in accord with how the sentences represent things to be and those not in accord with how the sentences represent things to be (setting vagueness aside, as nothing here turns on how to handle it). And a sentence provides putative information about how things are by virtue of this fact. If you come across the sentence and are confident, for whatever reason, that things are as the sentence represents them to be—it was produced by someone reliable who has no reason to dissemble, or perhaps it appears in a reputable encyclopedia—then you are in a position to infer that the way things are is in accord with how the sentence represents things to be. If, further, you know what that way is, if in that sense you understand the sentence, the information becomes available to you.

---

[1] There is a use of the term 'representation' in the philosophy of colour that holds that an opaque thing's looking red represents that it has so and so a surface reflectance property (if that is how the colour science turns out). This is not our use. An opaque thing's looking red does not provide putative information that that thing has so and so surface reflectance in the way that a map, say, provides putative information about where the train comes in. For more on this issue, see Jackson (2007a).

Although this picture of language, or of much of language, is compelling, it raises many questions. This essay is concerned with the question of what to say about three kinds of sentences, where how they represent things to be appears to differ markedly from the set of possibilities at which the sentences are true. Or, more particularly, it is concerned with what *not* to say about the problem raised by these sentences. Our negative message will be, Don't try and solve our problem by appeal to the distinction between metaphysical and conceptual possibility. I'll close, however, with a *very* short comment of a more positive kind. It concerns an ambiguity in what it is to be true at a possibility, but for now please read this notion in the currently dominant way that I'll be presuming until near the very end.

The three kinds of sentences we will look at are: sentences that employ personal pronouns to say how things are, those that employ proper names, and sentences using natural kind terms to say how things are. An example of the first is 'I am happy'. Similar issues arise for 'You are happy', 'He was alive for many years', and so on, but we will focus on present tense, first person examples. An example of the second kind is 'Clark Kent is in the room', under the usual philosophers' pretence in these contexts that the Superman comics are history; another is 'Frank Jackson is giving this talk'. An example of the third kind is 'Water is in the glass'. Similar issues arise for 'That ring is made of gold', 'Jade is uncommon', and so on, but we will frame our discussion mainly in terms of the case of water.

I'll start by noting how these kinds of sentences make trouble for the representational-cum-division of possibilities picture of language. I will then explain why it might be tempting to appeal to the distinction between conceptual versus metaphysical possibility and possibilities to solve the problem before I give the case for resistance. I will be covering some ground I've covered before but discussions with those who take the opposite position have convinced me that I need to say more and, especially, that I need to connect the discussion of representation with the issue of credence and show how the key points apply to sentences containing proper names as well as to sentences containing names of kinds and pronouns. (I should have talked about credence and proper names from the very beginning.[2])

I will mainly talk in terms of possibilities to allow vagueness about whether we should be thinking in terms of possible worlds or centred possible worlds, but when it matters I will distinguish. Mostly it won't matter.

2.

I come out of a coma in a state of dreadful confusion and suffering serious memory loss. I have no idea of who I am or when it is, though in fact I am Frank Jackson and

---

[2] Thanks here in particular to Scott Sturgeon and Scott Soames for opposition, with thanks to David Chalmers and David Braddon-Mitchell for helping me understand where the opposition is coming from, and thanks more generally to the discussions at the Australian National University and Brown University where earlier versions of some of the ideas here were presented. The previous occasions are the discussions in Jackson (1998, 70 f; 2007c: sect. vi; 2004).

it is 0800 on 2 January 2008. I feel thirsty and report this in the sentence 'I am thirsty (now)'. How am I representing things to be? I am not representing that Frank Jackson is thirsty at 0800 on 2 January 2008. I don't know and have no opinion concerning who I am, and I don't know or have any opinion about the time that I am thirsty. But the worlds where the sentence is true are the worlds where Frank Jackson is thirsty at 0800 on 2 January 2008.

The point just made shows that the set of worlds where the sentence is true gives too much content to 'I am thirsty'. It excludes worlds that should not be excluded, worlds where someone other than myself is thirsty and where the time of thirst is not 0800, 2 January 2008. The set is also too weak. A division—any division, not only the one just rejected—among possible worlds cannot capture the content of the sentence because possible worlds do not cut the possibilities finely enough. To capture the *representational content*—how the sentence represents things to be—of 'I am thirsty', we need a division among centred worlds. Worlds are too coarse-grained. Although I am making a claim about the kind of world I am in when I say that I am thirsty, for I am saying in part that I am in a world with at least one thirsty person, I am in addition making a claim about the kind of thing I am in this world, and this extra claim requires that the representational content of 'I am thirsty' makes a division among centred worlds—in this case, in a way that includes those with thirsty centres in the content—not worlds simpliciter.

This point is an old one but it is still sometimes treated as if it revealed some kind of mystery about the nature of our world, something that outruns science with its perspective-free account of our world, something irreducibly indexical in the sense of being an 'indexical fact' additional to those inventoried in science, whereas there is, in my view, instead an important lesson about representation. We do not learn something about how things are but something about how we represent things to be.[3]

Here is a way to see this. Imagine that God is looking down on a possible world and has the ability to find out everything there is to find out about what that world is like. In that world someone says 'I am thirsty'. How would God tell whether or not the person had spoken truly? God would check to see if the person who had produced the sentence token was or was not thirsty at the time of speaking. God would not need to investigate indexical facts or anything like that. All that would be required would be to ascertain whether or not a certain causal origin of the token sentence was thirsty. What is irreducible is the need for centred worlds to capture how things are being represented to be, not indexicality *qua* feature of a world.

Let's now look at sentences using proper names.

---

[3] As David Lewis said (Lewis 1979). The literature on the issue is a large one but see Perry (1979), and the discussion and references in Jackson (1998).

3.

The set of worlds at which 'Frank Jackson is giving this talk' is true is the set where that very person is giving this talk. But what unites those worlds is the presence of the person with my essential properties and that's not part of how a user of that sentence represents things to be. Most users of that sentence will have no idea of my essential properties.

Here is a way to bring the point out. The (rational) credence profile of 'Frank Jackson is giving this talk' does not line up with the distribution of credences over the worlds where the sentence is true. We know the kind of evidence that justifies us in using the sentence 'Frank Jackson is giving this talk' to represent how things are. It is the kind of evidence that you, the audience, have here and now (I first used this example at a lecture): the speaker was introduced by the chair using the words 'our speaker is Frank Jackson'; the poster advertising this talk contained the words 'Frank Jackson' in the spot where the name of the speaker is typically placed; if you ask the person next to you for the name of the speaker, the words 'Frank Jackson' come from their mouth; the name on the passport of the person giving the talk is 'Frank Jackson'; and so on. We know that this kind of evidence confers a very high probability that things are as we use the sentence 'Frank Jackson is giving this talk' to represent them to be. It had better, because it is precisely the kind of evidence we typically have. The alternative is the highly unpalatable one of holding that the claims we make using sentences like 'Frank Jackson is giving this talk' are largely unjustified. This point stands independently of the debate over the right semantic treatment of proper names. We don't have to adjudicate that debate to know when we are justified in using sentences of the form 'A is F' to make claims about how things are.[4] But this kind of evidence does not confer a very high probability that the set of worlds where Frank Jackson, that very person, is giving the talk includes the actual world. The trouble is that the contingently possessed properties you use to identify me—call them Jackson-as-presented-to-us, if you like—do not select from among the very many essential properties that might, for all you know, be my essential properties, and it is my essential properties that determine the set of worlds where 'Frank Jackson is giving this talk' is true.

Let $FJ_1, FJ_2, FJ_3, \ldots$ be the persons who might, for all you, know be me. Suppose that FJ_{17} *is* me. The trouble is that your evidence does not favour the actual world belonging to the set of worlds where 'FJ_{17} is giving this talk' is true over the actual world belonging to the set of worlds where 'FJ_x is giving this talk' for some $x \neq 17$, where FJ_x presents to you in the very way I do. There is nothing to make the difference between giving a high rational credence to the actual world belonging to one set over another.

I should confess that I think we could have made our key point very quickly using the Superman example. I think it is obvious that how Lois Lane represents things to be using 'Clark Kent is before me' differs markedly from how she represents things

---

[4] Which is not to say that points about the epistemology do not support some treatments over others, see Jackson (2007b).

to be using 'Superman is before me', and that the two sentences have very different credence profiles for her. For instance, when she is at the *Daily Planet* and looking at the apparently mild-mannered man wearing slightly nerdish glasses, she often gives a very high credence to 'Clark Kent is before me' being true but not to 'Superman is before me' being true, despite the fact that the two sentences are true at the very same worlds. But I have laboured the point as so many have, in what seems to me to be a triumph of tenuous theory over common sense, persuaded themselves that the two sentences represent alike and consequently have the same credence profiles.

I suppose that someone might object to the link I am making between credence and representation. Why suppose that how Lois Lane represents things to be using one or another sentence has anything particular to do with the credence she gives things being as the sentence represents things to be? But the credence one gives to a sentence is simply the credence one gives to things being as the sentence represents them to be. One isn't giving credence to the sentence *per se*. (More on this below.)

Let's now look at 'water' sentences.

4.

Consider competent English speakers in 1730, well before it was established that water is H_2O, saying, as it might be, 'There is water in the glass'. They were representing that things were a certain way, and, surely, they knew what that way was. This is how they knew on occasion that what they were saying was very likely true, was a matter of some importance, was something supported by so and so bodies of evidence, was a very useful thing to say, and so on. If they didn't know what they were saying, they could not have known any of these things.

Some have objected to me that this is to fail to understand the environmental nature of content. According to them, speakers in 1730 did *not* know what they were saying precisely because they did not know the key environmental fact that water is H_2O. But notice how implausible this claim is. It means that the philosophers around in 1730 should have warned English speakers that they do not know what they are saying when they use the word 'water' in sentences like 'There is water in the glass', perhaps adding as reassurance that scientists are working hard to find out what water is, and as soon as they have found the answer, we will know what we are saying when we use the word 'water'![5]

I think we must allow that people in 1730 did know what they were representing about how things are when they said 'There is water in the glass'. But they weren't representing that there is H_2O in the glass. They had no idea that water is H_2O and maybe didn't even have the concept of H_2O. What's more, they were very often entitled to believe that things are as they were representing them to be, but they were not entitled to believe that there was H_2O in the glass. They hadn't done the experiments; no one had. And think of those who subsequently did do the key

---

[5] For more on this, see Jackson (2007c).

experiments later on. At one point in time the experimenters were entitled to say something like 'There is water in the glass'. A little later, after obtaining two parts of hydrogen and one of oxygen on passing a current through the stuff in the glass, they were entitled to say 'There is H_2O in the glass' and accordingly to conclude that water is H_2O. We don't want to find ourselves in the position of having to charge these experimenters with arguing in a circle. But of course the worlds where 'There is water in the glass' and the worlds where 'There is H_2O in the glass' are one and the same. It follows that we have another case where the representational content of a sentence differs from the set of worlds where a sentence is true.

The implausibility of giving 'There is water in the glass' and 'There is H_2O in the glass' the same representational content also comes out when we think of the credences we give the two sentences. As we said above, when we attach a credence to a sentence, we are not attaching it to the sentence *per se*. We are attaching it to things being the way the sentence represents them to be. This is the sense in which language is diaphanous, to borrow a term from the philosophy of sensory experience; language points out into the world. To ask how much credence one should give 'The coin will land heads' is nothing over and above to ask how much credence one should give to the coin's landing heads. But this means that if the representational content of 'There is water in the glass' is one and the same as that of 'There is H_2O in the glass', the sentences must always have the same credence, including for those ignorant or in doubt about the identity of water with H_2O. This is very hard to believe. Indeed one might claim the possibility that there is a difference in credence is close to common ground. For it is close to common ground that it is *epistemically* possible that water is not H_2O, and that implies that 'water' and 'H_2O' sentences may differ in credence. What is more—and this is a point I owe to discussion with David Braddon-Mitchell—suppose a critic insisted, against appearances, that the two sentences had the same credence in 1730, what was that single credence? Suppose scientists of the time gave a very small credence of, say, 0.5 to water being H_2O, and suppose our speaker is 99.9% certain that there is water in some glass in front of her and knows that current science gives a chance of 0.5 to water being H_2O. She thinks, in consequence, that 'There is water in the glass' has 99.9% likelihood of being true, and that 'There is H_2O in the glass' has about 0.5% likelihood of being true. Our critic is insisting that in fact the two sentences have the very same credence—at least one of her opinions about the credence of the sentences in her mouth is false. But which credence—99.9% or 0.5%—is the wrong one? Or should we average, so both are wrong? It is impossible to give a principled answer.

One might be tempted to respond to the case for 'There is water in the glass' and 'There is H_2O in the glass' differing in content by arguing that what we have, rather, is the same (representational) content differently presented. Hearing where the mouse is and seeing where it is may represent the same location for the mouse but under different modes of presentation. But the case for differentiating the contents turned on differences in how things were represented to be by the two sentences, not differences in modes of presentation. The case turned on the fact that how 'There is water in the glass' represents things to be was known in 1730, and that what was known was something often reasonably believed, whereas neither is the case for how 'There is H_2O in the glass' represents things to be.

5.

There is an initially appealing way out of the problem posed by the above examples and although I will be rejecting it—indeed, doing that is the main business of this essay—we should note its attractions first.

Take the problem posed by the fact that 'There is water in the glass' and 'There is H_2O in the glass' are true at the very same possibilities. This is a consequence of the fact that 'Any water is H_2O' is necessarily true (I use the 'any' construction to avoid issues raised by worlds that lack water which are by the way here). However, that sentence is not *a priori*; it is *a posteriori*. As it is often put, the sentence is metaphysically necessary but not conceptually necessary. It is then tempting to express this by distinguishing the space of metaphysical possibilities from the space of conceptual possibilities, saying that 'Any water is H_2O' is true at every metaphysical possibility but not at every conceptual possibility. The space of conceptual possibilities is the space of possibilities that cannot be ruled out *a priori*, it might be urged, and the idea is that the lesson of Saul Kripke's convincing examples of the necessary *a posteriori* is that, as Scott Soames puts it, there are 'world states' that cannot be ruled out on conceptual grounds but which are, all the same, impossible: they are metaphysically impossible but conceptually possible.[6] Or consider how William G. Lycan expresses it:

Consider the standard picture of logical space, featuring ever-larger concentric circles. We can start with the usual three grades of possibility, nomic, metaphysical, and conceptual; the nomically possible worlds are a proper subset of the metaphysically possible, which in turn are a proper subset of the conceptually possible.[7]

But now, runs the line of thought,[8] we can make the representational content of 'There is water in the glass' different from that of 'There is H_2O in the glass' by identifying representational content with the set of conceptual possibilities at which a sentence is true instead of with the set of metaphysical possibilities at which a sentence is true. The fact that there are conceptually possible worlds where water is not H_2O then makes the content of the two sentences different—as desired. Also, we would seem to have a neat account of how their credence profiles can differ. For example, we can say that in 1730 people confronted with our glass gave 'There is water in the glass' a much higher credence than they gave to 'There is H_2O in the glass' because

---

[6] Soames (2005: *passim*, e.g. the beginning of ch. 5, p. 84 f.).

[7] Lycan (2009: 78).

[8] A line of thought opened up by Soames, Lycan, and Sturgeon (in discussion); I am not saying that they would endorse it although I am sure many would.

they gave lots of credence to their being in one of the conceptually possible worlds where water is not H_2O but is the stuff in the glass.[9]

Similar remarks might be made for other examples. Take the fact that I may be much more certain that 'I am thirsty' is true than that 'Frank Jackson is thirsty' is true. The idea would be to put this down to the substantial credence I give the conceptual possibility that I am not Frank Jackson. Or take the case where Lois Lane is much more confident of the truth of 'Clark Kent is before me' than she is of 'Superman is before me'. The idea is to put this down to the considerable credence she gives to her being in one of the conceptually possible worlds where Clark Kent is not Superman but is before her.

In sum, the idea is that we get the representational content of a sentence, S, right by identifying it with the set of conceptual possibilities where S is true, and we get the intimately related topic of credence right by distributing the credences over the space of conceptual possibilities. Our troubles have all been the product of asking the space of metaphysical possibilities to do the job of the space of conceptual possibilities. Indeed, the supporters of this idea might well add that the point was obvious from the beginning. Using the space of the metaphysically possible to model representation content would make metaphysics too much a part of semantics; it would allow metaphysics to intrude unduly into our representational capacities.

Why then do I reject the two logical spaces strategy? It is certainly initially appealing. (But note that the strategy implies that, on arguably the central sense of 'reference', it is false that 'water' refers to H_2O. For arguably the central sense of 'reference' is tied to what happens in the possibilities right for representation. This result doesn't worry me but will worry some.)

6.

My original reason was the conviction that the famous examples of the necessary *a posteriori*, while being good examples of *sentences* that were necessary *a posteriori*, did not show that we need to admit *world states* or *possibilities* or *possible worlds* that are metaphysically impossible while being conceptually possible.[10] True, one might naturally have thought that granting that the sentence 'Any water is H_2O' is necessarily true, while also granting that its being so is only *a posteriori* discoverable, commits one to possibilities that are metaphysically impossible and yet conceptually possible in the sense that their impossibility is not *a priori* available. For a natural thought is that

---

[9] Conceptual possibilities are often called epistemic possibilities. I think this is potentially confusing when discussing 'two spaces of possibilities' views. The obvious way to think of epistemic possibilities is as possibilities consistent with such and such an epistemic state; that says nothing about whether or not there are two spaces of possibilities, only that among the perhaps single space we can distinguish ones consistent from ones not consistent with such and such an epistemic state. I'm *not* suggesting that those who call conceptual possibilities epistemic possibilities are confused. They are thinking of conceptual possibilities as those that are in some sense believ*able*, those that cannot be ruled out *a priori*.

[10] See, e.g., Jackson (1992; 1994; 1998). The conviction came from reading supporters of two-dimensional treatments of the necessary *a posteriori*, especially Tichý (1983).

water's failing to be H_2O is precisely an example of something that is conceptually possible while being metaphysically impossible. But reflection on the origin of our conviction that the sentence 'Any water is H_2O' is necessarily true strongly suggests otherwise.

The conviction comes from a combination of three facts. One is that the word 'water' is a descriptive name for the typically potable, odourless substance that is a fluid at room temperature and is found in lakes, etc. This is what we use the word for—or something like that, with the usual caveats about cluster terms, vagueness and variation between users of the word, and about context. The second is that if something is H_2O in any possible world, then it is H_2O in every possible world in which it appears. Finally, there is the fact that the typically potable, odourless substance that is a fluid at room temperature and is found in lakes, etc. is H_2O. The first is a fact about words; the second is *a priori* (the argument is that our concept of being the same kind precludes sameness in kind surviving a change from being H_2O to not being H_2O); and the third is an *a posteriori* contingent fact. That is to say, the facts that tell us that the sentence 'Any water is H_2O' is necessary *a posteriori* are none of them something which is itself necessary *a posteriori*. Armed with the space of conceptual possibilities and a plausible view about how what the word 'water' picks out at a possibility is a function of how things actually are, we have an attractive account of why the sentence 'Any water is H_2O' is a necessary *a posteriori* truth. There is no need to add into the mix possibilities that are metaphysically impossible while being conceptually possible. Occam's Razor tells us to dispense with conceptual possibilities that are metaphysical impossibilities.[11]

I stand by this argument but I now think it gave an unnecessary hostage to fortune in its reliance on kind terms being descriptive names. The key issue is whether or not we should acknowledge two spaces of possibility: the space of metaphysical possibilities as a proper subset of the space of conceptual possibilities, with the second space being the right one for representation according to the view under examination; and we can argue against this position without taking an inevitably controversial stand on kind terms being descriptive names.[12]

7.

There are two problems for the two space view which we can press without recourse to the issue about the semantics of kind terms. The first concerns the identity of the possibilities that are claimed to be conceptually possible while being metaphysically impossible.

If any water's being H_2O (the possibility) is metaphysically necessary but not conceptually necessary, whereas any water's being water (the possibility) is both

---

[11] For replies to some objections some have to this argument, see Jackson (2003).

[12] For a different argument against the two spaces position but one that also steers clear of whether or not 'water' is a descriptive name, see Stalnaker (2003: §1).

metaphysically and conceptually necessary, any water's being H_2O is a different possibility from any water's being water, by Leibniz's Law. But then what makes the difference between the two possibilities? The only possible answer would seem to be that water differs from H_2O, but to hold that would be to take the necessity of water's being H_2O as a necessary connection between distinct properties—water and H_2O—and that seems exactly the wrong way to look at what is going on. Perhaps—*pace* Hume—there are necessary connections between distinct properties, but water and H_2O is not an example. Look as hard as you like at a glass of water and you won't discern two properties: water and H_2O, that somehow necessarily track one another. There are in fact only two live options for the type *water*: it is the type H_2O, in which case there is a single property, or it is the type *the typically potable, odourless substance that is a fluid at room temperature and is found in lakes, etc.*, in which case there are indeed two properties but they are not necessarily connected.

Here's another way of making essentially the same point. We should all agree that water's being H_2O is both conceptually and metaphysically possible, for the best of all possible reasons: water's being H_2O is actual. Now consider the relationship between that possibility and water's not being H_2O, the possibility that is allegedly conceptually possible while being metaphysically impossible—call them the first and second possibility, respectively. What makes the water in the second possibility the water in the first possibility? There are three answers one might give. First answer: its being H_2O. But H_2O's not being H_2O is conceptually impossible. Second answer: what makes the water in the second possibility the water in the first possibility is its being a kind that is typically potable, odourless, liquid at room temperature, and all that. But H_2O's not being such a kind is metaphysically possible. Third answer: what makes the water in the second possibility the water in the first possibility is its having some *sui generis* 'water-making' feature. But that's the extra property view we noted above is to be rejected. On no credible answer to our question do we have a possibility that is conceptually possible without being metaphysically possible.

A similar problem can be raised for other examples of possibilities claimed to be conceptually possible but metaphysically impossible. Many hold that some particular table's not being made of wood, in the case where it is in fact made of wood, is metaphysically impossible. But now we have: the possibility of that table's being made of wood is both conceptually and metaphysically possible, whereas the possibility of that table's not being made of wood is conceptually possible but not metaphysically possible. What makes the table in the second possibility that very table? If a table's constitution is an essential property of it (and if it isn't, we don't have an example of metaphysical impossibility to start with), part of the answer must be its being made of wood. But then the second possibility is that of a table made of wood not being made of wood, and that is *conceptually* impossible. That is, the second possibility isn't an example of something metaphysically impossible while being conceptually possible.

As one might expect, a similar problem also arises for cases involving proper names. Here's an example that points up the issue in an especially sharp form, or so it seems to me.

Fred knows a bit about American literature but not much. He opens a book that has on its title page: '*The Adventures of Huckleberry Finn* by MARK TWAIN'. In consequence, he gives the sentence 'Mark Twain is the author of *The Adventures of Huckleberry Finn*' a very high credence; he knows that most title pages are to be trusted. Fred also knows that it is unusual for one person to have two names. Putting the two points together, he gives the sentence 'Samuel Clemens is the author of *The Adventures of Huckleberry Finn*' a very low credence. This is exactly the right thing for him to do. But how can this be the right thing to do if the sentences are true at the very same worlds, bearing in mind our earlier point that the credence we give sentences isn't to words *per se* but to how they represent things to be? The two spaces position we are examining responds, first, that the worlds at which the sentences are true coincide through metaphysically possible space but not through conceptually possible space. The set of conceptually possible worlds where 'Mark Twain is the author of *The Adventures of Huckleberry Finn*' differs from the set of conceptually possible worlds where 'Samuel Clemens is the author of *The Adventures of Huckleberry Finn*'. Secondly, the two space position says that conceptually possible space is the right space for modelling representation and credence. It follows that there is no puzzle about the two sentences having different credences for Fred.

This response requires there to be conceptually possible but metaphysically impossible worlds where Mark Twain ≠ Samuel Clemens. But our world, the actual world, is conceptually possible as well as metaphysically possible, and it has Mark Twain being one and the same person as Samuel Clemens. Are the Mark Twain and Samuel Clemens of the conceptually possible worlds where Mark Twain doesn't equal Samuel Clemens, the very same people as *our* Mark Twain and Samuel Clemens? They cannot be. Two people can't be one person. At most, what is conceptually possible is that persons who present in the Mark Twain way (whatever precisely that way is, but presumably it will be in part to do with the connection between the person and the name) and who present in the Samuel Clemens way are distinct in those worlds, but that's metaphysically possible. It is metaphysically possible for persons who present in the Mark Twain way and the Samuel Clemens way to be different people. What's metaphysically impossible is for our very own Mark Twain and Samuel Clemens to be distinct persons. As before, we don't have a possibility that is conceptually possible while being metaphysically impossible.

Now for the second problem.

8.

The key idea behind the two spaces approach is that we get the representational content of language right by focussing on the space of conceptual possibilities, and ditto for credence. Metaphysical possibilities are by the way when representation and credence are our concern. The second problem is that the problems generated by personal pronoun sentences and by sentences containing proper names can be raised without moving outside the space of the conceptually possible, as we'll now see.

If conceptual possibilities are right to capture the representational properties of words and sentences, we better be able to use words to talk about conceptual possibilities and about objects and properties at conceptual possibilities. If we can't, we can be sure that conceptual possibilities are the wrong possibilities to capture the representational content of language. But in that case I can use 'I' and 'now' to name myself and a time of speaking across the space of conceptual possibilities. But in that case 'I am thirsty (now)' said by me at 0800 on 2 January 2008 is true at the conceptually possible worlds where Frank Jackson is thirsty at 0800 on 2 January 2008. We are back with the problems of too much content and too little content! Too much content because I am not saying who I am and when it is when I produce 'I am thirsty now' at 0800 on 2 January 2008; too little content because as we saw earlier we need centred possible worlds to capture the content, and divisions among centred worlds carry more information than divisions among worlds.

Similar points apply to the Mark Twain and Samuel Clemens example.

It had better be the case that we can name people rigidly across conceptual possibilities. Otherwise conceptual possibilities cannot be right for representation. That is, it had better be the case that we can give the very same person in conceptual space two different names. How else could we address a question like, What is conceptually possible for *Plato*? But our naming practices are not always transparent in the sense of revealing when we've named the same thing twice over, or thrice over or ... In consequence, our non-expert on American literature will (rightly by his lights) give the sentence 'Mark Twain is the author of *The Adventures of Huckleberry Finn*' a very high credence, and the sentence 'Samuel Clemens is the author of *The Adventures of Huckleberry Finn*' a very low credence. But the sentences will be true at exactly the same conceptually possible worlds, for we are naming across the conceptually possible; *mutatis mutandis* for Lois Lane, Hesperus, and all the other examples of that ilk.

9.

I hope I have convinced you that the two logical spaces approach—two space-ism—to solving our problem is a mistake (but I'll take giving you serious pause). I promised something very brief of a positive kind on what to say about our problem.

Instead of two logical spaces, I think we need to think in terms of one space carved out in two different ways. One way of carving gives us *A*-intensions or primary intensions; the other gives us *C*-intensions or secondary intensions. *C*-intensions are the possibilities at which sentences are true in the sense operative in the discussions above. *A*-intensions are what we need for representation and credence. That's the idea I have defended in a number of places on other occasions.[13] I have said nothing here

[13] Jackson (2007c; 1998; 2004).

in defence of this idea except to the extent that one way of defending an idea is to raise objections to an initially promising alternative to it. But I should note in closing, as promised near the beginning, that there is an ambiguity in the notion of truth at a possibility. Suppose that, for some sentences, their truth at a possibility is a non-trivial function of both the possibility and of which possibility is actual. Then there would be a non-trivial distinction between truth at a possibility and truth at a possibility if that possibility is actual. But truth is a matter of being true the way things actually are. 'Snow is white' is true at the worlds where snow is white, but it is true simpliciter because it is true at the actual world. It follows that to be true at a possibility under the supposition that that possibility is actual is a perfectly kosher reading of truth at a possibility, and of course a sentence's A-intension is the set of possibilities where a sentence is true under the supposition that they are actual.

References

Jackson, Frank (1992). Critical notice of Susan Hurley, *Natural Reasons*, Oxford University Press, 1989, *Australasian Journal of Philosophy* 70: 475–87.

—— (1994). 'Armchair Metaphysics', in Michaelis Michael and John O'Leary Hawthorne (eds.), *Philosophy in Mind (Philosophical Studies Series*, 60; Dordrecht: Kluwer), 23–42.

—— (1998). *From Metaphysics to Ethics: A Defence of Conceptual Analysis* (Oxford: Clarendon Press).

—— (2003). 'From H₂O to Water: The Relevance to A Priori Passage', in Hallvard Lillehammer and Gonzalo Rodriguez-Pereyra (eds.), *Real Metaphysics: Papers for D. H. Mellor* (London: Routledge, 2003), 84–97.

—— (2004). 'Why We Need A-Intensions', *Philosophical Studies* 118 (1-2): 257–77.

—— (2007a). 'Colour for Representationalists', *Erkenntis* 66: 169–85.

—— (2007b). 'On Not Forgetting the Epistemology of Names', *Grazer Philosophische Studien* 74: 239–50.

—— (2007c). 'Reference and Description from the Descriptivists' Corner', Review discussion of Scott Soames, *Reference and Description: The Case Against Two-Dimensionalism*, Princeton University Press, 2005, *Philosophical Books* 48: 17–26.

—— and Chalmers, David J. (2001). 'Conceptual Analysis and Reductive Explanation', *Philosophical Review* 110: 315–60.

Lewis, David (1979). 'Attitudes De Dicto and De Se', *Philosophical Review* 88: 513–43.

Lycan, William G. (2009). 'Serious Metaphysics: Frank Jackson's Defense of Conceptual Analysis', in Ian Ravenscroft (ed.), *Minds, Ethics, and Conditionals: Themes from the Philosophy of Frank Jackson* (Oxford: Oxford University Press) 61–83.

Perry, John (1979). 'The Problem of the Essential Indexical', *Noûs* 13: 3–21.

Soames, Scott (2005). *Reference and Description: The Case Against Two-Dimensionalism* (Princeton: Princeton University Press).

Stalnaker, Robert (2003). 'Conceptual Truth and Metaphysical Necessity', in *Ways a World Might Be* (Oxford: Clarendon Press, 2003), 201–15.

Tichý, Pavel (1983). 'Kripke on the Necessary A Posteriori', *Philosophical Studies* 43: 225–41.

5

Epistemic Modals
Are Assessment-Sensitive

John MacFarlane

1. Introduction

By "epistemic modals," I mean epistemic uses of modal words: adverbs like "necessarily," "possibly," and "probably," adjectives like "necessary," "possible," and "probable," and auxiliaries like "might," "may," "must," and "could." It is hard to say exactly what makes a word *modal*, or what makes a use of a modal *epistemic*, without begging the questions that will be our concern below, but some examples should get the idea across. If I say "Goldbach's conjecture might be true, and it might be false," I am not endorsing the Cartesian view that God could have made the truths of arithmetic come out differently. I make the claim not because I believe in the metaphysical contingency of mathematics, but because I know that Goldbach's conjecture has not yet been proved or refuted. Similarly, if I say "Joe can't be running," I am not saying that Joe's constitution prohibits him from running, or that Joe is essentially a non-runner, or that Joe isn't allowed to run. My basis for making the claim may be nothing more than that I see Joe's running shoes hanging on a hook.

Clearly, epistemic modals have something to do with knowledge. But knowledge presupposes a knower or knowers. So, one ought to ask, *whose* knowledge is relevant to the truth of claims made using epistemic modals?

I presented earlier versions of this paper at the University of Utah (2003), the University of Chicago (2005), Ohio State (2005), the Arché Center at St Andrews (2005), UC Santa Cruz (2005), the Eastern Division APA meeting in New York (2005), Berkeley's Logic Colloquium (2006), and the University of Michigan Linguistics and Philosophy Workshop (2006). I am grateful to all these audiences for stimulating questions. I would particularly like to thank Kent Bach, Chris Barker, Fabrizio Cariani, Richard Dietz, Branden Fitelson, David Hunter, Graham Priest, Brian Weatherson, Matt Weiner, Seth Yalcin, and two anonymous referees for useful comments. Finally, I acknowledge the financial support of an ACLS/Andrew W. Mellon Fellowship for Junior Faculty and a Berkeley Humanities Research Fellowship. Readers of Egan et al. (2005) will notice substantial overlap in our conclusions and arguments. We arrived at them independently (though I was inspired by Hawthorne (2004: 27 n. 68), which I read in draft in summer 2003, and they by MacFarlane (2003)). I shared with them an ancestor of this paper while they were writing theirs.

It is tempting to answer: *the speaker's.* On the resulting view, which I will call
SOLIPSISTIC CONTEXTUALISM, "Joe might be running" expresses a truth just in case
what the speaker knows does not rule out that Joe is running, and "Joe must be running" expresses a truth just in case what the speaker knows rules out that Joe is not
running. For present purposes, we can leave the notion of "ruling out" schematic: we
need not decide, for instance, whether knowledge that *p* rules out everything logically
inconsistent with *p*. Our discussion of Solipsistic Contextualism and its variants will
turn only on *whose* knowledge is at stake, not on what "ruling out" consists in.
Hence we will regard theories that understand epistemic modals as quantifiers over
"epistemically possible worlds" as versions of Solipsistic Contextualism, provided they
take the relevant set of worlds (together with an ordering, perhaps) to be determined
by the *speaker's* knowledge or evidence.[1]

Solipsistic Contextualism promises to explain two facts about epistemic modals that
would otherwise seem quite puzzling. First, it explains why we are normally prepared
to make epistemic possibility claims on the basis of our own ignorance. If someone
asks me whether Joe is in Boston, it is generally okay for me to reply, "He might be,"
unless I know that he is not. This is just what we should expect if the truth of "He
might be" depends on what the speaker knows. It is not what we should expect if the
truth of "He might be" depends in part on what others know, or on what one could
come to know. As we will see in what follows, the more "objective" we make claims
about epistemic possibility, the larger the gap between the circumstances in which we
are warranted in making them and the circumstances in which we actually do make
them. Solipsistic Contextualism explains why we are willing to assert "It might be
that *p*" in roughly the same cases as "For all I know, *p*."

Second, Solipsistic Contextualism beautifully explains why the following sentences
sound paradoxical:

(1) Joe might be in Boston, but I know he isn't.
(2) Joe might be in Boston, but he isn't.

According to Solipsistic Contextualism, (1) is a contradiction: when the second
conjunct expresses a truth, the first must express a falsehood. And, while (2)
isn't a contradiction—possibility had better not imply actuality!—it is pragmatically

---

[1] Solipsistic Contextualism is sometimes attributed to G. E. Moore (perhaps the first philosopher to
clearly distinguish epistemic uses of modals from others) on the basis of passages like this one, from his
Commonplace Book:

People *in philosophy* say: The *props.* that I'm not sitting down now, that I'm not male, that I'm dead, that I
died before the murder of Julius Caesar, that I shall die before 12 to-night, are "logically possible." But it's
not English to say, with this meaning: It's possible that I'm not sitting down now etc.—*this* only means "It's
not certain that I am" or "I don't know that I am." (Moore 1962: 184)

However, Moore did not accept the Solipsistic Contextualist analysis of "must." He denied that "It *must* be
that *p*" means the same as "It's impossible that not-*p*" (1962: 188), on the grounds that it is appropriate to
say the former only when one does not know *directly* (e.g. by seeing) that *p*. It seems that he also rejected
the solipsistic view for "probably" (1962: 402).

infelicitous, since in asserting that Joe isn't in Boston, one represents oneself as knowing that he isn't, contrary to what is conveyed by the first conjunct.[2]

However, there are serious problems with Solipsistic Contextualism. I won't be alone in pointing them out: most of them have been noticed already by nonsolipsistic contextualists and expressivists. But I think that the former have failed to appreciate how deep these problems are, while the latter have appreciated them but overreacted. As I will argue below, once the force of the objections to Solipsistic Contextualism have been properly appreciated, it becomes clear that there is no stable nonsolipsistic fix. Recognizing this, expressivists have abandoned the whole project of doing truth-conditional semantics for epistemic modals. But that is throwing the baby out with the bathwater: there is, as I will argue, a viable truth-conditional semantics for epistemic modals, provided one is willing to entertain the idea that truth varies not just with the context in which a claim is made, but with the context in which it is *assessed*.

2. Against Solipsistic Contextualism

I'll consider three arguments against Solipsistic Contextualism. All of them are facets of a single problem: Solipsistic Contextualism cannot explain why we take ourselves to be disagreeing with each other about what might be the case, even when we have very different bodies of background knowledge.

2.1. Third-person assessments

The first problem is that people don't assess others' epistemic modal claims in the way that they should if Solipsistic Contextualism were correct. They don't take them to be equivalent to claims about what is ruled out by what the speaker knows at the time of utterance.

I'd like you to imagine yourself in two slightly different scenarios. I'll ask a question about each; write down your answer.

> *First case:* You overhear George and Sally talking in the coffee line. Sally says, "I don't know anything that would rule out Joe's being in Boston right now" (or perhaps, more colloquially, "For all I know, Joe's in Boston"). You think to yourself: *I* know that Joe isn't in Boston, because I just saw him an hour ago here in Berkeley. *Question:* Did Sally speak falsely?

> *Second case:* Scene as before. Sally says, "Joe might be in Boston right now." You think to yourself: Joe can't be in Boston; I just saw him an hour ago here in Berkeley. *Question:* Did Sally speak falsely?

Did you answer "No" to the first question and "Yes" to the second? Of course we don't have grounds for supposing that Sally spoke falsely in the first case: she was

---

[2] Cf. DeRose (1991: 600); Stanley (2005).

simply commenting on what she knew. In the second case, though, it seems quite natural to reject her claim as false on the basis of the same information.[3]

Of course, we must take care that we are rejecting Sally's whole claim as false, and not just the (embedded) proposition that Joe *is* in Boston. Compare this dialogue:

"It's rumored that you are leaving California."

"That's completely false!"

Here the point of the response is to reject the thing that is rumored, not the claim *that* it is rumored. Could something similar be said about our inclination to reject Sally's claim?

We have ways of distinguishing between cases where the whole asserted content is being rejected and cases where the embedded proposition is being rejected. The easiest way is just to ask:

"Do you mean that it's false that you're leaving California, or that it's false that that's what's rumored?"

"The former."

So, since you are the protagonist in the two cases I described above, let me ask you. When you said (supposing you did) that Sally spoke falsely, did you mean that she spoke falsely in saying "Joe might be in Boston," or just that it's false that Joe *is* in Boston? It was the former, right? Perhaps there would be some ambiguity if you had assented to "That's false." But you assented to "Sally spoke falsely," which clearly concerns what Sally asserted, not its embedded complement.

2.2. Retraction

If that's not enough, try this test: Should Sally *retract* her assertion, or can she stand by it? Consider how odd it would be for your interlocutor in the rumor case to retract her assertion:

"It's rumored that you are leaving California."

"That's completely false!"

"Okay, then, I was wrong. I take back what I said."

Your interlocutor wasn't wrong about anything and can quite reasonably let her assertion about what is rumored stand:

"What a relief! But that *was* the rumor."

---

[3] This phenomenon was first called to my attention by a footnote in John Hawthorne's book *Knowledge and Lotteries*: "[A]s far as I can tell, ordinary people evaluate present tense claims of epistemic modality as true or false by testing the claim against their own perspective. So, for example suppose Angela doesn't know whether Bill is alive or dead. Angela says *Bill might be dead*. Cornelius knows Bill is alive. There is a tendency for Cornelius to say Angela is wrong. Yet, given Angela's perspective, wasn't it correct to say what she did? After all, when I say *It might be that P and it might be that not P*, knowing that Cornelius knows whether *P*, I do not naturally think that Cornelius knows that I said something false. There is a real puzzle here, I think, but this is not the place to pursue it further." (Hawthorne 2004: 27 n. 68)

By contrast, it seems entirely natural for Sally to retract her assertion that Joe might be in Boston after she hears what George has to say:

"Joe might be in Boston."
"No, he can't be in Boston. I just saw him an hour ago in Berkeley."
"Okay, then, scratch that. I was wrong."

Indeed, it would be very odd for Sally *not* to retract her claim (explicitly or implicitly):

"Okay, then, he can't be in Boston. But I still stand by what I said a second ago."

It's not plausible to say that the target of Sally's retraction (the thing she takes herself to have been wrong about) is the embedded proposition—that Joe *is* in Boston—for she didn't assert or believe *that*. It must, then, be the modal proposition she expressed by saying "Joe might be in Boston."

It is important here to distinguish *retracting* an assertion from claiming that one ought not to have made it in the first place. To say that one was wrong *in claiming* that p is not to say that one was wrong *to claim* that p. Sometimes it is right to make a claim that turns out to have been wrong (false). For example, suppose that all of the evidence available to Holmes overwhelmingly supports the hypothesis that the butler is the murderer. Then he was not wrong *to* claim that the butler was the murderer, even if it turns out that he was wrong *in* so claiming. Not only was he right to claim that butler was the murderer—following the evidence, as always—but he would have been wrong to withhold his view on the matter.

If you find it implausible that Sally would say "I was wrong" in the dialogue above, make sure you're not interpreting her as saying "I was wrong to say that." Of course she wasn't wrong to say what she did. But what she said was wrong, and that is what she is acknowledging.

2.3. Disputes

Here is a third reason for rejecting Solipsistic Contextualism. It seems that we sometimes *argue* and *disagree* about epistemic modal claims. A conversation might center, for a time, on the question whether Joe might be in Boston. The issue is not whether Joe *is* in Boston; everyone present acknowledges that he might be in Berkeley, and so no one thinks that there are going to be grounds for asserting that he *is* in Boston. The point of the conversation is to settle whether he *might be* in Boston. Reasons are offered on both sides, disputes are resolved, and perhaps a consensus is reached.

It is crucial to such disputes that the participants take themselves to be contradicting each other when one says "It might be that p" and the other says "No, it can't be that p." Solipsistic Contextualism cannot make sense of this. For it holds that the first participant's claim is about what *she* knows, while the second's is about what *he* knows.

A (broadly) Solipsistic Contextualist might account for this data by taking epistemic modals to work the way "local" seems to work. If your brother in Anchorage says "I went to a local bar, the Moose's Tooth," you (in Berkeley) can reply: "That's not local, it's five miles away from you!" (meaning *local to your brother*). In the same way, the Contextualist might say, epistemic modals can be used with reference to what someone else (say, one's interlocutor) knows. This move would help make sense of perceived disagreement.

It would do so, however, by construing disputes about what might be the case as disputes about what some particular person knows at some particular time. But then we should expect them to be asymmetrical in a way that they are not, since the person in question has privileged access to what she believes, and this is relevant to what she knows. Disputes about what might be the case do not feel as if they are "centered on" a particular person in this way. Indeed, they feel like continuous arguments, with a single topic, even as the participants gain relevant knowledge through discussion. Solipsistic Contextualism cannot account for this.

2.4. Semantic blindness?

All I am doing here is calling attention to how we use epistemic modals in practice. The defender of Solipsistic Contextualist could always acknowledge these facts but dismiss them as misleading guides to the semantics of epistemic modals. Perhaps third parties who assess Sally's claim mistakenly take her to have asserted what *they* would be asserting by saying "Joe might be in Boston." Perhaps Sally, assessing her own past assertion, mistakenly takes it to have the content she would *now* express if she used the same sentence. And perhaps the parties to a dispute about whether it's possible that Joe is in Boston are mistakenly taking themselves to contradict each other, when in reality they are simply talking past each other.

But that's a lot of error to impute to speakers. One wants some explanation of why speakers are systematically confused in this way, and why this confusion doesn't generalize to other cases that should be similar if Solipsistic Contextualism is correct. For example, if speakers are systematically blind to unobvious context sensitivity, why doesn't the following dialogue seem natural?

> "Joe is tall. In fact, he's the tallest graduate student in our department."
> "No, he isn't tall. He's shorter than nearly every NBA player."
> "Okay, then, scratch that. I was wrong."

One would also need to explain why the data that seems to support Solipsistic Contextualism (primarily data about when speakers take themselves to be warranted in making epistemic modal claims) should be taken so seriously, when the data about third-party assessments, retraction, and disputes are just thrown away. There is no clear reason to favor the "positive" data in this way. Quite the contrary, semantics is typically driven more by data about perceived incompatibilities and entailments than by data about when people are willing to accept sentences. I propose, then, to put this approach to defending Solipsistic Contextualism on the back burner, as a last resort should no alternative view prove viable.

3. Nonsolipsistic Contextualism

These problems with Solipsistic Contextualism are relatively well known. Indeed, practically no one who has staked out a serious position on the semantics of epistemic modals defends the view.[4] It is very common, however, to suppose that the problems with Solipsistic Contextualism lie with its solipsism, and that the solution is to move towards a form of contextualism that is less solipsistic and less subjective. If "Joe might be in Boston" doesn't mean "For all I know, Joe is in Boston," perhaps it means "For all *we* know, Joe is in Boston," or "For all we know or could easily come to know, Joe is in Boston." All of these can be thought of as variants on "What is known does not rule out Joe's being in Boston," with different glosses on "what is known."

In this section, I will consider some different ways in which a contextualist might try to meet the objections we have considered by moving away from the strict Solipsistic Contextualist position. I hope to persuade you that these are all bandaids on a gaping wound. The fundamental problem with Solipsistic Contextualism lies with its Contextualism, not its Solipsism.

3.1. *Widening the relevant community*

According to NONSOLIPSISTIC CONTEXTUALISM, "Joe might be in Boston" expresses a truth just in case what the contextually relevant group knows does not rule out Joe's being in Boston.[5] There are complications about what it means to say that a *group's* knowledge rules something out, but we will skip over these until Section 3.3. There are also complications about how these truth conditions can be generated compositionally: these will be discussed further in Section 6, but for our purposes here we need not settle them. The important thing is that we have replaced talk of the speaker's knowledge with talk of the knowledge of a group picked out by features of the context of use (including, on most versions, the speaker's intentions).

Nonsolipsistic Contextualism allows us to make sense of Sally's retraction of her claim in light of George's response, by supposing that the contextually relevant group includes not just Sally but all the parties to the conversation, George included. That would explain why, when Sally learns that George knew things that precluded Joe's being in Boston, she regards her own claim as having been refuted. It would also vindicate George's assessment of Sally's claim as false. Finally, it would make it possible to understand how a group can argue about whether Joe might be in Boston. According to Nonsolipsistic Contextualism, the group is trying to come to a consensus about what its shared knowledge excludes and leaves open.

Moreover, Nonsolipsistic Contextualism can explain the paradoxical ring of sentences (1) and (2) just as well as its Solipsistic cousin. For it is usually assumed that the speaker belongs to the contextually relevant group, and that the group counts as

---

[4] It appears that Stanley (2005: 128) does endorse it.
[5] See e.g. Hacking (1967: 148); Teller (1972); DeRose (1991).

knowing if any member does. On these assumptions, if the speaker knows that Joe isn't in Boston, then "Joe might be in Boston" cannot express a truth. It follows that (1) is a contradiction and that (2) is pragmatically infelicitous.

So far, the move away from solipsism seems well-motivated and plausible. The problem is that once we let data about third-party assessments and retraction motivate an expansion of the contextually relevant group to include more than just the speaker, there is no way to stop this machine. The same kind of arguments that motivate expanding the relevant group of knowers to include George (in our example above) will motivate expanding the relevant group of knowers to include anybody who will ever consider the claim.

Indeed, the problem can be seen in our very first example with Sally and George. When you overhear Sally telling George, "Joe might be in Boston," you think to yourself "She has spoken falsely." To make sense of this reaction, the Nonsolipsistic Contextualist will have to make the contextually relevant group of knowers include *you*, even though you are not part of the conversation, not known to Sally, and perhaps not even *noticed* by Sally. It seems, then, that we need to take Sally's claim to concern not just what she and George know, but what anyone within earshot of their conversation knows.

And why limit ourselves to earshot? It doesn't matter much to our story that you are in the same room as Sally. You'd assess her claim the same way if you were thousands of miles away, listening through a wiretap. Indeed, it seems to me that it does not even matter whether you are listening to the wiretap live or reviewing a recording the next day—or the next year.[6] To vindicate all these third-party assessments, the Nonsolipsistic Contextualist would have to extend the relevant group of knowers not just to those in earshot, but to all those who will one day hear of, read of, or perhaps even conjecture about, Sally's claim. There's no natural stopping point short of that.

Consideration of when speakers will retract their claims seems to point in the same direction. For it seems to me that the retraction data we considered in Section 2.2 is just as robust when we replace George by a hidden eavesdropper. Suppose Sally says, "Joe might be in Boston," and George replies, "Oh really? I didn't know that." At this point, Jane—who is hiding in the closet—emerges and says, "Joe can't be in Boston; I just saw him down the hall." It seems entirely natural for Sally to reply, "Oh, then I guess I was wrong. Thanks, Jane." It would be bizarre for her to say, "Thanks for telling us, Jane. I guess Joe can't be in Boston. Nonetheless, I stand by what I said a second ago." Clearly Sally did not have Jane in mind when she made her claim. So if we're going to make sense of these retractions, we must suppose that the force of Sally's claim was something like: *what we know—we who are or will be in a position to consider this claim—does not rule out Joe's being in Boston.*

---

[6] In that case it will be your knowledge of Joe's whereabouts on the day the recording was made that is relevant—but still *your* knowledge (not Sally's), and your knowledge *now*.

The same point can be made by considering *disputes* about what might be the case. Suppose two research groups are investigating whether a certain species of snail can be found in Hawaii. Neither group knows of the other's existence. One day they end up at the same bar. The first group overhears members of the second group arguing about whether it is "possible" that the snails exist on the big island, and they join the discussion. Although the two groups have different bodies of evidence, it does not intuitively seem that they are talking past each other when they argue. Nor does it seem as if the topic *changes* when the first group joins the discussion (from what was ruled out by the second group's evidence to what is ruled out by both groups' evidence). To accommodate these intuitions, the Nonsolipsistic Contextualist will have to take *all* the possibility claims made by both groups to concern what is ruled out by the collected evidence of everyone who is investigating the question (known or unknown)—for any of these investigators could show up at the bar, in principle.

To sum up: the arguments that motivate a move from the "for all I know" reading of epistemic modals to the "for all we know" reading also motivate extending the scope of "we" to include not just the participants in the conversation but eavesdroppers, no matter how well hidden or how distantly separated in time and space. "It is possible that *p*" becomes "*p* is not ruled out by what is known by anyone who will ever consider this claim."

But this is something like a *reductio ad absurdum* of Nonsolipsistic Contextualism. For if this is what epistemic modals mean, then most ordinary uses of them are completely irresponsible. Surely Sally would not be warranted in asserting "Nothing known by me *or by anyone who will ever consider this claim* excludes Joe's being in Boston." Indeed, she may have good reason to deny this. But intuitively Sally *is* warranted in asserting that Joe might be in Boston; her assertion is a paradigm use of an epistemic modal.

3.2. Objective factors

Hacking (1967) has a somewhat different argument for the same conclusion, that widening the relevant group of knowers to include the speaker's conversational partners will not suffice to save a contextualist semantics for epistemic modals:

Imagine a salvage crew searching for a ship that sank a long time ago. The mate of the salvage ship works from an old log, makes a mistake in his calculations, and concludes that the wreck may be in a certain bay. It is possible, he says, that the hulk is in these waters. No one knows anything to the contrary. But in fact, as it turns out later, it simply was not possible for the vessel to be in that bay; more careful examination of the log shows that the boat must have gone down at least 30 miles further south. The mate said something false when he said, "It is possible that we shall find the treasure here," but the falsehood did not arise from what anyone actually knew at the time. (1967: 148)

Hacking concludes that the truth of epistemic modal claims must depend not just on what is known, but on objective features of the situation—here, the presence of relevant information in the log.

This is another way in which contextualism might be made nonsolipsistic: instead of (or in addition to) widening the community of relevant epistemic agents, we relax the strength of the relation these agents must stand in to the relevant facts. In addition to looking at what they *do* know, we look at what they could *come* to know through a "practicable investigation" (as Hacking puts it), or what is within their "epistemic reach" (as Egan 2007 puts it). We might say that "it is possible that *p*" expresses a truth if what is within the speaker's epistemic reach (or perhaps the epistemic reach of a contextually relevant group) does not rule out *p*. Similar ideas can be found in DeRose (1991), which talks of "relevant way[s] by which members of the relevant community can come to know," and even in G. E Moore's *Commonplace Book*.[7]

On this view, the reason Sally speaks falsely when she says "Joe might be in Boston" is that she has within her "epistemic reach" facts that would have ruled out Joe's being in Boston. A "practicable investigation"—simply asking those around her—would have settled the matter. That also explains why Sally retracts her assertion when she hears what George has to say. Finally, it explains how it is that a group of people can argue about "whether Joe might be in Boston" without talking past each other or constantly changing the subject as they learn new things. The real topic is whether the facts that are within the group's "epistemic reach" suffice to rule out Joe's being in Boston.

I am skeptical that speakers make any implicit distinction in their use of epistemic modals between "practicable" and "impracticable" investigations, or between what they can easily come to know and what they can come to know only with difficulty or by the cooperation of fate. For example, it seems correct to say that people who used to think that it was possible that there were even numbers greater than 2 and less than 10^{17} that were not the sum of two primes were wrong—since we have now verified computationally that there cannot be any such numbers—even though this computation was not a practicable investigation for *them*. Similarly, we will judge Sally's claim false (on the basis of what we know) even if we are listening in remotely, so that Sally is unable to take advantage of our information about Joe's whereabouts. And Sally will retract her assertion that Joe might be in Boston just as surely if she finds an itinerary on the floor as she will in response to George's intervention—even if her finding this scrap of paper is completely fortuitous and not the result of a "practicable investigation" or a contextually relevant "way of coming to know."

Even leaving this worry aside, however, it seems to me that Hacking's is the wrong fix. Consider his own salvage ship example. It seems perfectly reasonable for the mate to say:

"It's possible that we shall find the treasure here, and it's possible that we shall find it farther south. Let's examine the log before we dive: maybe we can eliminate one of these locations."

[7] Moore writes: "Things which no-one in fact knows may be such that, owing to them, it is in fact likely or unlikely that p, provided they are such that the person who says p is likely or unlikely *easily might* know, or which the speaker & his hearers *couldn't easily know or have known*, is incompatible with p, doesn't prevent its being true that p is prob." (Moore 1962: 402, emphasis added).

In his second sentence, the mate is acknowledging the possibility that a "practicable investigation" will rule out one of the two possibilities. If Hacking is right, that is tantamount to acknowledging that one of the two conjuncts of the mate's first sentence might be false. So if Hacking's proposal is right, then the mate's speech should sound as infelicitous as "Jane is in Boston and Al is in New York. Maybe Jane is not in Boston." But it doesn't; it is perfectly felicitous.

3.3. Distributed knowledge

A different way in which one might handle cases like Hacking's, in which an epistemic modal claim seems to be false even though the proposition said to be possible is not ruled out by what anyone knows, is to appeal to *distributed* knowledge. We have been appealing, vaguely, to "what is known by a contextually relevant group G." But what is it for a group G to know that p? A variety of answers are possible:

> *Universal knowledge:* Every member of G knows that p.
>
> *Partial knowledge:* Some member of G knows that p.
>
> *Common knowledge:* Every member of G knows that p, and knows that the other members know that p, and that they know that the other members know that p, etc.
>
> *Distributed knowledge:* p is a consequence of the totality of facts known by various members of G.

Teller (1972) suggests that if we take epistemic modal claims to concern a group's *distributed* knowledge, we can explain why claims of the form "It is possible that p" sometimes seem false even though no one in the speaker's group is in a position to rule p out.

Consider the unfortunate murder of McRich (Teller 1972: 310). Sleuth knows that McRich's nephew was ten miles from the scene of the crime all evening, while Private Eye knows that the murder occured between 7 and 8 p.m. Both believe that it's possible that the nephew did it. When they compare notes, they realize that the nephew couldn't be the murderer. Teller points out how natural it would be for them to concede that they were wrong before, and that it had only *seemed* possible that the nephew was the murderer. The explanation, on Teller's view, is that the truth of their claims of epistemic possibility depends on what is known *distributively* by the two of them together, which rules out the possibility that the nephew is the murderer. "What we know," in this sense, can include facts not known to any of us individually.

Like broadening "epistemic reach," appealing to distributed knowledge in the semantics for epistemic modals can make epistemic modal claims more "objective." This helps account for the fact that we tend to assess them in light of information not possessed by the speaker or any members of the speaker's group. The problem, as before, is that it threatens to make them *too* objective. Given that Sleuth and Private Eye both have reason to believe that the other has information he does not have, it would be rash for either to assert or believe that what is known *distributively* by them fails to rule out the nephew as murderer. So if Teller is right about epistemic modals, it should seem rash for either of them to assert or believe that it's possible that the nephew did it. But it doesn't seem rash. It seems perfectly appropriate.

3.4. The puzzle

All of the proposals we've considered in this section are attempts to keep the core contextualist idea of Solipsistic Contextualism—the idea that epistemic modals are contextually sensitive to what is known at the context of use—while dropping the implausible Solipsism. And all of them face the same basic problem. The less solipsistic the theory becomes, the harder it is to explain why speakers feel entitled to make the epistemic modal claims they do.

The problem is that we have two kinds of data, and they seem to point in different directions. If we attend to facts about when speakers take themselves to be warranted in asserting that something is "possible," Solipsistic Contextualism looks like the right view. Unfortunately, it cannot account for the data about speakers' assessments of epistemic modal claims—including self-assessments that prompt retraction—or for the nature of disputes about questions expressed using epistemic modals. We can account for these data by making our Contextualism less solipsistic, but then we can no longer account for the data that originally motivated Solipsistic Contextualism.

Nor does there seem to be any stable position that balances these two competing desiderata. If we focus on *uptake* (third-party assessments, retractions, and disagreement), we are led to expand the relevant body of knowledge, seemingly without end. But if we focus on *production*, we are led to contract it (on pain of making ordinary, apparently reasonable assertions unwarranted). We are led to a kind of paradox: although the truth of a claim made using epistemic modals must depend somehow on what is known—that is what makes it "epistemic"—it does not seem to depend on any *particular* body of knowledge. And there is no way to account for this in the framework of contextualism, which requires that the relevant body of knowledge be determined by features of the context of use. The fundamental problem with Solipsistic Contextualism lies with its Contextualism, not its Solipsism.

4. Non-Truth-Conditional Approaches

If these arguments seem familiar, perhaps it's because they've been made before. Consider how Price (1983) argues against truth-conditional treatments of "probably." First, he points out that we do not treat claims about what is "probable" as claims about what is likely given the *speaker's* evidence:

If I disagree with your claim that it is probably going to snow, I am not disagreeing that given *your* evidence it is likely that this is so; but indicating what follows from *my* evidence. Indeed, I might *agree* that it is probably going to snow and yet think it false that this follows from your evidence. (1983: 403)

He then notes that if we fix this problem by expanding the relevant body of evidence to include, say, evidence that is available in principle, we can no longer understand how speakers take themselves to be justified in making the probability judgements they do:

consider the surgeon who says, 'Your operation has probably been successful. We could find out for sure, but since the tests are painful and expensive, it is best to avoid them.' The accessibility, in principle, of evidence which would override that on which the SP judgement is based, is here explicitly acknowledged. (1983: 405)

If we look at when speakers make "probably" claims, we are pushed towards a solipsistic semantics, while if we look at third-party assessments of such claims, we are pushed toward something more objective. The upshot is that there is no way of filling in the X in "Given evidence X, it is probable that q" that would yield plausible truth conditions for the unqualified "It is probable that q."

Price takes these arguments to be compelling reasons for the view that "probably" does not contribute to the propositional content of a speech act at all. His view is that "probably" contributes to the *force* of a speech act, not its content.[8] Other philosophers and linguists have taken similar views about "possibly" and other epistemic modals. So it is worth considering whether such approaches might provide a satisfactory resolution to the problems scouted in the preceding two sections.

4.1. Epistemic modals as force modifiers

It would be misguided to ask how "speaking frankly" contributes to the truth conditions of

(3) Speaking frankly, she's too good for him.

When (3) is used to make an assertion, what is asserted is simply *that she's too good for him*. "Speaking frankly" does not contribute anything to the content of the assertion; its role is rather to comment on the kind of speech act being made. We should not puzzle ourselves about when the proposition *that speaking frankly she's too good for him* is true, because there is no such proposition.

Perhaps asking how epistemic modals affect truth conditions is equally misguided. We have assumed so far that Sally is making an assertion, and this assumption leads directly to questions about the truth conditions of her claim. But we need not understand her speech act as an assertion. Perhaps she is simply signalling her unwillingness to assert that Joe *isn't* in Boston. As Hare argues, "We have a use for a way of volubly and loquaciously *not* making a certain statement; and perhaps there is one sense of 'may' in which it fulfils this function" (1967: 321). Or perhaps she is *perhapserting* the proposition *that Joe is in Boston*. Here a "perhapsertion" is a distinct kind of speech act, which we might understand as the expression of some minimal degree of credence, or advice not to ignore a possibility. If the linguistic role of epistemic modals is to signal

---

[8] In later work (1994) he suggests that the speech act can be *both* an assertion that it might be that p—in some minimal sense of "assertion"—*and* a non-assertive expression of positive credence in p.

that the speaker is making a perhapsertion, then we need not trouble ourselves about the contribution it makes to truth conditions.

Such views account quite well for our uses of (stand-alone) sentences involving epistemic modals, while allowing us to dodge the questions about the truth-conditional contribution of epistemic modals that we saw above to be so problematic. However, they leave us unequipped to deal with *embedded* uses of epistemic modals. And in general, they make it difficult to explain interactions between epistemic modals and expressions that have a content-expressing role.

4.2. *Interface problems*

Epistemic modals can occur embedded under quantifiers, truth-functional connectives, conditionals, attitude verbs, adjectives, and other constructions.[9] In this they differ greatly from "speaking frankly," which does not embed in these ways:

(4) (a) If it might be raining, we should bring umbrellas.
   (b) #If speaking frankly she's too good for him, she'll realize this.
(5) (a) It's not possible that Joe is in Boston.
   (b) #It's not the case that speaking frankly, Joe is in Boston.
(6) (a) Sally believes that it's possible that Joe is in Boston.
   (b) #Sally believes that speaking frankly, she's too good for him.

The force modifier approach tells us nothing about the contribution made by "might" in (4a) or "possible" in (5a). It is clear that "might" in (4a) is *not* indicating that anything is being perhapserted. In typical uses of (4a), the whole conditional is being asserted full stop, and the antecedent is neither asserted nor perhapserted. (It's perfectly coherent to say, "If *p*, then *q*. But not *p*.") There is clearly a difference between (4a) and

(7) If it is raining, we should bring umbrellas.

but the force-modifier account of "might" does not help us understand what it is, since "might" is not serving as a force modifier in (4a).

Similarly, the force-modifier account of

(8) It's possible that Joe is in Boston

gives us no guidance whatsoever about the meaning of (5a). Clearly "possible" occurs here within the scope of the negation—(5a) does not mean the same thing as

(9) It's possible that Joe is not in Boston

—but what sense can we make of the negation of a *speech act*?

Finally, in (6a), "possible" occurs in the description of the content of a cognitive state, not a speech act. Although it is fairly clear how we could leverage our understanding of the kind of speech act conventionally made by (8) into an understanding of (6a), this requires that we treat "believe" differently when its complement is modified

[9] However, there are some interesting restrictions. For example, von Fintel and Iatridou (2003) argue that in many contexts epistemic modals must take wide scope over quantifiers.

by an epistemic modal than when it is not. (Roughly: when "believes" takes a complement clause in which an epistemic modal takes wide scope, it will attribute credence above some minimal threshold, while in other cases it will attribute full belief.) Similar modifications will be needed for other attitude verbs. This complicates the (already difficult) project of giving a compositional semantics for attitude verbs by undermining the neat division of labor between force (supplied by the attitude verb) and content (supplied by the complement clause).

An advocate of the force-modifier approach might be able to tell separate stories, like the story sketched above about attitude verbs, about how epistemic modals behave in all of these other embedded contexts. But the resulting account is bound to be ugly and complex. The beauty of truth-conditional semantics is that it provides a common currency that can be used to explain indefinitely many interaction effects in a simple and economical account. We should be prepared to accept a messy, non-truth-conditional account of epistemic modals only if there is no truth-conditional account that explains the data.

4.3. Explaining retractions

In addition to these problems with embedded uses, the force-modifier approach has difficulty with the same retraction data that caused problems for contextualism. For, if the force-modifier view is right, why does Sally say "I was wrong" when George tells her about Joe's whereabouts? None of the answers that are available on the force-modifier view seem to work:

1. *She believed that Joe was in Boston, and he wasn't.* No, because she didn't believe this.
2. *She had a minimal degree of credence that Joe was in Boston, and he wasn't.* No, because there's nothing "wrong" about having a minimal degree of credence in a proposition that turns out to be false. For example, it's quite reasonable to have a minimal degree of credence in each of a number of incompatible alternatives, even though all but one of these are bound to be false.
3. *She had a minimal degree of credence that Joe was in Boston, and she shouldn't have, given her evidence.* But she should have! *Her* evidence didn't rule out his being in Boston.
4. *She raised to salience the possibility that Joe was in Boston, and she shouldn't have.* But she should have! It was reasonable and appropriate for her to do so.

In order to exhibit Sally's retraction as rational, we need to understand how she can reasonably take herself to have performed a speech act that is in some way incorrect. The force-modifier approach lacks the resources to do this.

5. A "Relativist" Approach

Advocates of force-modifier accounts are typically well aware of the interface problems canvassed in the last section. That is why they motivate their views by arguing *against* truth-conditional approaches. For example, Simon Blackburn says that although his expressivist theory of evaluative language will no doubt have "Ptolemaic" complexities, there is no "Copernican" theory that explains the data better (Blackburn 1984: 195–6). Price's argument for a force-modifier approach to "probably" proceeds along similar lines.

Such arguments work only if they can rule out all possible truth-conditional approaches. Typically, they assume that any such truth-conditional view must have a contextualist shape. In the case of epistemic modals, this means that the body of known facts relative to which the modal is assessed must be determined by features of the context of use (including the speaker's intentions). We have seen above how one might argue quite generally that no view with this shape accurately captures the way we use epistemic modals.

But must a truth-conditional semantics for epistemic modals have this shape? In this section, I want to explore the possibility of broadening our semantic frameworks to make room for a new kind of view, on which the truth of epistemic modal claims depends on a body of known facts determined not by the context of use, but by what I'll call the *context of assessment*. This semantics offers prospects for meeting the objections to contextualist views in a broadly truth-conditional framework, thereby undermining the motivation for the force-modifier approach.

5.1. Bicontextuality

We can understand the notion of a context of assessment by analogy with the familiar notion of a context of use:

Context of use: the setting for an actual or possible use of a sentence (or proposition) in a speech act or mental act.

Context of assessment: the setting from which such a use is being assessed for truth or falsity on some actual or possible occasion of assessment.

For many purposes, one can think of a context as a centered possible world—a world-time-agent triple—since all of the other contextual factors that are needed are determined once a centered world is given. We can then talk of "the speaker of the context of use," "the time of the context of assessment," or "the epistemic state of (the assessor at) the context of assessment." Alternatively, one can think of a context of assessment as an abstract sequence of parameters representing semantically relevant features of a (concrete) setting from which a speech act or other use of a sentence might be assessed. I will take the first approach here (following Lewis (1980) rather than Kaplan (1989)), but nothing hangs on it.

Since we do assess uses of sentences, and whenever we do this we occupy some particular context, there is little to object to in the concept of a "context of assessment." Semanticists of all stripes should be able to deploy this concept; the only question is whether it has a useful role to play. The question is whether truth, reference, and other semantic properties can depend not just on features of the context in which a sentence is used, but on features of the context in which it is assessed. To answer Yes to this question is to acknowledge a new kind of context sensitivity, which I have called *assessment sensitivity* to distinguish it from the familiar *use sensitivity*.[10]

It should be obvious where this is going. We started with the intuitively compelling idea that the truth of epistemic modal claims depends on *what is known*. That is why they are called "epistemic." But we ran into trouble when we tried to answer the question, "known to whom?". For it seemed that people tend to assess epistemic modal claims for truth in light of what *they* (the assessors) know, even if they realize that they know more than the speaker (or relevant group) did at the time of utterance. A straightforward way to account for this puzzling fact is to suppose that epistemic modals are assessment-sensitive: the truth of an epistemic modal claim depends on what is known by the assessor, and thus varies with the context of assessment. On this view, epistemic modal claims have no "absolute" truth values, only assessment-relative truth values. This is why they resist being captured in standard frameworks for truth-conditional semantics.

For the sake of concreteness, we'll work at first with the most austere kind of relativist view—what one might call SOLIPSISTIC RELATIVISM. (Later we'll consider some complications.) On this view, "Joe might be running" expresses a truth, as assessed by Sam, just in case what *Sam* knows (at the time of assessment) does not rule out that Joe is running. This is not yet a compositional semantics for "might," since we have not explained how to handle embedded occurrences. More on that later (Section 6). But we can already see from this sketch of a theory how Solipsistic Relativism will handle the data that seemed most problematic for the various forms of contextualism.

5.2. Explaining third-party assessments

Solipsistic Relativism has a very straightforward explanation of the data about third-party assessments. According to Solipsistic Relativism, the truth of an epistemic modal claim (relative to a context of assessment) depends on what the assessor knows, not what the speaker knew when making the claim. So it is appropriate for eavesdroppers to assess the truth of epistemic modal claims against the background of what they know, even if this is very different from what the speaker knew.

Recall that the contextualist could only handle the eavesdropper data by strengthening truth conditions for claims of epistemic possibility to the point where it became hard to understand why people would make them at all. The relativist does not have this problem. Sally's claim that Joe might be in Boston is true as assessed from the context in which she makes it, so we can understand why she makes it in the first place. In general, Solipsistic Relativism counts a sentence as true as used at c and assessed at c

---

[10] A sentence (or proposition) is *use-sensitive* iff its truth as used at c_U and assessed at c_A depends on features of c_U. A sentence (or proposition) is *assessment-sensitive* iff its truth as used at c_U and assessed at c_A depends on features of c_A.

just when Solipsistic Contextualism counts it as true as used at c. The relativist semantics will diverge from the contextualist semantics only when the context of assessment is distinct from the context of use. So the Solipsistic Relativist will be able to explain *production* of epistemic modals in much the same way as the Solipsistic Contextualist, while explaining *assessments* in a way that is not available to the contextualist.[11]

Hacking's salvage ship case can be handled in the same way. It is really just another third-party assessment case, in which *we* (Hacking's readers) are the third party. According to Solipsistic Relativism, the truth of the mate's claim (as assessed by us) depends on what *we* know. Since we know (from Hacking's narrative) that the treasure lies elsewhere, the mate's claim is false, relative to the context of assessment we occupy. That explains quite straightforwardly why we judge it to be false. The fact that there was a "practicable investigation" the mate could have carried out is simply irrelevant. What is crucial is something Hacking did not explicitly point out: that we, the readers, come to know, through Hacking's testimony, that the treasure lies elsewhere.

5.3. Explaining retractions

The Solipsistic Relativist has an equally simple explanation of why Sally should retract her claim in response to George's correction (Section 2.2, above). After Sally learns from George that Joe is not in Boston, she occupies a context of assessment relative to which her original claim is false (since she now knows more than she did). So it is proper for her to retract it.[12]

Note the change of perspective. The contextualist assumes that if what George says implies that Sally's claim is false, then George must be part of the group whose knowledge matters to the truth of Sally's claim. But as we have seen, this way leads to madness: there is no way to keep the group from expanding indefinitely. The relativist, by contrast, holds that what is important is not that *George* knew that Joe was in Berkeley, but that *Sally* comes to know this.

Hence it is irrelevant, for the relativist, that Sally comes to know this through the testimony of someone else who already knew it (at the time she made the claim). What is known by others is relevant only insofar as they are potential informants of the speaker (in this case, Sally). If they don't speak up, or if they do speak up but Sally doesn't believe them (and so doesn't acquire knowledge), then Sally has no objective reason to retract her assertion. Conversely, if the way Sally comes to know something incompatible with Joe's having been in Boston is not through others' testimony but

---

[11] This needs some qualification, since it's not clear that deliberation about whether to assert an assessment-sensitive proposition shouldn't take into account its truth value relative to contexts of assessment other than the one occupied by the speaker. For example, one might refrain from asserting something one knows one will have to retract almost immediately, when one's context changes, even if it is true relative to one's current context.

[12] Here I am relying on the normative account of assertion developed in MacFarlane (2005b), according to which one is obligated to retract an assertion that has been shown to have been false, relative to one's current context of assessment.

through her own observation, or through serendipitous discovery of evidence, she has just as much reason to retract her original claim, and it seems just as natural for her to do so. That the contextualist isn't getting the right generalization here comes out clearly in the need for epicycles: for example, the appeal to "contextually relevant ways of coming to know" and "distributed knowledge" in addition to a "contextually relevant group of knowers."

5.4. Explaining disputes

As we have seen, the contextualist has difficulty accounting for the fact that people take themselves to be arguing and disagreeing about epistemic modal claims. What are they arguing about? Not about what some particular one of them knows. Perhaps, then, what the group knows. But what if another group joins the discussion? This should seem like a change of subject, and it doesn't. Their disputes seem to concern a common topic—say, whether it is possible that infected birds have entered Alameda county—and this topic can't be reduced to a question about what anyone, or any group, knows.

The Solipsistic Relativist gets this right. On the relativist's account, epistemic modal claims aren't equivalent to any claims about what people know. The former are assessment-sensitive, and the latter are not.[13] The relativist can say that every group that is debating whether it is possible that infected birds have entered Alameda county (by such and such a date) is debating the truth of the same proposition. It's just that the truth of this proposition is perspectival.

5.5. Philosophical debts

Let's take stock. In Sections 2 and 3 we saw that contextualist semantics is structurally unable to explain our use of epistemic modals. In order to explain third-party assessments, retraction, and disputes, we need to widen the contextually relevant group of knowers—perhaps indefinitely—and put further, "objective" conditions on the truth of epistemic modal claims. But when we do this, it becomes impossible to explain our readiness to make epistemic modal claims even in situations where we are well aware that others may know more than we do. Historically, this problem was one motivation for the view that epistemic modals should be understood non-truth-conditionally, as modifiers of the force of a speech act rather than its content. However, as we saw in Section 4, this project requires a piecemeal account of the role of epistemic modals in embedded contexts. Such an account, if possible at all, is likely to be very complex. Moreover, force-modifier accounts don't do any better than Solipsistic Contextualism

---

[13] Not in the same way, anyway. In MacFarlane (2005a), I argue that knowledge-attributing sentences are assessment-sensitive, because their truth (relative to a context of assessment) depends on the epistemic standards relevant at the context of assessment. But even if this is right, their truth is not sensitive to the same features of contexts of assessment as epistemic modals, so they still won't be equivalent to any epistemic modal claims.

in explaining the retraction data. So we are left with no good account of the meanings of epistemic modals.

Solipsistic Relativism offers a way out. It neatly explains the data that proved impossible to accommodate in a contextualist framework, and it does so without giving up the advantages of a truth-conditional framework. But is it intelligible? If we are to use an assessment-relative truth predicate in our semantic theories, we must pay some philosophical debts. At the very least, we must answer these questions:

1. What changes does relativism require in standard theories of propositions, standard accounts of assertion and belief, and standard approaches to compositional semantics?
2. Isn't this kind of relativism about truth self-undermining, for reasons given by Plato in the *Theaetetus* and repeated by many philosophers since?
3. Even if talk of truth relative to a context of assessment is not self-undermining, do we really understand it? What is it to commit oneself to the truth of an assessment-sensitive proposition? Can the relativist make sense of the idea that belief "aims at" truth?
4. Can we really make sense of *disagreement* about assessment-sensitive claims? If so, what is the point of disagreeing about things whose truth is relative?
5. More broadly, what purpose is served by assessment sensitivity? What would we be lacking if we replaced our assessment-sensitive expressions with assessment-invariant ones (not talking about what might be the case, for example, but only about what various people do and do not know)?

I will not try to answer these questions here. I have addressed the first three in MacFarlane (2005b) and the last two in MacFarlane (2007). But there is much more clarificatory work to be done before we can be confident that we understand what we are saying when we characterize a claim as true "relative to a context of assessment."

6. Compositional Semantics

The rough characterization of Solipsistic Contextualism in the previous section refers only to stand-alone sentences in which the epistemic modal takes widest scope. But of course epistemic modals can also occur embedded under quantifiers, conditionals, and other kinds of operators. Since one of the advertised advantages of relativist semantics over the force-modifier approach is its capacity to explain embedded uses, it's worth looking at how standard semantic frameworks must be modified in order to make room for assessment sensitivity, and how a compositional semantics for epistemic modals might look in such a framework.

6.1. Baseline: solipsistic contextualism

As a baseline for comparison, let's start with a version of Solipsistic Contextualism. The aim is to give a finite definition of "true at context of use c" for a first-order language containing the epistemic modal operator "*Might* : " ("it is possible that") and an operator "FAK_t^x:" ("for all x knows at t"). Since "*Might* : ", "FAK_t^x:", and the quantifiers are not truth-functional, we can't simply give a recursive definition of truth at a context of use. Instead, we'll give a recursive definition of truth at a *point of evaluation*, then define truth at a context of use in terms of truth at a point of evaluation.[14] Here a *point of evalution* is an ordered quadruple $\langle c, w, i, a \rangle$, where c is a context, w a possible world,[15] i a set of possible worlds representing an *information state* (intuitively, the worlds not ruled out by the information), and a an *assignment* of objects from the domain relevant at c to the variables.

First, we define the extensions of the primitive terms and predicates of the language, relative to a point of evaluation:

- The extension of "Joe" at $\langle c, w, i, a \rangle$ = Joe.
- The extension of "I" at $\langle c, w, i, a \rangle$ = the agent of c.
- The extension of "now" at $\langle c, w, i, a \rangle$ = the time of c.
- The extension of "human" at $\langle c, w, i, a \rangle$ = the set of humans in w.
- And so on (finitely many of these).

We can now define truth at a point of evaluation recursively as follows:

- $\ulcorner \phi(a) \urcorner$ is true at $\langle c, w, i, a \rangle$ iff the extension of a at $\langle c, w, i, a \rangle$ belongs to the extension of ϕ at $\langle c, w, i, a \rangle$. (And similarly for polyadic predicates.)
- $\ulcorner \neg \Phi \urcorner$ is true at $\langle c, w, i, a \rangle$ iff Φ is not true at $\langle c, w, i, a \rangle$.
- $\ulcorner \Phi \wedge \Psi \urcorner$ is true at $\langle c, w, i, a \rangle$ iff Φ is true at $\langle c, w, i, a \rangle$ and Ψ is true at $\langle c, w, i, a \rangle$.
- $\ulcorner \exists a \Phi \urcorner$ is true at $\langle c, w, i, a \rangle$ iff for some assignment a' that agrees with a on every variable except possibly a, Φ is true at $\langle c, w, i, a' \rangle$.
- $\ulcorner Might : \Phi \urcorner$ is true at $\langle c, w, i, a \rangle$ iff for some w' in i, Φ is true at $\langle c, w', i, a \rangle$.[16]
- $\ulcorner FAK_\tau^a : \Phi \urcorner$ is true at $\langle c, w, i, a \rangle$ iff Φ is true at $\langle c, w', i', a \rangle$, where i' is the set of worlds not excluded by what is known by the extension of a at $\langle c, w, i, a \rangle$ at w and the time denoted by τ at $\langle c, w, i, a \rangle$, and w' is some world in i'.

Finally, we can define truth at a context in terms of truth at a point of evaluation:[17]

> An occurrence of a sentence Φ at a context c is true iff Φ is true at every point of evaluation $\langle c, w_c, i_c, a \rangle$, where

---

[14] Cf. Tarski (1944: §11); Kaplan (1989: 547).

[15] I won't worry here about how these worlds are to be individuated or whether the same set of worlds can be used in semantics for alethic modals. Though these are important questions, they cross-cut the questions of primary concern to us here.

[16] Here I depart from the more standard approach of quantifying over the domain of worlds w' such that Rww', where R is a contextually determined "accessibility relation." I have chosen to formulate Solipsistic Contextualism this way, with the domain of worlds provided by a separate information state parameter, in order to make Solipsistic Contextualism easier to compare with Solipsistic Relativism, which uses such a parameter (for the essential difference between the views, see Section 6.3, below). There are, however, some excellent reasons for doing the semantics this way, even if one does not want to be a relativist in the end (see Yalcin 2007).

[17] Compare Kaplan (1989: 522). In what follows, I'll use "Φ is true at c" interchangeably with "an occurrence of Φ at c is true."

- w_c = the world of c,[18]
- i_c = the set of worlds that aren't excluded by what is known (at c) by the agent of c,
- a = an assignment of objects from the domain relevant at c to the variables.

Note that truth at a point of evaluation is defined for all formulas, but truth at a context of use is defined only for sentences (formulas with no free variables).

Let's verify that this account accords with the rough initial statement of Solipsistic Contextualism from Section 1. Let Φ be the sentence "*Might : Joe is running*," let c be a context in which George is uttering Φ, and let i_c be the set of worlds left open by what George knows at c. Our definition of truth at a point of evaluation tells us that Φ is true at a point of evaluation $\langle c, w, i, a \rangle$ just in case there is some world $w' \in i$ such that "Joe is running" is true at $\langle c, w', i, a \rangle$. Feeding this into our definition of truth at a context, we get that an occurrence of Φ at c is true just in case there is some world w' in i_c such that "Joe is running" is true at $\langle c, w', i_c, a \rangle$ for all assignments a. In other worlds, just in case what George knows at c does not rule out the truth of "Joe is running."

Logical truth and logical consequence can be defined (after Kaplan) as truth and truth preservation at every context:

A sentence Φ is *logically true* iff for every possible context of use c, Φ is true at c.

A sentence Φ is a *logical consequence* of a set Γ of sentences iff for every possible context of use c, if every member of Γ is true at c, then Φ is true at c.

It is also useful to define a notion of logical necessity that quantifies over points of evaluation rather than contexts, and a corresponding notion of logical implication:[19]

A formula Φ is *logically necessary* iff for every point of evaluation π, Φ is true at π.

A formula Φ is *logically implied* by a set Γ of formulas iff for every point of evaluation π, if every member of Γ is true at π, then Φ is true at π.

If a sentence is logically necessary, it is logically true, but the converse is not guaranteed. Similarly, if Φ is logically implied by Γ, it is a logical consequence of Γ, but the converse is not guaranteed.

Using these definitions, we can show that $\ulcorner FAK_{now}^{I} : \Phi \urcorner$ and $\ulcorner Might : \Phi \urcorner$ are equivalent in the sense that each is a logical consequence of the other.[20] This is a nice

---

[18] The assumption that there is a unique "world of c" might prove problematic on some ways of thinking of the epistemic "worlds." I'm not going to pursue this issue further here.

[19] On the need for these two distinct notions, see Thomason (1970: 273) and Kaplan (1989: 548–50). Note that logical truth and consequence are defined only for sentences (closed formulas), while logical necessity and implication are defined for (open or closed) formulas.

[20] Proof: Let c be any context. Let w_c be the world of c, t_c the time of c, s_c the agent of c, and i_c the set of worlds not excluded by what s_c knows at c. Let a be an arbitrary assignment: since we won't be dealing with open formulas, any formula that is satisfied by a can be assumed to be satisfied by any assignment.

result, because Solipsistic Contextualism was motivated in large part by the intuition that "It might be that p" and "For all I know, p" are in some strong sense equivalent. (Note that they are not equivalent in the stronger sense of logically *implying* each other, for there are points of evaluation at which one is true and the other false. To see this, note that the truth value of $\ulcorner FAK^I_{now} : \Phi \urcorner$ at a point of evaluation $\langle c, w, i, a \rangle$ does not depend at all on the value of i, while the truth value of $\ulcorner Might : \Phi \urcorner$ at that point does depend on the value of i. This makes a difference in embedded contexts: for example, "For all John knows now, for all I know now it is raining" can diverge in truth value from "For all John knows now, it might be raining." $\ulcorner FAK^I_{now} : \Phi \urcorner$ is, however, *strongly* equivalent to $\ulcorner FAK^I_{now} : Might : \Phi \urcorner$: they are true at just the same points of evaluation. This, too, is satisfying, insofar as we seem to use these forms interchangeably in English.)

6.2. Nonsolipsistic contextualism

If we want to make our semantics less solipsistic, it's very easy to do so. We can leave everything in the recursive definition of truth at a point of evaluation just as it is. All we need to change is the definition of truth at a context:

An occurrence of a sentence Φ at a context c is true iff Φ is true at every point of evaluation $\langle c, w_c, i_c, a \rangle$, where

- w_c = the world of c,
- i_c = the set of worlds that aren't excluded by what is known *distributively* at c by *the group of knowers relevant at c*,
- a = an assignment of objects from the domain relevant at c to the variables.

We could add "objective factors" just as easily—again, by modifying the clause for i_c in the above definition. Or we could refrain from specifying exactly how the relevant information state is determined by features of context, and say simply:

- i_c = the information state relevant at c.

The differences between the various sorts of contextualism would then be cast as differences about what makes an information state "relevant" at a context. We might call this formulation FLEXIBLE CONTEXTUALISM.

6.3. Solipsistic relativism

Moving to a view on which "might" is assessment-sensitive is nearly as easy. Again, we need not modify the recursive definition of truth at a point of evaluation. The

---

By the definition of truth at a context, $\ulcorner FAK^I_{now} : \Phi \urcorner$ is true at c iff it is true at the point $\langle c, w_c, i_c, a \rangle$. By the recursive clause for $FAK :$, $\ulcorner FAK^I_{now} : \Phi \urcorner$ is true at $\langle c, w_c, i_c, a \rangle$ iff Φ is true at $\langle c, w', i', a \rangle$, where i' is the set of worlds not excluded by what is known by the extension of "I" at $\langle c, w_c, i_c, a \rangle$ at w_c and the time denoted by "now" at $\langle c, w_c, i_c, a \rangle$, and w' is some world in i'. But the extension of "I" at $\langle c, w_c, i_c, a \rangle$ is s_c and the time denoted by "now" at $\langle c, w_c, i_c, a \rangle$ is t_c. So $i' = i_c$. Thus $\ulcorner FAK^I_{now} : \Phi \urcorner$ is true at c iff for some world $w' \in i_c$, Φ is true at $\langle c, i_c, w', a \rangle$. But as we have seen, this is just the condition for $\ulcorner Might : \Phi \urcorner$ to be true at c.

only change needed is in the definition of truth at a context—or, now, at context*s*, for we can only ask about the truth of an occurrence of a sentence relative to some particular context of assessment. To move from Solipsistic Contextualism to Solipsistic Relativism, we need only substitute the context of assessment for the context of use in the clause governing the initialization of the i parameter:

> An occurrence of a sentence Φ at a context c_U is true as assessed from a context c_A[21] iff Φ is true at every point of evaluation $\langle c_U, w_{c_U}, i_{c_A}, a \rangle$, where
>
> - w_{c_U} = the world of c_U,
> - i_{c_A} = the set of worlds that aren't excluded by what is known (at c_A) by the agent of c_A,
> - a = an assignment of objects from the domain relevant at c to the variables.

It is trivial to verify that these definitions yield the result described earlier, that $\ulcorner Might : \Phi \urcorner$ is true as used at c_U and assessed at c_A iff what is known to the assessor at c_A is compatible with the truth of Φ at $\langle c_U, c_A \rangle$.

Logical truth and consequence can be defined as before, only we quantify over both contexts of use and contexts of assessment:

> A sentence Φ is *logically true* iff for every possible context of use c_U and context of assessment c_A, Φ is true as used at c_U and assessed from c_A.

> A sentence Φ is a *logical consequence* of a set Γ of sentences iff for every possible context of use c_U and context of assessment c_A, if every member of Γ is true as used at c_U and assessed from c_A, then Φ is true as used at c_U and assessed from c_A.

On this semantics, we no longer get the result that $\ulcorner FAK^I_{now} : \Phi \urcorner$ and $\ulcorner Might : \Phi \urcorner$ are logically equivalent. To see that they could not be, it suffices to notice that the latter is assessment-sensitive while the former is not. However, a weaker kind of equivalence holds: they are *diagonally equivalent*.[22]

> Two sentences Φ and Ψ are *diagonally equivalent* iff for any possible context c, Φ is true as used at and assessed from c just in case Ψ is true as used at and assessed from c.

That is, a speaker considering $\ulcorner FAK^I_{now} : \Phi \urcorner$ and $\ulcorner Might : \Phi \urcorner$ from a particular context c should hold that an occurrence of either at c would have the same truth value. This vindicates the intuition that it is correct to say "It is possible that p" just when what one knows does not exclude p.

6.4. Monadic "true"

The relativist semantics makes use of two relativized truth predicates: (1) truth of a formula at a point of evaluation and (2) truth of a sentence at a context of use

---

[21] In what follows, I'll use "i is true at context of use c_U and context of assessment c_A" interchangeably with "an occurrence of i at c_U is true as assessed from c_A."

[22] The proof is straightforward.

and context of assessment. These are theoretical notions that get their significance from the role they play in a larger theory of meaning.[23] But what about the *monadic* predicate "true" used by ordinary speakers—a predicate that applies to *propositions*, not to sentences? Can the relativist make sense of this? Yes—it's just another bit of vocabulary in the object language, and we can give semantics for it just as we can for other predicates.

First we need a proto-theory of propositions. We don't need to say in any detail what propositions are, or how they are individuated. We will assume only that there *is* such a thing as (for example) the proposition that Smith might be the murderer. Supposing there is such a proposition, what can we say about its truth? It is standardly assumed that propositions will have different truth values relative to different possible worlds. But the relativist will also take the truth of propositions to be relative to an information state, which we have been modeling by a *set* of worlds, those not excluded by "what is known."[24]

Of course, the object-language truth predicate does not have argument places for these; it is monadic. So an account of its semantics must explain how these argument places are to be filled in. The answer is obvious: we just extract these values from our points of evaluation.

> The extension of "True" at a point of evaluation $\langle c_U, w, i, a \rangle$ is the set of propositions p such that p is true at $\langle w, i \rangle$.

"True" so defined is disquotational: every instance of the following schema is logically necessary (true at every point of evaluation):

---

[23] For details, see MacFarlane (2005b).

[24] Note that this view about propositional truth is not what makes the relativist view "relativist," since it is compatible with a "nonindexical" form of contextualism (see MacFarlane 2009). Indeed, our Solipsistic Contextualist could embrace the idea that truth for epistemic modal propositions is relative to a world and an information state. The crucial issue between the contextualist and the relativist is whether truth varies with the context of assessment, and that is left open by this decision about propositional truth.

Egan et al. (2005) and Egan (2007) take truth for epistemic modal propositions to be relative to a world, time, and an individual as "center." This approach may seem simpler than the one proposed here, and less radical, so it is worth taking a moment to explain why I am not inclined to go this way. The basic problem is that, although a world-time-individual triple is guaranteed to determine a pair of a privileged world and information state—the set of worlds not excluded by what is known by the individual at the world and time—the reverse is not the case. Given an arbitrary world w and information state i, there is no guarantee that there will be a triple $\langle w, t, s \rangle$ such that i is the set of worlds not excluded by what is known by s at w and t. Indeed, we know that some combinations of i and w will not be determined by *any* $\langle w, t, s \rangle$. For, knowledge being factive, w must surely belong to the set of worlds not excluded by what is known by s at w and t, so centered worlds will not determine any $\langle w, i \rangle$ pairs where $w \notin i$.

Why does this matter? Well, suppose that at c_A we are assessing an assertion at c_U of the proposition that p. We should judge the assertion true just in case p is true at $\langle w_{c_U}, i_{c_A} \rangle$. If we are assessing a merely counterfactual assertion, so that the world of c_U is not our world, it may be that $w_{c_U} \notin i_{c_A}$. This is no problem if we take propositional truth to be relative to world-set pairs. But what do we do if we take propositional truth to be relative to world-time-individual triples? There's not going to be a triple that gives us the world *and* the set of non-excluded worlds we need. The problem, in short, is that centered worlds "entangle" parameters that need to be free to move independently in the semantic theory.

$$\forall x((x = \text{the proposition that } P) \supset (True(x) \equiv P))$$

(where P is replaced by a sentence).[25] This is a welcome result. A disquotational truth predicate is a useful expressive device, and it is reassuring that the relativist can make good sense of it.

It is a corollary of this result that when P is assessment-sensitive and a denotes the proposition expressed by P, $\ulcorner True(a) \urcorner$ will also be assessment-sensitive.

7. Tensed Epistemic Modals

I want to close with a discussion of two problems I regard as open and difficult. The first concerns the interaction of epistemic modals and tense; the second concerns the robustness of the data used to motivate the relativist semantics. I will not try to resolve these issues here; the aim is to provide a prolegomenon to further investigations.

On all of the views we've considered so far, the set of epistemically open worlds with respect to which epistemic modals are evaluated is supplied entirely by context. For the Solipsistic Contextualist, it is the set of worlds not excluded by what the speaker knows at the time of utterance; for the Nonsolipsistic Contextualist, it is the set of worlds not excluded by what the contextually relevant group knows at the time of utterance; for the Solipsistic Relativist, it is the set of worlds not excluded by what the assessor knows at the time of assessment. Let us suppose all these contextual factors have been fixed. Then either the set of non-excluded worlds contains worlds at which Fermat's Last Theorem is false or it does not. If it does, then the second conjunct of

(10) In 1980 it was possible that Fermat's Last Theorem was false, but this is not possible today.

is false. If it doesn't, then the first conjunct is false: the past tense has no effect, because there is no time variable associated with the epistemic modal. Either way, then, (10) is false. On all of these views, "possible" and "might" are temporally *rigid*: like "now" and "yesterday," they are unaffected by shifts in the time of evaluation.

This might be thought to be a bad consequence. I am not so sure. Note, first, that the information relevant to evaluating embedded occurrences of epistemic modals does not seem to shift with the *world* of evaluation. Here is a test case:

(11) It isn't possible that Jones is the murderer, but if no one had looked in this desk, it would have been possible that Jones was the murderer.

But if counterfactual changes in what we know do not induce counterfactual changes in what is epistemically possible, why should trans-temporal changes in what we know induce trans-temporal changes in what is epistemically possible? The (alethic) modal

---

[25] Proof: Take any sentence P and consider any point of evaluation $\langle c, w, i, a \rangle$ such that '$x = $ the proposition that P' is true at $\langle c, w, i, a \rangle$. '$True(x)$' is true at $\langle c, w, i, a \rangle$ iff $a(x)$ is true at $\langle w, i \rangle$. But this is so iff P is true at $\langle c, w, i, a \rangle$, because $a(x)$ is the proposition expressed by P at c. So '$True(x) \equiv P$' is true at $\langle c, w, i, a \rangle$.

rigidity of epistemic modals is some evidence for their temporal rigidity. Intuitions about (10) are not as clear, but to me it has the same odd feel as (11).[26] A much more natural thing to say would be

(12) In 1980 people thought it possible that Fermat's Last Theorem was false, but we know today that this is not possible.

Here is a similar test case with a contingent sentence embedded under the epistemic modal:

(13) We know now that Sarah murdered Jenkins by herself. But yesterday it was possible that she had an accomplice.

We do sometimes hear this kind of thing, especially in legal contexts. But my (admittedly contaminated) intuition is that it is, strictly speaking, false. What is meant is

(14) We know now that Sarah must have murdered Jenkins by herself. But yesterday it was possible *for all we knew* that she had an accomplice. (Or: yesterday it had *seemed* possible that she had an accomplice.)

If you're not convinced, consider asking someone who asserts (13) *at what time* it became impossible that Sarah had an accomplice, and what changed to make it so. I predict embarrassment. For the only answer is, "At N o'clock, when we learned such and such." And this answer commits the speaker to the view that by learning something, she *made it impossible* that Sarah had an accomplice. I believe that ordinary speakers (those not already indoctrinated into contextualist theories of epistemic modals) will find this consequence bizarre.

Here's a real-life example, from a *New York Times* article concerning *Science*'s retraction of a paper reporting the production of eleven lines of cloned human embryonic stem cells:[27]

The retraction did not include information revealed in South Korea at a news conference on Thursday. Until then, *it had seemed possible* that Dr. Hwang's group had created 2 cloned stem cell lines, not 11. On Thursday, the investigators in Seoul said that even those two were not clones. (emphasis added)

Notice how odd it would have been to say, "Until then, it had *been* possible that Dr. Hwang's group had created 2 cloned stem cell lines, not 11," despite the fact that the information revealing that no cloned lines had been created was not known until the press conference.

Thus it is far from clear that simple temporal embeddings like (10) and (13) should motivate us to make epistemic modals time-indexed. But there are more complex cases that are harder to dismiss in this way, for example:

---

[26] If we cash in "possible" for "might," it sounds even worse: "In 1980 Fermat's Last Theorem might have been false, but today it must be true." But this may be due to syntactic differences between "might" and "possible."

[27] Kolata (2005).

(15) I studied that book because it was possible that Fermat's Last Theorem would be refuted using its techniques.

Intuitively, it seems that one can truly and felicitously assert (15) even if one knows that Fermat's Last Theorem is true, provided it was not known at the time one studied the book that the theorem was true. But "becausal" contexts are generally considered to be factive: "*A* because *B*" implies, or perhaps presupposes, *B*. So, if (15) is true and felicitous, then it seems we are committed to the truth of "it was possible that Fermat's Last Theorem would be refuted using its techniques," even though we know now that the theorem would not be refuted.

It would be hasty to conclude, however, that the set of worlds relative to which an occurrence of "possible" needs to be evaluated shifts with the time of evaluation. Consider this close analogue of (15):

(16) I failed to prove the conjecture because it was impossible to prove it.

Here the set of worlds over which "impossible" quantifies is definitely not the set of worlds left open by the speaker's knowledge at the time of evaluation (that is, the time the proof was being attempted).

It is presumably important here that (15), unlike (16), gives the speaker's own reasons for doing something. In this kind of context, the presupposition of factivity is sometimes relaxed. Suppose Joe has just found out that the internet search company he invested in has gone bankrupt. He might felicitously say:

(17) I bought that stock because it was going to be the next Google!

Similarly, the utterer of (15) might say:

(18) I studied that book because it was going to show me how to refute Fermat's Last Theorem.

Was the book going to show her how to refute Fermat's Last Theorem? Presumably not, since the theorem is true. But the speech is still felicitous, in a context where the speaker is displaying the mental state that motivated a certain action. Given examples like (17) and (18), which do not contain epistemic modals, (15) and sentences like it do not motivate taking epistemic modals to be temporally "shifty."

Another challenging class of cases involves *binding*:

(19) He lectures in a bulletproof vest whenever it is possible that members of the audience are packing handguns.
(20) Whenever it was possible that Mary was drunk, the people she came with drove her home.[28]

It seems that in (19), "possible" needs to be evaluated with respect to the sets of worlds left open by what is known (presumably by the lecturer) on various occasions of lecturing. And in (20), "possible" needs to be evaluated with respect to what is known on various occasions of partying.

[28] I owe this example to Fabrizio Cariani.

Note that in addition to the bound readings of (19) and (20), there are readings where the occurrences of "possible" are, plausibly, assessment-sensitive. Suppose several groups of researchers have been compiling data on a lecturer's sartorial habits, and about the likelihood that members of various audiences are armed. The groups might disagree about whether, at some particular lecture where no bulletproof vest was worn, it was possible that the audience members were packing handguns, and because of this they might disagree about the truth of an occurrence of (19). They would *not* be disagreeing about whether the lecturer's knowledge left it open that the audience members were armed; they might all agree that it did. A similar scenario will generate an assessment-sensitive reading of (20). So it is not the case that the modals are *always* affected by tense (or, relatedly, quantification over events). Sometimes there is a kind of binding, and sometimes there is not. When there is not, the arguments for the assessment sensitivity of the modals apply as before.

Moreover, it is not just the time that gets bound, but the *knower*. This can be seen in the first of two possible bound readings of (20):

(21) Whenever it was possible [for all they knew then] that Mary was drunk, the people she came with drove her home.

(22) Whenever it was possible [for all I knew then] that Mary was drunk, the people she came with drove her home.[29]

So the simple expedient of indexing the epistemic modals to a time (that is, letting the set of worlds they quantify over be a function of the time of evaluation) is not going to be sufficient to generate all the bound readings.

The most straightforward approach for the relativist—one that works within the framework that has been presented above—is to get the various bound readings by appeal to "free enrichment" of (19) and (20) with appropriately placed FAK_t^a: operators. These operators provide agent and time variables that can be bound by the enclosing quantifiers. The idea, then, is that one can use the *sentence* (20) to express a number of different propositions, including at least two assessment-invariant propositions with binding of the variables in FAK_t^a: operators, as well as one assessment-sensitive proposition with no binding. The speaker relies on the audience's ability to figure out which proposition she intends to convey based on contextual clues. (When the ambiguity cannot be resolved contextually, the FAK_t^a: operators can be made explicit.)

To sum up: The simple-minded approach of taking the modals to be sensitive to what is known at the time of evaluation generates dubious predictions, and is neither necessary nor sufficient to explain what is going on in sentences (19) and (20). It is not sufficient, because the binding involves not just times but knowers. And it is not necessary, because the binding can be explained by positing an implicit FAK_t^a:

---

[29] If you're having trouble getting this reading, try continuing (20) with "This seems to have been a lucky coincidence, because they were usually too plastered to notice her condition."

operator. Since this explanation is consistent with the relativist semantics, interactions between temporal modifiers and epistemic modals do not give us any compelling reason to resist taking epistemic modals to be assessment-sensitive.

8. Doubts about the Data

The second set of worries I want to discuss concerns the robustness of the data used to motivate the relativist semantics.

8.1. Limits to retrospective correction?

Immediately after presenting his "salvage ship" case, discussed in Section 3.2, above, Ian Hacking writes:

> When one starts collecting examples like this, it begins to look as if, whenever it turns out to be false that *p*, we say, of an earlier era, that in those times it may have seemed possible that *p*, but it was not really possible at all.

If Hacking had endorsed this description of the data, he would have been well on the road to relativism. For only a relativist semantics can explain why earlier epistemic modal claims are *always* evaluated in light of what we know now (at the time of assessment), even when we know much more than was known at the time the claim was made.

However, Hacking thinks that this description of the data "would be too strong." Here's why:

> Consider a person who buys a lottery ticket. At the time he buys his ticket we shall say it is possible he will win, though probably he will not. As expected, he loses. But retrospectively it would be absurd to report that it only *seemed* possible that the man would win. It was perfectly possible that he would win. To see this clearly, consider a slightly different case, in which the lottery is not above board; it is rigged so that only the proprietors can win. Thus, however it may have seemed to the gullible customer, it really was not possible that he would win. It only seemed so. "Seemed possible" and "was possible" both have work cut out for them. (Hacking 1967: 148)

If Hacking is interpreting his example correctly, it spells trouble for the relativist. For it suggests that the retrospective assessment data used to motivate relativism do not extend as far as the relativist needs them to. In the case of the non-rigged lottery, it seems, we *don't* assess our earlier claim that it was possible that the man would win as false, despite the fact that what we know now (after the lottery) excludes his having won. This seems to favor some version of contextualism over relativism.

However, it is far from clear that Hacking's interpretation of the example is correct. Hacking says,

(23) It was perfectly possible that he would win.

and this seems right. But assent to (23) is only problematic for the relativist if "possible" in it is an epistemic modal. And there are at least three reasons for supposing that it is not:

1. The embedded clause ("that he would win") is in the subjunctive mood. Epistemic uses of "possible" characteristically take the indicative. So, let's try forcing an epistemic reading by putting the clause in the indicative (rephrasing it a bit to avoid grammatical difficulties): "It was perfectly possible that he had the winning ticket." Now my willingness to accept the sentence vanishes. We know he did not, in fact, have the winning ticket, so we can't assert that it was possible that he did.

2. Suppose the universe evolves deterministically. Does that assumption make a difference to your willingness to accept (23)? If it does—and it does for me—that is strong evidence that the modal in (23) is alethic. For whether the universe evolves deterministically is independent of the truth of epistemic modal claims. Determinism is compatible with universal ignorance about how things will evolve.

3. We will certainly not accept "It *is* perfectly possible that his ticket was going to be the winning one." So if we accept (23), we will have a case like (13), which we argued was strictly speaking false.

If "possible" in (23) is not an epistemic modal, then Hacking's example does nothing to call into question the evidence supporting an assessment-sensitive semantics for epistemic modals.

8.2. *Ignorant assessors*

Dietz (2008) has observed that although our intuitions about retrospective assessments seem to support relativist semantics when the assessor knows *more* than the original asserter, they do not do so when the assessor knows *less*. Here is a variation on one of Dietz's examples. Suppose that yesterday I proved Theorem X and asserted "Theorem X must be true." Today, however, my memory has gone fuzzy. I recall that I was working on Theorem X, but I don't remember whether I proved it, refuted it, or did neither. If Solipsistic Relativism is correct, I should be able to say:

(24) If I said "Theorem X must be true" yesterday, then what I said was false.

For what I know now (at the context of assessment) leaves open the possibility that Theorem X is false.[30] And this seems bizarre. Intuitively, I don't have warrant to pronounce on the falsity of claims made by my better-informed past self, even when these claims contain epistemic modals.

If epistemic possibility is perspectival, this data suggests, it is *asymmetrically* perspectival. The truth of epistemic modal claims can depend on what is known by the assessor, but only if the assessor knows more than the original asserter.

---

[30] Note that given the account of "True" from Section 6.4, above, it does not matter whether we say "is false" or "was false" in (24).

One way to capture this asymmetry in the relativist account would be to complicate the semantics, amalgamating the asserter's and the assessor's knowledge into a single body of known facts with respect to which the epistemic modal is to be evaluated. The definition of truth of an occurrence of a sentence in context would then look like this (only the second bulleted item has changed from Section 6.3):

> An occurrence of a sentence Φ at a context c_U is true as assessed from a context c_A iff Φ is true at every point of evaluation $\langle c_U, w_{c_U}, i_{c_U+c_A}, a \rangle$, where
>
> - w_{c_U} = the world of c_U,
> - $i_{c_U+c_A}$ = the set of worlds that aren't excluded either by what is known (at c_A) by the agent of c_A or by what is known (at c_U) by the agent of c_U.[31]
> - a = an assignment of objects from the domain of c to the variables.

The revised account, which is a kind of HYBRID between Solipsistic Relativism and Solipsistic Contextualism, would agree with Solipsistic Relativism on every case where the assessor is not ignorant of any relevant facts that the utterer knows. This includes all of the cases we used to motivate the relativist account.

One consequence of the move to the hybrid account is that it makes it difficult to *reiterate* epistemic modal claims. Suppose Sally says (at time t)

(25) It's possible that Joe is six years old.

How can we make a claim with the same truth conditions as Sally's—one that is guaranteed to have the same truth value as hers relative to every context of assessment? For the Solipsistic Relativist, this task is easy:

(26) It's possible that Joe is six years old at t

will do the trick. For the Solipsistic Contextualist, it is equally easy:

(27) For all Sally knows at t, Joe is six years old at t.

But on the hybrid account, neither of these sentences can be used to make a claim that can be counted on to have the same truth value as Sally's claim relative to every context of assessment. For the truth of (26), as uttered by us and assessed by Judy, will depend in part on what is known by us, while the truth of (25), as uttered by Sally and assessed by Judy, will not depend at all on what is known by us. And since (27) is not assessment-sensitive, it cannot serve to reiterate Sally's assertion of (25), which is. Thus, on the hybrid account, epistemic modal claims are perspectival in the very strong sense that a claim made from one perspective cannot be reiterated in another, except by the use of semantic ascent or anaphoric devices.

A more promising response to the objection—and one less concessive to contextualism—would be to hold that whose knowledge is relevant to the evaluation

---

[31] Another alternative would be to consider what is known *distributively* by the speaker at c_U and the assessor at c_A: $i_{c_U+c_A}$ = the set of worlds that aren't excluded by what would be known by a rational agent who knew everything known at c_A by the agent of c_A and everything known at c_U by the agent of c_U.

of epistemic modals is *itself* determined by features of the context of assessment.[32] We might call this more flexible and less commital view FLEXIBLE RELATIVISM:[33]

> An occurrence of a sentence Φ at a context c_U is true as assessed from a context c_A iff Φ is true at every point of evaluation $\langle c_U, w_{c_U}, i_{c_A}, a \rangle$, where
>
> - w_{c_U} = the world of c_U,
> - i_{c_A} = the set of worlds that aren't excluded by the information that is relevant at c_A,
> - a = an assignment of objects from the domain of c to the variables.

This is still a relativist view, because it is features of the context of assessment, not the context of use, that determine which information state is relevant for the evaluation of epistemic modals. But it refrains from making any additional commitments about what information is relevant. If it were always the information possessed by the agent of c_A, Solipsistic Relativism would be correct; if it were always a combination of the information possessed by the agents of c_A and c_U, the hybrid view would be correct. Flexible Relativism refrains from hard-wiring either choice into the semantics, holding instead that the choice will depend on features of the context of assessment.

This response is analogous to Keith DeRose's defense of epistemic contextualism[34] in the face of cases where epistemic standards seem to depend on the situation of the *subject* of the knowledge attribution, not the attributor. DeRose notes that the contextualist account, properly understood, can handle such cases without modification:

there is nothing in contextualism to prevent a speaker's context from selecting epistemic standards appropriate to the subject's practical situation, even when the subject being discussed is no party to the speaker's conversation—which is good, because speakers often do select such standards when their conversational purposes call for it. On contextualism, the speaker's context does always call the shot. . . . But sometimes speakers' own conversational purposes call for employing standards that are appropriate to the practical situation of the far-away subjects they are discussing, and so the shot that the speakers' context calls can be, and often quite naturally will be, to invoke the standards appropriate to the practical situation faced by the subject being discussed. (DeRose 2005: 189)

The essential point here is that it is the *speaker's* context that determines whether it is appropriate to take into account the situation of the subject. So the view is genuinely contextualist, not a hybrid of a contextualist and a subject-centered view.

Flexible Relativism affords a similar kind of response to worries about ignorant assessors. The idea is that, although in some cases the speaker's information *is* relevant to the evaluation of epistemic modal claims, it is the *assessor's* context that determines when this (or any other information) is relevant. In contexts where the primary point of the assessment is critical evaluation of a speaker's assertion (as when one is trying

---

[32] The following section was added after Dietz (2008) was in press.

[33] Compare Flexible Contextualism, Section 6.2, above.

[34] The view that the extension of "knows" depends in part on contextually determined epistemic standards.

to determine whether the speaker might be a trustworthy source of information), the relevant information state will generally be a composite of the speaker's and the assessor's information. And in contexts where the assessor is simply trying to guide her own inquiry, the relevant information state may be entirely determined by her own knowledge. But in each case, it is features of the context of assessment that determine which information is relevant. So the view is genuinely relativist, and not a hybrid of relativism and contextualism.

9. Conclusion

None of the standard accounts of epistemic modals works very well. Contextualist accounts can't make sense of retrospective assessments, retractions, and disagreement, no matter how much contextual flexibility they introduce; expressivist accounts flounder on some of the same data and require a Ptolemaic account of embedded uses of modals. Each view can be motivated by pointing to the shortcomings of the other, but neither is very satisfying in its own right.

Relativism looks like a promising alternative to these standard views. It seems to explain all of the data that motivate the others views, but it can also handle the problem cases that they can't handle.

Substantial problems remain. There are many difficult issues that arise in the compositional semantics—for example, concerning the interaction of epistemic modals with temporal modifiers—but these face all of the standard accounts as well. The *special* problems for the relativist are philosophical problems—for example, the problem of making sense of the assessment-relative truth predicate. Those have been kept off the table here. The present paper is an advertisement for their importance, not just for philosophers, but for natural language semanticists of all stripes.

References

Blackburn, Simon (1984). *Spreading the Word* (Oxford: Oxford University Press).

DeRose, Keith (1991). "Epistemic possibilities", *Philosophical Review* 100(4): 581–605.

——(2005). "The ordinary language basis for contextualism, and the new invariantism", *Philosophical Quarterly* 55: 172–98.

Dietz, Richard (2008). "Epistemic modals and correct disagreement", in Manuel García-Carpintero and Max Kölbel (eds.), *Relative Truth* (Oxford: Oxford University Press), 239–264.

Egan, Andy (2007). "Epistemic modals, relativism, and assertion", *Philosophical Studies* 133: 1–22.

——Hawthorne, John, and Weatherson, Brian (2005). "Epistemic modals in context", in G. Preyer and P. Peter (eds.), *Contextualism in Philosophy* (Oxford: Oxford University Press), 131–68.

von Fintel, Kai, and Iatridou, Sabine (2003). "Epistemic containment", *Linguistic Inquiry* 34: 173–98.

Hacking, Ian (1967). "Possibility", *Philosophical Review*, 76: 143–68.

Hare, R. M. (1967). "Some alleged differences between imperatives and indicatives", *Mind* 76: 309–26.

Hawthorne, John (2004). *Knowledge and Lotteries* (Oxford: Oxford University Press).

Kaplan, David (1989). "Demonstratives: An essay on the semantics, logic, metaphysics, and epistemology of demonstratives and other indexicals", in Joseph Almog, John Perry, and Howard Wettstein (eds.), *Themes from Kaplan* (Oxford: Oxford University Press), 481–566.

Kolata, Gina (2005). "Amid Confusion, Journal Retracts Korean's Stem Cell Paper", *New York Times*, Dec. 31.

Lewis, David (1980). "Index, context, and content", in Stig Kanger and Sven Öhman (eds.), *Philosophy and Grammar* (Dordrecht: Reidel), 79–100.

MacFarlane, John (2003). "Future Contingents and Relative Truth", *Philosophical Quartely* 53: 321–36.

—— (2005a). "The assessment sensitivity of knowledge attributions", *Oxford Studies in Epistemology* 1: 197–233.

—— (2005b). "Making sense of relative truth", *Proceedings of the Aristotelian Society* 105: 321–39.

—— (2007). "Relativism and disagreement", *Philosophical Studies* 132: 17–31.

—— (2009). "Nonindexical contextualism", *Synthese* 166: 231–550.

Moore, G. E. (1962). *Commonplace Book, 1919–1953* (London: Allen and Unwin).

Price, Huw (1983). "Does 'probably' modify sense?", *Australasian Journal of Philosophy* 61: 396–408.

—— (1994). "Semantic minimalism and the Frege point", in S. L. Tsohatzidis (ed.), *Foundations of Speech Act Theory: Philosophical and Linguistic Perspectives* (London: Routledge), 132–55.

Stanley, Jason (2005). "Fallibilism and concessive knowledge attributions", *Analysis* 65: 126–31.

Tarski, Alfred (1944). "The semantic conception of truth and the foundations of semantics", *Philosophy and Phenomenological Research* 4: 341–76.

Teller, Paul (1972). "Epistemic possibility", *Philosophia* 2: 303–20.

Thomason, Richmond H. (1970). "Indeterminist time and truth-value gaps", *Theoria* 36: 264–81.

Yalcin, Seth (2007). "Epistemic modals", *Mind* 116: 983–1026.

6

Perspective in Taste Predicates and Epistemic Modals

Jonathan Schaffer

Imagine that Ann, asked to name her favorite treat, answers:

    1. Licorice is tasty

Imagine that Ben, having hidden some licorice in the cupboard, whispers to Ann:

    2. There might be licorice in the cupboard

What if any role is played by *perspective*—whom the licorice is tasty to, whose evidence allows for licorice in the cupboard—in the semantics of such sentences?

I will argue that taste predicates like "tasty" and "fun" project syntactically real *experiencer arguments*, which specify the perspective at issue. Thus 1 basically means [licorice is tasty *to*——], with the blank filled in by the speech context. Relative to the context in which Ann is asked to name her favorite treat, the blank is most naturally filled in with "Ann." But relative to a context in which Ann is asked to suggest a snack for both her and Ben, the blank is most naturally filled in as "both Ann and Ben." The perspective may be specified explicitly, as in:

    3. Licorice is tasty to me
    4. Licorice is tasty to everyone

But when the perspective is not specified explicitly, as in 1, it is supplied by the context.

I will also argue that modals like "might" and "must" feature *restrictor arguments* in logical form, which specify the perspective at issue. Thus 2 basically means [there might, *given*——, be licorice in the cupboard], with the blank filled in by the speech context (cf. Kratzer 1977). Relative to the context in which Ben is whispering to

Thanks to Rajesh Bhatt, Berit Brogaard, Herman Cappelen, Fabrizio Cariani, Jonathan Cohen, Amy Rose Deal, Andy Egan, Kai von Fintel, Valentine Hacquard, John Hawthorne, Kyle Johnson, Chris Kennedy, Angelika Kratzer, Peter Ludlow, John MacFarlane, Sarah Moss, Daniel Rothschild, Jason Stanley, Crispin Wright, and audiences at the ANU Epistemic Modality Conference, the St Andrews Adjectives Conference, and the Arché Contextualism and Relativism seminar.

Ann about her prospects for licorice, the blank is most naturally filled in with "what Ann knows." But relative to a context in which Ben is professing his own ignorance as to where he hid the licorice, the blank is most naturally filled in with "what Ben knows." The restrictor may be specified explicitly, as in:

5. There might, given what I know, be licorice in the cupboard
6. There might, given what any of us know, be licorice in the cupboard

But when the restrictor is not specified explicitly, as in 2, it is supplied by the context.

I will thus be defending the view—which I will label *meaning perspectivalism*—on which perspective plays a semantic role with respect to the proposition expressed by sentences with taste predicates or epistemic modals. Such propositions are *always perspective-specific*. And the version of meaning perspectivalism that I will defend is *contextualist*, insofar as it allows that sentences like 1 and 2 can express different propositions in different contexts, in ways traceable to the occurrence of the taste predicate and epistemic modal, and involving differences in the perspective at issue.

Meaning perspectivalism contrasts with *truth perspectivalism* (including *truth relativism*), on which perspective does not necessarily factor into the proposition expressed, but rather plays a role later in the semantic machinery, in truth evaluation. The truth perspectivalist holds that sentences like 1 and 2 may express perspective-neutral propositions. But she adds that a given proposition may be *true for Ann*, and yet *false for Ben*.

Meaning perspectivalism also contrasts with *absolutism*, on which perspective plays no semantic role whatsoever, either in the proposition expressed, or in its truth evaluation. The absolutist holds that sentences like 1 and 2 may express perspective-neutral propositions, and that such propositions are objectively true or false in a completely perspective-independent way.

Of course mixed views are possible. For instance, one might be a meaning perspectivalist for taste predicates, and an absolutist for epistemic modals. It is a substantive claim that perspective plays the same semantic role in both taste predicates and epistemic modals. Indeed it is already a substantive claim that perspective plays the same semantic role in different taste predicates like "tasty" and "fun." Though in defending meaning perspectivalism for taste predicates and for epistemic modals, I shall in effect be defending a unified approach.

Overview: In § 1 I will provide an overview of the space of theories about the semantic role of perspective, by contrasting meaning perspectivalism, truth perspectivalism, and absolutism (and relating these to contextualism and relativism). In § 2 I will defend a contextualist form of meaning perspectivalism for taste predicates, by arguing that these project syntactically real experiencer arguments. In § 3 I will turn to epistemic modals, and defend a contextualist form of meaning perspectivalism by arguing that modals feature restrictor arguments in logical form. And finally in § 4

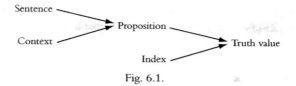

Fig. 6.1.

I will consider disagreement cases, which have been thought to trouble contextual-ist views, and even to require relativism. I will argue that the contextualist form of meaning perspectivalism I defend actually yields the best explanation of disagreement cases, once one moves beyond the one or two toy cases discussed in the literature, and considers the full range and dynamics of disagreements.

1. The Space of Theories

What if any role is played *by perspective* in the semantics of taste predicates and epistemic modals? It will help to situate this question within an orthodox Kaplanian seman-tical framework, on which a sentence type at a context expresses *a proposition*, and a proposition relative to an *index* takes a truth value (Kaplan 1989) (see Fig. 6.1).

This framework serves to usefully constrain where perspective might enter into the semantics. Consider a *bare sentence*—one which does not explicitly specify a perspective—such as:

1. Licorice is tasty
2. There might be licorice in the cupboard

Perspective can either enter the semantics of such bare sentences through the context and into the proposition expressed (as per meaning perspectivalism), or through the index and into truth evaluation (as per truth perspectivalism). There is no other entry point.

There are some useful analogies to be made between the space of theories con-cerning the semantic role of perspective, and the space of theories concerning the semantic role of *time*.[1] Consider a sentence that does not explicitly specify a time, such as:

7. It is raining

One might think that the time at issue can enter through the context and into the proposition expressed. This is *eternalism* (analogous to meaning perspectivalism), on which 7 basically means [it is raining *on*——], with the blank filled in by the speech context. Or one might think that the time at issue can enter through the index and into truth evaluation. This is *temporalism* (analogous to truth perspectivalism), on which 7 may express a time-neutral proposition, which might be *true on Monday*

---

[1] For more on the space of theories concerning the semantic role of time, see Richard (2003).

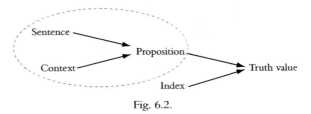

Fig. 6.2.

and yet *false on Tuesday*. And in principle one might also think—though this would be a deeply implausible view to hold for time—that 7 may express a time-neutral proposition, which is timelessly true or false. This is what the analogue of absolutism would be for time. (Absolutism is far more plausible in the case of perspective.)

In this section I will primarily focus on bare sentences like 1 and 2. In the assumed Kaplanian framework a full semantic treatment of such sentences must answer two questions. There is *the proposition question*, concerning what proposition the sentence in question expresses at a given context (§ 1.1). And there is *the index question*, concerning how the index is involved in evaluating propositions for truth (§ 1.2). There turn out to be important connections between the answers to these questions, which constrain the overall space of theories (§ 1.3). In particular, given the answer to the proposition question given by the meaning perspectivalist, the answer to the index question given by the truth perspectivalist will turn out to be unhelpful. If all the propositions of interest are perspective-specific, then adding a perspective coordinate into truth evaluation will do no work. I will conclude the discussion (§ 1.4) by connecting the theories under discussion to contextualism and relativism, which are related but strictly speaking orthogonal.

1.1. The proposition question

Imagine that Ann, asked to name her favorite treat, answers with 1. Imagine that Ben, having hidden some licorice in the cupboard, whispers 2 to Ann. What proposition is expressed by each these sentences in their respective contexts? In general, I am asking how the circled portion goes in Fig. 6.2 for bare taste sentences and bare modal sentences.

It is worth noting at the outset how this portion of the orthodox framework rules out certain views. (This is not to say that such views should be ruled out, but only to explain what assumptions would need to be waived to situate them.) First, there are views that deny that a sentence at a context always expresses a proposition. One example of such a view is *non-cognitivism,* according to which sentences like 1 and/or 2 are not in the business of expressing propositions at all.[2] A second example of this

---

[2] One prominent form of non-cognitivism for epistemic modals has them serving, not as elements of the proposition, but rather as extra-propositional *force markers* for a speech act weaker than assertion. Thus Hare claims: "We have a use for a way of volubly and loquaciously *not* making a certain statement; and perhaps

first sort of view is the *propositional radical* view, according to which sentences like 1 and/or 2 express gappy contents such as [licorice is tasty to——] and [there might, given——, be licorice in the cupboard], where the blanks are not filled in by the semantics.[3]

Second, there are views that deny that a sentence at a context always expresses just one proposition. These *are pluralist* views, on which sentences like 1 and/or 2 might express a plurality of propositions.[4] One pertinent example of a pluralist view is *content relativism*, on which sentences like 1 and/or 2 might express different propositions to different people. For instance, 1 might express [licorice is tasty to Ann] to Ann, and [licorice is tasty to Ben] to Ben.[5]

While I cannot possibly defend the orthodox framework on this point here, my defense of meaning perspectivalism will in effect yield the following partial defense: nothing in the semantic role of perspective requires deviating from orthodoxy in this respect. (Though I should confess that I would modify orthodoxy in two other respects: I think that there may be multiple speech contexts associated with a given sentence tokening (§ 1.4, § 4.2), and I don't think that an index is needed in the semantic machinery at all (§ 1.2). But these issues will prove largely independent of the current discussion. The meaning perspectivalist *can* be entirely orthodox.)

So, assuming that one and only one proposition is expressed by a sentence at a context, one might distinguish two main answers as to *which proposition is expressed*, for bare sentences like 1 and 2. The *perspective-neutralist* holds that, for a given bare sentence, there is a context relative to which it expresses a perspective-neutral proposition.[6] Note that her core claim is only about perspective-neutrality. She might hold that such sentences invariantly express *minimal propositions*, such as [licorice is tasty] and [there might be licorice in the cupboard]. But she might equally allow for further information in the proposition, as long as it does not concern perspective (and she might even allow for context sensitivity with respect to this further information). For instance, she might well allow that "tasty" takes a degree argument that is contextually supplied when left implicit: [licorice is tasty *to degree*——], as long as the degree argument is held to be unconnected to any perspective.[7]

there is one sense of 'may' in which it fulfills this function" (1967: 321). See § 3 for some arguments (from embeddings and from the univocity of modals) against this view.

[3] See Bach (1994) for further discussion of propositional radicals.

[4] See Soames (2005) for a defense of pluralism, based on the idea that the proposition expressed is only required to be "an acceptable completion" of a "propositional matrix."

[5] See Stephenson (2007), Egan (2009), and Weatherson (2009) for defenses of various forms of content relativism, and Egan, Hawthorne, and Weatherson (2005) for objections.

[6] Perspective-neutral propositions of the minimal sort are in the spirit of the insensitive semantics of Cappelen and Lepore (2005). Perspective-neutralism is also presupposed in the relativist framework of Wright (2001), and in the truth relativist semantics of Lasersohn (2005) and MacFarlane (2007).

[7] See Kennedy (2007) for a defense of degree arguments for gradable adjectives, and Glanzberg (2007) for a discussion of the idea that the scale associated with the degree argument might get constructed in ways that are connected to the perspective at issue.

Note also the quantification: the perspective-neutralist is only committed to the claim that there are perspective-neutral propositions expressed at *some* contexts. She can allow that there are other contexts relative to which bare sentences express perspective-specific propositions. She can thus be a full-blown contextualist, in allowing that sentences like 1 and 2 can express different propositions in different contexts, in ways traceable to the occurrence of the taste predicate and epistemic modal, and involving differences in the perspective at issue. (This is part of the reason why contextualism and relativism are compatible doctrines, and why contextualism is strictly orthogonal to the present debate: § 1.4.)

The alternative to perspective-neutralism is the *perspective-specific* view on which sentences like 1 and 2 express perspective-specific propositions at every context. (This is the view of the meaning perspectivalist: § 1.3.) The friend of perspective-specific propositions may or may not also posit further information. For instance, she might also posit a degree argument for "tasty", and so hold that 1 basically means [licorice is tasty *to degree* ———— *to* ————], with the degree and experiencer blanks filled in by the speech context.

The perspective-specific theorist will presumably trace the perspectival information, in a compositional way, to the occurrence of the taste predicate and the epistemic modal. There are at least two subtly different ways in which this might work. First, she might treat the terms in question ("tasty", "fun", "might", "must", etc.) as themselves *indexicals* (analogous to "I", "here", and "now"), whose reference is not determined by linguistic meaning alone, but for which context plays a reference determining role.[8] Second, she might treat the terms in question as *relational*, where the terms in question are themselves invariant in reference, but bring with them further arguments which context may evaluate. And a relationalist treatment further subdivides between *syntactic relationalism*, where the further argument is syntactically realized, and *semantic relationalism*, where the further argument is not syntactically realized but is still present in an "enriched" logical form.

While my own sympathies are with syntactic relationalism for taste predicates, and are divided between syntactic and semantic relationalism for epistemic modals, these distinctions will not matter for what follows. I am only concerned with defending the perspective-specific view generally. (I will use relationalist formulations for definiteness, but nothing should turn on this.) That said, it is important to distinguish these views, as they posit different logical forms. Thus a fuller taxonomy of answers to the proposition question (amongst those that preserve the orthodox idea of one and only one proposition per context) would be as shown in Fig. 6.3.

---

[8] In this vein, DeRose (1991) defends the related view that "possible" in the epistemic sense functions as a context-sensitive term. Rothschild and Segal (2009) provide an indexicalist semantics for "red" and a class of related predicates, which could naturally be extended to taste predicates.

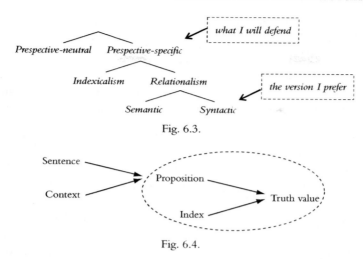

Fig. 6.3.

Fig. 6.4.

1.2. The index question

Suppose that one has answered the proposition question. One has determined whether bare taste claims and bare epistemic modal claims sometimes express perspective-neutral propositions, or always express perspective-specific propositions. It remains to ask how these (and other) propositions are to be evaluated for truth. I am now asking how the circled portion in Fig. 6.4 works.

An index is some n-tuple of coordinates. In Kaplan's (1989) formal fragment, propositions are evaluated for truth relative to world and time coordinates $<w, t>$. Moreover, the positions of these coordinates are initialized by the speech context. Operators may shift the positions of these coordinates (e.g. a modal operator may shift the position of the world coordinate). But an operator-free proposition expressed at $<w_i, t_j>$ will be evaluated for truth relative to $<w_i, t_j>$.[9]

There are thus two subquestions of the index question that will prove useful to separate. First, there is *the number subquestion*, concerning which coordinates are listed in the index. Second, there is *the setting subquestion*, concerning how the positions of these coordinates are initialized.

As to the number subquestion, there are two main views to distinguish. The *baseline* view does not posit any coordinates that provide a perspective. What (if any) coordinates it does posit will not matter here, so Table 6.1 shows four versions of the baseline view that I will not further distinguish.

For definiteness I will follow orthodoxy and invoke the Kaplanian $<w, t>$ two-tuple version of the baseline view.[10]

---

[9] Kaplan himself was willing to add further coordinates to the index (1989: 504). He uses $<w, t>$ pairs solely because his formal fragment was equipped with only modal and temporal operators.

[10] I myself am a schmentencite but cannot possibly defend this view here. The interested reader might consult King (2003) for doing without all but worlds, and then consider the systems of von Stechow (2002)

Table 6.1

Lewis (1980)	the index is a world, time, location, and precision four-tuple $<w, t, l, p>$
Kaplan (1989)	the index is a world, time two-tuple $<w, t>$
King (2003)	the index is just a world one-tuple $<w>$
schmentencite	the index is a zero-tuple (propositions are true or false *simpliciter*)

The alternative to the baseline view is *the supplemented view* which adds a *judge coordinate* to provide a perspective.[11] (This is the view of the truth perspectivalist: § 1.3.) Given a Kaplanian $<w, t>$ baseline, the supplementer holds that the index is a $<w, t, j>$ triple. A proposition true at $<w_m, t_n, j_{Ann}>$ but false at $<w_m, t_n, j_{Ben}>$ may be said to be *true for Ann* but *false for Ben* (relative to $<w_m, t_n>$).

Turning to the setting subquestion as to how the positions of these coordinates are initialized, everyone in the debate agrees that the settings of the baseline coordinates are initialized from the speech context. But what about the alleged judge coordinate of the supplemented view? If the judge coordinate is treated on the precedent of the world and time coordinates it too will be initialized from the speech context. Call this *the speaker view*. On the speaker view, absent any judge-shifting operators, propositions are evaluated for truth relative to the perspective of the speaker.[12] (This is the view of the *non-indexical contextualist*: § 1.3.)

But *truth relativists* (MacFarlane 2003 and 2005a; Lasersohn 2005; Egan, Hawthorne, and Weatherson 2005, *inter alia*) want propositions to be evaluated for truth not from the perspective of the speaker but from the perspective of the *assessor*. What is radical about truth relativism is not so much the added judge coordinate, but rather the idea that the default setting of this coordinate is to the assessor. Call this *the assessor view*. While the supplemented view challenges the baseline answer to the number subquestion, the assessor view further challenges the generality of the "default to the speech context" rule with respect to the setting subquestion.[13] Thus a fuller taxonomy of answers to the index question would be as shown in Fig. 6.5.

and Schlenker (2005a) and arguments of Percus (2000) and Speas (2004b) according to which verbs syntactically project not just a time but also a world argument. See Schaffer (forthcoming and MS) for further discussion, and Cappelen and Hawthorne (2009) for a different version of the view that propositions are true or false *simpliciter*, which does not invoke world arguments.

[11] The term 'judge' is from Lasersohn (2005: 663). MacFarlane (2007) invokes *standards of judgement*, and Egan (2007) speaks *of individuals* (who presumably serve as the judges). Nothing in what follows will turn on this distinction. In the main text I will follow Lasersohn's terminology for the sake of definiteness.

[12] Strictly speaking all the speaker-view is committed to is that the position of the judge coordinate is initialized from the speech context. This could work by taking in the speaker's intentions to speak of a given perspective (not necessarily her own), rather than automatically taking in the speaker's own perspective.

[13] MacFarlane (this volume: §5.1) describes the truth relativist position in terms of *bi-contextuality*, with the idea that the default setting of $<w_{utter}, t_{utter}, j_{assess}>$ is arrived at by piecing together bits of two proper contexts $<w_{utter}, t_{utter}, j_{utter}>$ and $<w_{assess}, t_{assess}, j_{assess}>$ This is how he generates the $<w_{utter}, t_{utter}, j_{assess}>$ default. (The other positions of the two proper contexts—$<..., j_{utter}>$ and $<w_{assess}, t_{assess}, ...>$—do no further work.)

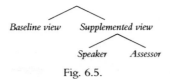

Fig. 6.5.

1.3. The space of theories

Answers to the proposition and index questions are not independent. The primary connection of interest is that the perspective-specific view of propositions renders the supplemented view of the index unusable. Consider a given perspective-specific proposition, such as [licorice is tasty to Ann]. All the perspectival information is already provided. Whether or not such a proposition is true should be constant across any alleged perspectives of evaluation. No matter how Ben or Claire or anyone else views licorice, whether [licorice is tasty for Ann] is "true for Ann", "true for Ben", or "true for Claire" (etc.) should depend only on how Ann views licorice.

The analogy with the semantics of time may be useful. Consider a given time-specific proposition, such as [it is raining on Monday]. Whether or not such a proposition is true should be constant across any times of evaluation. No matter what the weather is like on Tuesday or any other time, whether [it is raining on Monday] is true on Tuesday or Wednesday or five hundred years from now (etc.) should depend only on what the weather is like on Monday. [14]

More precisely, if the friend of the supplemented view thinks that Ann has expressed the proposition [licorice is tasty to Ann], and treats [to Ann] as an intensional operator serving to fix the position of the judge coordinate on Ann (Lasersohn 2005: 666, 668), then she will find her judge coordinate fixed on Ann *at every point of assessment* (Lasersohn 2009: 362). So it will make no difference whatsoever as to which perspective such a proposition is evaluated from for truth. The posit of a judge coordinate will thus be unusable, in that it will do no semantic work whatsoever.

Thus one reaches the space of theories shown in Table 6.2 (with the 'X'-ed box eliminated because the supplemented view of the index requires perspective-neutral propositions to do any work).

Moreover, truth perspectivalism divides between the speaker and assessor answers to the setting subquestion of the index question. The speaker answer yields the theory

---

[14] In this respect my argument for meaning perspectivalism mirrors one of the standard arguments for eternalism, which invokes the semantic treatment of tense to argue that all propositions are time-specific (cf. Partee 1973). As King concludes: "[I]f the proper way to treat tenses is *not* as index shifting sentence operators, then there is no need for temporal coordinates in indices of evaluation" (2003: 223).

Table 6.2

	Perspective-specific propositions	Perspective-neutral propositions
Baseline view of the index	Meaning perspectivalism	Absolutism
Supplemented view	X	Truth perspectivalism

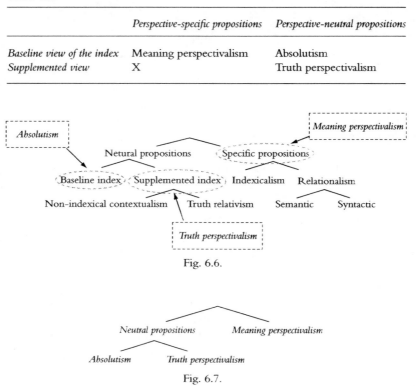

Fig. 6.6.

Fig. 6.7.

sometimes labeled *non- indexical contextualism*, with a given perspective-neutral proposition being evaluated for truth relative to a supplemented index (e.g. $<w, t, j>$), with
j defaulting to the speaker.[15] The assessor answer yields *truth relativism*.[16]

Thus one reaches the overall theory tree shown in Fig. 6.6. Lopping off
the branches I am lumping together, and re-labeling as per the boxes yields
Fig. 6.7.

Recall that this is only the space of theories arising on the assumption that each
sentence expresses one and only one proposition per context (§ 1.1). To make room
for non-cognitiuism, content relativism, and other approaches that reject this bit of
orthodoxy, one would need a lot more tree.[17]

---

[15] Non-indexical contextualism is introduced (though not defended) by MacFarlane (2009).
Brogaard (2008) defends a version of this view for moral claims.

[16] See Lasersohn (2005) and MacFarlane (2007) for developed versions of truth relativism.

[17] Note that meaning perspectivalism and truth perspectivalism are only characterized under the assumption that a sentence at a context expresses one and only one proposition. If this bit of orthodoxy is rejected,
there is room for a view that holds *both* (i) that every proposition at issue is perspective-specific, but that (ii)

1.4. Contextualism and relativism?

The reader expecting discussion of the debate between contextualists and relativists may wonder at the idiosyncratic way I have mapped out the space of theories. (Though I hope that the reader familiar with the debate over the semantic role of time will see the parallel.) There are three main reasons why I have *not* tried to set up any division between contextualists and relativists. The first and most important reason is that there is no division between contextualism and relativism. The theories are compatible. The relativist can allow that bare taste sentences and bare epistemic modal sentences (like 1 and 2) express different propositions in different contexts, in ways traceable to the occurrence of the taste predicate and epistemic modal, and involving differences in the perspective at issue (§ 1.1). She need only add that such bare sentences can also express perspective-neutral propositions in some contexts (and that propositions are evaluated for truth via a judge-supplemented index, with the judge defaulting to the assessor). She would thereby be a relativistic contextualist. Of course most contextualists are also anti-relativists, and most relativists are also anti-contextualists, but such an opposition is not required by relativism or by contextualism *per se*.

The second reason I have not tried to set up any division between contextualists and relativists is that I fear that "contextualism" may be losing its usefulness as a label for doing semantics. The label "non-indexical contextualism" has become attached to what I am calling the speaker version of truth perspectivalism, but this theory is not contextualist in any standard sense. At least as I use "contextualism" (drawn from the literature on the semantics of "know"), it is basically a claim that a single sentence can express different propositions in different contexts. More precisely, contextualism for taste predicates (/epistemic modals) is the view that a single taste (/epistemic modal) sentence can express different propositions in different contexts, in ways traceable to the occurrence of the taste predicate (/epistemic modal), and involving differences in the perspective at issue. The view labeled "non-indexical contextualism" makes no such claim. I see how this view shares certain underlying motivations with contextualism (for instance in being speaker-centric rather than assessor-centric), but the views work quite differently from the perspective of the semantic machinery. So I think it would be misleading to speak of contextualism and the view labeled "non-indexical contextualism" as species of a common semantic genus.

Third, I also doubt that "relativism" is a useful label for doing semantics. I am more than happy to speak of "truth relativism" and "content relativism", and consider each view on its own merits. But, while these views may share certain underlying motivations (being assessor-centric), they too work quite differently from the perspective of the semantic machinery. So I think that it would be misleading to treat them as species of a common semantic genus.

propositions are evaluated for truth via a judge-supplemented index. Indeed content relativism—at least in the form developed in Stephenson (2007)—upholds both views.

Indeed my own view of the semantics—while certainly contextualist—is consistent with content relativism. In this vein, Stephenson (2007)—who is a content relativist for taste predicates (though not for epistemic modals)—agrees that there is perspectival information specified in the proposition. She just adds a new way for such information to be specified, by positing a new phonologically null element PRO_{judge}, whose denotation is read off an assessor sensitive judge coordinate. Stephenson allows PRO_{judge} as one possible contextually supplied value for the syntactically realized experiencer argument of taste predicates, and one may extend her view by allowing [what PRO_{judge} knows] as one possible contextually supplied value for the restrictor argument for epistemic modals. For present purposes I have no dispute with such a view. That said, to the extent that content relativism is motivated by disagreement cases, I will in effect be arguing that one can already handle disagreement cases well enough without any of the added machinery of content relativism, and so without a need to posit anything like PRO_{judge}, specify the constraints on its distribution, add a judge coordinate and the assessor defaulting needed to interpret it, or allow for the open-ended plurality of propositions per single sentence-context pair that results (§ 4.3).[18]

Moreover, while I myself am opposed to both truth relativism and content relativism, there is a form of relativism that I would not necessarily oppose: *context relativism*. According to context relativism, a given sentence tokening may be assigned a different speech context by different assessors. For instance, if the preacher stands before Ann, Ben, Claire, and Dave, and says "Jesus loves you" (with singular "you"), context relativism has it that Ann should interpret this sentence relative to a speech context in which she is the one and only addressee, Ben should likewise interpret this sentence relative to a speech context in which he is the one and only addressee, etc.[19] Though note that this form of relativism does not require any judge coordinate in the index, or any sense in which a given proposition may be true for Ann but false for Ben, or any deviation from the thesis that a sentence-context pair generates a unique proposition. This is just to point out yet another way in which the label "relativism" may pick out theories that look extremely different at the level of the semantic machinery.

That said, there is at least the following point of connection between my taxonomy and 'contextualism versus relativism.' The meaning perspectivalist will almost certainly be a contextualist. After all, given that she holds that perspective enters the semantics of bare sentences through the context, she will almost certainly

---

[18] A different version of content relativism, discussed in Egan (2009), also agrees that there is perspectival information specified in the proposition. It just allows that sometimes what might be expressed is an incomplete propositional radical, which different assessors will fill in different ways. And see Weatherson (2009) for a subtly different third form of content relativism. It is a nice question for all these forms of content relativism as to what constrains the distribution of their silent assessor-sensitive element.

[19] See Egan (2009) for further discussion of these matters.

allow for contextual sensitivity. Strictly speaking she need not. She could in principle hold that every single context supplies the very same perspective (perhaps God's?). But I take it that any plausible form of meaning perspectivalism will be contextualist, and the form of meaning perspectivalism I defend is paradigmatically contextualist.

2. Meaning Perspectivalism for Taste Predicates

Imagine that Ann, asked to name her favorite treat, answers:

1. Licorice is tasty

Imagine that Claire, asked to name her favorite amusement park ride, answers:

8. Roller coasters are fun

I will now argue that these two taste predicates ("tasty" and "fun" respectively) project syntactically real *experiencer arguments*, which specify the perspective at issue. Given that such arguments are assigned specific values by the semantics at every context, meaning perspectivalism follows. Relative to any context, the proposition expressed by 1 and the proposition expressed by 8 will involve a specified experiencer.

Four qualifications should be made from the start. First, I should confess that I do not know exactly what defines a taste predicate. I will follow Lasersohn (2005: 645) in assuming that "tasty" and "fun" are kindred in this respect, and remaining neutral on what (if any) other predicates are of this kind. If there is to be a natural lexical kind of which "tasty" and "fun" are paradigmatic members, it might be *adjectives derived from experiencer verbs*.[20] Thus "tasty" comes from the verb "to taste", which comes from the Latin "taxtare", meaning *to evaluate*. "Fun" comes from the Middle English "to fon", meaning *to befool*. (Here is already some *prima facie* reason to suspect experiencer arguments. Given that experiencer verbs project experiencer arguments, and that the verbal structure survives within its adjectival derivative, one should expect experiencer arguments within the adjectival derivatives. At any rate I will argue that this is what one finds with "tasty" and "fun." The experiencer argument is still alive and kicking, even when left implicit.)

Second, I take no stance on how to evaluate covert experiencer arguments, save to piously intone that these are evaluated by context. Presumably the contextual evaluation of covert arguments is something we are stuck with in any case, so at least no new mysteries are created. There may well be stereotypical conventions associated with certain covert positions.[21] Indeed, I suspect that covert experiencer

---

[20] Thanks to Peter Ludlow for suggesting this point.

[21] *Point of clarification*: not all covert arguments need behave in the same way. For instance, the covert subjects of passives and the covert object of "Pam ate" are both existentially closed, while the covert object of "Pain noticed" is deictic. The covert experiencer of "John is an enemy" and of "licorice is tasty" can both come as either free variables or as closed under various quantifiers. One diagnostic for possible settings is negation. Thus "the ship was not sunk" seems to only allow the interpretation that the ship was not sunk *by anyone*. This suggests that the subject of the passive must be existentially closed (below where the negation

arguments are stereotypically set to either (i) the speaker, via a covert *de se* pronoun (PRO), or (ii) the typical person, via a covert *generic* pronoun (PRO$_{ARB}$). Though sufficient contextual cues can override the stereotypical settings. In particular, embedding under attitude verbs *tends* to shift the experiencer to the subject of the lowest attitude. Thus in both "Ann thinks that licorice is tasty" and "Ben thinks that Ann thinks that licorice is tasty", the most natural reading has the experiencer being Ann.

Third, when I render these experiencer arguments overtly, I will use "to"-phrases with "tasty" (e.g. "tasty to Ann") and "for"-phrases with "fun" (e.g. "fun for Ben"). Some readers may prefer other renderings. I think there is a fair amount of idiolectical variation among English speakers on this score. In any case, I take both "to" and "for" to function purely as case assigners (e.g. "to Ann" is the way English renders "Ann" in the dative case), which get deleted in semantic evaluation. Basically "to" and "for" are just different stylistic variants for slipping past the case filter.

Fourth, I will be using four diagnostics to test for covert experiencer arguments in bare taste claims like 1 and 8. These are: the existence of bound readings where the argument in question is bound to a quantifier (§ 2.1), the licensing of overt counterparts where the experiencer argument goes explicit (§ 2.2), the possibility of using the experiencer argument to control the subject of infinitival clauses (§ 2.3), and the existence of sluicing constructions targeting the experiencer argument (§ 2.4). It should be acknowledged from the start that all of these diagnostics are defeasible, embody controversial theoretical assumptions, and require judgments that may be contested. Such is unavoidable in empirical inquiry. The *best-case result* is when all the diagnostics converge. I will be claiming just such a best-case result for taste claims.

2.1. The binding test

One leading diagnostic for covert arguments is the possibility of binding them (Partee 1989; Stanley 2000). To see the binding test in action, start with pronouns. Thus consider:

9. Every boy called his mother

9 has a natural reading—the bound reading—on which it basically says that boy$_1$ called boy$_1$'s mother, boy$_2$ called boy$_2$'s mother, etc. The denotation of "his" is bound to the quantifier. On this reading there needn't be a single mother who received all the calls. Each mother only needs to have received as many calls as she has boys. (The bound reading is not the only possible reading of 9. There is also for instance the deictic reading on which there is a single mother who received all the calls—imagine the speaker pointing to a particular boy while saying "his." What is relevant is only that the bound reading is a possible reading of the sentence.)

can reach). But "licorice is not tasty" seems to allow multiple interpretations, including: licorice is not tasty *to me*, licorice is not tasty *to the typical person*, licorice is not tasty *to anyone*, etc. This suggests that the experiencer can come free or closed under generic and universal quantifiers, etc. I am indebted to Kyle Johnson for discussion here.

Now consider "local." According to Partee (1989), "local" projects a potentially covert argument [local *to* ——]. One major source of evidence for such an argument is the prospect of a bound interpretation for sentences such as:

10. Every girl went to a local playground

10 has an interpretation on which it means that $girl_1$, went to a playground local to $girl_1$, $girl_2$ went to a playground local to $girl_2$, etc. On this reading there needn't be a single locale featuring all of these playgrounds. $Girl_1$, could have been in Canberra and $girl_2$ could have been in Reykjavik, as long as $girl_1$ went to a Canberra playground and $girl_2$ went to a Reykjavik playground. The evidence for "local" providing location-specific information via a covert argument is that it provides the best explanation for the existence of the bound reading of 10.

To see that something special is happening with "local" that allows for a bound reading, it might help to contrast 10 with:

11. Every man is mortal

11 does not have any natural bound reading, or at least any that I can hear. That is, there is no natural reading of 11 on which the mortality in question shifts as one cycles through the quantifier domain. This is presumably because "mortal" does not project any covert arguments, or at least none of the relevant sort to be bound by the quantifier phrase.

The standard view of binding is that it is syntactic relation, requiring the right syntactic environment (basically, co-indexing and c-command: Chomsky 1981). On this view the possibility of bound readings is excellent evidence for the syntactic reality of the argument in question. And likewise the impossibility of binding—assuming that the proper syntactic environment can be constructed—is excellent evidence for syntactic irreality. But alternative semantic views of binding have also been proposed (cf. Schlenker 2005b). For present purposes I will remain neutral as between syntactic and semantic views of binding. I only assume that bound readings require the existence of arguments in logical form, whether or not these arguments are syntactically projected. In particular I assume that bound readings reveal the *pre-existence* of the argument in the question in the material under the quantifier, as opposed to the spontaneous creation of new material. In a slogan, I assume that the quantifier reveals structure rather than creating it.[22]

Thus one way to test whether taste predicates project experiencer arguments—as the meaning perspectivalist maintains—is to see if there are taste claims with a bound experiencer reading. I think the result is a fairly clear *yes*. Start with "tasty." To set the scene, imagine that the Smiths go out for ice cream. Ma only likes chocolate, Pa only likes vanilla, Suzy only likes rum raisin, and Billy only likes mint chip. Today they are in luck. Each finds their favorite flavor. So Ma, by way of celebrating their good fortune, says:

---

[22] Though see Recanati (2004) for the claim that the higher quantifer can bring into logical form the very arguments it then binds.

    12. Everyone got something tasty

12 has a natural bound reading relative to Ma's speech context, which basically says that Ma got something tasty to Ma, Pa got something tasty to Pa, etc. There needn't be a single thing which is tasty to all of them (indeed, the story builds in that there is no single thing tasty to all of them).

    To see that something special is happening with "tasty" that allows for a bound reading, it might help to contrast 12 with:

    13. Everyone got something frozen

Imagine Ma expressing her pleasure that no one got any melted ice cream soup. 13 may well be true relative to such a context. But 13 (like 11) does not have a natural bound reading, at least to my ears. That is, there is no natural reading of 13 on which the frozenness varies across family members, because there is no sense in the notion of "frozen to Ma" or "frozen to Pa."[23] For other examples without a bound reading, consider:

    14. Everyone got something round
    15. Everyone got something artificially sweetened

Hence I conclude that "tasty" bears a potentially covert experiencer argument. This is the best explanation for the bound reading of 12, and the contrast between 12 and 13–15 as to the availability of a bound reading.

    With "fun", imagine that the Smiths go to the amusement park. Ma only likes Ferns wheels, Pa only likes roller coasters, Suzy only likes bumper cars, and Billy only likes merry-go-rounds. Fortunately this amusement park has it all. So they split up and happily do their own thing. On the drive home, Pa, remarking on what a great outing they had, says:

    16. Everyone did something fun

16 has a natural bound reading relative to Pa's speech context, which basically says that Ma did something fun for Ma, Pa did something fun for Pa, etc. There needn't be a single thing which is fun for all of them (indeed, the story builds in that there is no single thing fun for all of them).

    For a contrast without a bound reading, consider:

    17. Everyone did something legal

17 may well be true relative to Pa's speech context. Thus imagine Pa expressing his relief that Suzy and Billy refrained from their usual delinquencies. But 17 does not support any natural sort of bound reading. Further contrasts could be obtained with examples such as:

---

[23] *Caveat*: given the presence of a degree argument, there may be a somewhat unnatural but still possible bound reading which targets the degree argument. But there should at least be a clear contrast between 12 and 13, as to whether or not there is a natural bound reading available.

18. Everyone did something sedentary

19. Everyone did something environmental

Hence I conclude that "fun" bears a potentially covert experiencer argument. This is the best explanation for the bound reading of 16, and the contrast between 16 and 17–19 as to the availability of a bound reading. Overall it seems that both "tasty" and "fun" pattern with "local" and with pronouns in allowing bound readings.

There are several potential confounds to consider. But I will just address what might be the most obvious potential confound, which is that the bound argument might be a situation argument rather than an experiencer argument. For instance, one might maintain that the bound reading on 12 is basically: Ma was in a Ma-containing situation of getting something tasty, Pa was in a Pa-containing situation of getting something tasty, etc.

I believe in situation arguments and believe that they can be bound. I just do not believe that this can be what explains the relevant bound readings of 12 and 16, for two main reasons. First, such an alternative could not possibly explain the contrasts between 12 and 13–15, or between 16 and 17–19, as presumably every single one of these cases involves a situation argument. Taste predicates seem to be adding something special, and this needs to be explained. Second, one can append higher adverbial quantifiers binding the situation argument, as per:

20. Usually everyone gets something tasty

Thus imagine 20 uttered by Billy in answer to Ma's utterance of 12, to indicate that this sort of outcome does not call for celebration. One natural way of reading 20, relative to Billy's speech context, requires us to look across situations and see whether or not most of these situations involve everyone getting something tasty. This requires assessing the bound reading of "everyone got something tasty" *at a single situation*.

2.2. The licensing test

A second diagnostic for covert arguments is the possibility of making them explicit. To see the licensing test in action, consider passives such as:

21. The ship was sunk

21 is sometimes thought to feature a covert agent argument, and one way to argue for this is to argue that there are overt counterparts of 21 in which the agent is made explicit:

22. The ship was sunk by the pirates

To see that something special is happening with passives that licenses agent-specifying "by"-clauses, it might help to contrast 21 with an unaccusative construction:

23. The ship sank

The unaccusative construction does not license an agent-specifying "by"-clause:

24. *The ship sank by the pirates[24]

Arguably, the best explanation for the contrast between the presence of overt agent-specifying counterparts of 21, and the absence of such counterparts for 23, is that 21 involves a covert agent argument but 23 does not.[25]

Thus one way to test for whether taste predicates project experiencer arguments—as the meaning perspectivalist maintains—is to see if there are taste claims with overt experiencer arguments. This is only a one-way test, in that the presence of overt counterparts would indicate the presence of an experiencer argument, but the absence of an overt counterpart would not necessarily indicate the absence of an experiencer argument. The experiencer argument might be required to remain unarticulated, like the subject argument of infinitival clauses (PRO). Indeed one plausible view of the "by"-clause in 22 is not as saturating the subject argument, but rather as an adjunct phrase that is required to be co-referential with the (still covert) agent argument. Though note that such a view still posits a syntactically realized covert agent argument for passives.

It might *seem* evident that there are overt counterparts for bare taste claims. Thus recall:

3. Licorice is tasty to me
4. Licorice is tasty to everyone

And likewise:

25. Roller coasters are fun for me
26. Roller coasters are fun for the whole family

But what is not yet obvious is that these experiencer phrases provide experiencer *arguments*. Thus the absolutist may well regard the experiencer phrases as merely optional adjuncts, and the truth perspectivalist may well regard the experiencer phrases, not as arguments of "tasty" or "fun", but rather as intensional operators that shift the position of the judge coordinate (Lasersohn 2005: 666, 668). So to use the test from overt counterparts properly, we will need to consider the best interpretation of the experiencer phrases.

The experiencer phrases do not seem to be adjuncts, as the absolutist maintains. It should be acknowledged that there are no uncontroversial tests for arguments versus adjuncts, and that the distinction itself faces some difficult cases.[26] But at least one decent test concerns whether another adjunct phrase can be interposed in the middle. This is not permitted with an argument, but is with an adjunct. (To apply the test one

---

[24] There is a grammatical reading of 24 which should be disregarded, in which the "by"-clause is interpreted, not as specifying who sank the ship, but rather in specifying the location of the sinking (e.g. "the ship sank nearby the pirates").

[25] For some further discussion see Bhatt and Pancheva (2006: especially 556–9).

[26] Among the difficult cases for the argument versus adjunct distinction are benefactors. Thus compare: "Billy built a slingshot", "Billy built Suzy a slingshot", and "Billy built a slingshot for Suzy." The status of the benefactor (Suzy) in these constructions is at best unclear. See Ludlow (2008: especially § 1) for a skeptical take on the distinction.

already needs to have judged that the interposed phrase is an adjunct. So this is circular as a general test for arguments versus adjuncts, but it can be used on a case-by-case basis given a background agreement on the status of the interposed phrase.) For an especially clear illustration of this test, consider "student." This is a relational noun. It takes an argument, as given in "of history" or "of medicine." The phrase "with a nose ring" is an adjunct. Or so befits the following pattern:

27. The student of history with the nose ring failed
28. *The student with the nose ring of history failed

The best explanation for the badness of 28 is that it involves an attempt to interpose the adjunct phrase "with the nose ring" between "student" and its argument "of history." [27]

To apply this form of argument to experiencer phrases, I will assume that "when sober" serves as an adjunct phrase for "tasty" and for "fun" (similar results can be obtained with "when dancing" and "at home"). Now consider:

29. Licorice is tasty to me when sober
30. *Licorice is tasty when sober to me
31. Roller coasters are fun for me when sober
32. *Roller coasters are fun when sober for me

It should be acknowledged that the contrast between 29 and 30, as well as between 31 and 32, is not quite as clear (to my ears at least) as the contrast between 27 and 28. But what is relevant is that there is still a perceptible contrast. So I think there is some good evidence that the experiencer phrases are not merely adjuncts, on grounds that interposition of an adjunct is at least somewhat bad.

Moreover, these phrases do not seem to be intensional operators, as the truth perspectivalist maintains. First, intensional operators should not be restricted as to which sentences they can operate on. So we should find that 3 is equally as acceptable as:

33. *Licorice contains anise to me
34. *Roller coasters are at amusement parks for me [28]

The contrast between 3 and 33, and between 8 and 34, are akin to the contrasts seen between the passive and unaccusative constructions in 22 and 24, with respect to the licensing of agent-specifying "by"-phrases. In both cases a special story seems required about the argument structure of the constructions in question (viz., passives involve agent arguments, taste predicates involve experiencer arguments). A general story about intensional operators seems to miss the crucial contrasts. The friend of the intensional operator story can of course claim that the experiencer phrases in 33 and 34 are *vacuous* intensional operators, given that the sentences embedded happen

---

[27] This test, in the first instance, concerns syntactic adjaceny rather than semantic role. But it is reasonable to assume that syntactic adjacency and semantic argument status are at least typically correlated.

[28] 34 has an unintended but acceptable (if bizarre) reading which should be disregarded here, on which it says that roller coasters are placed at amusement parks for my benefit.

to be true or false in a constant way across perspectives. But at most this should make 33 and 34 conversationally infelicitous. To the extent that one can have discerning intuitions about these matters, I would say that 33 and 34 are grammatically odd, or at any rate not merely conversationally infelicitous.

A second reason to reject an intensional operator construal of experiencer phrases is that intensional operators iterate in a characteristic way, while arguments do not iterate at all (once the argument place is saturated, no additional argument of the sort in question is licensed). Thus consider:

    35. *Licorice is tasty to Ann to Ben
    36. *Roller coasters are fun for Ann for Ben for Claire

If these experiencer phrases were intensional operators, then 33 should basically say that by Ben's light, licorice is tasty by Ann's light (that is, that Ben holds that Ann holds licorice to be tasty). And 34 should basically say that by Claire's light, according to Ben, roller coasters are fun by Ann's lights (that is, that Claire holds that Ben holds that Ann holds that roller coasters are fun). Nothing like these readings seems available.

2.3. The control test

A third diagnostic for covert arguments is the possibility of having them control the covert subject of infinitival clauses. This test packs in two widely accepted but heavy theoretical assumptions. The first assumption is that infinitival clauses involve a phonologically null but syntactically realized subject argument (PRO). The second assumption is that PRO is subject to relations of *control*, where the controllers must be syntactically realized, and must be arguments of the predicate that select the infinitival clause.[29]

To see the control test in action, consider pronouns and agents of passives, as per:

    37. He tried to eat all the ice cream
    38. The ship was sunk to collect the insurance

In 37, the pronoun is controlling the covert subject of "to eat all the ice cream." In 38 it seems as if the person who sank the ship is the one aiming to collect the insurance. This provides further evidence for a (syntactically realized) agent argument, as controlling the covert subject of "to collect the insurance." Indeed, just as in the passive of 22 and the unaccusative of 24, there is a robust contrast between the passive of 38 and the unaccusative variant:

    39. *The ship sank to collect the insurance [30,31]

---

[29] See Landau (2000) for further discussion of these matters.

[30] Again there is an unintended and bizarre regarding to be disregarded. The reading in question is one in which the ship, as an intentional agent, submerged itself for the money.

[31] Another related contrast pertaining to the existence of covert agent argument for passives: "the ship was sunk deliberately" versus *"the ship sank deliberately." I thank Rajesh Bhatt for discussion on these issues.

So one way to test whether taste predicates project experiencer arguments is to see if there are bare taste claims on which the experiencer controls PRO. I think the result is a very clear *yes*, at least for "fun."[32] Thus consider:

40. It is fun to dance

The natural reading—indeed perhaps the only reading—of 40 involves exactly the sort of control sought, where the person doing the dancing is the person who experiences the fun (cf. Epstein 1984). Thus Bhatt and Pancheva describe the PRO found in 40 as "controlled by a non-overt benefactive/experiencer argument of fun" (2006: 574).

To see that "fun" is doing something special—namely projecting an experiencer argument—which is generating the control relation, contrast 40 with:

41. It is popular to dance

41 simply comments on the social regard of the practice of dancing. There is no control reading of 41, presumably because "popular" does not project any argument that could control PRO. Hence I conclude that the best explanation for the control reading of 40, and the contrast between 40 and 41, is that taste predicates project syntactically real experiencer arguments.

2.4. The sluicing test

A fourth diagnostic for covert arguments—and the final one considered here—is the prospect for sluicing constructions targeting them. To see the sluicing test in action, consider agents of passives again, with respect to:

42. The ship was sunk, but by whom?

The standard sluicing analysis of constructions like 42 is that they involve elliptical reconstruction of the first conjunct (*the source*) into the second conjunct (*the target*). The "whom" portion of the target is understood via *wh*-fronting an element recovered in the elliptical reconstruction (with pied-piping of "by"). This requires that this element (the agent who sank the ship, for 42) be present in the source to be reconstructed at the target and then *wh*-fronted.[33]

For a second illustration, one argument that "Pain ate" contains a covert direct object (for the patient, what was eaten) is that one can get sluicing constructions targeting it, as in:

43. Pam ate, but what?

---

[32] Unfortunately it is not possible to run the control diagnostic on "tasty", at least in the form considered here. This is because, while "fun" is licensed on both objects and actions (video games can be fun, and playing video games can be fun), "tasty" is only licensed for objects not for actions (cakes can be tasty, but baking cakes cannot). The control diagnostic I am using involves the frame "it is——to Φ" which concerns actions.

[33] For a sustained discussion of sluicing and ellipsis see Merchant (2001). Whether sluicing calls for syntactic realization or mere semantic involvement depends on whether one holds a purely syntactic copy theory of ellipsis (cf. Fiengo and May 1994), or thinks of ellipsis as semantic.

43 may be usefully contrasted with an attempt to sluice a direct object for an intransitive verb like "dined":

    44. *Pam dined, but what?

With bare taste claims, there are sluicing constructions that target the experiencer. Thus imagine that Ron has ten housemates. Yesterday he saw a big hunk of really stinky cheese in the communal fridge, and worried it was rotten. Today he sees that most of the cheese has been eaten, and concludes that someone must have loved it. This leads him to say:

    45. The stinky cheese is tasty, but to whom? [34]

The standard analysis of 45 (as in 42) would involve a second conjunct formed from (i) *wh*-fronting (with pied-piping of "to"), plus (ii) ellipsis on the sister constituent of the *wh*-phrase from the source. An experiencer variable is needed in the source, to be *wh*-fronted at the target.

To get a minimal pair, contrast 45 with a case in which the predicate obviously does not select for an experiencer:

    46. *The stinky cheese is French, but to whom?

46 should elicit middling-to-strong judgments of ungrammaticality. This is presumably because "blue"' does not project the right sort of argument for the sort of *wh*-fronting found in the second conjunct. Further examples of contrasts could be obtained with:

    47. *The stinky cheese is circular, but to whom?

    48. *The stink cheese is blue, but to whom?

For an example with "fun", imagine that Sam has ten housemates. Yesterday he saw a big pile of paper clips on the floor, and wondered what on earth they were there for. Today he learns that the paper clips have been played with over and over, and concludes that someone must have enjoyed playing with them. This leads him to say:

    49. The paper clips are fun, but for whom? [35]

Again an experiencer argument is needed in the source, to be *wh*-fronted in the target. 49 should be contrasted with constructions such as:

    50. *The paper clips are metallic, but for whom?

    51. *The paper clips are magnetic, but for whom?

    52. *The paper clips are shiny, but for whom?

---

[34] Since Ron does not actually taste the cheese, some may prefer an epistemic modal construction serving as an evidential marker of indirectness, viz.: "The stinky cheese must be tasty, but for whom?" Also some find sluicing constructions more natural when the sluice is embedded in an attitude verb, "The stinky cheese is tasty, but I can't imagine for whom." The same points should arise either way.

[35] Again some may prefer a marker of evidential indirectness: "The paper clips must be fun, but for whom?"

Now I must mention that the sluicing diagnostic is at risk of overgenerating. Notice that one can sluice out temporal, locative, and even causative 'arguments' for "Pam ate":

53. Pam ate, but when?
54. Pam ate, but where?
55. Pam ate, but why?

Overall, sluicing constructions seem to diagnose the prospect *of either* arguments *or* optional adjuncts.[36] So the same confound recurs here from the licensing test (§ 2.2), in that the absolutist may well regard the sluicing constructions in 45 and 49 as merely targeting an optional adjunct. But, given the argument above that experiencer phrases are not adjuncts, this confound is already resolved.

Putting this all together. All four of the diagnostics I have invoked—binding, licensing, control, and sluicing—have converged on the claim that taste predicates project experiencer arguments. This is a best-case result. I thus would conclude that the evidence for meaning perspectivalism for taste claims is very strong. Anytime there is a taste predicate, there is an experiencer specified, even if only covertly.

3. Meaning Perspectivalism for Epistemic Modals

Imagine that Ben, having hidden some licorice in the cupboard, whispers to Ann:

2. There might be licorice in the cupboard.

Imagine that Claire, listening into the conversation, leaps to the conclusion:

56. There must be licorice in the cupboard.

I will now argue that these two modals ("might" and "must") feature *restrictor arguments*, which—as long as they are read as epistemic modals—specify the perspective at issue. Given that such arguments are assigned specific values by the semantics at every context, meaning perspectivalism follows. Relative to any context—so long as the modals are read as epistemic modals—the proposition expressed by 2 and the proposition expressed by 56 will involve a specified body of evidence. In this regard I am upholding the view of Kratzer (1977), according to which:

[W]hat we have ... is not an absolute 'must' but a relative 'must in view of.' This relative modal phrase 'must in view of' has two arguments: a phrase like 'what is known' or 'what is good for us' etc. and a sentence. (1977: 341)

Five qualifications should be made from the start. First, I will only be considering the modal auxiliaries "might" and "must." English has many other ways of expressing modality. There are further modal auxiliaries, including: "may", "can", "could", "will", "would", "shall", and "should." There are quasi-modal verbs such as: "have

---

[36] Thanks to Daniel Rothschild for an insightful discussion on this point.

to", "ought to", and "need to." And there are modal sentential adverbs, for instance: "possibly", "probably", "certainly", and "necessarily" (which pattern with phrases like: "it is possible that", "it is probable that", "it is certain that", and "it is necessary that"). Indeed, English can even generate modality without *any* overt modalizing element, in certain non-finite constructions such as: "Sandy is the person to call for computer help" (cf. Bhatt 2006). I will not be considering any of these other ways of expressing modal meanings.

Second, I do not believe that there is any such thing as an "epistemic modal" *per se* (see § 3.2 for further discussion). Still following Kratzer (1977), I take modals to involve a tripartite structure: [*Quantifier: Restrictor*] [*Scope*]. I take the *Restrictor* and the *Scope* positions to be occupied by propositions. This structure may then be read as: In *Quantifier* of the worlds such that *Restrictor, Scope*. Thus a natural epistemic reading of "Kate might be in Canberra" may be glossed via: In some of the worlds such that what is known holds, Kate is in Canberra. So called "epistemic modals" are merely modals whose restrictor involves some sort of epistemic proposition.[37]

Third, I take no stance on how to evaluate implicit restrictor arguments, save to piously intone that these are evaluated by context. I suspect that among the stereotypical settings for epistemic restrictors are (i) the speaker's knowledge, and (ii) universal knowledge, with strong contextual cues needed to override the stereotypical settings. But nothing will turn on this.[38]

Fourth, while my sympathies are with syntactic relationalism for taste predicates (with a syntactically real experiencer argument), I am divided between syntactic and merely semantic relationalism for epistemic modals. Krazter herself does not posit syntactic realization (p.c.). In my terminology (§ 1.1), she is a *semantic* relationalist. Von Fintel and Heim, on the other hand, do posit syntactic realization in their online lecture notes, speaking of modals as involving logical forms with "a kind of invisible pronoun, a free variable that stands for a set of possible worlds" (2007: 31). They continue: "The covert variable next to the modal picks up a contextually salient set of worlds, and this functions as the quantifier's restrictor" (2007: 32). Thus they are syntactic relationalists. I will remain neutral on the syntactic status of restrictor arguments in what follows.

---

[37] *Point of clarification*: I will continue to speak of "epistemic modals" as modals restricted by an epistemic property. The point I am making is that no single element of the proposition expresses "epistemic modality", Rather the epistemic modality of the proposition is determined compositionally by the modality of the modal plus the epistemicality of the restrictor.

[38] Embedding under attitude verbs *strongly tends* to shift the restrictor to an epistemic state of the subject of the lowest attitude. Thus in both "Ann thinks that there might be licorice in the cupboard" and "Ben thinks that Ann thinks that there might be licorice in the cupboard", by far the most natural restrictor is to an epistemic state of Ann's. I do not know why other readings are so difficult to generate.

Fifth (and perhaps most importantly), I will be relying almost exclusively on the binding test to argue for implicit restrictor arguments in bare epistemic modal claims like 2 and 56 (§ 3.1). The other tests used on taste predicates in § 2 are either inapplicable (for instance, the restrictor argument is not of the right type to control PRO), or unclear in verdict (for instance, the restrictor phrase can be made explicit, but it is unclear whether the phrase serves as an argument of the modal or an adjunct). Thus I can claim some decent evidence for meaning perspectivalism for epistemic modals, but nothing like a best-case result. The case for meaning perspectivalism for epistemic modals is not nearly as strong as the case with taste predicates. Though I will add a further broad-scale consideration for meaning perspectivalism for epistemic modals, based on *the unity of the modals* (§ 3.2).

3.1. The binding test

Recall (§ 2.1) that one leading diagnostic for semantic arguments is the possibility of binding them. I have illustrated with binding with respect to pronouns, "local", "tasty", and "fun." It might prove useful to add one more illustration, involving quantifier domain restriction. Thus consider:

57. In every room, every wall is blue

Perhaps the only natural reading of 57 is the bound reading, on which 57 basically says that in $room_1$, every wall in $room_1$ is blue, in $room_2$, every wall in $room_2$ is blue, etc. There needn't be a single room containing every wall. The domain of the second quantifier is bound to the domain of the first. The existence of such a bound reading is the primary argument for the syntactic reality of quantifier domain restrictors in the influential discussion of Stanley and Szabó (2000). But—maintaining neutrality as between syntactic and semantic accounts of binding—I would at least say that the existence of the bound reading of 57 is excellent evidence for the presence of quantifier domain restrictor arguments in logical form. To the extent that modals serve semantically as quantifiers over worlds, it would be unsurprising to find a parallel case for modal restrictor arguments.

But there are complications in applying the binding test to epistemic modals, which stem from the fact that epistemic modals tend to move to the left periphery of the syntax, out-scoping any quantifiers that might on surface seem able to bind them. Thus consider:

58. Everyone must be guilty

Surface form notwithstanding, the "must" has managed to out-scope the quantifier. That is, 58 basically means that it must be the case that everyone is guilty. In general, according to von Fintel and Iatridou's (2003) *epistemic containment principle*, a quantifier cannot have scope over an epistemic modal (more technically: a quantifier cannot bind its trace across an epistemic modal).[39] Thus to apply the binding test properly,

[39] Epistemic modals project well above root (e.g. deontic and dynamic) modals. This may be illustrated via the following minimal pair, due to Brennan (1993):

one must create *islands*, which form syntactic barriers to modal movement. Here are five examples of epistemic modals marooned on islands:

59. If Billy and Suzy might be coming over, then you should hide the cookies
60. It is not the case that Billy must be guilty
61. If Billy might be the one who stole the cookies, then Suzy might be too
62. Ma thinks that Suzy must be the cookie thief
63. Any child who might be the cookie thief should provide an alibi immediately

The reader may confirm that giving the epistemic modal widest scope in any of 59–63 would produce unavailable readings. For instance, 60 clearly means that Billy's innocence is still open. It does not go so far as to say that Billy's innocence is certain. But giving the epistemic modal wide scope would produce just such a reading. Likewise giving the epistemic modal wide scope in 62 would give the reading that it must be the case that Ma thinks that Suzy is the cookie thief.

One can thus apply the binding test, as long as one is careful to keep the epistemic modal marooned beneath the higher quantifier. I begin with an extension of the pattern in 62. (I take 62 first to display a further confound for the binding test, which will be addressed by extending the patterns in 59–61 and 63.) Imagine that all the boys in Billy's class have had a bad day. Billy failed the quiz, Tommy forgot his homework, Larry lost his glasses, and Kenny can't find his notebook. Now consider:

64. Every boy thinks he must be stupid

64 has a bound reading, in which it basically means that Billy thinks he must be stupid in view of failing the quiz, Tommy thinks he must be stupid in view of forgetting his homework, etc. There need not be a single reason for believing oneself stupid common to every boy.[40] For another example (with "might" instead of "must"),

---

   (a) Every radio may get Chicago stations and no radio may get Chicago stations
   (b) *Every radio can get Chicago stations and no radio can get Chicago stations

Sentence(a) is fine, because the epistemic modal has out-scoped the quantifier, to produce a reading that basically says that it may be the case either way, as to whether every radio gets Chicago stations or none do (cf. von Fintel and Iatridou 2003). But sentence (b) is semantically incoherent, because the dynamic modal has stayed under the quantifier. In Cinque's (1999) hierarchy of projections, epistemic modals always merge above tense, while root modals always merge below aspect. The tendency of modals with epistemic restrictors to project so high may seem like evidence that they are extra-propositional force markers. It is as if they are fleeing the proposition entirely. But see Hacquard (2006) for an insightful account (within an overall Kratzer-style semantics) of why epistemic modals project so high, involving event binding and interaction with aspect. In any case I will shortly be offering multiple examples of *embedded* modals with epistemic restrictors. This is further evidence that they contribute to propositional content.

[40] This style of example is borrowed from Speas, who comments:

> The set of propositions on which the conclusion "x must be stupid" is based . . . is different for every boy. [64] means that every boy has gone through some process of inference wherein some epistemic modal base led him to conclude that he is stupid. The content of this modal base will co-vary with the assignment of values to boys. Jim might think "Based on my report card full of F's, the fact

imagine that all the girls in Suzy's class have had a good day. Suzy aced the quiz, Tara got all the homework questions right, Liz found Larry's lost glasses, and Anna hid Kenny's notebook. Now consider:

65. Every girl thinks she might be brilliant

65 has a comparable bound reading to 64.

But a second complication arises with respect to the bound readings of 64 and 65, since it might be thought that what is being bound is not the modal restrictor but rather some argument of the attitude verb. The presence of the attitude verb creates a syntactic barrier to the movement of the modal (the modal gets stuck inside the complement phrase). But could it be that the attitude verb is not *merely* creating a syntactic barrier to the leftward movement of the modal, but is also projecting the very argument being bound? Indeed, Lasersohn (2009: 365) suggests that certain attitude verbs project a judge variable, and so he might well hold that what is being bound in 64 and 65 is *not* any restrictor of the modal but rather the judge of the attitude. So the truth perspectivalist has an elegant way of accommodating 64 and 65.

Indeed the truth perspectivalist account of 64 and 65 can look very promising, since the existence of bound readings for 64 and 65 does not survive the removal of the attitude verb, but does survive the removal of the modal. That is, one does not find bound readings for:

66. Every boy must be stupid
67. Every girl might be brilliant

But one does find bound readings for:

68. Every boy thinks he is stupid
69. Every girl thinks she is brilliant

The friend of restrictor arguments for modals need not be too troubled by this. As mentioned with 58, the absence of bound readings for 66 and 67 is simply be due to the fact that the modal has managed to out-scope the quantifier. Moreover the presence of bound readings for 68 and 69 may well be due to the fact that the attitude verb has supplied a bindable argument (such as a world argument). But a clear example of binding *on a restrictor argument* is still needed.

At this point it is crucial to consider a wider range of syntactic tricks for creating barriers to modal movement, beyond embeddings in complements of attitudes. Here the patterns in 59–61 and 63 prove crucial. *There is binding of modal restrictors with other*

---

that I can't understand basic algebra and the fact that I can't read anything but comic books, I must be stupid." Jason might think "Based on the fact that I don't understand what Chomsky's saying in 'Derivation by Phrase' despite having read it 3 times, I must be stupid." Joe might think "Based on the fact that I thought for a while that Tiffany might actually go out with me, I must be stupid." (2004b: 268) *syntactic barriers to modal movement, even without attitude verbs.* Take 59, where the modal is stuck within an "if-"clause instead. Now consider:

> 70. Anytime you are going for a walk, if it might rain, you should bring an umbrella
>
> 71. Whenever you have cookies in the house, if Suzy might come over, you should hide the cookies

Both 70 and 71 feature an epistemic modal stuck within an "if"-clause, and a higher situation quantifier. Both have natural bound readings. 70 basically says that in any situation in which you are going for a walk, if it might rain *given the evidence in that situation*, you should (in that situation) bring an umbrella. And 71 basically says that in any situation in which you have cookies in the house, if Suzy might come over *given the evidence in that situation*, you should (in that situation) hide the cookies.[41]

Here is another case to consider, extending the pattern of 63 in using free relatives to embed modals:

> 72. Every boy has a father who might be a genius

72 has a natural bound reading, which allows that different boys might have different and even incompatible rationales for regarding their respective fathers as geniuses (imagine 72 uttered by the school psychologist while pontificating on the general admiration boys have for their various fathers).

The remaining patterns in 60 and 61 can likewise be extended to produce bound readings under situation quantifiers, as per:

> 73. Sometimes it is not the case that Billy must be guilty
>
> 74. Usually if Billy might be the one who stole the cookies, then Suzy might be too

Hence I conclude that the argument of the attitude verb cannot explain all of the binding phenomena. Overall it seems that modal restrictors pattern with quantifier domain restrictors in allowing for bound readings, on any way whatsoever of preventing the modal from out-scoping the quantifier. The best explanation of the overall pattern is that modals take restrictor arguments.

3.2. The unity of the modals

A second consideration that I think favors meaning perspectivalism for epistemic modals concerns *the unity of the modals.* After all, modals are not always interpreted in an epistemic way. Thus consider:

---

[41] Egan, Hawthorne, and Weatherson provide a similar example, involving a military instructor training troops for jungle warfare who says: "Before you walk into an area where there are lots of high trees, if there might be snipers hiding in the branches, clear away the foliage with flamethrowers." They offer the following gloss involving a bound reading: "Generally in situations where you are walking into an area where there are lots of high trees, if it's consistent with *your party's* knowledge that there are snipers hiding in the branches, use your flamethrowers to clear away the foliage" (2005: 143–4). They maintain their truth relativism (with its required perspective-neutralism about propositions) via skepticism of the binding test. My dispute with them might then spill over into a larger dispute concerning the proper diagnostics for semantic argument structure.

75. Billy might offer his cookies to Suzy

75 can be read as involving an epistemic modal (imagine a speech context where we are trying to guess what unpredictable Billy might do with his cookies). But 75 can also be read as involving a deontic modal, where it basically means that Billy is permitted to offer his cookies to Suzy (nothing wrong with offering cookies!), and 75 can also be read as involving a dynamic modal, where it basically means that Billy has the ability to make the offer (he is not so selfish as to be incapable of it), *inter alia*.

How does a sentence like 75 allow for all of these different readings? One option is to maintain that modals are *ambiguous*—or at least *polysemous*—so that there are at least three different sentences associated with 75, viz.:

75a. Billy might$_{epistemic}$ offer his cookies to Suzy
75b. Billy might$_{deontic}$ offer his cookies to Suzy
75c. Billy might$_{dynamic}$ offer his cookies to Suzy

But exactly how many sentences will we wind up with, in the end? In this vein, Kratzer asks:

How many kinds of 'must' do we have to distinguish? How many deontic ones? How many epistemic ones? How many dispositional ones? And how many preferential ones? Obviously many, many of each group. We do not just refer to duties. We refer to duties of different kinds. To different duties different persons have towards different persons at different times. We do not simply refer to a bit of knowledge and information—once and forever the same. We refer to different kinds of knowledge or information in different situations. (1977: 339)

Going down the ambiguity path for modals like "might" seems to threaten an explosion of meanings.

Moreover, going down the ambiguity path seems to miss a crucial generalization. In all of these readings of sentences like 75, "There is something in the meaning [that different occurrences of modals have] which stays invariable" (Kratzer 1977: 340). Kratzer's key insight is that the unity of the modals lies in their quantificational force. For instance, "must" always expresses the universal quantifier over worlds. As von Fintel aptly summarizes this canonical view, "Modality is a category of linguistic meaning having to do with the expression of possibility and necessity" (2006: 20).

Indeed, the modals form a system within English. For instance, "must", "necessarily", and "it is necessary that" pattern together, as do "might", "possibly", and "it is possible that", etc. This would be a remarkable coincidence given anything like ambiguity.[42] Why for instance should the various different meanings of "might"

---

[42] *Caveat*: There are some idiosyncracies amongst the modals. In the English modal system, some modal terms have lexicalized selection restrictions on the flavor of their restrictors. For instance, in English "it is possible that" does not naturally take deontic restrictors. Some of this may be due to lexical competition from terms like "permitted" and "allowed." Still, the general contours of a system are in place.

Table 6.3 The modal system of English

	Epistemic	Deontic	Circumstantial	Future
Strong	Must	Must	Must	Will
Weak	Can	Can	Can	Might

Table 6.4 The modal system of St'át'imcets (Lillooet Salish)

	Epistemic	Deontic	Circumstantial	Future
Strong	K'a	Ka	—	Kelh
Weak	K'a	Ka	Ka–a	Kelh

systematically correlate with the various different meanings of "possibly" and "it is possible that", in the same way on each modal meaning?

Moreover there is considerable unity to the modal systems found across natural languages. As Papafragou observes: "An interesting fact about the root and epistemic types of meaning is that they often tend to be expressed by a single class of modal expression in the languages of the world" (1998: 371), from which she concludes: "[a] purely ambiguous approach to the English modals can quickly be discredited" (1998: 371).

There is actually one very suggestive parameter of difference between modal systems of different natural languages. While some languages (including English) lex-icalize the modal but do not lexicalize the restrictor, other languages (such as Salish) evince the opposite pattern, where the modal is implicit but the restrictor is what gets made explicit.[43] In Salish, the default quantificational force of modality is the universal quantifier of necessity, though the existential quantifier of possibility can be contextually cued. What one explicitly says is whether one is speaking of epistemic, deontic, circumstantial, or future modality. This pattern is elegantly summarized by Matthewson Rullmann, and Davis (2005), via Tables 6.3 and 6.4.

Given the unity of the modals, treatments requiring a special "epistemic modal" element may be eliminated from the start. Thus one cannot posit special index-ical characters for "epistemic modals" (contra the meaning perspectivalist semantics of DeRose 1991), treat "epistemic modals" as special extra-propositional force mark-ers (contra the expressivist semantics of Hare 1967), or give "epistemic modals" any special semantical clauses (contra the truth relativist semantics of MacFarlane this vol-ume). Given unity, the only possible treatment of epistemic modality must derive epistemic modality compositionally, as a consequence of the quantificational force

---

[43] This can be understood as a variant form of the licensing test (c.f. § 2.2), in that there are other languages in which the argument in question cannot be left implicit. I thank Chris Kennedy for discussion here.

of the modal plus the epistemic property in the restrictor (cf. von Fintel and Heim 2007: 31–2).

Moreover, given the unity of the modals, at least some level of contextualism is required for sentences like 2 and 75. 75, for instance, is a single sentence that can express different propositions in different contexts, depending at minimum on the flavor of modality the context supplies.

But if the context must supply the flavor of modality for a sentence like 75, it is hard to see how context could do so in any way that avoids meaning perspectivalism. For if context flavors modals by supplying restrictor arguments, and if context flavors modals epistemically by providing a body of information relative to which the prejacent counts as possible (/necessary/etc.), then this body of information just *is* the specified perspective.

I do not mean to suggest that the truth perspectivalist and absolutist have no possible way to account for the unity of the modals. Perhaps there are contexts that flavor a modal epistemically, but supply an inspecific restrictor argument, that says that a body of information is relevant (thus imparting epistemic flavor) without saying which body of information is relevant. But I do not know how this story could go.[44] So I think it fair to conclude that the truth perspectivalist and absolutist owe a worked out account of how context can flavor a sentence like 75 in ways that do not yet yield meaning perspectivalism. Meaning perspectivalism is, at the least, a very natural consequence of the unity of the modals.

4. Meaning Perspectivalism and Disagreement Cases

So far I have argued for meaning perspectivalism for taste predicates (§ 2) and for epistemic modals (§ 3), maintaining that the perspective at issue is always specified in the proposition. My approach has been a contextualist approach, insofar as I take the experiencer argument of the taste predicate, and the restrictor argument of the modal, to be supplied by context (in a non-constant way) when left implicit. But contextualist theories (and absolutist theories) are sometimes charged with mishandling disagreement cases, by not allowing for the prospect *of faultless disagreement* (Wright 2001, Kölbel 2004, MacFarlane 2007 *inter alia*). Indeed faultless disagreement has emerged as perhaps *the* major impetus towards relativist views. So in what remains I will discuss disagreement cases, and argue that the contextualist form of meaning perspectivalism I defend actually yields the best explanation, once one considers the full range and dynamics of disagreements. Thus I will conclude on a happy note: both the linguistic tests for argument structure, and the test of best explaining disagreement cases, converge on the meaning perspectivalist view.

---

[44] Though I see how the story could go for the content relativism, if context could supply a restrictor argument involving PRO_{judge} or some other element with an assessor-determined denotation.

Faultless disagreement is supposed to arise in dialogues involving taste predicates, like the following (imagine that Ann is a licorice lover, and Ben a licorice hater):

Tasty Licorice
Ann: Licorice is tasty
Ben: No, licorice is not tasty

Ann and Ben seem to be in disagreement, and yet one might also think that neither side is at fault, or in any way mistaken. As Lasersohn comments on cases of this nature, Ann and Ben are in some sense "disagreeing, even contradicting each other" (2009: 360), and yet "each of them is entitled to his or her views on this matter... neither one is 'making a mistake'" (2009: 360).

The absolutist is said to have trouble capturing the intuition that neither side is in any way mistaken. Given absolutism, and assuming that what Ann says is the perspective-neutral proposition [licorice is tasty], then this proposition will simply be true or false (for a given world and time). Ann and Ben would be in disagreement over whether it is true or false. No matter how much Ann loves licorice, and no matter how much Ben hates it, one of them would just be flat wrong about the real tastiness of licorice.

The contextualist is said to have trouble capturing the intuition that there is any disagreement in the first place.[45] Given contextualism, and assuming that what Ann says is the perspective-specific proposition concerning her perspective [licorice is tasty to Ann], and that what Ben says is the perspective-specific proposition concerning him [licorice is not tasty to Ben], then there is no conflict whatsoever. Ann and Ben would merely be talking past each other (Wright 2001: 51). As MacFarlane puts the point, in a way that emphasizes the crucial role it plays in the debate:

The relativist's central objection to contextualism is that it fails to account for the possibility of *disagreement* in subjective discourse—for our sense that when I say that carrots are delicious and you deny this, we are genuinely *disagreeing* with each other, and not making compatible claims about our respective tastes.   (2007: 2)[46]

Though note that this particular way of putting the objection to contextualism assumes a simple and inflexible contextualist theory, on which the covert experiencer argument is always evaluated as the speaker.

The relativist, though, is said to be able to capture the phenomenon of fault-less disagreement, by combining perspective-neutral propositions with a judge-supplemented index. Ann and Ben are said to be in disagreement over the perspective-neutral proposition [licorice is tasty]. But neither Ann nor Ben need be mistaken,

---

[45] The non-indexical contextualist is said to suffer a similar fate. Though it may be worth considering versions of non-indexical contextualism on which the position of the judge coordinate is initialized from the speech context in a more subtle way, perhaps via which perspective the speaker intends to discuss (§ 1.2), which need not always be her own.

[46] Though see Lasersohn (2009) and Weatherson (2009) for some further truth relativist arguments, which I will not attempt to address here.

since [licorice is tasty] may be true at $<w^*, t^*, j_{Ann}>$ but false at $<w^*, t^*, j_{Ben}>$. So the idea is that Ann has said what is *true for Ann*, Ben has said what is *true for Ben*, and so neither is at fault in the dispute.

Similar cases arise with epistemic modals (imagine that Ann has no idea where the licorice is, but Ben has just checked the cupboard and is certain that it is licorice-free):

Mighty Licorice
Ann: The licorice might be in the cupboard
Ben: No, the licorice cannot be in the cupboard

For parallel reasons, it is said that the absolutist cannot capture the idea that no one is at fault, while the contextualist cannot capture the idea that there is real disagreement. And the relativist is said to be the only one who can do justice to faultless disagreement, by combining perspective-neutral propositions as the common object of disagreement, and a judge-supplemented index as the basis for faultlessness.

I will primarily be interested in comparing the prospects for an anti-contextualist truth relativist treatment of disagreement cases, with the kind of contextualistic meaning perspectivism I defend. I will argue that the case for relativism relies on a misrepresentative sample of underdeveloped cases. Once one considers a wider range of disagreements, and situates them in larger dialogues, the contextualistic meaning perspectivalist approach will prove far superior to its anti-contextualist truth relativist rival. Thus in § 4.1 I will offer a wider range of cases, and situate them in larger dialogues. In § 4.2 I will maintain that the contextualist meaning perspectivalist view I have advocated achieves a nearly best-case result, in handling virtually all of the cases very well. And in § 4.3 I will argue that the anti-contextualist truth relativist meets with a nearly worst-case result, in having trouble with every single one of these cases.

I should mention—in light of my best-case result for meaning perspectivism for taste predicates (§ 2), but weaker result for meaning perspectivism for epistemic modals (§ 3)—that the following opportunity to buttress the case for epistemic modals arises. Given that meaning perspectivism holds for taste predicates, and that the disagreement cases work in parallel ways for taste predicates and epistemic modals, the type of disagreement seen in both cases must at least be compatible with meaning perspectivism. So meaning perspectivism for epistemic modals can thereby be sheltered from objection. In other words, given the best-case result for experiencer arguments for taste predicates, coupled with the appearance of faultless disagreement over taste claims, the question should no longer be *if* contextualism for epistemic modals can handle disagreement cases, but merely *how*.

4.1. Disagreement cases

Is *Tasty Licorice* or *Mighty Licorice* a case of faultless disagreement? I doubt there is a fact of the matter. These cases, without any specified contexts or continuations to consider, are too under-described. Note first that these cases are *dialogues*. It will help to illuminate what is happening in *Tasty Licorice* and *Mighty Licorice* to consider the role of dialogue (as opposed to Ann and Ben merely soliloquizing in separate rooms), as well as the various contexts they might be embedded in, and the various continuations available.

So imagine instead that Ann and Ben are merely soliloquizing in separate rooms, and drop the discourse marker "no" that Ben employs:

Soliloquies on Tasty Licorice
Ann [sitting alone in the living room, dreaming of licorice]: Licorice is tasty
Ben [standing alone in the kitchen, eyeing the licorice]: Licorice is not tasty

Soliloquies on Mighty Licorice
Ann [alone in the living room, dreaming of licorice]: The licorice might be in the cupboard
Ben [alone in the kitchen, eyeing an empty cupboard]: The licorice cannot be in the cupboard

By my lights at least, there is far less of a feeling of disagreement in these cases than in their dialogue counterparts.

For a more dramatic illustration of a case without disagreement—on the not implausible assumption that "sexy" is a predicate of personal taste—suppose that Ann and Ben are both heterosexual adults with some knowledge of the world, and consider:

Soliloquies on Fabio
Ann [alone in the living room, dreaming of Fabio]: Fabio is sexy
Ben [alone in the kitchen, considering his sexuality]: Fabio is not sexy

I think there should be very little feeling of disagreement in this case. If either were to learn of the others' view, neither would feel compelled to provide arguments or to resolve any difference of opinion. Both would simply understand from the start that their sexual tastes differ. Indeed, it would be *utterly bizarre* to imagine a dialogue counterpart:

Sexy Fabio
Ann [leering at the cover of her romance novel]: Fabio is sexy
Ben [eyeing Ann's novel and noting that Fabio does not excite him]: No, Fabio is not sexy

Ben, who is being assumed to have some knowledge of the world, simply would not respond in this way. If he did he would be at fault, in that he would have missed Ann's point, or misunderstood something important about heterosexuality.

What the various *Soliloquy* cases show is that dialogue is playing a role in our intuitions of disagreement in the original *Tasty Licorice* and *Mighty Licorice* cases. In particular, it matters that Ann is speaking *to* Ben, and it matters that Ben is replying *to* Ann, and is prefacing his reply with a "no." This needs explanation.

Now let us return to the dialogue cases, but go beyond the mere two-line exchange, and consider the various contexts these dialogues might be embedded in, as well as the various continuations Ann might offer. It seems to me that there are at least three main styles of continuation that are potentially available (assuming Ann continues this line of conversation at all), in ways that are shaped by the question under discussion. First, it is open to Ann to *entrench*, as in:

Entrenched Tasty Licorice
Ann: Licorice is tasty
Ben: No, licorice is not tasty
Ann: Listen, I was just saying that *I* like it

Entrenched Mighty Licorice
Ann: The licorice might be in the cupboard
Ben: No, the licorice cannot be in the cupboard
Ann: Look, I just meant that *I* thought it might be there.[47]

Such a continuation is especially likely if Ann feels a need to defend herself. For instance, she might have been asked to name her favorite treat:

Entrenched Tasty Licorice in Context
Ben: Hey Ann, I'd like to buy you a gift. What's your favorite treat?
Ann: Licorice is tasty
Ben: No, licorice is not tasty
Ann: Listen, I was just saying that *I* like it

Or she might have been asked to explain why she is running so hopefully towards the cupboard:

Entrenched Mighty Licorice in Context
Ben: Hey Ann, why on earth were you running towards the cupboard?
Ann: The licorice might be in the cupboard
Ben: No, the licorice cannot be in the cupboard. So that cannot be the explanation.
Ann: Look, I was just saying that *I* thought it might be there

Situated in this way, I think it is hard to sustain any original intuition that Ann and Ben were in real disagreement. Ann seems to be telling Ben that he has misunderstood what she was saying. And she seems right.

Entrenchment is especially plausible in cases like the following:

Mighty Agent
Bush [just before invading Iraq]: Tell me, to the best of your current knowledge: do the Iraqis have weapons of mass destruction?

---

[47] In this vein, von Fintel and Gillies note: "The basic observation is that *solipsistic* readings for the modals—readings on which the modals quantify over the evidence available to the speaker at the time of utterance—are virtually always available" (2008: 82).

> *Honest Agent*: We just don't know. Our intelligence is extremely poor. The Iraqis might have weapons of mass destruction. But it is difficult to say anything with confidence.
>
> [Months pass, Bush invades, the Iraqis prove not to have such weapons. Bush summons Honest Agent back to the Oval Office.]
>
> *Bush*: What you told me before proved false. You're fired.

Clearly Honest Agent has been mistreated. She evidently was only speaking of the current knowledge of the CIA at the time. She should complain that Bush has quite blatantly misunderstood and mistreated her. Or consider "might and might not" constructions such as:

> *Might-or-Might-noty Agent*
>
> *Bush* [just before invading Iraq]: Tell me, to the best of your current knowledge: do the Iraqis have weapons of mass destruction?
>
> *Honest Agent*: We just don't know either way. Our intelligence is extremely poor. The Iraqis might have weapons of mass destruction. But they might not. It is difficult to say anything with confidence.
>
> *Cheney*: We are going to invade. We will find out whether or not the Iraqis have weapons of mass destruction. At that point one of the things you just said will prove false. So you're fired right now.

Again Honest Agent has been mistreated. She should complain that Cheney has quite blatantly misunderstood and mistreated her. Indeed anyone who utters a "might or might not" sentence will have said something incoherent by absolutist lights, and something doomed to falsification (should the truth emerge) by the lights of the truth relativist.

A second possible continuation open to Ann is to *retract* her original claim, as in:

> *Retracted Tasty Licorice*
>
> *Ann*: Licorice is tasty
>
> *Ben*: No, licorice is not tasty
>
> *Ann*: Okay, I was wrong

> *Retracted Mighty Licorice*
>
> *Ann*: The licorice might be in the cupboard
>
> *Ben*: No, the licorice cannot be in the cupboard
>
> *Ann*: Fair enough, I was wrong

Such a continuation is especially likely if Ann was asked to speak on behalf of both Ann and Ben:

> *Retracted Tasty Licorice in Context*
>
> *Claire*: Hey Ann and Ben, I'd like to buy you two a treat. What would you two like?
>
> *Ann*: Licorice is tasty
>
> *Ben*: No, licorice is not tasty
>
> *Ann*: Okay, I was wrong

Retracted Mighty Licorice in Context
Claire: Hey Ann and Ben, why were you two both running over to the cupboard?
Ann: The licorice might be in the cupboard
Ben: No, the licorice cannot be in the cupboard
Ann: Fair enough, I was wrong

Retraction is especially plausible in cases where Ann defers to Ben's expertise on the topic. Thus imagine that Ben is a wine connoisseur, and Ann is attending Ben's seminar on wine:

Retracted Tasty Wine in Context
Ben: Thanks for coming to my seminar, Ann. Let's see what you've learned! Tell me about this Mad Dog strawberry kiwi flavored wine.
Ann: The wine is tasty
Ben: Hmmm . . . no, the wine is not tasty
Ann: Okay, I obviously have a lot to learn! Tell me what you are reacting to in the flavor.

Situated in this way, I think it is hard to sustain any original intuition that Ann's claim is faultless. Or at least, Ann seems to be conceding fault.

A third possible continuation open to Ann is to *debate*, which might take a substantive form.

Substantive Debate on Tasty Licorice
Ann: Licorice is tasty
Ben: No, licorice is not tasty
Ann: But consider the warmth of the anise

Substantive Debate on Mighty Licorice
Ann: The licorice might be in the cupboard
Ben: No, the licorice cannot be in the cupboard
Ann: But consider the suspicious bulge under the napkins

Or the debate might degenerate into mere denial:

Mere Denial on Tasty Licorice
Ann: Licorice is tasty
Ben: No, licorice is not tasty
Ann: Yes it is

Mere Denial on Mighty Licorice
Ann: The licorice might be in the cupboard
Ben: No, the licorice cannot be in the cupboard
Ann: Yes it might

Such continuations are especially likely if Ann was asked to speak on behalf of the expert, and neither Ann nor Ben defers to the other on the matter at issue. Thus consider:

Substantive Debate on Tasty Wine in Context

Claire: Hey Ann, you know wines, is this wine tasty?

Ann: The wine is tasty

Ben: No, the wine is not tasty

Ann: But consider the subtle hints of blackberry

Substantive Debate on History in Context

Claire: Hey Ann, you know your politics, did Bush know that the Iraqis had nothing to do with the terrorist attacks of September 11th?

Ann: Bush might have known that

Ben: No, Bush could not have known that

Ann: But consider the idiocy and cynical hypocrisy he evinced on so many other occasions

Here at last we see sustained disagreement, with no concession of fault. But the conversation has only just begun. It is Ben's turn now, and he himself could entrench, retract, or continue the debate (substantively, or by mere denial). If Ben entrenches then there is no longer disagreement. If Ben retracts then he has conceded fault. *Only if both sides are in principle disposed to debate forever can any appearance of faultless disagreement arise.*

In summary, there seem to be several divisions to be drawn among disagreement cases, in ways—for the dialogues—which are connected to the question under discussion (See Fig. 6.8).

A successful account of disagreement cases needs to explain not only the appearance of faultless disagreement that might perhaps arise if both parties are in principle disposed to debate forever, but overall needs to explain the following six points:

D1 Why soliloquies produce less of an intuition of disagreement than dialogues

D2 Why entrenchment is possible, especially in certain contexts

D3 Why retraction is possible, especially in certain contexts

D4 Why substantive debate is possible, especially in certain contexts

D5 Why mere denial is possible, especially in certain contexts

D6 Why mere denial cases can generate an appearance of faultless disagreement

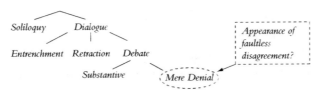

Fig. 6.8.

4.2. Meaning perspectivalism and disagreement

I will now argue that the sort of contextualistic meaning perspectivalism I advocate provides a natural and plausible explanation for D1–D5, and has considerable prospects for explaining the appearance of faultless disagreement as per D6. This is a nearly best-case result.

Starting with the role of dialogue in D1, this is essentially a context effect. Compare *Tasty Licorice* to *Soliloquies on Tasty Licorice*. For the meaning perspectivalist, the fact that Ann has said "Licorice is tasty" *to Ben* makes it seem less likely that Ann is merely intending to report her own personal taste, and more likely that she is intending to report some shared standard (all else being equal). The fact that Ben both speaks *to Ann*, and marks his reply with "no" signals his intention to be understood as negating Ann's claim. This is a context-driven difference between dialogue and soliloquy, and it explains why in soliloquies we often do have the intuition that the two parties are talking past each other. And this is why disagreement turns bizarre in dialogues where it is obvious to all that there is no shared standard, such as *Sexy Fabio*. All else is not equal. The addition of dialogue does not make it seem any more likely that Ann is intending to report some shared standard, which is why Ben's "no" becomes bizarre.

Turning to the possibility of entrenchment as per D2, this is possible to the extent that an interpretation of the perspective at issue is available which excludes Ben. This includes solipsistic speaker-only interpretations, but also interpretations that involve wider groups:

Entrenched Tasty Licorice in a Group-Reading Context

Ben: Hey Ann, I'd like to buy you and Claire a gift. What sort of treat do you two like?

Ann: Licorice is tasty

Ben: No, licorice is not tasty

Ann: Listen, I was just saying that *we* like it

In such cases Ann has every right to tell Ben that he has misunderstood her. This is why—to return to the original *Entrenched Tasty Licorice in Context*—setting the context with a question about what Ann likes (as opposed to a question about what Ann and Ben both like) helps to license entrenchment. Such a context makes the [licorice is tasty to Ann] reading much more likely.

Moving on to the possibility of retraction in D3, this is possible to the extent that the one subject may grant that the other has better information about the perspective at issue. This can even happen in solipsistic readings, in the unusual case where someone grants that another person has better information about their own perspective than they do. Thus consider:

Retracted Frog Legs in Context

Ma: Hey Pa, what are you going to order at this fine French bistro?

Pa: Frog legs are tasty

Ma: Now Pa, you know that you don't like that sort of thing—you know you prefer salads

Pa: Of course you are right Ma. What would I do without you?

Or consider *Retracted Tasty Wine*. Why can Ann retract? Because she might have expressed something like [licorice is tasty to the expert], and regard Ben as having better access to the expert perspective. If so she should retract, by her own lights. This is why setting the context with explicit deference helps to produce retraction. Such a context makes a reading involving a public standard much more likely.

Continuing with the possibility of substantive debate as with D4, this is possible to the extent that each subject may consider herself at least as informed as the other, with respect to the perspective at issue. Thus consider *Substantive Debate on Tasty Licorice*. In such cases Ann has every right to explain to Ben what features of the licorice she is recognizing. This is why setting the context with explicit invocation of an expert standard helps to produce substantive debate, at least for those articulate enough to engage in it.

Indeed, the prospects for mere denial in D5 receive the same explanation as the prospects for substantive debate, and the contextual effect is the same in both cases. Mere denial is just an inarticulate version of substantive debate.

So far, so good. The sort of contextualistic meaning perspectivalism I advocate provides a natural and plausible explanation for D1–D5. It remains to consider the appearance of faultless disagreement as per D6. I think my approach has at least three possible ways to explain this appearance. First, the faultlessness in question might be *merely epistemic*. Perhaps Ann and Ben are disputing the proposition [licorice is tasty to the expert], and perhaps each has some reason to uphold their side of the dispute. In that sense each would be disputing responsibly, on the basis of what they took to be the good evidence. But they would just fail to converge on a common conclusion. Such a model is akin to the scenario in *Substantive Debate on History in Context*, and other cases where different historians might draw different conclusions about the historical record, or cases where different political partisans might draw different conclusions, such as:

Mere Denial on Politics in Context

Claire: Hey Ann and Ben, I know you have different political views—what do you guys think about Bush? Was he a mere puppet of the oil industry and other moneyed interests?

Ann: Bush was a mere puppet of the moneyed interests

Ben: No, Bush was not a mere puppet of the moneyed interests

Ann: Yes he was

Ben: No he wasn't

In such a case there is a single factual claim in dispute (I assume that [Bush was merely a puppet of the moneyed interests] is not a matter whose truth or falsity depends on your perspective—but change the example if you think otherwise). One of Ann or Ben is speaking falsely. But each might still be speaking responsibly, insofar as each might conceivably find some support from the historical record (again, change the example if you think otherwise). The opponent of meaning perspectivalism needs to explain how the matter of faultless disagreement relevantly differs from the kind of intractable disputes one finds between political partisans concerning what are evidently matters of objective fact.

Second and relatedly, the dispute in question might only concern *implicatures* (or other matters downstream from the propositions at issue). Thus consider:

Anchovy Pizza?
Ben: Hey Ann, which topping should we get on the pizza?
Ann: Anchovies are tasty
Ben: No, anchovies are not tasty
Ann: Yes they are
Ben: No they aren't

In such a context it strikes me as plausible that Ann and Ben are each speaking about their own perspective, so that Ann's first assertion, relative to its speech context, expresses [Anchovies are tasty to Ann], while Ben's first assertion, relative to its speech context, expresses [Anchovies are not tasty to Ben]. Does this mean that Ann and Ben are talking past each other? *Not at all.* They are indirectly disputing which topping to get on their pizza. The 'debate' over what is tasty is playing a political role—via implicature—as to how Ann and Ben should coordinate their actions.[48]

Third and finally, the meaning perspectivalist might consider deviating from orthodoxy in allowing there to be a plurality of speech contexts that are in some way associated with a given sentence tokening. On one version of this view, it might be *indeterminate* as to which is the exact speech context. Thus von Fintel and Gillies offer "the metaphor of 'a cloud of admissible contexts' with respect to which the sentence might be interpreted" (2008: 96). Or there might be a *determinate* plurality of speech contexts. Or one might even adopt the *context relativist* view (§ 1.4), on which the unique and determinate speech context *for Ann* might differ from the unique and determinate speech context *for Ben*. Any such approach—in order to avoid the charge of *ad hoccery*—must provide independent motivation for positing this plurality of contexts, and independent evidence that such can lead to an appearance of faultless disagreement. Of special interest is the case of singular "you" sentences

---

[48] Such a treatment is especially plausible with epistemic modals, given the known tendency of denials to merely target the implicated scopal proposition. Thus Simons speaks of the scopal proposition as often constituting "the main point of the utterance" (2007: 1035; cf. von Fintel and Gillies 2008: 82–3). She offers the following examples:

   Ann: Why isn't Louise coming to our meetings these days?
   Ben: Henry thinks that she's left town.
   Claire: a. But she hasn't. I saw her yesterday in the supermarket.
             b. No he doesn't. He told me he saw her yesterday in the supermarket. (2007: 1041)

addressed to a crowd, such as when the preacher tells the congregation "Jesus loves you" (§ 1.4). If this is to be understood vis-à-vis a plurality of speech contexts (perhaps even via context relativism), and can be shown to lead to an appearance of disagreement between members of the congregation, then such independent evidence and motivation would exist. Thus imagine that there is a Jesus, who in fact loves Ann but not Ben, and consider:

> Faultless Disagreement in the Pews?
> Preacher: Jesus loves you
> Ann [in the audience, feeling beloved]: Yes, that's true
> Ben [in the audience next to Ann, feeling nothing]: No, that's not true

Ann and Ben seem at least superficially to be in disagreement, but only because (given context relativism) they are evaluating the preacher's sentence at different contexts.

4.3. Truth relativism and disagreement

The sort of contextualistic meaning perspectivalism I advocate achieved a nearly best-case result across the full range of disagreement cases, providing a natural and plausible explanation for D1–D5, and considerable prospects for explaining the appearance of faultless disagreement in D6. It is time to consider whether anti-contextualistic truth relativism can do better. I will now argue that such an approach fails to explain any of D1–D4, and has even worse prospects for providing a principled explanation of D5–D6. This is a nearly worst-case result.

Starting with the intuitive difference between soliloquies and dialogues in D1, it would seem that everything the truth relativist says about the dialogue case should apply equally to the soliloquy case. In both cases the truth relativist—given her anti-contextualism—would treat the proposition expressed as perspective-neutral, and in both cases the propositions expressed will have the status of being true for Ann but false for Ben. Thus for instance in both *Soliloquies on Fabio* and in *Sexy Fabio* she will presumably see Ann and Ben both expressing [Fabio is sexy], with that content true for Ann but false for Ben. But if that is the basis for faultless disagreement, why is *Sexy Fabio* so obviously not a case of faultless disagreement? In general the truth relativist seems to accord no role to dialogue.

Turning to the possibility of entrenchment as with D2, it is mysterious how the truth relativist can allow for entrenchment. She sees Ann as initially expressing a perspective-neutral proposition such as [licorice is tasty], and that retreating to a different perspective-specific proposition [licorice is tasty to Ann] with very different truth conditions. Ben ought to feel cheated. Given truth relativism, Ben ought to be able to rejoin: "Well, *that* may be true but that is another matter entirely. That is not what you said. Quit changing the topic." Yet obviously Ben cannot so rejoin.

Moreover, the truth relativist offers no account of why entrenchment is more acceptable in some contexts than others. For instance, in *Entrenched Tasty Licorice in Context*, the fact that Ann was asked a question about what she likes seems to play a role in allowing her to entrench, and likewise the context in *Mighty Agent* seems to play a role in making entrenchment so likely. But if we are dealing with perspective-neutral propositions evaluated from judge positions either way (given an anti-contextualist approach), then no role is allotted to context.

Moving on to the possibility of retraction as per D3, it is mysterious how the truth relativist could motivate retraction. Consider *Retracted Tasty Licorice in Context*. For the truth relativist, Ann has expressed the perspective-neutral proposition [licorice is tasty], and this proposition presumably remains true for Ann—her taste buds have not suddenly transformed. Perhaps Ann discovers that this proposition is false for Ben. But when she evaluates the proposition, she is still the judge, so she should continue to find it true. Yet obviously Ann may well retract. Moreover, the truth relativist offers no account of why retraction is more acceptable in some contexts than others. For instance, in *Retracted Tasty Licorice in Context*, the fact that Ann was asked a question about what both she and Ben like seems to play a role in leading her to retract.

Continuing with the possibility of substantive debate in D4, it is mysterious how the truth relativist could motivate any substantive debate. With *Debated Licorice*, if the underlying facts are that [licorice is tasty] is true for Ann but false for Ben, then what is Ann doing appealing to something like the warmth of the anise? Why is she providing reasons at all? She should just recognize that Ben doesn't like licorice and be done. And again the impact of context seems ignored. An explanation is needed for why debate is more acceptable when the question concerns the taste of the expert.

The prospect of mere denial in D5 seems likewise mysterious. In general, if two people merely occupy different positions with respect to a baseline index coordinate, and evaluate a proposition differently purely on this basis, then there seems no sense in which they would disagree at all. Thus—continuing to work with the baseline assumption of world and time coordinates in the index—imagine two people at different times, evaluating a time-neutral proposition. For instance, imagine that it is raining on Monday but no longer raining on Tuesday, and that Ann evaluates [it is raining] as true on Monday, while Ben evaluates [it is raining] as false on Tuesday. There is no sense in which they are in any disagreement. If Ben were to take himself as contradicting Ann's claim from the previous day ("Hah! Ann was wrong!"), he would merely be displaying a misunderstanding.[49]

For a more dramatic illustration of a case where merely occupying different positions with respect to the time coordinate produces no sense whatsoever of disagreement, imagine that Suzy is hopping up and down on her pogo stick, with Ma and Pa proudly providing a running commentary.

---

[49] For a comparable case involving different positions on the world coordinate, consider the proposition [Kennedy is dead], and suppose that it is affirmed by Ann at 1980 in actuality, but denied by Dave at 1980 in a world in which Kennedy was never assassinated and lived past 1980. If Ann imagines Dave's scenario, she presumably would not imagine herself and Dave to be in disagreement, or feel any pressure to provide reasons. She would simply appreciate that Dave is being imagined to speak of a very different possibility.

Pogo

Ma [at t1]: She's up!

Pa [at t2]: She's down!

Ma [at t3]: She's up!

Pa [at t4]: She's down!

[. . . and so on for the next hour]

It would be utterly bizarre to imagine that Ma and Pa are in any disagreement in *Pogo*. (Imagine Billy listening to all of this, and demanding that Ma and Pa stop arguing with each other. That would display a deep misunderstanding on Billy's part.)

Of course the truth relativist need not think that her judge coordinate works the same as a time or world coordinate, vis-à-vis generating a sense of disagreement that could trigger mere denial. But now she has no precedent to draw upon, and is in danger of proceeding in a purely *ad hoc* manner, to find some way to handle the one bit of disagreement data that her theory still has some prospect of handling. This is not a good result, especially for a theory whose main selling point has been accounting for disagreement cases.[50]

The appearance of faultless disagreement asked after in D6 is thus elusive as well, for the truth relativist. Ma and Pa are not in disagreement at all in *Pogo*, and so *a fortiori* not in faultless disagreement. Any attempt at denial would be utterly bizarre:

Pogo in Denial

Ma [at t1]: She's up!

Pa [at t2]: No, she's not—she's down!

Ma [at t3]: That's false—she's not down, she's up!

Pa [at t4]: How wrong you are! She's down!

It is no accident that truth relativism has no explanation for the role of dialogue, or for the possibility of entrenchment, retraction, or substantive debate, or for the ways in which the question under discussion in the context may shape these possibilities. This is because truth relativists have typically worked with just one or two underdeveloped cases along the lines of *Tasty Licorice* and *Mighty Licorice*, and have assumed that all disagreement cases are mere denials, as emerges in the following passage from MacFarlane:

This account captures the distinctive phenomenology of disagreement about matters whose truth is relative. The challenger thinks (rightly) that he has absolutely compelling grounds for

---

[50] Along these lines, MacFarlane (2007)—noting that the occupation of different world or time positions does not yet engender a sense of disagreement—proposes the following as a working definition of disagreement:

If (there are parties $s1$ and $s2$, a proposition p, and a context c, such that (i) $s1$ accepts p but $s2$ denies p, and (ii) $s1$'s acceptance of p and $s2$'s denial of p cannot both be accurate as assessed from c), then there is disagreement between $s1$ and $s2$ over p with respect to c.

This does by and large allow the relativist to at least explain mere denials. But it seems to me *ad hoc*, and certainly can claim no precedent for the special role it accords the assessor.

thinking that the assertion was not accurate. But the original asserter thinks (also rightly, from her point of view) that the challenger's grounds do nothing to call into question the accuracy of the assertion. The asserter's vindication will seem to the challenger not to show that the assertion was accurate, and the challenger will continue to press his claim. (Until the game gets boring.)   (2007: 20)

Perhaps MacFarlane is right about "the distinctive phenomenology" of one very particular sort of disagreement, which degenerates into an endless series of mere denials. My point is that there are many other ways that disagreements may unfold in various contexts, which the literature seems not to have yet considered, and which the truth relativist seems unable to explain.

There is one last move that the truth relativist might consider, which is to waive her anti-contextualism, and thereby handle D1–D4 as all concerning perspective-specific propositions (with the perspective at issue supplied by context). She would reserve perspective-neutral propositions and the relativist machinery for handling D5–D6.[51] This strikes me as awfully heavy machinery to haul in for a very small job, especially given the various alternative explanations of the appearance of faultless disagreement available to the meaning perspectivalist without recourse to truth relativism (§ 4.2), and how problematic the truth relativist explanation of D5–D6 turns out to be on closer inspection. While I cannot rule out this option completely, I suspect that few who have been attracted to truth relativism would be happy to see its explanatory role diminished to such an extent. Though perhaps other completely independent rationale could be provided for truth relativism. I have only argued that disagreement cases provide no such rationale.[52]

I can thus conclude on a happy note. Both the linguistic tests for argument structure, and the test of best explaining disagreement cases, converge on a contextualist meaning perspectivalist view.

References

Bach, Kent (1994). "Conversational Impliciture", *Mind and Language* 9: 124–62.

Bhatt, Rajesh (2006). *Covert Modality in Non-finite Contexts* (Berlin: de Gruyter).

——and Pancheva, Roumyanal (2006). "Implicit Arguments", *The Blackwell Companion to Syntax* (Oxford: Basil Blackwell), 554–84.

[51] In effect this is comparable to the position of content relativists (e.g. Stephenson 2007, Egan 2009), except that they do not recognize perspective-neutral propositions, but rather a plurality of propositions with different specified perspectives for different assessors. They too would presumably reserve their machinery for D5–D6.

[52] MacFarlane has also argued for a relativist treatment of future contingents (2003) and knowledge claims (2005b). I cannot discuss these issues here. Though it may be worth noting that MacFarlane's arguments in all these areas draw heavily on disagreement cases, so to the extent that I have shown that truth relativism does not provide a plausible account of disagreement, I have cast doubt on the case for truth relativism in all these domains. That said, it is certainly compatible with the arguments of the main text that some other rationale could be provided for truth relativism in these or other domains.

Brennan, Virginia (1993). *Root and Epistemic Modal Auxiliary Verbs,* Ph. D. thesis, University of Massachusetts-Amherst.

Brogaard, Berit (2008). "Moral Contextualism and Moral Relativism", *Philosophical Quarterly* 58: 385–409.

Cappelen, Herman, and Hawthorne, John (2009). *Relativism and Monadic Truth* (Oxford: Oxford University Press).

Cappelen, Herman, and Lepore, Ernest (2005). *Insensitive Semantics: A Defense of Semantic Minimalism and Speech Act Pluralism* (Oxford: Basil Blackwell).

Chomsky, Noam (1981). *Lectures on Government and Binding* (Dordrecht: Foris).

Cinque, Guglielmo (1999). *Adverbs and Functional Heads: A Cross-Linguistic Perspective* (Oxford: Oxford University Press).

DeRose, Keith (1991)."Epistemic Possibilities", *Philosophical Review* 100: 581–605.

Egan, Andy (2007). "Epistemic Modals, Relativism, and Assertion", *Philosophical Studies* 133: 1–22.

—— (2009). "Billboards, Bombs, and Shotgun Weddings", *Synthese* 166: 251–79.

—— Hawthorne, John and Weatherson, Brian (2005). "Epistemic Modals in Context", in Gerhard Preyer and Georg Peter (eds.), *Contextualism in Philosophy: Knowledge, Meaning, and Truth* (Oxford: Oxford University Press), 131–68.

Epstein, Samuel (1984). "Quantifier-Pro and the LF Representation of PROarb", *Linguistic Inquiry* 15: 499–505.

Fiengo, Robert, and May, Robert (1994). *Indices and Identity* (Cambridge, Mass.: MIT Press).

von Fintel, Kai (2006). "Modality and Language", in Donald Borchert (ed.), *Encyclopedia of Philosophy* (2nd edn., Detroit: Macmillan Reference), x. 20–7.

—— Gillies, Anthony (2008). "CIA Leaks", *Philosophical Review* 117: 77–98.

—— Heim, Irene (2007). *Intensional Semantics,* Online Lecture Notes, MIT.

—— Iatridou, Sabine (2003). "Epistemic Containment", *Linguistic Inquiry* 34: 173–98.

Glanzberg, Michael (2007). "Context, Content, and Relativism", *Philosophical Studies* 136: 1–29.

Hacquard, Valentine (2006). *Aspects of Modality,* Ph. D. thesis, Massachusetts Institute of Technology.

Hajicová, Eva, Partee, Barbara, and Sgall, Petr (1999). *Topic-Focus Articulation, Tripartite Structures, and Semantic Content* (Dordrecht: Kluwer).

Hare, R. M. (1967). "Some Alleged Differences between Imperatives and Indicatives", *Mind* 76: 309–26.

Kaplan, David (1989). "Demonstratives", in Joseph Almog, John Perry, and Howard Wettstein (eds.), *Themes from Kaplan* (Oxford: Oxford University Press), 481–563.

Kennedy, Chris (2007). "Vagueness and Grammar: The Semantics of Relative and Absolute Gradable Adjectives", *Linguistics and Philosophy* 30: 1–45.

King, Jeffrey C. (2003). "Tense, Modality, and Semantic Values", *Philosophical Perspectives* 17: 195–245.

Kölbel, Max (2004). "Faultless Disagreement", *Proceedings of the Aristotelian Society* 104: 53–73.

Kratzer, Angelika (1977). "What 'must' and 'can' must and can mean", *Linguistics and Philosophy* 1: 337–55.

—— (1991). "Modality", in Arnim von Stechow and Dieter Wunderlich (eds.), *Handbook of Semantics* (New York: de Gruyter), 639–50.

Landau, Idan (2000). *Elements of Control: Structure and Meaning in Infinitival Constructions* (Dordrecht: Kluwer).

Lasersohn, Peter (2005). "Context Dependence, Disagreement, and Predicates of Personal Taste", *Linguistics and Philosophy* 28: 643–86.

—— (2009). "Relative Truth, Speaker Commitment, and Control of Implicit Arguments", *Synthese* 166: 359–74.

Lewis, David (1980). "Index, Context, and Content", in Stig Kanger and Sven Ohman (eds.), *Philosophy and Grammar* (Dordrecht: Reidel), 79–100.

Ludlow, Peter (2008). "Cheap Contextualism", *Philosophical Issues* 18: 104–29.

MacFarlane, John (2003). "Future Contingents and Relative Truth", *Philosophical Quarterly* 53: 321–36.

—— (2005a). "Making Sense of Relative Truth", *Proceedings of the Aristotelian Society* 105: 321–39.

—— (2005b). "The Assessment Sensitivity of Knowledge Attributions", *Oxford Studies in Epistemology* 1: 197–233.

—— (2007). "Relativism and Disagreement", *Philosophical Studies* 132: 17–31.

—— (2009). "Non-Indexical Contextualism", *Synthese* 166: 231–50.

—— (this volume). "Epistemic Modals are Assessment-Sensitive", Ch. 5.

Matthewson, Lisa, Rullmann, Hotze, and Davis, Henry (2005). "Modality in St'at'imcets", in J. C. Brown, Masaru Kiyota, and Tyler Peterson (eds.), *Papers for the 40th International Conference on Salish and Neighboring Languages* (Vancouver: University of British Columbia Linguistics Department), 166–83.

Merchant, Jason (2001). *The Syntax of Silence: Sluicing, Islands, and the Theory of Ellipsis* (Oxford: Oxford University Press).

Papafragou, Anna (1998). "The Acquisition of Modality: Implications for Theories of Semantic Representation", *Mind and Language* 13: 370–99.

Partee, Barbara (1973). "Some Structural Analogies between Tenses and Pronouns in English", *Journal of Philosophy* 70: 601–10.

—— (1989). "Binding Implicit Variables in Quantified Contexts", *Proceedings of the Chicago Linguistics Society* 25: 342–65.

Percus, Orin (2000). "Constraints on Some Other Variables in Syntax", *Natural Language Semantics* 8: 173–229.

Recanati, François (2004). *Literal Meaning* (Cambridge: Cambridge University Press).

Richard, Mark (2003). "Introduction to Part I", in Aleksandar Jokic and Quentin Smith (eds.), *Time, Tense, and Reference* (Cambridge, Mass.: MIT Press), 25–48.

Rothschild, Daniel, and Segal, Gabriel (2009). "Indexical Predicates", *Mind and Language* 24: 467–93.

Schaffer, Jonathan (*forthcoming*). "Necessitarian Propositions", *Synthese*.

—— (MS) "Confessions of a Schmentencite: Towards an Index-Free Semantics."

Schlenker, Philippe (2005a). "The Lazy Frenchman's Approach to the Subjunctive: Speculations on Reference to Worlds and Semantic Defaults in the Analysis of Mood", in Twan Geerts, Ivo van Ginneken, and Haike Jacobs (eds.), *Romance Languages and Linguistic Theory* 2003 (Amsterdam: John Benjamins Publishing), 269–309.

—— (2005b). "Non-Redundancy: Towards a Semantic Reinterpretation of Binding Theory", *Natural Language Semantics* 13: 1–92.

Simons, Mandy (2007). "Observations on Embedding Verbs, Evidentiality, and Presupposition", *Lingua* 117: 1034–56.

Soames, Scott (2005). "Naming and Asserting", in Zoltán Gendler Szabó (ed.), *Semantics Versus Pragmatics* (Oxford: Oxford University Press), 356–82.

Speas, Margaret (2004a). "Evidentiality, Logophoricity, and the Syntactic Representation of Pragmatic Features", *Lingua* 114: 255–76.

—— (2004b). "Evidential Paradigms, World Variables, and Person Agreement Features", *Rivista di Linguistica* 16: 253–80.

Stanley, Jason (2000). "Context and Logical Form", *Linguistics and Philosophy* 23: 391–434.

—— and Zoltán Gendler Szabó (2000). "On Quantifier Domain Restriction", *Mind and Language* 15: 219–61.

von Stechow, Arnim (2002). "Binding by Verbs: Tense, Person and Mood under Attitudes", in Makoto Kadowaki and Shigeto Kawahara (eds.), *Proceedings of NELS* 33 (Amherst, Mass. GLSA), 379–403.

Stephenson, Tamina (2007). "A Parallel Account of Epistemic Modals and Predicates of Personal Taste", *Proceedings of Sinn und Bedeutung* 11: 583–97.

Weatherson, Brian (2009). "Conditionals and Indexical Relativism", *Synthese* 166: 333–57.

Wright, Crispin (2001)."On Being in a Quandary", *Mind* 110: 45–98.

7

Conditional Propositions and Conditional Assertions

Robert Stalnaker

One standard way of approaching the problem of analyzing conditional sentences begins with the assumption that a sentence of this kind expresses a proposition that is a function of the propositions expressed by its component parts (plus, perhaps, some features of the context in which the sentence is uttered). The task is to characterize this function. But there is also a long tradition according to which conditional sentences—at least some conditional sentences—are used to perform a special kind of speech act. A conditional assertion is not a standard kind of speech act (assertion) with a distinctive kind of content (a conditional proposition), but rather a distinctive kind of speech act that involves just the two propositions, the ones expressed by the antecedent and the consequent. There has been considerable controversy about which of these two strategies for explaining conditionals is better.

There is a second controversial issue that interacts with this one: conditional sentences have traditionally been divided into two categories, usually labeled "subjunctive" and "indicative" even though it has long been recognized that while there is a clear grammatical contrast between the two kinds of conditionals, the difference is not a simple matter of grammatical mood. The issue concerns the relationship between the conditionals of the two kinds. Some theorists have treated the problem of analyzing indicative and subjunctive conditionals as separate problems, each to be treated on its own terms. Others have sought some kind of unified analysis. It is clear that the two kinds of conditionals have much in common, but also clear that there are semantic differences between them, since there are minimal pairs, differing only in that one is "subjunctive" and the other "indicative" that seem, intuitively to say

Thanks to Thony Gillies, Isadora Stojanovic, Andy Egan, and the editors of *New Work on Modality* (where an earlier version of this chapter was published) for helpful comments. Thanks also to the editors of this volume, Andy Egan and Brian Weatherson, for their helpful and stimulating comments and suggestions. Finally, thanks to Jonathan Bennett for conversation and correspondence over the years about conditionals that helped me to get clearer about many issues.

quite different things.[1] So while it is uncontroversial that the contrast between the two kinds of conditionals is not a simple and superficial one, there remains a question whether one can explain the semantic and pragmatic differences within a unified theory of conditionals, or whether one should treat the two kinds of "ifs" as different concepts that happen to be expressed by the same word. The issue about whether conditionals express propositions interacts with the question whether we can give a unified account of the two kinds of conditionals, since the considerations favoring the propositional analysis of conditionals are much stronger in the case of subjunctive conditionals, while the considerations favoring the conditional assertion account are much stronger in the case of indicative conditionals.

Some philosophers—David Lewis and Frank Jackson, for example—make no attempt to give a unified account that covers both kinds of conditionals, but still support the hypothesis that indicative conditionals have truth conditions. Lewis gave the following reason for this decision:

> I have no conclusive objection to the hypothesis that indicative conditionals are non-truth-valued sentences, governed by a special rule of assertability. . . . I have an inconclusive objection, however: the hypothesis requires too much of a fresh start. It burdens us with too much work still to be done, and wastes too much that has been done already. . . . We think we know how the truth conditions for compound sentences of various kinds are determined by the truth conditions of constituent subsentences, but this knowledge would be useless if any of those subsentences lacked truth conditions. Either we need new semantic rules for many familiar connectives and operators when applied to indicative conditionals—perhaps rules of truth, perhaps special rules of assertability like the rule for conditionals themselves—or else we need to explain away all seeming examples of compound sentences with conditional constituents. [2]

Lewis's methodological concern might be generalized. It is not only that if we treat indicative conditionals as truth-conditional, we can draw on the resources of compositional semantics to explain the embedding of conditionals in other constructions; it is also that we can draw on standing accounts of speech acts, such as assertion, and of propositional attitudes such as belief, and epistemic states such as knowledge to explain the assertion of, belief in, and knowledge of conditionals. Speech acts and propositional attitudes are standardly factored into content and force, or content and kind of attitude. By treating a conditional as a distinctive kind of content, one avoids the problem of giving an account of distinctive kinds of conditional force, and distinctive conditional mental states.

---

[1] By a *semantic* difference, I mean here a difference in the assertive content that utterances of the contrasting conditional sentences would have in a similar situation. This is compatible with the hypothesis that the abstract semantics for the two conditionals is the same, but that the difference in content is explained by a difference in contextual determinants relative to which the contrasting kinds of conditionals are interpreted.

[2] Lewis (1976): 305.

But these methodological considerations cut both ways. While there are some complex constructions with indicative conditionals as constituents, the embedding possibilities seem, intuitively, to be highly constrained. For example, simple disjunctions of indicative conditionals with different antecedents and conditionals with conditional antecedents are sometimes difficult to make sense of. The proponent of a non-truth-conditional account needs to explain what embeddings there are, but the proponent of a truth-conditional account must explain why embedded conditionals don't seem to be interpretable in full generality. And while the truth-functional analysis of indicative conditionals favored by Lewis, Jackson, and Paul Grice can make sense of negations and disjunctions with conditionals as parts, it is in those kinds of constructions that the consequences of the truth-functional analysis are most difficult to reconcile with intuitions about examples.

On the speech act and attitude issue: it would be an advantage to reduce the problem of conditional assertion, promise, command, belief, intention, knowledge, and so forth to the single problem of analyzing a kind of content—conditional propositions—that they all share, but on the other hand, it may distort the phenomenon of conditionality to do so. As is often noted, conditional bets and questions are not properly understood as bets on or questions about the truth of a conditional proposition, and conditional promises do not seem to be promises to make true a conditional proposition. It may also be that a proper account of belief, intention, and knowledge must make room for conditional versions of these attitudes that cannot be reduced to categorical belief, knowledge, and intention.

So there are costs and benefits on both sides to be weighed in comparing the truth-conditional and non-truth-conditional accounts of conditionals. My aim in this paper is to try to get clearer about what is at stake in this debate, focusing on the case of indicative conditional assertions. More generally, I hope to get clearer about the relation between speech acts and the propositions and propositional attitudes that are expressed in them. My strategy will be to sketch a specific account of each kind within a common framework, and then to consider exactly how they differ. One of my conclusions will be that while there are real differences between the accounts, they may be less significant than they have seemed.

In Section 1, I will sketch a conditional assertion account, which will require saying something about how categorical assertion should be understood. In Section 2 I will sketch a non-truth-functional propositional account of indicative conditionals, an account that is basically the same as one I proposed some years ago. While this account has problems, it is not so easily refuted as has been suggested. I will respond to some arguments against it, but also say what I think the real problems with the account are. There are tensions, I will suggest, between the roles of public knowledge (or common ground) and of the knowledge and beliefs of individual speakers in determining what is said in indicative conditional statements. I will conclude, in Section 3, with an example that brings out this tension, and that is a problem for both propositional and conditional assertion accounts.

1. Conditional Speech Acts

W. V. Quine, in an often quoted remark, said that

An affirmation of the form 'if p then q' is commonly felt less as an affirmation of a conditional than as a conditional affirmation of the consequent. If, after we have made such an affirmation, the antecedent turns out true, then we consider ourselves committed to the consequent, and are ready to acknowledge error if it proves false. If on the other hand the antecedent turns out to have been false, our conditional affirmation is as if it had never been made.[3]

G. H. von Wright, in a 1957 article on conditionals, proposed to treat the conditional as a "mode of asserting," and tentatively suggested that conditional sentences do not express propositions: "I shall never speak of a conditional as a proposition which is being asserted, but only of propositions being asserted conditionally, relative to other propositions."[4] J. Mackie characterized a conditional assertion, if p, then q, as an assertion of q within the scope of the supposition that p.[5] But how exactly is the speech act of conditional assertion to be understood?

To better understand what needs to be said to answer this question, it will help to say a little bit about how the speech act of categorical assertion is to be understood. There are two ways of approaching the task of giving an account of a speech act such as assertion, both of which have their roots in J. L. Austin's work on speech acts. Speech acts obviously alter the situation in which they take place, and one might try to explain what it is to make an assertion by saying how it changes, or is intended to change, the context. Alternatively, one might characterize assertions in terms of the way they are assessed. Speech acts are generally assumed to be moves in a rule-governed institutional practice, and one might focus on the constitutive norms that constrain the practice. A speech act might be successful in the sense that it succeeds in changing the context in the way that assertions are intended to change the context, but still be defective in some way—still be an assertion that failed to meet some standard or norm that assertions are supposed to meet. A full account of assertion should include an account of such standards or norms.

David Lewis, in his "Scorekeeping in a language game," sketches a framework for answering the first question. He suggested that we think of a conversation as like a game with an evolving score, and of speech acts as moves in the game. A characterization of a speech act of a certain kind will be an account of how the speech act changes the score of the game. My account of assertion in "Assertion"[6] fits this pattern. A discourse context is represented by a set of possible situations—a context set—representing the relevant alternatives, or live options that the conversational participants intend to distinguish between in their speech acts. The essential effect of an

---

[3] Quine (1959: 12).

[4] von Wright (1957: 131).

[5] Mackie (1973).

[6] Stalnaker (1999: ch. 4), originally published in 1978.

assertion is to add the content of the assertion to the information that is henceforth to be presupposed—to eliminate from the context set those possible situations that are incompatible with the content of the assertion. On this account, one might think of an assertion as something like a proposal to change the context set in that way, a proposal that is adopted if it is not rejected by one of the other parties to the conversation.

Different theorists might accept this account of the effect of assertions, but give different answers to the question about how assertions are assessed, and one might distinguish different speech acts in terms of the way they are assessed, even if they change the context in the same way. For example, parties to a conversation might agree to accept certain things that they may not be in a position to assert. ("It's probably going to rain—let's assume that it will." Or lawyers in a court proceeding may agree to stipulate certain facts). This kind of speech act changes the context in the same way as an assertion, but may be subject to different norms.[7]

Here are some contrasting answers to the question about the norms of assertion that have been given:

(1) Some claim that the only norm for assertion is truth. That is, an assertion of something false is defective, subject to criticism, but a true assertion achieves all that assertions essentially aim at. This account need not say that a speaker who makes a false assertion is always subject to criticism—she might have had good reason to believe that her action conformed to the norm. And conversely, the account will allow that speakers may be subject to criticism even for true assertions, if they did not have good enough reason to believe that they were true. There are general norms that one should take care, in one's actions, to ensure that one meets the standards that apply to those actions. The claim is that the only specific norm governing assertion is the norm of truth.[8]

(2) Others—most prominently, Timothy Williamson—have argued that successful assertions must meet a higher standard: the speaker represents himself as knowing the content of the assertion, and so the assertion fails of its aim if the speaker does not have this knowledge.[9] Again, speakers who make assertions without knowledge may not be subject to criticism, should they be justified in believing that they knew the truth of what they asserted, but their assertions will still be defective when the speaker lacks knowledge.[10]

---

[7] I don't want to suggest that there is a sharp or deep line between the two kinds of questions about speech acts (how do they change the context, and how are they assessed). If two speech acts are subject to different norms, then they will inevitably change the context in different ways as a result. For example, if knowledge is a mutually recognized norm of assertion, then an assertion that P will normally change the context by making it common ground that the speaker has represented herself as knowing that P. But different theorists have emphasized one or the other of these questions, and I think it is useful to view their answers as complementary parts of a full account of a speech act.

[8] See Weiner (2005) for a defense of this thesis.

[9] Williamson (1996) and (2000: ch. 11).

[10] The difference between the truth norm and the knowledge norm is subtle, and some might argue that there is really no difference, given that to meet the norm of truth (together with the general norm that

(3) Robert Brandom and others have argued that one who makes an assertion undertakes a commitment to defend the truth of the assertion in response to reasonable challenges—a proposed norm that is weaker in some respects, and stronger in others than the norm of knowledge.[11] Thus an assertion by one who is uncertain of the truth of what he asserts, but who is prepared to give arguments, and to withdraw the claim in the face of good counterarguments satisfies this norm, while failing to satisfy the knowledge norm. On the other hand, one who says "I will tell you what I know, but you will just have to take my word for it" may satisfy the knowledge norm, while failing to live up to this one.

(4) A Bayesian might say that assertability is a matter of degree.[12] The higher the degree of belief that the speaker has in the truth of the content of the assertion, the more asssertable it is. How high is high enough will depend on context—on the balance of the costs of being wrong, and the benefits of getting it right.

Now with those models of what an account of a speech act might look like, how might one explain conditional assertion? First, here is an answer to the first question, paralleling the account of the effect of categorical assertion on the context: First, one adds the content of the antecedent, temporarily, to the context; that is, one sets aside the possibilities in the context set in which the supposition is false.[13] (What if the supposition is incompatible with the prior context, so that the whole context set is set aside? In this case, just as in the case of a categorical assertion that is incompatible with the prior context, the speech act will be inappropriate unless there is a way to adjust the context to make it compatible with the supposition.) Then the content of the consequent is treated like the content of a categorical assertion: one eliminates, from this temporary or derived context those possible situations that are incompatible with the content of the consequent. Finally, one adds back the possibilities that one had set aside.

David Lewis and other defenders of the material conditional analysis might point out that on this account, the effect of a conditional assertion is exactly the same as the effect of the categorical assertion of the corresponding material conditional. Is this just an example of Lewis's methodological point that a non–truth–conditional account will have to do over again work that has already been done? The defender of the conditional assertion analysis will argue that it is not. Even if the effect of a conditional assertion is exactly the same as the effect of a categorical assertion of the

one should have sufficient reason to believe that one is conforming to any specific norm), one must have sufficient reason to believe that one's assertion is true, and that might be hard to distinguish from sufficient reason to believe that one had knowledge. But Williamson argues that there is a difference, and that it is important.

[11]   Brandom (1983).

[12]   I don't mean to suggest that anyone who accepts a Bayesian account of belief and degree of belief is committed to any particular line on norms of assertion.

[13]   Swanson (2004) argues that we should think of conditional assertions as two different speech acts—an act of supposition followed by an assertion under the scope of the supposition.

corresponding material conditional, that does not mean that the overall account of conditionals is the same on the two accounts. It was, after all, Lewis's point that the material conditional analysis yields an account of the role of conditionals in embedded contexts, while the conditional assertion account (without further supplementation) does not. And it is with embedded conditionals that the material conditional account runs into trouble.

The most striking counterexamples to the material conditional analysis of conditionals are negations of conditionals. My favorite is an argument for the existence of God cited by Dorothy Edgington, and attributed to W. D. Hart: If there is no god, then it is not the case that if I pray, my prayers will be answered. I don't pray; therefore, there is a god. The premisses seem more reasonable than the conclusion, but if the conditional is the material conditional, the argument is valid.[14] On the conditional assertion account, as Lewis observed, there is no straightforward interpretation of the negation of an indicative conditional, but it is natural to interpret it as a conditional denial. To deny that if I pray, my prayers will be answered is the same as to assert that my prayers will not be answered, conditional on my praying. (In the argument, the negation of the conditional is also embedded in a conditional context, but the conditional assertion account has no problem with conditionals with conditional consequents. "If A, then if B, then C" is a conditional assertion of C on condition B, made in the context of a supposition that A.) The defender of the material conditional analysis may try to explain the discrepancy between intuitive judgments about negations of conditionals and what is implied by his analysis by paraphrasing the negative conditional, putting the negation on the consequent (perhaps using some kind of general bracketing device, such as Grice proposed in his defense of the material conditional analysis[15]), but to do this is to give up the methodological advantage that Lewis claimed for a truth-conditional account.

Negations of indicative conditionals often seem interpretable, and when they are, are most naturally interpreted as conditionals with the negation on the consequent. In contrast, disjunctions of indicative conditionals (with different antecedents) are hard to make sense of. Suppose I were to say "Either he will win if he carries Ohio, or he will carry Ohio if he wins." If you can make sense of this at all, does it seem to be a tautology (as it is, on the material conditional analysis)? On the other hand, *sometimes* disjunctions of indicative conditionals seem fine, especially when they are future oriented, where the semantic difference between indicative and subjunctive is more subtle. Suppose there are two switches, one of which controls the light but I don't know which it is. I say "if I flip switch A, the light will go on, or if I flip switch B the light will go on." The syntax may be a bit awkward, but the meaning seems clear enough.[16]

---

[14] Edgington (1986), 187.
[15] Grice (1989: ch. 4).
[16] This point was made by an anonymous referee, with this example.

The conditional assertion account yields no natural interpretation for a disjunction of conditionals with different antecedents. (If the antecedents of the disjoined conditionals are the same, then they might naturally be interpreted as an assertion of the disjunction of the consequents, conditional on their common antecedent.) If you find such conditionals intuitively bewildering, this is a point (at least a small point) in favor of the conditional assertion account, but it is a point against that you need to explain the cases that seem okay.

So the conditional assertion account yields the result that the effect of a conditional assertion is the same as the effect of a categorical assertion of a material conditional, but this does not imply that the two accounts are equivalent for just the reason that Lewis emphasized: if conditionals have truth conditions they may be embedded in other truth-conditional contexts. The two accounts may also differ in what they say about how conditional assertions should be assessed. What are the norms of conditional assertion? Each of the alternative accounts of the norms of categorical assertion suggests a natural extension to an account of the norms of conditional assertion. Let me consider them in turn.

(1) If truth is the sole norm of assertion, then the natural extension to conditional assertion would be to say that a conditional assertion is subject to a conditional norm of truth (of the consequent), conditional on the truth of the antecedent. This is the norm suggested by the remark from Quine quoted above. The sense in which the conditional affirmation is "as if it had never been made" in the case where the antecedent is false is that it is then not subject to criticism for violating the norm. On this account, the norm for conditional assertion is, in effect, the same as the norm for a categorical assertion of a material conditional.[17]

(2) If knowledge is the norm for categorical assertion, then it seems reasonable to require that a speaker have conditional knowledge of the consequent, conditional on the truth of the antecedent. But what is conditional knowledge? In the case where a person is unsure whether a condition A is true or false, then it seems reasonable to say that she has knowledge of B, conditional on A, just in case she has categorical knowledge of the material conditional, $(A \supset B)$, so at least in the case where the speaker is uncertain about the truth of the antecedent, the norm will be, in effect, the same as the norm for the categorical assertion of the corresponding material conditional. But what about situations where the speaker knows the antecedent to be false? In this case, she knows the truth of the material conditional, but if we can make sense of conditional knowledge in this kind of situation, then there might be cases where one

---

[17] There will always be general Gricean norms of cooperative speech, constraining both categorical and conditional assertions, but these will not be norms that are specific to a kind of speech act, but general constraints on rational cooperative behavior. As Grice noted, it is normally misleading to assert a (material) conditional on the basis of knowledge of the falsity of the antecedent, and he offered an explanation for this in terms of general conversational maxims. Similar explanations could be given by a defender of the conditional assertion account for why it would normally be inappropriate to make a conditional commitment on the basis of knowledge that the condition will remain unfulfilled.

would satisfy the norm for the categorical assertion of the material conditional, while violating the norm for conditional assertion.

One might be tempted to think that a conditional assertion, made by a speaker who knows that the antecedent is false, would always violate some Gricean maxims, since such a speaker is always in a position to assert that the antecedent is false, and if the falsity of the antecedent were asserted and accepted, the conditional assertion would no longer be appropriate (since it requires that what is supposed be compatible with the context set). But it might happen that even when the speaker in fact knows that A is false, the addressee is not prepared to accept that A is false—it might be a point of contention in the conversation, in which case the assertion that the antecedent is false will not be accepted, and that proposition cannot be presupposed (by the speaker) without begging the question. In such a case, even though the speaker knows that the antecedent is false, she may have well-grounded conditional beliefs—well-grounded belief revision policies—which might constrain her conditional assertions.

For example, I take myself (correctly, let us assume) to know that Shakespeare wrote *Hamlet*. O'Leary, however, disputes it. It is common ground between O'Leary and me that the play was written by someone, and I take myself to know that it was, even conditional on the hypothesis that Shakespeare was not the author. Partly in the interest of ultimately convincing him that I am right about who wrote *Hamlet*, I might engage in debate with O'Leary about who the author of the play was or could have been if it wasn't Shakespeare. ("Well, we can rule out Christopher Marlowe for the following reasons . . . "). It makes sense to talk about conditional belief, conditional on hypotheses that are not only counterfactual, but contrary to the subject's knowledge. Can we also make sense of conditional *knowledge* in such cases? And if we can, should cases of conditional knowledge be reduced to cases of categorical knowledge of some kind of conditional proposition? Perhaps, but it is clear that it would be wrong to identify the relevant proposition with the corresponding counterfactual proposition. For while I take myself to know that even if Shakespeare didn't write *Hamlet*, *someone* did, I also take myself to know that if Shakespeare hadn't written *Hamlet*, that play would never have been written.[18] We will return to the issue of conditional knowledge after putting our proposition-expressing hypothesis on the table.

(3) The commitment-to-defend hypothesis for the norm of categorical assertion suggests the following extension to a norm of conditional assertion: In the case of conditional assertions, one undertakes a commitment to defend the truth of the consequent against reasonable challenges, but only with one additional resource available to support it: the proposition expressed in the antecedent. This resource is not itself subject to challenge—the defense is conditional on it.

This account of a norm of conditional assertion also seems to yield the result that a conditional assertion is essentially the same, in the way it is assessed, as the categorical

---

[18] Examples of this kind were first given by Ernest Adams. The Shakespeare example is from Jonathan Bennett.

assertion of a material conditional. For if one could defend a material conditional against reasonable challenges, then one could use modus ponens to defend the consequent, with the additional help of the antecedent. And if one could defend the consequent with the help of the antecedent, then by a division of cases, one could defend the material conditional without the help of the antecedent.

(4) Finally, the Bayesian account of assertability suggests a natural extension to an account of conditional assertability, an account that has been one of the primary motivations for the development and defense of the non-propositional account of conditionals. If ordinary assertion goes by degree of belief, then conditional assertion goes by conditional degree of belief. Here, as proponents of the Bayesian account emphasize, we get a divergence between conditional assertability and the assertability of the material conditional, since the probability of a material conditional might be high (because of the low probability of the antecedent) when the conditional probability of consequent on antecedent is low (because the probability of the conjunction of the antecedent and consequent is much lower than the probability of the antecedent).

This completes our survey of the alternative accounts of norms of conditional assertion. We will look back at them after sketching a truth-conditional account that treats conditional propositions as propositions that are stronger than the material conditional.

2. Conditional Propositions

The propositional account I will sketch is the one given in my 1975 paper, "Indicative Conditionals."[19] The account is very simple, and has two components: first, a standard possible worlds and selection-function semantics for the conditional; second, a pragmatic constraint on the selection function that applies only to the case of indicative conditionals. The abstract semantics postulates a set of possible worlds and a selection function, f, taking a possible world α and a proposition A into a possible world, $f(A,\alpha)$. Propositions are represented by subsets of the set of possible worlds. The semantic rule for the conditional is this:

$(A > B)$ is true in possible world α if and only if B is true in $f(A, \alpha)$.

The abstract semantics imposes a number of constraints on the selection function, motivated by the idea that the selection possible world should be a world in which the antecedent proposition is true, but that is otherwise minimally different (in relevant respects) from the base world from which it is selected. These constraints are common to conditionals of both kinds—indicative and subjunctive.

As we have noted, the pragmatic framework that provides the setting for an account of the effect of speech acts assumes that assertions occur in a context, which determines a set of possible worlds—the *context set* that represents the live options among which speaker and addressee intend to distinguish between in their conversation.

---

[19] Reprinted as Stalnaker (1999: ch. 3).

Propositions true in all of the worlds in the context set are (pragmatically) *presupposed* by the speaker. They include the information that is available, or that the speaker takes to be available, for the interpretation of utterances that occur in the discourse. If the language used is, in any way *context-dependent*, then the speaker will be assuming that the features of the context on which interpretation depends will be available, which requires that they be presupposed, which is to say that the information is entailed by the context set.

The second component of the account of indicative conditional propositions, a pragmatic constraint on selection function that determines the interpretation of conditionals, is as follows:

If A is compatible with the context set, $\mathbf{C}$, then if $a \in \mathbf{C}, f(A, a) \in \mathbf{C}$.

The constraint is a partial specification of the respects of similarity and difference that are relevant to the interpretation of indicative conditionals: possible worlds compatible with the context are more similar to other possible worlds compatible with the context than they are to possible worlds outside the context set.

In the account of conditional assertion sketched above, we said that a supposition creates a *derived context*. There will also be a derived context on the propositional account (for both indicative and subjunctive conditionals). The derived context, $\mathbf{C}(A)$ for conditional supposition, A made in context $\mathbf{C}$, will be defined as follows: $\mathbf{C}(A) = \{f(A, a) : a \in \mathbf{C}\}$. The effect of the pragmatic constraint is to ensure that in the case of indicative conditionals, the derived context set is a subset of the basic context set. Intuitively, this means that all the presuppositions of the basic context will be preserved in the derived context (assuming this is possible, which it will be provided that the supposition is compatible with the basic context set). The pragmatic constraint is motivated by the hypothesis that the role of the special morphology (the combination of tense, aspect, and mood that distinguishes "If pigs could fly, they would have wings" from "If pigs can fly, they have wings," and that we have gotten into the habit of calling "subjunctive") is to signal that some of the presuppositions of the basic context are being suspended in the derived context. The idea is that the default assumption is that presuppositions of a basic context carry over to the derived context created by the supposition. In the absence of indication to the contrary, the pragmatic constraint will hold.[20]

---

[20] On this theory, both kinds of conditionals ("subjunctive" and "indicative") have the same abstract semantics, but a context-dependent parameter of the interpretation—the selection function—is differently constrained by the different grammatical constructions. So, on this theory, the difference between the two kinds of conditionals is a *semantic* difference in two different senses, but a purely *pragmatic* difference in a third sense. The difference is semantic, first in the sense that there will normally be a difference in the proposition expressed by the contrasting conditional sentences, even when uttered in similar situations. And it is semantic also in the sense that the difference is marked by a conventional linguistic device (the tense/aspect/mood difference). But the distinction is pragmatic in that the device works by the way it constrains features of the context. The semantic rule that gives the truth conditions of the conditional as a function of the contextual parameter will be the same for both kinds of conditionals.

It is required, on this account, that one use the so-called subjunctive morphology whenever presuppositions are being suspended, which is to say whenever the derived context is not a subset of the basic context. This implies that the conditional cannot be *counterfactual*, where what I mean by "counterfactual" is that the antecedent of the conditional is presupposed to be false. This does *not* imply, however, that speakers cannot suppose (in the indicative way) things that are incompatible with what they take themselves to know, or even to be common knowledge. All that is implied is that the conversational players must accommodate, expanding the basic context to include possible worlds compatible with the antecedent, if a speaker supposes something incompatible with the prior context. There is a difference between a counterfactual supposition (where we create a derived context disjoint from the basic context) and an "indicative" supposition of something incompatible with the prior context (where we expand the basic context so that the derived context can be a subset of it). To use the Shakespeare example again, when I say "If Shakespeare hadn't written *Hamlet*, English literature would have been the poorer than it actually is," I continue to presuppose, in the basic context, that Shakespeare did write *Hamlet*. But when I say, "If Shakespeare didn't write *Hamlet*, it must have been written by Marlowe," I adjust my basic presuppositions to accommodate the possibility that someone else wrote it. (I could not intelligibly say, for example, "If Shakespeare didn't write *Hamlet*, then it was written by a different person than the one who actually wrote it.")

The combination of the selection function semantics with the pragmatic constraint on selection functions yields an overall account of indicative conditionals that reconciles the thesis that the proposition expressed by a conditional is stronger than the material conditional with the fact that the acceptance of the material conditional seems to be sufficient for the acceptance of the corresponding indicative conditional (at least in contexts in which the negation of the antecedent was not accepted). Once a disjunction of the form (*not-A or B*) is accepted in a context (becomes part of the common ground), then the pragmatic constraint on the selection function ensures that the corresponding indicative conditional, (*if A, then B*), will be true in all of the possible worlds in the context set, and so it will be accepted as part of the common ground that the indicative conditional is true. Dorothy Edgington, in an influential general critique of truth-conditional analyses of conditionals (Edgington 1986), used the prima facie conflict between this thesis about conditional propositions (that they entail, but are not entailed by, the corresponding material conditional) and this fact about the acceptance conditions for indicative conditionals (that acceptance of the material conditional is sufficient for the acceptance of the indicative conditional) to argue against the thesis. She acknowledged that the account I had developed provided a way around her criticism, but she argued that it did so at too high a cost, the cost of making indicative conditionals unacceptably context-sensitive. Her criticisms of my account do point to real problems, but in detail, they are off the mark, missing two distinctions that are important, whatever the ultimate fate of the truth-conditional analysis.

Edgington claims that this analysis gets *acceptance* conditions right only "by making 'truth' and 'truth conditions' radically information-dependent." Specifically, she claims, "If one party is certain that if A, B, and another is not (but regards A as possible), they *cannot* be disagreeing about the obtaining of the same truth conditions. They *must* be equivocating. For the former's context set must rule out $A\&\sim B$, and the latter's must not" (Edgington 1986: 199). But this is not correct; it confuses the context set (which, in a non-defective context is the same for speaker and addressee) with the beliefs of the speaker and addressee (which will always be different, if they have any reason to communicate with each other). The pragmatic constraint applies only to the context set—the common ground, which in a non-defective case, coincides with the possible situations compatible with what is presupposed. Even if one party is certain that if A, then B, if the other is not, and if it is recognized by both that at least one party to the conversation is not in a position to exclude the possibility that $(A\&\sim B)$, then it will not be *presupposed* by either party that if A, then B (or that $\sim(A\&\sim B)$). The two may still understand the conditional in the same way.

Edgington may reply that one cannot fully reconcile the truth-conditional account with the phenomena about the acceptance conditions for indicative conditionals unless one extends the pragmatic constraint so that it applies to the private beliefs of speakers as well as to the common ground. The fact she appeals to is that all one needs to know in order to be in a position to make a conditional assertion (in a situation in which one is uncertain whether the antecedent is true) is that the material conditional is true. To account for this fact, on the assumption that the conditional expresses a proposition with a selection-function semantics, one must assume that the speaker's selection function will give priority to possible situations compatible with her beliefs, as well as to possible situations compatible with the common ground. But we can accept this extension of the constraint while still denying that speakers with relevantly different beliefs are equivocating or misunderstanding each other. What must be granted is that in some cases, indicative conditionals are implicitly about the speaker's beliefs. We must allow that what I say when I say something of the form "*if A, then B*" may not be the same as what you would have said, using the same words. But whether one is defending a truth-conditional account or a conditional assertion account, one needs to recognize that indicative conditionals are conveying information about the speaker's epistemic situation. On either kind of account, we should distinguish *assertion* conditions (conditions under which one is in an epistemic position to make a conditional assertion) from *acceptance* conditions (conditions under which one in a position to accept a conditional assertion made by someone else). I may be in a position to *assert* a conditional while at the same time be prepared to *accept* one that appears to conflict with it, if asserted by you.[21]

---

[21] Here I am indebted to the comments of the editors of *New Work on Modality* (where an earlier version of this paper was published) for helping me to see the issue more clearly.

Once we acknowledge that our indicative conditional statements are in part about our individual epistemic situations, then one thing that needs to be explained is the fact that conditional statements with the same antecedent and contrary consequents that are made by different speakers in the same context seem to conflict with each other. I think that our account of proposition-expressing indicative conditional statements, together with an account of the dynamics of conversation, can account for such conflicts, as well as for cases where one first *accepts* one conditional, and then *asserts* one that seems to conflict with it.

What I *would have said* had I said "*if A, then B*" may be different from what you say with the same words, but once you have said it, the context changes, and if I still am unsure about the truth of the antecedent, I cannot say "*if A, then not-B*" without disagreeing with you. On the other hand, if I learn from what you say that the antecedent is false, then I may accept the truth of your conditional, while continuing to affirm one that appears to conflict with it. The following example illustrates this phenomenon. You say "one if by land, two if by sea," meaning that if the British are coming by land, there will be one lantern in the tower, and if they are coming by sea, there will be two lanterns in the tower. I *accept* what you say, and knowing already that there is just one lantern in the tower, I conclude that the British are coming by land. Before, I was in a position to *assert* "if the British are coming by sea, there is still only one lamp in the tower," and I am still prepared to say this. If the British are coming by sea, then there must have been some mistake about the signal. There is context-shifting and radical information-dependence here, but a truth-conditional account of what is going on can explain the phenomena, and does not have to say that there is equivocation or misunderstanding.[22]

Edgington's second complaint is that the pragmatic constraint requires an anti-realist conception of truth.

> If a context set is sufficiently bigoted or bizarre, any old (non-contradictory) conditional can come out 'true': 'If we dance, it will rain tomorrow', for instance. We dance, and the drought continues unabated. Given what we now know, we would not have uttered those words. But the context is different—in its own context, what was said was 'true'. (Edgington 1986: 199)

But this complaint is misguided, equivocating on what is meant by saying that something is true in a context. A context, in the general framework in question, is represented by a set of possible situations—the context set—which encodes the information that speaker and addressees take to be common ground. Context-sensitive utterances will have truth conditions that are sensitive to the context set, so that there are utterance that might have had different truth values (in the actual world) if their contexts had been different. For example, in one context it is common ground that the speaker intended to refer with "that man" to George W. Bush when she said "that man won the election", while in another context, the speaker uttered the same

---

[22] The Paul Revere example is discussed briefly in Stalnaker (1984: 108).

sentence, but there it is common ground that he intended to refer to John Kerry. One might say that the sentence was true in the first context, and false in the second. This is the most straightforward sense of "true in a context." On the other hand, since the context is represented by a set of possible worlds, one might mean by "true in a context" what is true in all of the possible worlds in the context set that represents that context. On this interpretation, to say that something is true in a context is to say that it is presupposed in that context—which is to say that it was taken to be common ground (whether it is actually true or not). In the second sense, "that man won the election" will be true in both of the above contexts, assuming that the assertion was accepted in both contexts. Truth in a context, in the second sense, is not a special notion of truth, but is just truth with respect to certain nonactual situations.

Edgington's rain dance example is an example of a conditional that is presupposed, and presumably believed, to be true, but that is in fact false. So it is "true in the context" only in the second (somewhat misleading) sense. This is no more a problem for a realist notion of truth than the fact that "John Kerry won the election" is true in possible situations compatible with the beliefs of people who think that he won. The pragmatic constraint on selection functions does imply that the actual truth of a conditional will sometimes be context-sensitive, but only when the actual world is compatible with the context, since it constrains the truth conditions of the conditionals only in the possible worlds in the context set—those compatible with what is presupposed.[23] The constraint has no consequences for the truth conditions of conditionals in possible worlds outside the context set, including the actual world, should that world be incompatible with what is presupposed.[24] But while the pragmatic constraint is not relevant to the actual truth value of the conditional in Edgington's example, the abstract semantics requires that it be false with respect to any context, since the antecedent is true, and the consequent false.

I have emphasized, in this response to Edgington's objection, that the pragmatic constraint that I proposed has consequences only for the truth conditions of conditionals in possible worlds that are compatible with what is presupposed in the context (possible worlds in the context set). One might worry that this constraint is therefore much too weak, saying nothing, in most cases, about the actual truth of indicative conditionals. The worry is that it seems reasonable to believe that in almost all contexts, speakers will be making at least one false presupposition, even if an irrelevant one. Consider a discussion between two creationists about the Kennedy assassination. They falsely presuppose the truth of some creationist doctrines, let us assume. Even though these presuppositions are irrelevant to their current discussion, they imply that the actual world will be outside of the context set, so the constraint will be silent on

---

[23] The truth value of a conditional statement will presumably be context-sensitive in some cases, even when the actual world is outside the context set, but my point is that this one specific pragmatic constraint does not imply that it is.

[24] This reply to Edgington's criticism is developed in Block (2008).

the *actual* truth value of a statement like "If Oswald didn't shoot Kennedy, someone else did." But it seems clear that this statement, made in such a context, would be true, and the explanation for why it is true should be the same as in the case where all the presuppositions are true.[25]

There is a more general issue here concerning the assessment of the truth value of statements, particularly context-sensitive statements, that are made in a context in which some presuppositions are false.[26] One way to limit the effect of irrelevant presuppositions (a way that is independently motivated) is to adopt a more coarse-grained analysis of the possible situations that define a context set.[27] The possibilities, on this kind of account, will be cells of a partition of the space. Possible worlds will be members of the same partition cell if they are equivalent in all respects that are relevant to what is at issue in the context. The actual situation will be the partition cell that contains the actual world. In a model of this kind for the creationist example, the actual situation will be compatible with the context, since the presuppositions that are relevant to the current discussion are all true.

So this truth-conditional account of indicative conditionals is not quite so quickly refuted as Edgington thought, and does not require any kind of non-standard conception of truth. No truth-conditional account will have a problem with examples (such as Edgington's rain dance example) with true antecedents. But there are related problems, brought most clearly into focus by Allan Gibbard's famous example of Sly Pete, the Mississippi Riverboat gambler. This is an example of a pair of apparently contrary conditionals with false antecedents, but which are made in a context in which the actual situation is compatible with what is presupposed. Here is Gibbard's story:

Sly Pete and Mr. Stone are playing poker on a Mississippi riverboat. It is now up to Pete to call or fold. My henchman Zack sees Stone's hand, which is quite good, and signals its contents to Pete. My henchman Jack sees both hands and sees that Pete's hand is rather low, so that Stone's is the winning hand. At this point the room is cleared. A few minutes later Zack slips me a note which says 'if Pete called, he won,' and Jack slips me a note which says 'if Pete called, he lost.' . . . I conclude that Pete folded.[28]

Jack and Zack, in this story, each have only partial information about the situation but each recognizes the way in which his information is partial, and neither is making any mistake. So the actual situation is compatible with the beliefs of both henchmen, and we may presume it is also compatible with the contexts in which each communicates with the narrator of the story (call him "Allan"). So the putative problem for the truth-conditional account is this: Suppose that indicative conditionals express

---

[25] This concern was pressed by the editors in their comments. The creationist example is theirs.

[26] See Yablo (2006) for a take on the general problem.

[27] I am drawing here on the work of Seth Yalcin on what he calls "modal resolution." See Yalcin (2008). See also work by Jonathan Schaffer, who argues that we need to enrich the idea of a context to include a partition of the space of possibilities that is determined by the alternative answers to the questions that are at issue in the context.

[28] Gibbard (1981: 231).

propositions, and that a conditional assertion is the categorical assertion of a conditional proposition. Then it seems that (1) Zack is not in a position to rule out what is in fact the actual situation in which Pete folds with a losing hand, and it does not seem that he is ruling it out. But (2) it seems that he is in a position to assert "if Pete called, he won" (thus ruling out all possible situations incompatible with the truth of the proposition expressed). But then it must be that (3) the conditional proposition expressed is true in the actual situation. Similarly for Jack, with his assertion of an apparently contrary conditional proposition. So it seems that when Jack says, "If Pete called, he lost," he speaks the truth, but also that Zack speak the truth when he says "if Pete called, he won." If we further assume that the conditional sentences are interpreted with a selection-function semantics, then we must assume that the selection function relevant to interpreting Zack's conditional is different from the one relevant to the interpretation of Jack's. To explain the truth and assertability of the conditionals, each selection function must be constrained, not only by the presumed knowledge that they share—the common ground—but also by their private beliefs or knowledge. But the information necessary to interpret a context-sensitive expression is supposed to be presumed by the speaker to be available to the addressee, and so to be presupposed. In general, a speaker's private beliefs and knowledge may be expressed in his assertions, but where they are not common ground, they cannot be presumed to be available for the interpretation of what is expressed.

But as we have seen, there is no conflict between the assumption that the selection function for interpreting conditional propositions is constrained by a speaker's private beliefs and the assumption that the relevant selection function must be public knowledge. As I suggested above, in discussing Edgington's first objection, the assumption that the selection function is constrained by the speaker's private beliefs *does* imply that a conditional in one speaker's mouth may say something different from what would have been said by a different speaker, in the same context, with the same conditional sentence. But it does *not* imply that the information necessary to interpret each speaker's conditional is not publicly available. For if it is a general constraint that selection functions for indicative conditionals should, where possible, be closed under the speaker's knowledge or beliefs, then it will be common ground that this constraint will hold. Even if the addressee does not know what the speaker knows, he will know, and it will be common ground, that the world selected from a given possible world in the context set will be constrained by what the speaker knows or believes in that possible world.

Let me spell the point out in detail, in terms of the riverboat example[29]: Let a, β, and γ be three possible worlds in which Pete in fact folded. a is the actual

[29] In Gibbard's telling of the story, he adds that Allan knows that the notes come from his trusted henchmen, but doesn't know which note came from which (and so presumably does not know anything about the basis for their conditional claims). To simplify the analysis (avoiding a proliferation of alternatives), I assume that Allan knows that the note came from Jack, and something about Jack's epistemic situation. I don't think anything essential is lost by this simplification of the story.

world in which Jack knows that Pete had a losing hand, β is a possible world in which Jack knows that Pete had a winning hand, and γ is a possible world in which Jack does not know whether Pete has a winning or a losing hand. Let f_J be the selection function relevant to interpreting Jack's conditional statements, let P be the proposition that Pete called, and let L be the proposition that he lost. Possible worlds of the three kinds (α, β, and γ) are compatible with the knowledge of Allan, the narrator, and with the context in which Jack's message is passed to Allan. But even though Allan does not know, and Jack does not presuppose, that the actual world is α, rather than β or γ, Allan does know, and it is common ground, that $f_J(P, \alpha)$ is a possible world in which L is true, and that $f_J(P, \beta)$ is a possible world in which L is false. (Nothing is implied by the constraints we are considering about $f_J(P, \gamma)$.) When Allan receives Jack's message, he understands it, and when he accepts it, he rules out possible world β. (He also, of course, rules out possible worlds in which Pete called and won.)

What about possible worlds like γ? Suppose that, in γ, Jack does not know anything that gives him reason to exclude either the possibility that Pete called and won, or the possibility that Pete called and lost. Then nothing we have said implies that the literal content of Jack's conditional statement is true, or that it is false, but Allan will still be able to exclude that possibility on the ground that Jack would not be in a position to assert the conditional if world γ were actual.

Even though Jack would not have made the conditional statement if world γ were actual, we still might ask whether (on the truth-conditional account) the conditional proposition he expressed (in α) was true or false in γ. It seems intuitively clear that the corresponding *counterfactual* conditional proposition, "if Pete had called, he would have lost" will be true (whatever Jack knew or believed) just in case Pete had a losing hand, but what about the indicative conditional? Here, the most natural intuitive judgment may be that the question does not arise—no non-arbitrary truth value can be assigned. This may seem to lend support to the conditional assertion account, according to which nothing has been asserted when the antecedent is false, but a proponent of the truth-conditional account might say the same thing, allowing (as seems plausible for both counterfactual and indicative conditionals) that selection functions may sometimes be only partially defined. A cautious version of the kind of truth-conditional account of indicative conditionals that I have been promoting might hold that, with indicative conditionals, *all* selection functions compatible with the epistemic and contextual constraints are admissible, and that indicative conditionals are true if and only if true with respect to all admissible selection functions, and false if and only if false for all. This version of the truth-conditional account will be essentially equivalent to a version of the conditional assertion account.

It is not that I want to defend this cautious version of the truth-conditional analysis, which implies that non-trivial indicative conditionals will be true or false *only* in possible worlds that are compatible with what is presupposed in the context. The point is just to note that we can see the conditional assertion account as equivalent to a limiting case of the truth-conditional account. One may not have to choose between the two alternatives: it may be that one can have some of the advantages of both. One advantage, in particular, to bringing the truth-conditional and conditional assertion accounts together is that it may facilitate a more unified theory of conditionals, and an explanation of the relations between indicative and "subjunctive" conditionals.

To account for the phenomena, we must assume, as Edgington noted, that conditionals are information-sensitive, both to public and private information. The pragmatic constraint imposed in my original account of indicative conditionals concerned only the relation between common ground—publicly available information—and the interpretation of conditionals. The aim there was limited to an explanation of the force of a certain argument, and more generally, to an exploration of one case of the interaction of context and content in the dynamics of discourse. But the Gibbard example, and others, make clear that indicative conditionals, if they are given a truth-conditional account, will be sensitive also to the knowledge or beliefs of individual speakers and thinkers, and so to information that is not, in general, publicly available. This kind of speaker-relativity means that indicative conditionals are, implicitly, in part about the speaker's epistemic situation, but this does not require any non-standard notion of proposition, or of truth, and it does not imply that speakers and addressees who are ignorant of each other's private beliefs do not understand each other.

The two kinds of constraints on the interpretation of indicative conditionals (by the common ground, and by the speaker's individual epistemic situation) will interact, and there will in some cases be tensions between them. I will conclude by considering an example that illustrates one such tension—an example that raises a problem for both truth-conditional and conditional assertion accounts. I am not sure what to say about this example, but will make a tentative suggestion.

3. Public vs Private Information

There are only three possible suspects for the murder—the butler, the gardener, and the chauffeur—and it is common knowledge that whoever did it acted alone. Alice was with the gardener at the time of the murder, so she is absolutely certain that he is innocent. Bert has conclusive evidence that rules out the chauffeur, which he has shared with Alice, so it is common knowledge between Alice and Bert that either the butler or the gardener did it. Alice concludes (privately) that since it wasn't the gardener, it must have been the butler. But Bert has what is in fact misleading evidence that he takes to exonerate the butler, so he infers that it must have been the gardener. Alice and Bert each tell the other who he or she believes was the guilty party, but neither is convinced by the other. Alice, in particular, is far more certain of the innocence of the gardener than she is of the guilt of the butler; were she to learn, to her surprise, that the butler was innocent, she would conclude that the chauffeur's alibi must not be as good as it looks, and that he is the guilty party. But that won't happen, since in fact, the butler did it.

Bert says, "We disagree about who did it, but we agree—it is common knowledge between us—that either the butler or the gardener did it, and each possibility is compatible with our common knowledge. So even though you are convinced that the butler is the guilty party, you should agree that if the butler didn't do it, the gardener did." Bert is just giving what I have called the direct argument, which all of the accounts on the table have assumed to be compelling.

Alice agrees that it is common knowledge that either the butler or the gardener did it, and that each of the two possibilities is compatible with their common knowledge. But she will be reluctant to accept the conditional, which conflicts with her conditional belief—perhaps with her conditional knowledge—that even if the butler didn't do it, the guilty party is still not the gardener.

If, in this case, we assume that common knowledge (what Alice and Bob both know, know that they know, know that they know that they know, etc.) coincides with the common ground (the context set), then if Alice reasonably refuses to accept Bert's conditional conclusion ("if the butler didn't do it, the gardener did"), we have a counterexample to the pragmatic constraint imposed in my original truth-conditional account of indicative conditionals. The example also seems to conflict with our conditional assertion account, which implies that one should accept B, conditional on A, if A, added to the common ground, entails B. But on the other hand, if Alice accepts the conditional that Bert invites her to accept, she will be apparently violating a conditional knowledge norm, and (from the point of view of the Bayesian account of assertability) asserting something unassertable.[30] On the truth-conditional analysis, what we seem to have is a case where the requirement to select a possible world from the context set conflicts with the requirement to select a possible world from the set of possibilities compatible with the individual's conditional knowledge.

I am not sure what the best response to this problem is, but I am inclined to think that one should question the assumption that everything that is common knowledge is common ground. That is, I am inclined to think that some possible situations that are incompatible with the common knowledge of the parties to a conversation are nevertheless "live options" in that conversation. When it becomes clear that the guilt of the butler is in dispute, so that it is a live option in the context that the butler didn't do it, Alice should insist that we reopen the possibility that the guilty party

---

[30] I assume that in an appropriate Bayesian account, conditional probabilities may be defined even when the probability of the condition is 0. Such conditional probabilities represent conditional degrees of belief, on conditions that are entertainable, even though they are taken to be certainly false. Alice is disposed, should she be surprised by the information that the Butler was certainly innocent, to revise her beliefs so that she would still assign very low credence, relative to that condition, to the proposition that the gardener did it.

was the chauffeur. ("I am sure it was the butler, but if it wasn't the butler, it might have been the chauffeur.") The context set should be expanded to include possibilities compatible with the conditional knowledge of the parties on any condition compatible with the context. This would be a way of reconciling the conflicting constraints, and seems to be intuitively plausible.[31]

The riverboat example was an example of the pooling of information. The different parties knew different things, but had no disagreements. The murder example is a case where the different parties know what each other thinks, but they disagree, so their beliefs continue to diverge. This kind of case may require a more complex account of the common ground.

References

Block, E. (2008). "Conditionals in context", *Mind* 117: 783–94.

Brandom, R. (1983). "Asserting", *Noûs* 17: 637–50.

Edgington, D. (1986). "Do conditionals have truth conditions?", *Critica* 18: 3–30; rep. in F. Jackson, *Conditionals* (Oxford: Oxford University Press, 1991), 176–201. Page references to the reprinted version.

——(1995). "On conditionals", *Mind* 104: 235–329.

Gibbard, A. (1981). "Two recent theories of conditionals", in W. L. Harper, R. Stalnaker, and G. Pearce (eds.), *Ifs: Conditionals, Belief, Decision, Chance and Time* (Dordrecht: Reidel), 211–47.

Grice, P. (1989). *Studies in the Way of Words* (Cambridge, Mass.: Harvard University Press).

Lewis, D. (1976). "Probabilities of conditionals and conditional probabilities", *Philosophical Review* 85: 297–315.

——(1979). "Scorekeeping in a language game", *Journal of Philosophical Logic* 8: 339–59.

Mackie, J. L. (1973). *Truth, Probability and Paradox* (Oxford: Clarendon Press).

New Work on Modality (2005). (MIT Working Papers in Linguistics and Philosophy, 51).

Quine, W. V. (1959). *Methods of Logic* (rev. edn., New York: Holt, Rinehart and Winston).

Stalnaker, R. (1984). *Inquiry* (Cambridge, Mass.: MIT Press).

——(1999). *Context and Content* (Oxford: Oxford University Press).

Swanson, E. (2004). "A suppositional theory of conditionals" (MS).

von Wright, G. H. (1957). *Logical Studies* (New York: The Humanities Press).

Weiner, M. (2005). "Must we know what we say?", *Philosophical Review* 114: 227–51.

---

[31] Thony Gillies pointed out that, if we expand the context set in this way, then Bert could attempt to close it again simply by asserting the disjunction, "either the butler or the gardener did it." Alice, it might seem, should accept this disjunctive assertion, since its content is entailed by something she accepts. But the response I am tentatively proposing must say that Alice should reject the assertion, despite the fact that it is entailed by something she believes. Given that her assertion that the butler did it was rejected, she should not be willing to accept this particular weakening of her assertion. "If we can't agree that the butler did it, we also can't agree that it was either the butler or the gardener." It is surprising that one might reasonably reject an assertion even if one would assert or accept one that entails it, but this still may be the right response. Compare Grice's discussion of what he calls "substitutive disagreement," where one rejects a disjunctive statement, "either Wilson or Heath will be the next Prime Minister" in favor of another that shares one of the disjunctions ("I disagree, it will be either Wilson or Thorpe."). Grice (1989: 64).

Williamson, T. (1996). "Knowing and asserting", *Philosophical Review* 105: 489–523.

—— (2000). *Knowledge and Its Limits*, (Oxford: Oxford University Press).

Yablo, S. (2006). "Non-catastrophic presuppostion failure", in A. Byrne and J. Thomson (eds.), *Content and Modality* (Oxford: Oxford University Press).

Yalcin, S. (2008). *Modality and Inquiry*. PhD Thesis, MIT, Department of Linguistics and Philosophy.

8

How Not to Theorize about the Language of Subjective Uncertainty

Eric Swanson

When we theorize about linguistic communication it's routine to focus on cases in which someone who is certain or nearly certain that ϕ conveys that ϕ to someone else. But we often communicate from positions of significant subjective uncertainty, and it isn't obvious what features the 'communication of uncertainties' shares with the communication of certainties or near certainties. Indeed, the case of belief suggests that we should expect to see significant differences between these kinds of communication: to be uncertain whether ϕ is not to believe a proposition, and so it would be surprising if it turned out that to express uncertainty about ϕ was to express a proposition.

This paper argues that the following four desiderata must not be neglected when we theorize about the language of subjective uncertainty.

1. We must successfully explain the effects this language can have on addressees' subjective uncertainty.
2. We must successfully explain the effects this language can have on (what I will call) conversational uncertainty.
3. We must explain the 'third grade of modal involvement' exhibited by epistemic modals and by epistemic adjectives.
4. We must explain the norms governing the language of subjective uncertainty, and explain the differences between them and the norms governing the language of subjective certainty.

Taken together, these constraints suggest that neither truth conditional nor traditional force modifier theories of the language of subjective uncertainty will be adequate.

For helpful discussion, thanks to audiences at University of Michigan, Ann Arbor, Harvard University, and University of California, Berkeley, to Selim Berker, Aaron Bronfman, Andy Egan, Adam Elga, Thony Gillies, John MacFarlane, Dilip Ninan, Rich Thomason, Tim Williamson, Steve Yablo, Seth Yalcin, and to the MATTI reading group at MIT. Thanks especially to Kai von Fintel, Ned Hall, Sarah Moss, Mark Richard, and Bob Stalnaker.

Because some ways of theorizing about the language of subjective uncertainty are incompatible with ways of theorizing about language broadly construed, the force of these constraints is more general than it might appear to be. As constraints on theorizing about an important part of language, they are constraints on theorizing about language: a theory of language that rules out every plausible theory of the language of subjective uncertainty is ipso facto implausible. I will argue that important features of the language of subjective uncertainty do not sit well with standard ways of thinking about language broadly construed. And so I take these constraints to have purchase on anyone who theorizes about language.

1.

The literature on epistemic modality tends to focus on modals that can also be used to express non-epistemic modalities, like 'can,' 'might,' 'have to,' and 'must'. But epistemic modals far outstrip the familiar operators '$\Box$' and '$\Diamond$':

'It's not unlikely that ϕ.'	'It's highly probable that ϕ.'
'It's a little more likely than not that ϕ.'	'Probably ϕ.'
'There's at least a 10% chance that ϕ.'	'Five to one that ϕ.'

To some extent Angelika Kratzer recognizes this, discussing some of the ways in which epistemic modality can be "graded" in her (1981). Unfortunately she seems not to recognize just how finely grained the language of subjective uncertainty can be. In many contexts it matters, for example, whether we use "Five to one that ϕ" or "Six to one that ϕ" to indicate our uncertainty with respect to the proposition that ϕ. Kratzer's treatments of modals like 'there is a good possibility' and 'there is a slight possibility' cannot be extended to these explicitly quantitative expressions of uncertainty. So her approach leaves much of the language of subjective uncertainty unilluminated.

How broadly *should* we construe the language of subjective uncertainty? What phenomena should a theory of this language explain? Many modals have both epistemic and non-epistemic uses, but the quantitative aspects of the language of subjective uncertainty are quite distinctive. This suggests that in order to uncover ways of expressing subjective uncertainty we would do well to look at the quantitative aspects of subjective uncertainty itself. Where there are aspects of one's doxastic state that are worth communicating, there are likely to be expressions that can help us communicate them.

There is a wide range of thought about what doxastic uncertainty is, how it can be measured, and how it should be represented. But by and large it is agreed that doxastic uncertainty cannot be characterized purely in terms of propositional content.[1] The

---

[1] Many also think it is a mistake to characterize "uncertain evidence" purely in terms of propositional content. (See especially Jeffrey 1968: 36.) For a contrary view on uncertain evidence, see (Williamson 2000: 213–21).

prevailing theories use probability spaces to represent uncertainty, thereby offering straightforward correlates to quantitatively specified expressions of subjective uncertainty. Given a standard probabilistic theory of uncertainty, for example, it's natural to think that in order to express my 0.8 credence in the proposition that it rained in Seattle yesterday I say

(1) There's an 80% chance that it rained in Seattle yesterday.

The most straightforward analyses of a sentence like (1) will give as its semantic value something that determines a function from the proposition that it rained in Seattle yesterday to 0.8.

It's compatible with such an analysis that (1) and other 'doxastically hedged' sentences have truth conditions, if those truth conditions are not supposed to give their meaning.[2] But the stronger view that truth conditions are sufficient to give the meaning of such sentences comes with heavy burdens to discharge. To begin with, we need the right kind of differences between the semantic value of (1), the semantic value of

(2) There's a 90% chance that it rained in Seattle yesterday.

and so on. So to give truth conditions for doxastically hedged sentences like these we would need to give a function $f(\cdot)$ from degrees of uncertainty and propositions into propositions, such that a believer is uncertain to degree n about a given proposition just in case she is certain or nearly certain of the proposition that is the image of that degree/proposition pair under $f(\cdot)$. That is, to provide truth conditions for (1) and (2) is to provide propositions that one is (nearly) certain about just in case one is uncertain to degree 0.8 or 0.9 about the proposition that it rained in Seattle yesterday. Construing subjective uncertainty about whether ϕ in terms of near certainty about some other proposition seems wrongheaded. But unless the truth conditional theorist can find such propositions, there is no reason to suppose that an assertion of a doxastically hedged sentence will inculcate the appropriate partial belief in the addressee. And the project of finding such propositions looks quixotic if not impossible.

In fact I have considerably understated the challenge, in a few different ways. First, unless she provides a function from *intervals* in [0, 1] and propositions into propositions, the advocate of a truth conditional theory cannot explain how to arrive at the semantic values of sentences like

(3) There's an 80 to 90% chance that it rained in Seattle yesterday.

Second, we can say

(4) It's likelier that it rained than that it snowed.
(5) It's twice as likely that it rained than it is that it snowed.
(6) It's between two and three times likelier that it rained than that it snowed.

---

[2] David Lewis takes this sort of view on imperatives in his (1970: 220–6).

To give such comparatives truth conditions we would need a function from intervals in the positive reals and pairs of propositions into propositions. Finally, consider

(7)   However likely it is that ϕ, it's every bit as likely that ϕ and ψ.

Epistemic comparatives of this form can be used to express the often important information that one's conditional probability of ψ on ϕ is high: if $P(\phi \wedge \psi) \geq P(\phi)$ then $\frac{P(\phi \wedge \psi)}{P(\phi)} \geq 1$, so $P(\psi|\phi) \geq 1$, so $P(\psi|\phi) = 1$. The familiar triviality results that follow from the claim that conditional probability is the probability of a proposition apply, mutatis mutandis, to such epistemic comparatives.[3] So we have many relatively specialized bits of language that we use to communicate our subjective uncertainty that are hard to theorize about in purely truth conditional terms.

Ironically, the project of giving truth conditions for doxastically hedged sentences also threatens to undermine an important initial motivation for truth conditional semantics. Propositions—i.e., truth conditions—are supposed to represent ways the world could be.[4] On the standard picture, to specify the content of a belief using a proposition is to say how the belief represents the world as being, by specifying the conditions under which the belief would successfully represent the world. The ways the world could be are, in principle, exactly the things eligible to be the content of a full belief. In light of subjective uncertainty we should not expect doxastic states to simply represent or misrepresent the world. Instead, they represent the world more or less *accurately* (Joyce, 1998). In just the same way, we should not expect the language of subjective uncertainty to simply represent or misrepresent the world.

Here's one way to see why. As a heuristic, represent a given full belief using an ordered pair consisting of 1 and the proposition that is believed. Let $\mathcal{F}$ be the set of all such ordered pairs. Represent partial beliefs by extending this set to the set $\mathcal{P}$ of all the ordered pairs consisting of some $n \in [0, 1]$ and a proposition. Obviously $\mathcal{F}$ is a proper subset of $\mathcal{P}$. By stipulation the elements of $\mathcal{F}$ exactly suffice to represent all the ways the world could be. So the members of $\mathcal{P}$ can represent *more* than this: for each way the world could be the members of $\mathcal{P}$ can represent *all the degrees of belief that one could stand in* to that way the world could be. The advocate of a truth conditional theory of the language of subjective uncertainty holds, in effect, that there are not only propositions to play the representational role played by the elements of $\mathcal{F}$, but also propositions to play the role of the elements of $\mathcal{P} \setminus \mathcal{F}$. Such a view is quite distant from the thought that propositions represent ways the world could be. One fundamental ambition of truth conditional semantics—to help explain how language represents the world by providing the conditions under which language successfully

---

[3]   For helpful presentations of various triviality results, see Edgington (1995) and Bennett (2003).

[4]   Obviously I am taking for granted a possible worlds conception of propositions. Many doubt that unstructured propositions are adequate to all the tasks propositions are supposed to discharge. But because the debate over whether propositions are structured has little to do with subjective uncertainty, I will freely talk in terms of possible worlds propositions. These can be thought of as equivalence classes of more finely-grained structured propositions.

represents the world—thus looks inconsistent with giving a truth conditional theory of the language of subjective uncertainty.

The first desideratum, then, is that theories of the language of subjective uncertainty must not neglect its quantitative aspects. It will be difficult if not impossible for truth conditional theories to capture these aspects of the language of subjective uncertainty, and no extant truth conditional theory comes close.

2.

Conversation is fundamentally a group activity, and uncertainty within a group is quite different from the uncertainty of particular individuals. So although it's crucial that we connect the language of subjective uncertainty to subjective uncertainty itself, it's also important not to overlook *conversational* uncertainty and the ways in which the language of subjective uncertainty interacts with it.

Following Robert Stalnaker, I hold that a conversational participant presupposes that ϕ just in case she takes it to be common belief among the conversational participants that for purposes of conversation they treat it as true that ϕ. On this analysis of presupposition, a conversational participant can presuppose that ϕ, can presuppose that $\neg\phi$, and can presuppose neither that ϕ nor that $\neg\phi$. This last state can be realized in a variety of ways; what's essential is simply that the participant *neither* take it to be common belief that all treat it as true that ϕ nor take it to be common belief that all treat it as true that $\neg\phi$.

In the simplest cases, where the conversational participants all make the same presuppositions, we can say that a conversation is uncertain as to whether ϕ just in case the participants presuppose neither that ϕ nor that $\neg\phi$. Conversational uncertainty of this sort directly affects what can be felicitously presupposed. For example, in a conversation that is uncertain about whether John is married, uses of 'John's wife' will generally be infelicitous unless presupposition accommodation occurs. Conversational uncertainty also makes a difference to which lines of inquiry it's natural to take up in a conversation. Whatever the individual credences of the participants in a conversation, a conversation that is uncertain about whether ϕ will be, ceteris paribus, more receptive to inquiry into the question whether ϕ than a conversation that is certain about whether ϕ.

Doxastically hedged assertions can influence not only the subjective uncertainty of the individuals in a conversation, but also which propositions the conversation is uncertain about. In a normal conversational context in which no one demurs, for example, an utterance of 'It might be that ϕ' ensures that the conversational participants do not presuppose that $\neg\phi$. To see this, consider the following dialogue:

BETTY: I saw Ron walking his dog last night with Sam.

CLARA: Are you sure it was Ron's dog? It might have been a neighbor's.

BETTY: # I think it was Ron's dog, but I might be wrong. Anyhow, Ron's dog was really misbehaving. . .

Betty's response is infelicitous because the presuppositions carried by the definite expression 'Ron's dog' are neither in place nor easily accommodated. Betty's admission that it might not have been Ron's dog ensures that the context set includes worlds in which Betty was wrong to think that the dog she saw was Ron's dog. In this particular case, it ensures that the conversation is uncertain about whether the dog she saw was Ron's dog. And this prevents Betty from appropriately presupposing that 'Ron's dog' denotes the dog she saw.[5]

We can see the context-changing effects of 'might' in other places as well. We often use 'might' statements when we reject assertions:

> SMITH: The weather report says it will definitely rain tomorrow, so it will rain tomorrow.
>
> JONES: It might not rain tomorrow—weather reports are sometimes wrong.

Given a Stalnakerian picture of assertion, the conversational participants have 'taken on board' Smith's assertive utterance that it will rain tomorrow only if the common ground comes to exclude worlds in which it doesn't rain tomorrow, because to assertively utter a non-hedged sentence 'ϕ' is to propose that the common ground exclude worlds in which $\neg\phi$. Against this background, Jones exploits the context change potential of 'It might not rain tomorrow' to make her rejection of that conversational proposal manifest. She in effect proposes that the common ground *include* some worlds in which it doesn't rain tomorrow. By making a proposal that is inconsistent with an intended effect of Smith's assertion, she rejects that assertion.

Stretching the original meaning of "context change potential" somewhat, I will call the aspiration of 'It might be that ϕ' to ensure that it is not presupposed that $\neg\phi$ the context change potential of 'might' statements.[6] This context change potential—combined with the crucial fact that speakers can often felicitously use 'might' statements without having much evidence that bears on the truth of the embedded claim—gives 'might' statements a surprising kind of power. Someone who gives very little credence to the proposition that ϕ may nevertheless still be obligated to admit that it *might* be that ϕ: "I might be a bodiless brain in a vat, but I really doubt it." So it's easy to make a *conversation* uncertain as to whether ϕ even if all the conversational participants think it's quite likely that $\neg\phi$. This is one reason why it's hard to argue with conspiracy theorists, skeptics, and the like. Give them an inch of credence, and they are entitled to take a mile of presupposition:

---

[5] Notice that these would-be failed presuppositions can be supplied by the antecedent of a conditional, as in:

> BETTY: I think it was Ron's dog, but I might be wrong. Anyhow, if it was Ron's dog, his dog was really misbehaving...

[6] Irene Heim's original way of thinking about context change potentials is significantly less inclusive than this one, in part because she assumes that applying a context change potential to a context will always yield a subset of the initial context. She writes, for example, that "There is an intimate connection between the CCP of a sentence and its truth conditional content: ... To be a true sentence is to keep the context true" (1983: 253).

RICHARD: My hand hurts.

TOM: Are you sure you have a hand? You might be a bodiless brain in a vat.

RICHARD: # I think I have a hand, but I might be wrong. Anyhow, my hand has been hurting for several days now.[7]

Richard's response to Tom is not as marked as Betty's response to Clara ("Anyhow, Richard's dog was really misbehaving")—but only insofar as Richard is conveying that he'd prefer not to play the skeptic's game today. In a conversation that is persistently uncertain about a 'hinge' proposition like that expressed by 'I have a hand,' it will be unclear just what we *can* presuppose. And although this is merely a conversational effect—Richard needn't give any less credence to the proposition that he has a hand than he did before Tom raised his skeptical challenge—it makes it difficult if not impossible for Richard to converse normally without seeming to beg the question.

Although subjective uncertainty comes in degrees, conversational uncertainty does not. When I use a definite noun phrase like 'John's wife' I *simply presuppose* that John is married. Presupposition failure may have more or less serious consequences for the course of a conversation, and presupposition accommodation may be more or less surprising and more or less reasonable to expect, but what is actually presupposed is not a matter of degree. In fact this is fortunate: adding degrees to pragmatic presupposition would require a complete overhaul of the standard analysis, and it's unclear how such an overhaul would go. On the standard analysis, a conversational participant pragmatically presupposes that ϕ just in case she takes it to be common belief that all the conversational participants treat it as true, for purposes of conversation, that ϕ. Common p-belief—a notion that adds 'degrees of common-ness' to common belief[8]—is orthogonal to the language of subjective uncertainty: in ordinary conversations someone who says 'It might be that ϕ' simply makes it common belief that for purposes of conversation we accept that it might be that ϕ. And analyzing degrees of presupposition in terms of common belief about degrees of treating as true for purposes of conversation would require, implausibly, that we coordinate not only on the content of presuppositions but also on the point-valued degrees (and, perhaps, intervals) to which a proposition is presupposed. (See Seth Yalcin's 2005 and 2007 for sketches of views like this.)

This difference between conversational and subjective uncertainty is reflected in the fact that expressions with (what for present purposes we can count as) the same context change potential can express different degrees of subjective uncertainty. Consider

(8) It's raining.

(9) It must be raining.

---

[7] Notice that the antecedent of a conditional can be used here, too, to supply the relevant presuppositions:

> RICHARD: I think I have a hand, but I might be wrong. Anyhow, if I have a hand, my hand has been hurting for several days now.

[8] See Monderer and Samet (1989) and Morris and Shin (1997).

If I have inferred that it is raining merely on the basis of seeing some wet umbrellas, it is generally inappropriate for me to say (8), even though (9) is appropriate. And, unsurprisingly, (9) makes a relevantly uninformed addressee less sure that it is raining than (8) does. But despite this difference in strength, (8) and (9) *both* induce the presupposition that it's raining. Similarly for

(10) It isn't raining.

(11) It couldn't be raining.

Both (10) and (11) aspire to make it presupposed that it isn't raining, but they exhibit a difference in strength parallel to that between (8) and (9). My point is not that 'must' and 'couldn't' always signal uncertainty, but that they sometimes do. So a successful treatment of 'must' must at least accommodate such uses.[9]

Phenomena like these spell trouble for the idea that 'doxastic change potential'—be it truth conditions or something probabilistic—can be read off of context change potential.[10] Because sentences like (8) and (9) and like (10) and (11) have the same effects on context (abstracting away from the different form of words), characterizations of their effects on context should make no distinction between them. But such characterizations will omit the differences between their effects on doxastic states. And doxastic change potentials (henceforth, 'DCPs') can't supplant context change potentials for all the reasons usually marshalled to think that truth conditions aren't up to the task: the DCP of 'ϕ and ψ,' for example, does not determine its CCP. So although there are systematic relationships between DCPs and CCPs, the language of subjective uncertainty shows that neither determines the other.

Given that context and context change are non-degreed, there is no hope of recovering doxastic change potential from context change potential. And given that doxastic change potential should not encode—for example—the order of conjuncts, there is no hope of recovering context change potential from it. The second desideratum for theorizing about the language of subjective uncertainty, then, is that we must not neglect the phenomena of conversational uncertainty.

---

[9] F. R. Palmer classifies 'must' as a "Deductive" modal, noting that "it is the notion of deduction or inference from known facts that is the essential feature of *must*, not just the confidence of the speaker, which is expressed by the adverbs *certainly, definitely,* etc." (Palmer 2001: 34–5; see also Karttunen 1972; Coates 1983: 41, 131, and 177; and Westmoreland 1998: 59–66). Epistemic 'have to' also has this feature, and under wide scope negation, epistemic 'can' and 'could' do as well. This rescues the hypothesis that 'can' and 'could' are duals of 'must' from the arguments to the contrary in Westmoreland (1998). For more on wide scope negation over epistemic modals, see von Fintel and Iatridou (2003: 184); cf. Cinque (1999: 198). See also Swanson (2008) on the evidentiality of weak epistemic modals like 'should' and 'ought.'

[10] The hypothesis that CCP determines doxastic change potential goes back to Irene Heim:

I will suggest that, while the CCP [context change potential] of "if" cannot be derived from its other properties, one *can* derive the content property from the CCP. More generally, the truth conditional aspect of the meaning of any expression is predictable on the basis of its CCP. (1983: 253)

In later work Heim goes so far as to claim that "The meaning of a sentence is its context change potential" (1992: 185)—a fundamental principle of dynamic semantics. At this point it's not clear to me how separating doxastic change potential from CCP—as I am urging here—would affect dynamic semantics.

3.

'Force modifier' analyses of epistemic modals may look like good candidates for satisfying both of the desiderata I have discussed so far. According to such analyses, epistemic modals indicate "the speaker's assessment of the truth of the proposition expressed in the [sentence's] residue or the nature of the speaker's commitment to its truth" (Huddleston and Pullum 2002: 767); they are "modulators of assertive force" (Yalcin 2005: 251).[11] Perhaps subjective uncertainty could be expressed by an assertion with tempered force, and perhaps an assertion with tempered force could have the appropriate kind of context change potential. We then would have avoided the task of finding (inter alia) for each proposition P and each degree of credence n, a proxy proposition that garners high credence just in case one has credence n in P.

One familiar objection to force modifier approaches is that they give unsystematic, ad hoc stories about doxastically hedged clauses that are embedded in a larger linguistic context. For example, if 'believes' expresses a relation that holds between a believer and a proposition, then a force modifier account makes it obscure what (12) could mean.

(12) I believe it might have rained in Seattle yesterday.

For present purposes I want to bracket this family of objections, because I think it is in fact not very hard to achieve compositionality in sentences like (12). Obviously we have to drop the assumption that the semantic value of 'believes' is simply a relation between a believer and a proposition. But 'believes' could denote a relation between a believer, a proposition, and an interval in [0, 1], and thus could be sensitive, in some way, to the ways in which epistemic modals are supposed to "modulate force."

The really hard problems of compositionality for force modifier approaches arise at the "third grade of modal involvement": the grade in which we see a quantifier scoping over a modal expression (Quine 1953). The fact that epistemic modals can exhibit such scope relations shows that the essential doctrine of force modifier approaches— that in asserting a statement headed by an epistemic modal, a speaker puts forward a non-hedged proposition with less than the usual authority or certainty—is untenable.

Contra the "descriptive generalization" argued for in von Fintel and Iatridou (2003), quantifiers can scope over epistemic modals:

(13) Al might be the best candidate, Betty might be the best candidate, and Clara might be the best candidate. So most people here might be the best candidate. (MOST PEOPLE HERE $> \Diamond$)

(14) Lots of people we don't know might be the murderer, so no one we know *has* to be the murderer. (LOTS OF PEOPLE WE DON'T KNOW $> \Diamond$, NO ONE WE KNOW $> \Box$)

---

[11] For contemporary examples of such views, see Westmoreland (1998), Drubig (2001), von Fintel (2003), Yalcin (2005), Davis et al. (2007), and Huitink (2008). In the end von Fintel does not endorse a force modifier approach.

(15) Be careful where you step, because every inch of the floor might have paint on it. (EVERY INCH OF THE FLOOR $>$ $\lozenge$)

To see why this kind of scope relation is important, note that a speaker who says (15) needn't commit herself to the claim that it might be that every inch of the floor has paint on it. When I paint, even if I have been sloppy enough so that paint could be anywhere, I'm nevertheless absolutely sure that I haven't splattered paint everywhere. But there is no proposition, put forward with *whatever* force, that gives the meaning of the relevant reading of (15). The proposition that at least one inch of the floor has paint on it is clearly too weak, and the proposition that every inch of the floor has paint on it—again, put forward with whatever force—is too strong, since I may be certain that there are paint-free square inches of the floor. This shows that doxastically hedged statements cannot in general be analyzed as ways of putting forward non-hedged propositions with less than the usual certainty, force, or authority. So the language of subjective uncertainty, appropriately broadly construed, cannot be handled by standard force modifier accounts, according to which a doxastic hedge modulates the force of the speaker's commitment to a given proposition.

We see similar phenomena with epistemic adjectives:

(16) This is an easy job; the person we hire for it doesn't need any special quali-fications. So even though only one person will be hired for the job, most of the applicants are possible hires.

The speaker here says that only one person will be hired for the job—thus *denying* that it's possible that most of the applicants are hires—and yet consistently with that says that most of the applicants are *possible* hires. So

(17) Most of the applicants are possible hires.

has a reading on which the quantifier scopes over the epistemic adjective. Similar problems arise in other domains where non-truth conditional theories may be attract-ive: consider 'Everyone should take a break, but not everyone should take a break at the same time.'[12]

A positive account of the meaning of sentences like these must pay close attention to the nature of quantification. Just as one can believe that most people are nice without knowing who is nice, one can believe that most of the applicants are possible hires without having any idea *which* of the applicants are possible hires. Some pointers toward a treatment can, I think, be gleaned from noticing the connections between quantification and disjunction. The proposition that most people in the set $\{a, b, c\}$ are hires *is* the proposition that exactly a and b are hires, *or* exactly a and c are hires, *or*

---

[12] For an extensive discussion, see Swanson (2010). The as yet quite obscure view that quantifiers can 'scope into speech acts' might help here. (For work in this vein see Karttunen (1977) and Krifka (2001 and 2004).) But one cannot consistently construe the logical form of (15) as (i) and hold that doxastic hedges simply serve to modify the 'force' associated with the assertion of a single proposition.

(i) [For every inch of the floor]$_i$, it might be that [that inch]$_i$ has paint on it.

exactly b and c are hires, *or* exactly a, b, and c are hires. Given plausible assumptions, to believe that most of the applicants are hires is to believe this disjunction. Similarly, to believe that most of the people in the set $\{a, b, c\}$ are *possible* hires is to believe the disjunction 'Exactly a and b are possible hires, or exactly a and c are possible hires, or exactly b and c are possible hires, or exactly a, b, and c are possible hires.'

Note that one can believe that a and b are possible hires without believing that it's possible that a and b are hires. Note also that one can believe an ordinary disjunction—one without any doxastic hedges, for example—while having significantly less than full belief in each of its disjuncts. But to *sustain* a belief in an ordinary disjunction a believer must be disposed to update her credences in a way that vindicates certain inferences. For example, a believer who sustains her belief that ϕ or ψ in the face of learning that $\neg\phi$ must come to believe that ψ. Similarly, a believer who sustains her belief that a is a possible hire or b is a possible hire in the face of learning that a is *not* a possible hire must come to believe that b is a possible hire. So a believer who sustains her belief in the disjunction that I am suggesting should be associated with 'Most of the people in the set $\{a, b, c\}$ are possible hires' must—to take just one example—come to believe that exactly a and b are possible hires in the face of learning that c is not a possible hire. This is so despite the fact that one can believe that exactly a and b or exactly a and c or exactly b and c or exactly a, b, and c are possible hires without believing that a is a possible hire, or that b is a possible hire, or that c is a possible hire. Put a little less abstractly: you can consistently believe that most of the people in the set $\{a, b, c\}$ are possible hires without believing that any particular one of them is a possible hire. But if in such a state you learn that c is not a possible hire, and you sustain your belief that most of the people in the set $\{a, b, c\}$ are possible hires, you're rationally constrained to believe that a and b are possible hires.[13]

The similarities between quantification and disjunction suggest one way of giving a compositional, non-truth conditional theory that can handle the third grade of epistemic modality. The thought is that quantified doxastically hedged sentences express something like disjunctions, each disjunct of which is a non-quantified doxastically hedged sentence. (For the details of a semantics that works in this way, see Swanson (2006).) The important point for present purposes is that a compositional

---

[13] Is believing that it might be that ϕ lending credence greater than zero to ϕ, as in Yalcin (2005)? Or is it lending credence greater than or greater than or equal to some non-zero threshold to ϕ? Suppose, for reductio, that to believe that it might be that ϕ it's sufficient that one lend non-zero credence to the proposition that ϕ. Consider then a believer who believes that *either* it might be that ϕ or it might be that ψ, without believing that it might be that ϕ and without believing that it might be ψ. Either she assigns non-zero credence to ϕ or she does not, and either she assigns non-zero credence to ψ or she does not. But given our reductio assumption she cannot assign non-zero credence to either without contradicting the stipulation that she does not believe that it might be that ϕ and does not believe that it might be that ψ. So she must assign zero credence to both. But this is surely wrong: there is a difference between believing that either it might be that ϕ or it might be that ψ and believing that $\neg(\phi \vee \psi)$. As a result it's crucial that believers be able to assign sub-threshold credence to a proposition without assigning *zero* credence to that proposition.

semantics—a semantics the effects of which could not be mimicked by a force modifier approach—needn't traffic solely in truth conditions.

Another point against force modifier approaches is the syntactic flexibility of epistemic adjectives. To begin with, consider

(18) Al is a possible hire.

The only plausible force modifier treatment of (18) that I can see gives it the logical form of (19).

(19) [It's possible that [Al is a hire]].

From a purely syntactic point of view it would be better (ceteris paribus) to say that 'possible' combines with 'hire' to form the complex predicate 'possible hire':

(20) [Al [is a possible [hire]]].

The costs of adopting syntactically revisionary theories of epistemic adjectives are even more evident in (21), which is doxastically hedged in two different ways.

(21) Al is a likely candidate and a possible hire.

In normal circumstances, an addressee's belief state after interpreting (21) will be no different (modulo beliefs about the mode of expression) than it would have been if the speaker had said

(22) It's likely that Al is a candidate. It's possible that Al is a hire.

This suggests, plausibly enough, that in some sense (21) and (22) have the same or very similar *content*. But it is quite another thing to say that they have the same underlying syntactic structure. I see no way for force modifier views to avoid this implausible commitment.

Epistemic adjectives raise no special problems for truth conditional theories. But to my knowledge no advocates of force modifier approaches have tried to extend their theories to cover epistemic adjectives, and the prospects for such an extension look dim. So much the worse for force modifier approaches: epistemic modals and epistemic adjectives are equally a part of the language of subjective uncertainty, and they are interesting for many of the same reasons. For obvious reasons the presence of epistemic adjectives is closely related to the ability of quantifiers to scope over epistemic modals. These features of natural language make it crucial that a theory of the language of subjective uncertainty not ignore Quine's "third grade of modal involvement" in the epistemic realm.

4.

So far I tried to make it clear that it is not only counterintuitive but also deeply mistaken to theorize about the language of subjective uncertainty as though it were all of a piece with the language of subjective certainty. Taking the language of subjective certainty (or near certainty; I will leave off this qualification in what follows). Taking the language of subjective certainty as paradigmatic will likely give us a distorted picture of the language of subjective uncertainty. But it is also deeply mistaken to theorize about communication as if it consisted solely of the communication of certainties. We can see this starkly when we consider the norms that govern assertion. The norms of assertion for doxastically hedged statements are not explained by—indeed, they are not even consistent with—many otherwise attractive accounts of the norms of assertion for non-hedged statements.

We can start by considering some distinctive features of the norms governing the use of 'might' statements. Suppose I have no idea where my car keys are, and neither does my housemate. He gets home from work—and so has no good sense of where I've looked—and I ask him if he knows where my keys are. He says

(23) The keys might be on the kitchen table.

Now his utterance in this case may or may not be *helpful* to me, because I may have already scoured the kitchen table looking for my keys. But whether or not his 'might' statement is helpful to me, it is *appropriate,* and he *knows* that it is appropriate. It wouldn't be fair for me to say in response "No, I've already looked on the kitchen table. They're not there. So why did you say they might be there?" All I can say is something like "No, I've already looked on the kitchen table. They're not there."

Truth conditional semantics for 'might' have considerable trouble making the right predictions about this case. To see why, consider two simple semantics for 'might,' in the spirit of Kratzer (1977, 1981, and 1991).

- A *solipsistic* semantics: 'The keys might be on the table' is true iff it's consistent with what the speaker knows[14] that the keys are on the table.
- A *non-solipsistic* semantics: 'The keys might be on the table' is true iff it's consistent with what the speaker and the addressee know, pooled together, that the keys are on the table.

Given standard assumptions about the norms governing assertion, both these semantics wrongly predict that my housemate's utterance was inappropriate. According to the solipsistic semantics, he asserted a proposition that (we can suppose) he rightly believed would be uninformative to me: I already knew that he didn't know whether the keys were on the table. But assertions that the speaker believes will be uninformative are generally not appropriate.[15] According to the non-solipsistic semantics, my housemate asserted a proposition concerning not only what *he* knows about the location of the keys, but also what *I* know. Given standard assumptions about the norms

---

[14] The arguments to come are also sound if we substitute, e.g. 'believes' for 'knows' throughout.

[15] See e.g. Grice (1987: 26). The right formulation of this constraint on appropriate assertion is a delicate matter, since it is appropriate for me to use

(i) Liem, you ate all the cookies.

simply to let my son know that *I* know that he ate all the cookies. But in such a circumstance I do believe that my utterance of (i) will change my son's beliefs and conversational presuppositions. Appropriate uses of 'might' statements do not require this.

governing assertion, on this semantics my housemate must be certain (or nearly certain) *that I am uncertain* as to whether the keys are on the table, if his utterance is to be appropriate. And in the situation as described he plainly is not certain about this. This brings out the crucial point that a semantics for the language of subjective uncertainty is not plausible unless it leaves room for uncertainty about epistemic states.

Moreover, it's nearly standard to think that a speaker cannot say truly that it might be that ϕ if relevant others know that $\neg\phi$ (Hacking 1967: 146, 148–9; see also Teller 1972: 310–11; DeRose 1991: 586–96, and von Fintel and Gillies, this volume). But then my housemate would take a serious risk of saying something false with his 'might' statement, presumably would know of this risk, and presumably would be criticizable if I knew that the keys weren't on the table.

But even if we abstract away from particular semantic theories for 'The keys might be on the table,' this example raises acute problems for some putative norms of assertion. For suppose that my keys are in fact not on the table, that I know this, and that my housemate, while not being unreasonable to think that my keys might be on the table, has no special reason to think that they might be there. Then although he may well *believe* that they might be on the table, we wouldn't say that he *knows* that they might be on the table.[16] Nevertheless he can appropriately say "The keys might be on the table." This suggests that the knowledge norm of assertion—"One must assert p only if one knows p" (Williamson, 2000: 243)—is not right. Similarly, Robert Brandom is not right to claim that in asserting speakers "undertake a specific task responsibility, namely the responsibility to show that they are *entitled* to the commitment expressed by their assertions, should that entitlement be brought into question" (1994: 173). Clearly my housemate can say that my keys might be on the table without any special epistemic entitlement—let alone the responsibility to show that he has such an entitlement—and without making any special commitments. Gary Watson voices a similar view—"To assert that p is, among other things, to endorse p, to authorize others to assume that p, to commit oneself to defending p, thereby (typically) giving others standing to criticize or challenge what one says. One exercises one's epistemic authority" (2004: 58). And John McDowell claims that the contents of assertion are "epistemic surrogates for represented states of affairs" (1980: 45). These views are subject to similar objections. Obviously I could go on with examples like these, in part because these are *not* implausible things to say about the language of subjective certainty. But when we pay attention to the distinctive features of the language of subjective uncertainty, it becomes clear that we should not generalize too liberally from the language of subjective certainty.

The defender of invariably stringent norms of assertion might well respond that 'might' statements are not, strictly speaking, assertions, and hence that they are not

---

[16] Compare Keith DeRose's example of knowing whether it's possible that ϕ: " 'I don't know whether it's possible that John has cancer; only the doctors know. I'll find that out tomorrow when the results of the test are revealed' " (1991: 584).

subject to the norms governing assertion. But this response would make it utterly mysterious what we should say about sentences like (24) and (25).

(24) Half these tires are worn, and might have punctures, too.

(25) Most of the candidates are possible hires, and well-credentialed too.

The norms governing the hedged parts of these sentences are different than the norms governing their non-hedged parts. But neither sentence naturally splits into a pair of syntactic units, so the claim that each involves two speech acts does not look promising. So we should count (24) and (25) both as assertions. They both aim to effect two kinds of doxastic change, which are governed by different norms.

Strictly speaking, 'belief' and 'reasonable belief' norms of assertion do better. As a general rule it seems inappropriate for my housemate to say that my keys might be on the table in circumstances in which he doesn't even believe that they might be there. But I suspect that this is being found innocent on the basis of a technicality: advocates of belief norms typically take themselves to be proposing that full (or near full) belief is necessary for appropriate assertibility. Otherwise their disagreement with advocates of knowledge norms would be much more dramatic than they have taken it to be: it's generally (though I think wrongly) presupposed that one knows that ϕ only if one gives full (or near full) credence to the proposition that ϕ.[17]

Why is it that the norms governing the appropriate use of 'might' statements are less stringent than the norms for statements that aren't doxastically hedged? When they make non-hedged assertions, at least, speakers seem to claim some authority (or to act as though they were claiming some authority). But a cooperative speaker who does not take herself to have much authority with respect to a given subject matter will signal her own ignorance by saying, for example, that it might be that ϕ, or that it's probably not true that ϕ (as opposed to simply saying that ϕ, or that $\neg\phi$). In so doing she claims less authority than she would have if she had used the language of subjective certainty. By claiming less authority she gives her addressees less stringent claims on her, and so the norms governing her assertion are looser as well.

The relationship between the language that a speaker uses and the authority she thereby claims is in fact a bit more complicated than what I have just said might suggest. To begin with, a speaker who says

(23) The keys might be on the kitchen table.

claims less authority (holding context, intonation, stakes, background conditions, and other relevant factors fixed) than does a speaker who says

(26) The keys are very likely on the kitchen table.

As I suggested earlier, even someone who is ignorant of relevant facts can appropriately (and in some cases helpfully) say (23). By contrast, a speaker has to be in a relatively

---

[17] Though see again DeRose's examples of 'knowing whether it's possible that ϕ' (1991: 584).

good epistemic position to appropriately say (26). Another way to see this contrast is to compare (27) and (28) as responses to "Have you seen my keys?"

(27) I don't know, they might be on the kitchen table.

(28) I don't know, they're very likely on the kitchen table.

I find (27) fine, and (28) quite strange. It's plausible that the explicit disavowal of epistemic authority in these sentences—"I don't know..."—is compatible with 'might' and clashes with 'very likely.'

However, many uses of the language of subjective uncertainty do not indicate that the speaker claims less than the usual epistemic authority. A climatologist who, after years of painstaking study, gives precise odds for the average temperature in southeastern Michigan 5,000 years ago justly claims a significant amount of authority when she says

(29) It's 90% likely that the average was between 46 degrees and 50 degrees.

She is using the language of subjective uncertainty *although she is an expert* on the subject matter at hand. (Similarly, we can use such language to make authoritative claims about objective chance.) On the other hand, if I, as a cooperative non-expert, were to opine on the climate, I might say something like

(30) The average temperature was probably between 46 degrees and 50 degrees.

My "probably" is more vague than the climatologist's "90% likely," and also specifies a wider range of acceptable credences. Of course it's difficult to say just where the lower bound on the range is, and its precise location is no doubt partly a function of context, the interests and values of the conversational participants, and so on. But a believer with *any* credence between that lower bound (say, 0.6, in a particular case) and 1 can be truthfully counted as thinking that probably the average temperature was between 46 and 50 degrees. And it would be misleading, at least, for me to say (30) if my credence weren't in that range.

When I do say (30), however, I am *not* aiming to ensure that my addressees give a credence within that range to the proposition that the average temperature was between 46 and 50 degrees. By saying only (30) I present myself not as an expert, but as a person with a not wholly unreasonable hunch. If I were to say (30)— unwittingly—to a group of climatologists, I would happily defer to them if they made their expertise manifest and demurred. But in such a case I would not have violated norms of conversation as badly as I would have if I'd presented myself as an expert, giving *precise* odds on the climate.

Or recall the car keys case. I do not know where my car keys are, and neither does my housemate; he does not know where I've looked; he says "Your keys might be on the kitchen table." In many cases he will have spoken appropriately even if I have already searched the kitchen table and know that my keys are not there. I can't criticize him for giving bad advice about the kind of doxastic state to have. So my housemate intends his advice to have *no force* if I already know that the keys are not on the table. He is attempting to ensure only that I not *inadvertently* rule out or overlook the possibility that my keys are on the kitchen table.

One important lesson to draw from these examples is that often speakers have quite modest intentions when they use doxastically hedged statements. Often, their hedging indicates that they are communicating from a position of ignorance. But this indication not only conveys a credence other than certainty or near certainty. It also indicates a kind of epistemic and communicative modesty—a disposition to take one's own credence as less than authoritative, and an intention that one's addressees take the expression of that credence as less than authoritative—that attenuates the authority that she claims with her assertion, and hence the norms that govern it.

Moreover, different expressions of subjective uncertainty attenuate the speaker's claim to authority to different degrees. With respect to authority claimed, 'might' is like 'doesn't have to be,' 'must' is like 'couldn't be,' and so on: holding other relevant factors fixed, it's more committal to say that the keys couldn't be in the living room than it is to say that they don't have to be in the living room, and it is still more committal to come right out and say that they *aren't* in the living room. This leads to the following generalization.

AUTHORITY REFLECTS RANGE:

The *authority* that a speaker claims in asserting that ϕ decreases with increases in the size of the *range* of credences such that 'S believes that ϕ' is true (holding fixed context, content of the prejacent,[18] vagueness of expression, intonation, stakes, background conditions, and other factors that help determine the authority that a speaker claims).[19]

A simple assertion with no doxastic hedges is maximally specific. Doxastically hedged statements exhibit degrees of specificity: 'Might ϕ' is less specific than 'Very likely ϕ,' which is less specific than 'There's a 50% chance that ϕ.' Accordingly, a speaker who says 'Might ϕ' claims less authority than one who says 'Very likely ϕ,' and so on. 'It might be that ϕ' admits a wide range of credence assignments, so that by saying it a cooperative speaker signals that she does not have the epistemic authority to express anything that is particularly committal about the right credence to have in ϕ. This generalization also lets us explain why my housemate's suggestion that the keys might be on the table is not criticizable in the ways that non-hedged assertions are.

By appealing to the ways in which the language of subjective uncertainty can modulate the authority of an assertion, we can explain aspects of cases that are commonly used to motivate relativist theories of the content of doxastically hedged statements. Consider

[18] Ceteris paribus, "Judy might be in Tangiers" generally claims more authority than "Judy might be in her office."
[19] For simplicity, here I'm abstracting away from mixed cases like (21), (24), and (25).

EAVESDROPPING:

The White spies are spying on the Red spies, who are spying on the gun for hire. The gun for hire has left evidence suggesting that he is in Zurich, but one clever White spy knows that he is in London. After finding the planted evidence, one Red spy says to the others, "The gun for hire might be in Zurich," and the others respond "That's true." The clever White spy says "That's false—he's in London" to the other White spies, and explains how he knows this.[20]

One argument a relativist could give here is that in order to explain the ways in which judgments about the Red spy's utterance are affected by the assessor's epistemic position, the truth value of 'what is said' must be sensitive to the assessor's epistemic position. But note that the Red spy significantly tempers the authority he claims when he says that the gun for hire might be in Zurich, by using an epistemic 'might.' As a result, I respond to the hypothetical relativist, we're inclined to judge the Red spy in a lenient way. It's nevertheless appropriate for the White spy—an observer with more relevant information, and hence more justifiable claim to authority—to say that because the gun for hire is in London, he *couldn't* be in Zurich, and to say that (there is a sense in which) the Red spy spoke falsely. Indeed, I find that my relativist-friendly truth value judgments, such as they are, weaken as the authority claimed is strengthened: I'm more inclined to judge "The gun for hire can't be in London" as straightforwardly false—even if the case is set up so that Red spy's belief is fully justified—than I am inclined to judge false "The gun for hire might be in Zurich." AUTHORITY REFLECTS RANGE can help explain why we have relativist-friendly judgments about expressions that claim less than the usual authority: the less authority we claim when making an assertion, the more lenient the norms that govern the assertion.

5.

In theorizing about natural language there is an understandable tendency to take one problem at a time. In many cases this approach is helpful—even essential—if we want to make any progress. But we can get a false impression of understanding when we toil away on one problem without considering the constraints on solutions that other problems impose. So in general it's important not to work on problems in *too* piecemeal a way. I worry that much theorizing about the language of subjective uncertainty has been too piecemeal. Focusing on one issue at a time has made the space of plausible solutions look bigger than it in fact is.

---

[20] A more complicated but in some respects better way to set up this example is with the Red spy using wide-scope negation over a necessity modal. Suppose he had thought that the gun for hire was in London, but on finding the planted evidence says "The gun for hire doesn't have to be in London." This modification to the example undercuts the thought that the demonstratives in the "That's true" / "That's false" responses target the modal's prejacent clause.

In particular, the first two constraints—that we explain both the doxastic and conversational changes associated with the language of subjective uncertainty—together suggest that doxastic change potential is not determined by context change potential, and thus that semantics should not deliver one or the other, but both. The third constraint shows that even as we move on from truth conditional semantics, we must do so without abandoning compositionality. Whatever one's thoughts about the plausibility of compositionality 'across the board,' it's not plausible that compositionality breaks down in simple structures of the form 'Most Fs are Gs.' And although philosophers and linguists often talk as though compositionality demands a truth conditional semantics, clearly it doesn't: truth conditional semantics yields objects that are functions from possible worlds into truth values, but a compositional semantics (that proceeds, as is familiar, via functional application) might well yield functions from sets of possible worlds into real values, or intervals, or the characteristic functions of sets of such functions.[21] But this does not mean—recalling the second constraint—that changes to the context need reflect such fine-grained semantic values. And it does not mean that we must abandon truth conditional semantics: indeed, we should generalize to the worst case while effectively *embedding* truth conditional semantics within a probabilistic theory. Finally, because the norms governing a speech act are a function of (inter alia) its meaning, semantic theories of the language of subjective uncertainty need to deliver objects that can be well used by a theory of the norms that govern it. This provides a further constraint on those theories. And again, it would be unproductive, I think, to try to satisfy this desideratum while ignoring the others.

In the 1970s, semantic proposals were generally given for a fragment of a natural language. Since then, the tacit codification of the methods of formal semantics has made it easy to forget that fruitful semantic techniques and frameworks are *fruitful relative to* such a fragment. Indeed, the worth of a framework for a particular fragment may be downright misleading when we begin to consider other and larger fragments of a language. I suspect that this is the case with the language of subjective uncertainty. Purely truth conditional semantics has given us considerable insight into the language of subjective certainty. But that is no reason to think that we must strictly adhere to that framework in theorizing about the language of subjective uncertainty. The next step is to develop frameworks and theories that aspire to illuminate the language of subjective uncertainty and the language of subjective certainty together.

References

Bennett, Jonathan (2003). *A Philosophical Guide to Conditionals* (Oxford: Oxford University Press).

Brandom, Robert B. (1994). *Making It Explicit* (Cambridge, Mass.: Harvard University Press).

---

[21] In Swanson (2006) I treat sentences as denoting functions of type $\langle\langle st, v\rangle, t\rangle$, where $D_v = [0, 1]$ (67–8), but other denotations would work equally well.

Cinque, Guglielmo (1999). *Adverbs and Functional Heads: A Cross-Linguistic Perspective* (Oxford: Oxford University Press).

Coates, Jennifer (1983). *The Semantics of the Modal Auxiliaries* (London: Croom Helm).

Davis, Christopher, Potts, Christopher, and Speas, Peggy (2007). "The pragmatic values of evidential sentences:", in Masayuki Gibson and Tova Friedman (eds.), *Proceedings of Semantics and Linguistic Theory (SALT)* 17, 71–88.

DeRose, Keith (1991). "Epistemic possibilities", *Philosophical Review* 100(4): 581–605.

Drubig, Hans Bernhard (2001). "On the syntactic form of epistemic modality." MS University of Tübingen. URL <http://www.sfb441.uni-tuebingen.de/b2/papers/DrubigModality.pdf>.

Edgington, Dorothy (1995). "On conditionals", *Mind* 104: 235–329.

von Fintel, Kai (2003). "Epistemic modals and conditionals revisited", MS., Massachusetts Institute of Technology. URL <http://web.mit.edu/fintel/www/umass-handout.pdf>.

—— Gillies, Anthony S. (this volume). "'*Might*' made right", Ch. 3.

—— Iatridou, Sabine (2003). "Epistemic containment", *Linguistic Inquiry*, 34(2): 173–198.

Grice, Paul (1987). "Logic and conversation", in *Studies in the Way of Words* (Cambridge Mass.: Harvard University Press).

Hacking, Ian (1967). "Possibility", *Philosophical Review* 76(2): 143–68.

Heim, Irene (1983). "On the projection problem for presuppositions", repr. in Portner and Partee 2002: 249–60.

—— (1992). "Presupposition projection and the semantics of attitude verbs", *Journal of Semantics* 9: 183–221.

Huddleston, Rodney and Pullum, Geoffrey K. (eds.) (2002). *The Cambridge Grammar of the English Language* (Cambridge: Cambridge University Press).

Huitink, Janneke (2008). "Scoping over epistemics in English and in Dutch", *Current Issues in Unity and Diversity of Languages* (Korea: Linguistic Society), 2077–89.

Jeffrey, Richard C. (1968). "Probable knowledge", in *Probability and the Art of Judgment* (Cambridge: Cambridge University Press), 30–43.

Joyce, James M. (1998). "A nonpragmatic vindication of probabilism", *Philosophy of Science* 65 (4): 575–603.

Karttunen, Lauri (1972). "*Possible* and *must*", in J. Kimball (ed.), *Syntax and Semantics* (New York: Academic Press) volume 1: 1–20.

—— (1977). "Syntax and semantics of questions", *Linguistics and Philosophy* 1: 3–44.

Kratzer, Angelika (1977). "What *must* and *can* must and can mean", *Linguistics and Philosophy* 1: 337–55.

—— (1981). "The notional character of modality", in H.-J. Eikemeyer and H. Rieser (eds.), *Words, Worlds, and Contexts, New Approaches to Word Semantics* (Berlin: de Greyter), 38–74, repr. in Portner and Partee 2002: 289–323.

—— (1991). "Modality", in Arnim von Stechow and Dieter Wunderlich (eds.), *Semantics: An International Handbook of Contemporary Research* (Berlin: de Gruyter), 639–50.

Krifka, Manfred (2001). "Quantifying into question acts", *Natural Language Semantics* 9: 1–40.

—— (2004). "Semantics below and above speech acts", MS., Humboldt Universität.

Lewis, David K. (1970). "General semantics", in *Philosophical Papers*, vol. i. (Oxford: Oxford University Press) 189–229.

McDowell, John (1980). "Meaning, communication, and knowledge", in *Meaning, Knowledge, and Reality* (Cambridge, Mass.: Harvard University Press), 29–50.

Monderer, Dov, and Samet, Dov (1989). "Approximating common knowledge with common beliefs", *Games and Economic Behavior* 1: 170–90.

Morris, Stephen, and Hyun Song Shin (1997). "Approximate common knowledge and co-ordination: Recent lessons from game theory", *Journal of Logic, Language, and Information*. 6: 171–90.

Palmer, F. R. (2001). *Mood and Modality* (2nd edn. Cambridge: Cambridge University Press).

Portner, Paul, and Partee, Barbara H. (eds.) (2002). *Formal Semantics: The Essential Readings* (Oxford: Blackwell).

Quine, W. V. O. (1953). "Three grades of modal involvement", in *The Ways of Paradox* (New York: Random House) 158–76.

Swanson, Eric (2006). *Interactions with Context*, PhD thesis, Massachusetts Institute of Technology.

—— (2008). "Modality in language", *Philosophy Compass* 3(6): 1193–1207. DOI: 10.1111/j.1747-9991.2008.00177.x.

—— (2010). "On scope relations between quantifiers and epistemic modals", *Journal of Semantics* 27(4): 529–40.

Teller, Paul (1972). "Epistemic possibility", *Philosophia* 2: 302–20.

Watson, Gary (2004). "Asserting and promising", *Philosophical Studies* 117: 57–77.

Westmoreland, Robert R. (1998). *Information and Intonation in Natural Language Modality*, PhD thesis, Indiana University.

Williamson, Timothy (2000). *Knowledge and Its Limits* (Oxford: Oxford University Press).

Yalcin, Seth (2005). "Epistemic modals", in Jon Gajewski, Valentine Hacquard, Bernard Nickel, and Seth Yalcin (eds.), *New Work on Modality*. MIT Working Papers in Linguistics, vol. 51, 231–72.

—— (2007). "Epistemic modals", *Mind* 116: 983–1026.

9

A Problem about Permission and Possibility

Stephen Yablo

This chapter explores the prospects for a unified theory of deontic and (so-called) epistemic modality. That we use similar language for the two sorts of modality is a familiar point. The audiovisual system made it for me once, when it projected these words onto the screen:

IF THIS EQUIPMENT IS OFF CAMPUS, IT MAY BE STOLEN.

The intended reading, of course, is that a certain *hypothesis* is not ruled out: that the projector is stolen. But another possible reading is that a certain *course of action* is not ruled out: that the projector *be* stolen.[1] Compare in this respect "Sabotage is not ruled out," as uttered by an FAA investigator after the crash, to the same sentence uttered by rebel leader Natasha before the crash. The investigator is saying that sabotage is not ruled out descriptively, as it would be if he'd asserted "There was no sabotage." Natasha is saying that it is not ruled out *prescriptively*, as it would be if she'd commanded her underlings not to engage in sabotage. That the two readings of "may" correspond to two readings of "not ruled out" is suggestive; it suggests that "That may be *so*" and "That may be *done*" have semantic properties in common.

What does it matter, though, if the one "may" has properties in common with the other? It matters because descriptive "may" is extremely confusing; and the questions

I am grateful to Seth Yalcin, Eric Swanson, Bob Stalnaker, Peter Railton, Allan Gibbard, Rich Thomason, Thony Gillies, Kai von Fintel, Sarah Moss, Sally Haslanger, Caspar Hare, Carrie Jenkins, Kit Fine, George Bealer, Andy Egan, Brian Weatherson, John MacFarlane, Tim Williamson, Gideon Rosen, Bob Hale, Elizabeth Fricker, Frank Jackson, Crispin Wright, Josh Dever, Nicholas Asher, Adam Morton, David Beaver, Cleo Condoravdi, Danny Fox, Brian Hedden, Nina Emery, Daniel Greco, Susanna Rinard, Andrew Graham, Alejandro Pérez Carballo, Paolo Santorio, and two anonymous referees for this volume. Bob Stalnaker was kind enough to show me remarks he made in response to Lewis's presentation of his permission problem at Cornell. Some of this material figured in my 2007 Nelson Lectures at Michigan and 2008 Hempel Lectures at Princeton; thanks to the audiences at both places. I learned a lot from participants, beyond those already mentioned, in the 2006 Austin Workshop on Epistemic Modals and the 2006 Arché Conference on Modality; particular thanks to my Arché commentator David Efird. This paper descends from a paper appearing, with David's comments, in an Oxford volume on modality edited by Bob Hale and Aviv Hoffman.

[1] Of course, it is a different sort of ruling out that's intended; stealing the projector is not *forbidden*.

we are driven to as we attempt to understand it are questions that, as it happens, have been much discussed in connection with deontic "may."

The standard semantics for "It may be (or might be, or is possible) that φ"[2] has it expressing something in the vicinity of the speaker's failing to know that $\sim\varphi$. Thus Moore:

It's possible that I'm not sitting down now... means 'It is not certain that I am' or 'I don't know that I am'.[3]

Later versions of the standard semantics allow the knower(s) and/or the information against which φ is tested to vary:[4]

"It is possible$_A$ that p" is true if and only if what A knows does not, in a manner that is obvious to A, entail not-p.[5]

"It is possible that p" is true if and only if (1) no member of the relevant community knows that p is false, and (2) there is no relevant way by which members of the relevant community can come to know that p is false.[6]

There is undoubtedly something right about this approach. But there are things wrong with it too.

One problem with the standard semantics is that it gets the subject matter wrong. When I say, "Bob might be in his office," I am talking about Bob and his office, not myself or the extent of my information.[7] The difference in subject matter makes for a difference in attitude. Imagine that the building is on fire and everyone other than Bob has escaped down the back stairs. I am afraid that Bob might still be in his office. I am not afraid that I don't know he's elsewhere.

Two, the proposed truth conditions in their naïve Moorean form are too weak. The mere fact that I don't myself know that $\sim\varphi$ doesn't make it true in my mouth that φ might be so. Suppose you question my claim on the basis that Bob was just seen stepping onto a plane. It would be no reply at all to say that my information really was as limited as I suggested; I really and truly didn't know that Bob was not in his office. Evidently the information that needs to comport with φ for a might-claim

---

[2] I will generally use "might" rather than "may" when the (so-called) epistemic reading is intended.

[3] Moore (1962: 184).

[4] DeRose (1991); Hacking (1967); Teller (1972); von Fintel and Gillies (2007).

[5] Stanley (2005: 128).

[6] DeRose (1991: 593-4).

[7] It might seem the worry could be sidestepped by putting speaker's knowledge into the mechanism by which the content is generated, rather than the content itself (Kratzer 1981). Speaker's knowledge would play the same sort of role in the evaluation of "might"-claims as speaker's attention plays in the evaluation of "you"-claims. Andy Egan pointed out that this solution may swing too far in the other direction. For the Kratzer-proposition can be seen as a consistency-claim: φ *is consistent with* K, where K is the relevant body of knowledge. The modal and evidential properties of "might"-claims look rather different from those of consistency-claims. Clouds are evidence that it might rain, but not evidence for the consistency of φ with K. Consistency-claims are necessary or impossible, but the gathering clouds hardly make it a necessary truth that it might rain.

to be correct can extend beyond what the speaker personally knows at the time of utterance. The proposal should really be that "It might be that φ" is true iff φ is not ruled out by any *pertinent* facts—where the test of pertinence is, presumably, that the speaker is prepared to acknowledge that she was mistaken if these facts really do/did obtain.[8]

But, and this is the third problem, the truth conditions are now so strong that speakers generally have no idea whether they are satisfied; they have no business, then, asserting that φ might be the case. The principle here is that I should not assert that χ, if (a) I am aware of a ψ such that χ is false if ψ is true, and (b) I consider ψ entirely likely to be true.[9] When χ is "It might be that φ," I am virtually always aware of a ψ like that, viz. "Somewhere out there, there is evidence that rules φ out." ψ meets condition (a) because I freely accept that my might-claim is mistaken if φ is ruled out by the evidence, including evidence I don't myself possess. (I freely accept, for instance, that *if* Bob was seen getting on a plane at 11:55, then it is not true after all that he might now (at noon) be in his office.) ψ meets condition (b) because I do not, when I say that it might be that φ, take myself to know that my evidence is relevantly complete; obviously I might be missing something which makes φ unlikely.[10] (When I say that Bob might be in his office, I do not take myself to know that no one has just seen him get on a plane.) The problem is this: if I think it entirely likely that there is evidence that exposes my statement as false, how in good conscience can I make the statement? Who would dare make a might-claim, if the claim was entirely likely to be mistaken?

The fourth problem with the standard semantics is that it is too *epistemic*. I have a thing about the sanctity of the ballot box, imagine, so when you ask me whether I am going to vote for Kucinich, I say, "I might and I might not," despite knowing perfectly well what I've decided, and not trying to hide the fact that I know.[11] Or suppose that I run into a creditor who demands that I give him a check by the end of the day. I know perfectly well that I am going to do what he asks—I have the check in my pocket—but still I say, "I might or I might not; it might have to wait until tomorrow," for the loan is not strictly due until Friday. I say it not because I don't know I'll give him the check today, but because I reserve the right not to; it's not a limit in my information I'm indicating, but a limit in what I'm prepared to commit to. One final example. Imagine I am pitching a story line to a Hollywood mogul. "Now comes the good part," I tell him. "The Raskolnikov character brutally murders the pawnbroker." "Not a chance, not if we want PG-13," comes the reply. "OK," I say in a concessive

---

[8] For more on these issues, see Egan (2007); Egan, Hawthorne, and Weatherson (2005); MacFarlane (2011); and von Fintel and Gillies 2007.

[9] Sarah Moss uses a principle like this in Moss (forthcoming).

[10] If that kind of knowledge were required, I would not say "It might be that φ and it might be that $\sim\varphi$" unless I thought that φ was *objectively undecidable*, in the sense that all the evidence in the world left it an open question whether φ.

[11] If I say I don't know whether I'll vote for Kucinich, you can properly accuse me of lying. But it is not a lie to say I might vote for him or I might not.

spirit, "so he might just rough her up a bit." The "might" here is not to mark the limits of my knowledge. There is nothing to know in this case; we are tossing around ideas. I say "might just rough her up" to convey that I am scaling back the proposal.

A fifth problem is more logical in nature. Suppose that φ is consistent with all pertinent information. Then so is everything φ entails. One would expect, then, that if φ entailed ψ, "It might be that φ" would entail "It might be that ψ." "Bob might be in his office," for instance, should entail "Bob might be in his office or in an opium den." And yet "Bob might be in his office or in an opium den" seems to make a *stronger* claim, roughly to the effect that Bob might be at the one place *and* in addition he might be at the other. There is of course a similar puzzle about permission: how is it that "You can go or stay" entails (or seems to) that you can do whichever you want, that is, it is open to you to go *and* it is open to you to stay.[12]

The sixth problem I learned from Seth Yalcin.[13] An advantage sometimes claimed for the standard semantics is that it explains the paradoxicality of "φ and it might be that $\sim\varphi$." To say that φ and it might be that $\sim\varphi$ is to say this: φ but I don't know that φ. And the problem with "φ but I don't know that φ" we more or less understand; it's an instance of Moore's paradox. But there are reasons to doubt that "φ and it might be that $\sim\varphi$" is no more than a form of Moore's paradox. That paradox is thought to arise because the Moore-sentence is *unassertable*. The proof that it's a problem of assertability rather than truth is that there is nothing to stop me from *supposing*, in the antecedent of a conditional, that φ and I don't know it: If I am unbeknownst to myself dreaming that I am typing this paper, then I am most likely at home in bed. If "φ and it might be that $\sim\varphi$" were paradoxical only for Moorean reasons, one would expect it to be supposable too. And it isn't. "If I am dreaming that I am typing, but might not be dreaming that I am typing . . . " makes no sense. The sixth problem is that "φ and it might be that $\sim\varphi$" is not coherently supposable, and the standard semantics offers no explanation of this.[14]

The traditional "static" semantics for epistemic modals has its problems. This has led some to propose a *dynamic* semantics; the meaning of "might φ" is given not by its truth conditions but by its effect on context or shared information. The best-known version of this is Frank Veltman's *default semantics*.[15] Veltman thinks of "might φ" as checking on φ's consistency with the going information state. Uttered in information state S, it returns S if S is consistent with φ, and it returns the null information state if S is not consistent with φ. Both parts of this seem prima facie at odds with the way "might" is used.

---

[12] Kamp (1973); Zimmermann (2000); Fox (2006).

[13] Yalcin (2007).

[14] Yalcin thinks that there is a problem here for any truth-conditional semantics. For the following is an invalid argument: *It might be the case that $\sim A$, therefore $\sim A$*. A one-premise argument *X, therefore Y* is invalid, one would think, only if the conclusion can be false while the premise is true—only if there is a possible scenario where $\neg Y \& X$. In this case, that means a possible scenario where *A and it might be that $\sim A$*. And there is no such scenario.

[15] Gillies (2004); Veltman (1996).

Consider first the idea that "might φ" returns the null state when S is inconsistent with φ. Suppose it is understood all around that John, Paul, George, and Ringo will be at the party. Then someone runs in with the news that Ringo might not be able to make it. Ringo's not making it is inconsistent with John, Paul, George, and Ringo being there. All our information is demolished, then, according to default semantics. But the information that John, Paul, and George will be at the party surely remains when we learn that Ringo might not attend.[16]

The idea that "might φ" returns S if φ is consistent with S seems questionable, too. It's consistent with John, Paul, George, and Ringo being at the party that either Ringo or Elton John stays away; for it might be Elton John that stays away. Nevertheless, if someone runs in with the news that Ringo or Elton John might not be attending, we will not keep on assuming that all four Beatles will be there. Our shared information is weakened to: John, Paul, and George will be at the party.

It seems from these examples that "might φ," uttered in information state S, has or can have the effect of cutting S down to a weaker information state S'; and it can have this effect both when φ is consistent with S and when φ is inconsistent with S. If information states are modeled as sets of worlds, then the effect of "might φ" is to add on additional worlds. The question, of course, is *which* additional worlds. Our reason for looking at *deontic* modals is that the analogous question about them was raised years ago by David Lewis, in a paper called "A Problem about Permission."

Lewis starts by describing a simple language game. The players are Master, Slave, and Kibitzer, though we'll be ignoring Kibitzer (he's used to it). Master issues commands and permissions to Slave, thereby shrinking and expanding what Lewis calls the *sphere of permissibility*, the set of worlds where Slave behaves as he ought. Behaving as he ought is Slave's only purpose in this game, and given how we defined the sphere of permissibility, that comes to behaving so that the actual world lies within the sphere. Slave can't work to keep the actual world within the sphere, though, unless he knows where its boundaries lie. Let's try to help him with this: how does the sphere evolve over time?

When the game begins, all worlds are in the sphere of permissibility. Now Master begins issuing commands and permissions. Our job is to figure out the function that takes a given sequence of commands (written !φ) and permissions (written ¡φ) to the set of worlds permissible after all those commands and permissions have been given. That fortunately boils down to two simpler-seeming sub-tasks: first, figure out the effect of a *command* on the sphere of permissibility; second, figure out the effect of a *permission* on the sphere of permissibility.

You might think the second sub-task would be the easier one: after all, a sphere of *permissibility* would seem to be more directly responsive to *permissions* than commands.

---

[16] The counter-response is that we would take steps to avoid this disaster by scaling back to an information state consistent with Ringo's non-attendance. I agree that this is what we would do; the question is whether scaling back should be understood as a repair strategy we use when disaster threatens, or as part of "might"'s basic semantic functioning. See Fuhrmann (1999). Thanks here to Thony Gillies.

But it is actually the first sub-task that's easier. Suppose the going sphere of permissibility is S and Master says, "Mop that floor!" Then presumably the new sphere S' is the old one S, restricted to worlds where the floor gets mopped. The rule stated generally is

$$!\varphi: S \rightarrow S \cap \|\varphi\|,$$

or, to formulate it as an identity:

(C) $!\varphi(S) = S \cap \|\varphi\|$.

The left-to-right inclusion here ($!\varphi(S) \subseteq S \cap \|\varphi\|$) follows from two extremely plausible assumptions:

(c1) commands shrink (i.e. don't expand) the sphere, and

(c2) commands to φ make *all* $\sim\varphi$-worlds impermissible.

The right-to-left inclusion ($!\varphi(S) \supseteq S \cap \|\varphi\|$) follows from (c1) and a third plausible assumption

(c3) commands to φ make *only* $\sim\varphi$-worlds impermissible.

All of this is treated by Lewis as relatively undebatable, and nothing will be said against it here; it serves as background to the problem to come.

That problem concerns permission. If commands go with intersection, the obvious first thought about permissions is that they would go with unions:

$$!\varphi: S \rightarrow S \cup \|\varphi\|,$$

or, the corresponding identity,

(P) $¡\varphi(S) = S \cup \|\varphi\|$.

The left to right inclusion ($¡\varphi(S) \subseteq S \cup \|\varphi\|$) is uncontroversial; it follows from

(p1) permissions expand (i.e., do not shrink) the sphere, and

(p2) permission to φ renders *only* φ-worlds permissible.

But the right to left direction requires along with (p1) the principle

(??) permission to φ renders *all* φ-worlds permissible.

And while it is hard to argue with

(p3) permission to φ renders *some* φ-worlds permissible,

(??) seems clearly wrong. Lewis explains why:

Suppose the Slave had been commanded to carry rocks every day of the week, but on Thursday the Master relents and says to the Slave, '¡The Slave does no work tomorrow'.... He has thereby permitted a holiday, but not just any possible sort of holiday... [not] a holiday that starts on Friday and goes on through Saturday, or a holiday spent guzzling in his wine cellar. (2000: 27)

So (??) allows in too much. (p3) on the other hand, although correct, can't be the whole story. Not any old expanded sphere that contains φ-worlds will do—for the sphere whose sole φ-world has Slave staying on holiday through Saturday won't do.

Some worlds where the Slave does not work on Friday have been brought into permissibility, but not all of them. The Master has not said which ones. He did not need to; somehow, that is understood. (2000: 27)

If it is understood, there must be a way we understand it: there must be a rule or principle of sphere-evolution that captures our shared implicit understanding of how permissions work.

Now we reach the problem of Lewis's paper. What is that rule? Or, to put it negatively, what exactly is wrong with a rule R that tells us that, having been permitted to take Friday off, Slave can take that and other days off? Lewis looks at five answers.

(1) R lets in **more worlds** than necessary

Putting in a Saturday-off world enlarges the sphere more than necessary to allow Friday-off worlds. It's a "gratuitous enlargement" in the sense of adding more worlds than necessary.

Lewis replies that any reasonable enlargement will be gratuitous in that sense, since the only non-gratuitous enlargement adds in just a single world. This is fair enough, but it is not, I think, the "real" problem. If it were, then limiting ourselves to non-gratuitous (single-world) enlargements would address it. And it doesn't; for we could pick as our single world a world where Slave takes Saturday off too.

(2) R lets in worlds **more remote** than necessary

Putting the Saturday-off world in is a gratuitous enlargement in a *qualitative* sense. We should allow in only the *closest* worlds where the permitted action is done.

This, Lewis says, is too restrictive. Suppose Slave had previously been ordered to carry rocks around. Then he is forced to spend his vacation lifting weights! For weight-lifting worlds are closer to rock-carrying worlds than lying-around-at-the-beach worlds are to rock-carrying worlds.

One can put the problem like this. A permission should *cleanly cancel* relevant earlier commands. But on the present approach, supposedly canceled commands continue, from beyond the grave as it were, to exert an effect. The *clean cancelation requirement*, as I will call it, will come up again.

(3) R lets in worlds **more impermissible** than necessary

Putting the Saturday-off world in is a gratuitous enlargement not in a qualitative but a prescriptive sense. We should put in the *least impermissible* worlds where the permitted action is done. Taking Friday and Saturday off was more impermissible than taking Friday off, so the two-day-off worlds aren't added in.

The objection Lewis offers is that this "solution" just restates, indeed aggravates, the problem: figuring out how comparative impermissibility evolves under the impact of commands and permissions is no easier (and possibly harder) than figuring out how straight permissibility does.

But there is again a prior worry—a version of the clean cancelation problem. Suppose Master first says not to eat any animals, then relents and permits eating lobster. Before lobster-eating was permitted, it was less impermissible to nibble on lobster than to eat a lobster in its entirety. So afterward is it only permissible to nibble on lobster?

(4) R lets in worlds **more disagreeable to Master** than necessary

Putting the Saturday-off world in frustrates Master's known or guessable purposes.

Lewis objects that either Slave knows Master's purposes or he doesn't. If he does, there's no need for commands; he can work unsupervised. If he doesn't, then the principle cannot be what's guiding him.

Once again, there is a prior worry. Let's say that Master has frequently ordered Slave to carry rocks up the hill. Presumably she did this because she wants the rocks up the hill. But the Friday-off worlds that best serve the purpose of getting the rocks up the hill are ones where Slave invites his friends to play a game where two teams compete to see who can carry more rocks up the hill. This is again a version of the clean cancelation problem.

(5) R lets in worlds **violating more commands** than necessary

This takes a bit more explanation. It's a given that Master doesn't issue commands and permissions unless she needs to. She doesn't issue the command to φ if it is already impermissible for Slave not to φ; and she doesn't give permission to φ if Slave is already permitted to φ. In particular, then, Master would not have permitted Slave to take Friday off unless taking Friday off would otherwise have been an act of *disobedience*, an act in violation of some explicit or understood command. So, proposal: the effect of permitting φ should be to invalidate any commands that forbid φing—that are inconsistent with φ—while leaving other commands in place. The problem with an update rule that lets Saturday-off worlds into the sphere is that it invalidates more commands than necessary. To make Slave's taking Friday off permissible, it is enough to invalidate the work-*Friday* command; the work-Saturday command doesn't care if Slave takes Friday off, so it should be left in place.

Call this the *remainder* rule, because it defines S^+ as the set of worlds satisfying the commands that remain when all φ-inconsistent commands are invalidated. Lewis doesn't like the remainder rule either; here is why. Clearly, to apply the rule, we need there to be a list of commands $\psi_1, \ldots, \psi_k$ such that a world is permissible iff it complies with all of them, that is,

$$S = \| \psi_1 \| \cap \| \psi_2 \| \cap \ldots \cap \| \psi_k \|.$$

For the way the rule works is we delete from this list all the ψ_is inconsistent with φ, and let the commands that remain define S^+. So if the φ-incompatible commands are $\psi_{j+1}, \psi_{j+2}, \ldots \psi_k$, the new sphere is

$$S^+ = \| \psi_1 \| \cap \| \psi_2 \| \cap \ldots \cap \| \psi_j \|.$$

Where is the initial set of commands supposed to come from, though, the one we thin out to arrive at the reduced command-set that defines the S^+-worlds? It would be one thing if "$_i\varphi$" were the first permission uttered; for then Master's earlier utterances were all commands, and we can let the ψ_is be those commands. Ordinarily, though, "$_i\varphi$" is preceded by commands *and other permissions*. One could try considering just the commands that have already been given, ignoring the permissions, but these will not define the current sphere of permissibility, because the update effects of earlier permissions will have been ignored.

It seems, then, that we are driven to *contriving*, reverse-engineering if you like, a package of commands that define the current sphere, a set of ψ_is that together define S. Unfortunately the relation between S and packages of commands defining S is one-many; lots of them will issue in the same sphere of permissibility. How does Slave know which package to use? It makes a difference, because the effect on S of permitting φ varies enormously with our choice of implicit commands ψ_i.

So, for instance, suppose that the current sphere S = the worlds where Slave works all day, every day from Monday to Sunday; but we arrived at that sphere by a complicated series of enlargements and contractions that offers no clues to what the right ψ_is, the right implicit commands, are. Slave *might* think that initially, before he is given Friday off, the commands in effect are

ψ_1: Slave carries rocks on Monday.
ψ_2: Slave carries rocks on Tuesday.
ψ_3: Slave carries rocks on Wednesday.
ψ_4: Slave carries rocks on Thursday.
ψ_5: Slave carries rocks on Friday.
ψ_6: Slave carries rocks on Saturday.
ψ_7: Slave carries rocks on Sunday.

The one command here inconsistent with "Slave takes Friday off" is "Slave carries rocks on Friday." Suspending that one command leaves the commands to work other days still in place. Clearly on this way of doing it, Slave has *not* been permitted to take other days off, which was the desired result. But Slave might also think that the implicit commands are

χ_1: Slave carries rocks on weekdays.
χ_2: Slave carries rocks on the weekend.

Now the φ-inconsistent rule, the one to be canceled on the present hypothesis, is "Slave carries rocks on weekdays." But then the sphere of permissibility expands to include all worlds where Slave works on the weekend. And that seems crazy. Master meant to give Slave Friday off, not Monday–Thursday as well.

Lewis's objection in a nutshell is that the implicit commands are too unconstrained for the remainder rule to be of any use. He may be right in the end. I wonder, though, whether there are constraints he is missing—constraints that don't come into view until you raise the problem he is pointing to in the starkest possible terms. Let's look, then, at the most extreme cases of badly chosen implicit commands. At the one extreme we have commands *each* of which is inconsistent with φ; at the other we have commands *none* of which is inconsistent with φ. An example of each-inconsistent is

θ_1: Slave carries rocks every morning of the week.

θ_2: Slave carries rocks every afternoon of the week.

Neither of these is compatible with Slave taking Friday off. Canceling the φ-inconsistent commands, then, is canceling all commands whatsoever. If all commands are canceled, then everything is permitted. Master wanted to let Slave take Friday off, but winds up giving Slave his freedom.

Now consider commands none of which individually requires Slave to work Friday, but whose *joint* effect is to require Slave to work every day of the week. For instance,

σ_1: Slave carries rocks every morning if any afternoon.

σ_2: Slave carries rocks every afternoon if every morning.

σ_3: Slave carries rocks some afternoon.

σ_1 allows Slave to take Friday off, provided he never carries rocks in the afternoon. σ_2 allows him to take Friday off, provided he omits to carry rocks some morning. σ_3 allows him to take Friday off, provided he carries rocks some afternoon. Each of the σ_is is consistent with φ, so none of them is canceled on the present rule. But then the sphere of impermissibility never changes. Master tried to give Slave permission to take Friday off, but it turns out he still has to work on Friday.

What can we conclude from this? The remainder rule—the one that says to cancel all and only pre-existing commands that forbid φ—can give very silly results. But we can make that work in our favour, by letting the results' very silliness help us tighten the rule. Call a command-list *reasonable* if running it through the remainder rule yields an expansion satisfying (p1)–(p3) above.

(p1) permissions (expand) do not shrink the sphere, and

(p2) permission to φ renders only φ-worlds permissible.

(p3) permission to φ renders some φ-worlds permissible.

It is not hard to establish the following (proof in Appendix):

FACT If S is defined by a reasonable list of commands, then $S = \|\sim\varphi\| \cap \|\psi\|$ for some ψ. Equivalently, any reasonable command list is of the form (up to equivalence) "You must not φ," "You must ψ."

This transforms the problem in a helpful way. Before we had one equation in several unknowns (corresponding to the several choices of implicit commands ψ_i). Now we have one equation in one unknown. For we know what S is; it's the present, pre-permission-to-φ, sphere of permissibility. And we know what $\|\sim\varphi\|$ is; it is the set of worlds where the permitted behavior does not occur. The one unknown is $\|\psi\|$, that is, the new sphere of permissibility S^+.

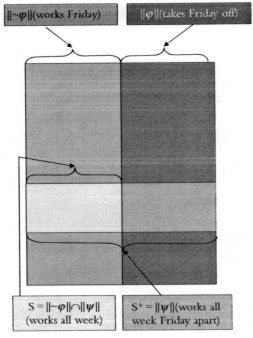

Fig. 9.1.

So, to review. Whenever a permission to φ is issued, it's as though the initial command list had consisted of two commands:

first, one saying (precisely) *do not* φ.

second, a command ψ that allows φing.

Our job as sphere-redrawers is to throw out the *do not* φ command and form the set of worlds allowed by the command that remains. This is nothing like an algorithm, because there is more than one way of choosing the command ψ that remains. (There are many sets whose intersection with $\|\sim\varphi\|$ is S.). But it is instructive nevertheless.

One way the equation $S = \|\sim\varphi\| \cap \|\psi\|$ helps is by showing us how to conceive the task diagrammatically (see Fig. 9.1). We are given

(i) the $\|\varphi\|$-region—that's the worlds where Slave takes Friday off, as he has been permitted to do:

(ii) the $\|\sim\varphi\|$-region—that's the worlds where Slave works Friday, in accord with his pre-permission obligations; and

(iii) the S-region—that's the set of initially permissible worlds, the ones where Slave works all week (Monday–Sunday).

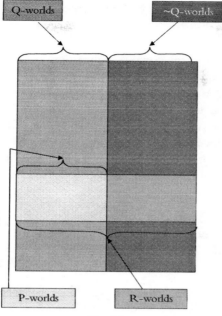

Fig. 9.2.

Our job is to extrapolate the S-region beyond the bounds imposed by the $\|\sim\varphi\|$ region, thus arriving at the set $\|\psi\|$ of worlds that are permissible after Master cancels the command to work Friday.

How is this to be done? The question here has nothing special to do with permission; it concerns logical extrapolation as such. To state it in full generality (see Fig. 9.2): Suppose P is a proposition implying Q, represented by a subregion of the Q-region of logical space. When does a proposition R count as extrapolating P beyond Q to the rest of logical space?[17]

Here is a proposal about that, developed elsewhere. For R to extrapolate P beyond Q—for it to go on in the same way, as it were—R should meet three conditions:

(i) within Q, R is true (false) in the same worlds as P
(ii) within Q, R is true (false) for the reasons Q&P holds rather than Q&~P (. . .)
(iii) outside Q, R is true (false) for the same reasons as within.

(i) says that R is equivalent to P within Q, so call it *Equivalence*. (ii) speaks to the reasons why R is true (false) within Q, so call it *Reasons*. (iii) takes a bit more explanation. For R to acquire new truthmakers (or falsemakers) when it left the Q-region would

---

[17] "R" is meant to suggest *remainder*.

mean that R was true (false) for one kind of reason in Q-worlds and another in non-Q-worlds. R would in that sense have changed direction as it crossed the Q-border; (iii) is thus a kind of *Orthogonality* condition.

Now we construct a possible-worlds proposition P—Q that satisfies (i), (ii), and (iii).[18] As the notation suggests, P—Q can be thought of as the *remainder* when Q is subtracted from P. It suffices to say in which worlds P—Q is true and in which worlds it is false. Consider first the Q-worlds. Clearly P—Q's truth value in any Q-world w must be the same as P's (by *Equivalence*). What is not so obvious is how to evaluate P—Q in worlds where Q is false (and therefore P, which implies Q, is false). The proposal: P—Q is false in a world where P and Q are both false if and only if P "adds falsity" to Q where X adds falsity to Y iff X&Y has a Y-compatible falsemaker in w. Equivalently,

X *adds falsity* to Y in w iff Y⊃X has a Y-compatible falsemaker in w.

X adds truth to Y in w iff its negation adds falsity there, that is, ∼X&Y has a Y-compatible falsemaker in w, which can equally be conceived as a Y-compatible truthmaker for Y⊃X:

X *adds truth* to Y in w iff Y⊃X has a Y-compatible truthmaker in w.

P—Q is true in w iff P adds truth to Q in w without adding falsity to Q in w. P—Q is true, in other words, iff P adds truth and only truth to Q in w. Assuming as above that P implies Q, this gives "—" the quasi-truth-table shown as Fig. 9.3.

The proposed update rule for permissions can now be stated very simply: *the effect of permitting φ is to subtract $\| \sim \varphi \|$ from the going sphere of permissibility.*

(UR$_i$) Assuming φ was initially impermissible, $S + {}_i\varphi = S - \| \sim \varphi \|$.

How does the rule work in practice? How, for instance, do we find the worlds that are still impermissible after Master permits φ? A world is still impermissible after Master permits φ iff $S-\| \sim \varphi \|$, which defines the new and enlarged bounds of permissibility, is false in that world. $S-\| \sim \varphi \|$ is false in w iff S is false in w for a reason not implying $\| \varphi \|$; equivalently, w is impermissible for a reason not implying $\| \varphi \|$. So a world is *still* impermissible iff it *was* impermissible for reasons *additional* to any violation of the ban on φing, reasons that could still have obtained even if that ban had been observed.

Consider a world where Slave continues his holiday through the weekend. That world *was* impermissible for reasons compatible with Slave's working Friday, such as his failure to show up on Saturday; so it *remains* impermissible after permission is given to take Friday off. A world where Slave takes just Friday off, however, does not remain impermissible, for it *was* impermissible only for φ-entailing reasons, and φ-entailing impermissibility-makers are deactivated when Master permits Slave to φ.

---

[18] (i) can be read off the definition. (ii) and (iii) depend on P—Q being assigned the appropriate truth- and falsemakers. Details are given elsewhere.

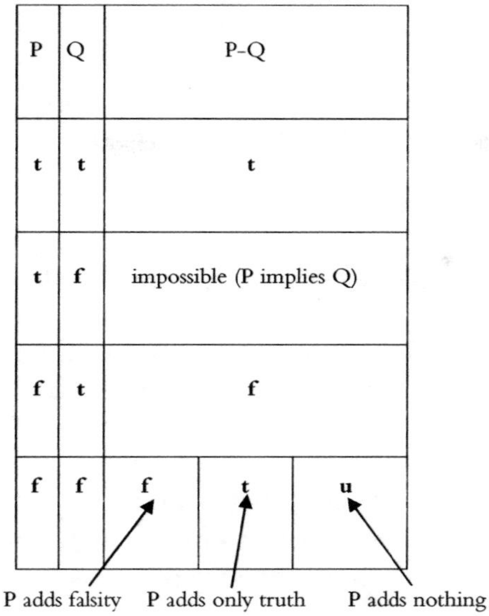

P	Q	P–Q		
t	t	t		
t	f	impossible (P implies Q)		
f	t	f		
f	f	f	t	u

P adds falsity   P adds only truth   P adds nothing

Fig. 9.3.

I said that a world where Slave takes just Friday off "does not remain impermissible." Is that the same as becoming permissible? Not quite. An impermissible world is one where S−‖∼φ‖ is false, and a permissible world is one where S−‖∼φ‖ is true; and for a remainder-proposition to avoid falsity is not yet for it to achieve truth. S−‖∼φ‖ is non-false in a world w iff

(a) S adds no falsity to ‖∼φ‖ in w, that is, S has no ‖∼φ‖-compatible falsemakers there,

For S−‖∼φ‖ to be true in w requires further that

(b) S adds truth to ‖∼φ‖ in w, that is, ‖∼φ‖⊃ S has ‖∼φ‖-compatible truth-makers there.

A world where Slave works Monday–Thursday and the weekend does indeed become permissible after Master permits Slave to take Friday off, because (a) and (b) are both satisfied, and for similar reasons. (a) is satisfied because Slave's working Monday–Thursday and the weekend means that ‖Slave works all week‖ is false in w *only because Slave took Friday off in it*; and Slave's taking Friday off is obviously not compatible with his working Friday. (b) is satisfied because Slave's working Monday–Thursday and the weekend is a truthmaker for ‖Slave works Friday‖⊃‖Slave works all week‖ that is compatible with Slave's working Friday. But although conditions (a) and (b) come to roughly the same in the case at hand, they are by no means equivalent.

Imagine that Master initially commands Slave to carry exactly one shovel and to keep it shiny clean. Permission is then given *not* to carry exactly one shovel. What should we say about a world u where Slave carries *two* shovels, one clean and one dirty? It meets condition (b) but not (a). It meets (b) because u does contain a truthmaker for ‖Slave carries exactly one shovel‖ ⊃ ‖Slave carries exactly one shovel and keeps it clean‖ that is compatible with Slave's carrying exactly one shovel, viz. the fact that *Slave carries a clean shovel*. It violates (a) because the fact that Slave *also* carries a dirty shovel is a ‖Slave carries exactly one shovel‖-compatible *falsemaker* for ‖Slave carries exactly one shovel and keeps it clean‖. A world v where Slave carries *no* shovels meets (a) but not (b). It meets (a) because the one and only reason ‖Slave carries exactly one shovel and keeps it clean‖ is false in v is that *Slave carries no shovel* there, and carrying no shovel is obviously not compatible with carrying exactly one shovel. It violates (b) because the one and only reason ‖Slave carries exactly one shovel‖ ⊃ ‖Slave carries exactly one shovel and keeps it clean‖ is true in v is again that *Slave carries no shovel* there. The upshot is that while it is not *impermissible* for Slave to carry no shovels, it is not positively permissible either; the deontic status of a world where Slave carries no shovels is left indeterminate in this case. And while it *is* impermissible for Slave to carry two shovels, one dirty and one clean, it is not as thoroughgoingly impermissible as carrying two dirty shovels, since S adds some truth in the first scenario, but it adds only falsity in the scenario where Slave keeps both of his shovels dirty.

Now I want to explore the epistemic analogue of Lewis's Master–Slave game. Here is how I understand the new game to work.

(1) The players this time are Teacher and Student, and the sphere of permissibility becomes the sphere of believability.

(2) The old game had Slave constantly adjusting his plans to fit with changes in what was permissible; the new one has Student constantly adjusting his theory to fit with changes in what is believable.

(3) It contracted the sphere of permissibility when Master said, "Do ψ"; the sphere expanded when Master said, "You may do φ." Likewise it contracts the sphere of believability when Teacher says, "ψ is so"; the sphere expands when Teacher says, "φ might be so."

(4) There was no great mystery about the *kind* of contraction brought on by "Do ψ"; one simply rejected as impermissible worlds where ψ failed. Similarly there is no great mystery about the kind of contraction brought on by "ψ is so"; worlds where ψ fails are rejected as unbelievable.

(5) It was initially mysterious how "You may do φ" enlarged the sphere of permissibility. Similarly it is mysterious to begin with how "φ may be so" enlarges the sphere of believability.

Let's continue the pretense that "φ might be so" has no effect on a sphere of believability that contains φ-worlds; it is only when all believable worlds are $\sim\varphi$ that we get an expansion. The question is, what expansion do we get? I propose that the update rule is pretty much as before.

($UR\Diamond$) Assuming φ was initially unbelievable, $S + \Diamond\varphi = S - ‖\sim\varphi‖$.

To see how it works, imagine that Teacher starts by saying it will be dry all week, meaning Monday–Sunday. She thereby banishes from the sphere of believability all worlds where it rains on one or more days. When Teacher learns that her evidence as regards Friday was shaky, she says, "Hold on, it might rain on Friday after all." Which worlds has she put back into the sphere of believability? To put it another way, what remains of Teacher's original prediction of no rain all week, once she has conceded it might rain on Friday? Our update rule says that

$$\|\text{It will be dry all week}\| + \Diamond(\text{It will rain on Friday}) = \|\text{It will be dry all week}\| - \|\text{It will be dry on Friday}\| \,.$$

Now, P—Q is non-false in w iff P adds no falsity to Q in w, and true iff P furthermore adds truth to Q in w; and P adds falsity (truth) to Q in w iff P is false in w for a Q-compatible reason (Q ⊃P is true for a Q-compatible reason). Thus the worlds Teacher is representing as no longer unbelievable are those in which ∥It will be dry all week∥ is false only because it rains on Friday, which is to say the worlds where it is dry on Monday, Tuesday, Wednesday, Thursday, Saturday, and Sunday. These worlds are also now believable, for its being dry on those days is a dry-Friday-compatible truthmaker for the conditional hypothesis that it will be dry all week if it is dry on Friday.

I want to return now to a limitation of the Lewis game noted earlier. Lewis stipulates that permission to φ has no impact unless φ was antecedently forbidden. That makes nonsense both of out-of-the-blue, discourse-initial, permissions, and permissions that soften commands that didn't strictly forbid the now-permitted behavior. Suppose, for instance, that Master, having first commanded Slave to work all week, allows him to go to the beach on his birthday; this wasn't strictly forbidden because Slave's birthday might still be a few months off. Similar worries can be raised about our epistemic analogue of the Lewis game. We have been assuming that "might φ" has no impact on the sphere of believability unless φ was antecedently denied. But then what is going on in a conversation like this:

A: Where is Bob?
B: Hmmm, I don't really know, but he might be in his office.
[A:* I never said he wasn't.]

Or this:

A: Bob will be at the office tomorrow.
B: Not so fast, he said he might stay home on his birthday.
[A: *That's compatible!]

Call this the problem of *unforced retractions*. I see two ways of addressing it. The first is simply to strike "Assuming φ was initially impermissible, ... " from the update rule for permissions, and to strike "Assuming φ was initially unbelievable ... " from the update rule for "might." These provisos might have been thought indispensable. For $S + \Diamond\varphi = S-(\sim\varphi)$; and didn't our definition of P—Q assume that P implied Q?

What is true is that *we* were assuming that P implied Q when we gave the definition. But the definition itself can be written in a way that makes sense either way. P—Q is the proposition that is false in w iff Q⊃∼P is true there for a Q-compatible reason, and true in w iff Q⊃ P is true there for a Q-compatible reason. Nothing here depends on P implying Q.

I suspect this first response to the problem of unforced retractions is ultimately to be preferred. But let me try a different response, one that is more in keeping with Lewis's approach in "A Problem About Permission." Lewis confronts there something like the dual of the present difficulty. Having laid it down that commands can only shrink the sphere of permissibility, he remarks that

> One sort of commanding may seem to require special treatment: commanding the impermissible. Suppose that ‖φ‖ contains no worlds that are... permissible ... The Master may nevertheless wish to command ... that φ.... Having commanded at dawn that the Slave devote his energies all day to carrying rocks, the Master may decide at noon that it would be better to have the Slave spend the afternoon on some lighter or more urgent task. If the master simply commands ... that φ, then no world ... remains permissible; the Slave, through no fault of his own, has no way to play his part by trying to see to it that the world remains permissible... Should we therefore say that in this case the sphere evolves not by intersection but in some more complicated way? I think not ... What the Master should have done was first to permit and then to command that φ. (2000: 27)

He notes a possible fix: whenever φ is impermissible, "a command that φ is deemed to be preceded by a tacit permission that φ, and the sphere of permissibility evolves accordingly" (2000: 27). Our present concern can be put in similar language:

> One sort of permitting may seem to require special treatment: permitting the not impermissible. Suppose that the sphere of permissibility contains φ-worlds ... The Master may nevertheless wish to permit ... that φ ... Having at dawn permitted the Slave to take the day off, the Master may decide at noon that the Slave should be permitted to visit his mother this week. If the Master simply permits ... the Slave to visit his mother this week, then no additional worlds ... become permissible; for there are already permissible worlds where the Slave visits his mother, namely worlds where the Slave visits his mother today ... Should we therefore say that in this case the sphere evolves not by the remainder rule but in some more complicated way?

I propose to avoid saying this by a maneuver similar to Lewis's: whenever φ is already permissible, permission to φ is deemed to be preceded by a tacit command not to φ, with the sphere of permissibility evolving accordingly. Likewise whenever φ is already believable, "it might be that φ" is imagined to be in response to the unspoken assertion that ∼φ.

How much justice does this kind of maneuver do to our feeling of still *conveying* something when we permit the not previously permissible, or suggest that things *might* be a way that no one had ever said they weren't?

The first thing to notice is that, just as permitting and then immediately commanding that φ can (even by our existing rules) change the sphere of permissibility, forbidding and then permitting φ can change the sphere of permissibility too. Mathematically speaking, there is no reason whatever to expect that $S^{+-} = {}_i\varphi(!\sim\varphi(S)) = (S\cap\|\sim\varphi\|)-\|\sim\varphi\|$ will just be S again. Indeed there is reason to expect it often won't; for the equation

$$(^*)\ (P\&Q) - Q = P$$

fails when P and Q overlap.[19] Suppose, to start with a case of total overlap, that P and Q are one and the same proposition. Then $(P\&Q) - Q = (P\&P) - P = P - P$. $P - P$ is presumably the null proposition; anyway it is not P as $(^*)$ would require. Or let P be the conjunctive proposition Q&R, where R is thoroughly independent of Q. $((Q\&R)\&Q)$—Q should be Q&R, according to $(^*)$. But we know by Boolean algebra that $(Q\&R)\&Q$ is Q&R; and the result of subtracting Q from Q&R is not going to be Q&R again.

In principle, then, forbidding and then permitting φ can change the sphere of permissibility. Here is an example where it happens. Imagine that Master starts out by commanding Slave to work on her (Master's) birthday. The initial sphere S is thus the set of worlds where Slave works on Master's birthday. Then Master further commands that Slave is to work on Friday. $S + !\sim\varphi = S\cap\|\sim\varphi\| =$ the set of worlds where Slave works on Master's birthday and on Friday. *Then* Master permits Slave not to work on Friday after all. The resulting sphere $(S\cap\|\sim\varphi\|)-\|\sim\varphi\|$ is not S = the set of worlds where Slave works on Master's birthday, but $S_* =$ the set of worlds where Slave works on Master's birthday *unless it falls on a Friday*. (The added worlds *were* impermissible only because Slave took Friday off in them, when Friday was Master's birthday; worlds that were impermissible only because they violate a certain ban do not remain so when the ban is lifted.) Forbidding and then immediately permitting Slave to take Friday off can thus have a non-trivial effect on the sphere of permissibility. Like remarks apply to asserting it will rain on Friday and then immediately taking it back, having previously asserted that it will rain on Teacher's birthday.

I have argued that forbidding and then immediately permitting φ can change the sphere of permissibility, and also that asserting φ and then immediately allowing that maybe $\sim\varphi$ can change the sphere of believability. But there are also cases where permitting what I've just forbidden (admitting that a previous assertion might be wrong) leaves the sphere just as it was. An example might be this. Nothing has been said about Bob's location, but I know you want to find him. What is accomplished by saying "He might be in his office," when no one has suggested otherwise? Likewise what is accomplished by announcing out of the blue that it is permitted to climb trees in order to rescue kittens?

It seems to me these things are not so mysterious, once we distinguish what *has* been forbidden, in the sense that the command has been given, from what *is* forbidden,

---

[19] I write "P&Q" instead of "P∩Q" to remind us that P∩Q considered as a proposition is the conjunction of P and Q.

in the sense that it's against the rules but Counselor may not have got around to announcing it yet. The children may know to begin with that nothing *has been* forbidden, but they have no idea what might or might not *be* forbidden, in the sense of being off limits or against the rules. When they hear that tree climbing after kittens is permitted, they learn an upper bound on what *is* forbidden, namely that it doesn't include tree climbing after kittens. This is not, to my mind, because the counselor has *said* climbing after kittens is not forbidden; she has the ability to forbid but not, as we're imagining the game, the ability to comment on the extent of the forbidden. What Counselor has done is "shown" that climbing after kittens is not forbidden by staging a confrontation with an imagined off-screen forbidder, and *canceling* that imagined person's decree.

Something similar is going on when I tell the seeker after Bob that he might be in his office. The distinction we need this time is between what has been asserted, and what is understood to be so even if no one has got around to announcing it yet. Before I spoke, my friend might have been wondering whether an assertion that Bob was not in his office was in the cards. I satisfy her curiosity not by *saying* that an assertion to that effect is not in the cards; my subject matter is Bob and his office, not assertions about them. I satisfy my friend's curiosity by *showing* that an assertion to that effect is not in the cards, by staging a confrontation with someone imagined to have made the assertion, and undoing what they are imagined to have done.

Let's return now to some of the problems raised at the outset, starting with problems for the standard semantics (SS). One problem was that SS gave "might φ" the wrong subject matter. "Bob might be in his office" seems intuitively to be about whatever "Bob is in his office" is about. Neither concerns the speaker or the extent of her knowledge. The present view construes "might φ" as a device for retracting or canceling an assertion of $\sim\varphi$. φ has the same subject matter negated as unnegated, and retracted as unretracted.

A second worry was that the truth conditions assigned by SS, in its naïve Moorean version, were too weak. If "might φ" says only that *my* information doesn't rule φ out, why do I accept correction by observers with information that I did not possess?[20] It is indeed puzzling why the speaker should accept correction, if his "mistake" was to have misstated the epistemic facts. But suppose that "might φ" is not a statement of fact. Suppose it is a cancelation order, an attempt to undo or block the assertion that $\sim\varphi$, to expel or bar $\sim\varphi$ from the common ground. If *that* is what the better-informed observer is taking issue with, then her objection makes perfect sense; for however well-intentioned, the cancelation order was unfortunate. The observer knew that $\sim\varphi$, hence that it would have been better *not* to block $\sim\varphi$'s addition to the common ground.

As already discussed, the standard semanticist's response to the "too weak" objection is to make the truth conditions stronger: φ should be consistent not only with

---

[20] See however the "Mastermind" example in von Fintel and Gillies (2007).

my information, but all *pertinent* information—where the test of pertinence must presumably be that the speaker concedes that he was in error if that information really does obtain. The third worry was that these revised truth conditions are too strong. If "might φ" is false when φ is ruled out by pertinent facts, then speakers should restrain themselves except when such facts are known not to obtain. I shouldn't say that Bob might be in his office, if there is a chance that Bob has unbeknownst to me been seen elsewhere. Clearly, though, speakers do *not* restrain themselves in this way. (Or "might"-claims would hardly ever get made.) Why not? Well, how careful I need to be depends on the threat I'm confronting. If I am concerned that my claim might be *false*, then I should indeed hold back until I have tracked down all the pertinent facts. But what if falsity is not the issue? What if I am concerned rather that my claim will turn out to have been ill advised, or counterproductive, given the purposes of the conversation? A blocking order is ill advised just to the extent that the assertions it blocks are better-informed than one's attempt to block them. The abstract possibility of evidence against φ *somewhere* out there does nothing to suggest that my utterance of "might φ" is ill advised in this sense; it does nothing to suggest that I am frustrating the efforts of better-informed co-inquirers. And the fact is that I *do* restrain myself when I run the risk of blocking better-informed assertions to the contrary. You will not hear me telling geophysicists that Mt St Helens might be about to blow.

The fourth problem was that SS is too epistemic. It reckons "I might vote for Kucinich and I might not" false unless I am genuinely undecided about how I am going to vote. The present theory can say that I am showing my audience, by example as it were, that no assertion is to be expected on the topic of how I am going to vote. I do it by giving myself the opportunity to make that sort of assertion and then visibly passing it up.

The fifth problem was that "It might rain on Tuesday" does not seem to entail "It might rain on Tuesday or Wednesday," even though a disjunction is compatible with the relevant body of information if one of its disjuncts is. If anything, the implication goes the other way: "It might rain on Tuesday or Wednesday" makes a stronger claim than "It might rain on Tuesday."[21] How are we to make sense of this? A "stronger claim" in the context of the cancelation theory is a might-claim that cancels more. To show that $\Diamond(\varphi \vee \psi)$ is stronger than $\Diamond\varphi$, we show that whereas $\Diamond\varphi$ cancels only $\sim\varphi$, $\Diamond(\varphi \vee \psi)$ cancels $\sim\varphi$ and $\sim\psi$ both.

Teacher starts out by telling us that it will not rain at all this week. This initializes the sphere of believability to S $= \sim$M&$\sim$T&$\sim$W&$\sim$R&$\sim$F&$\sim$A&$\sim$U.[22] The weather

---

[21] The analogous phenomenon with permission is better known. Suppose you are hungry and I tell you: You may have a piece of cake or a piece of pie. You reach for the pie and I snatch it away. What gave you the idea that *that* was a permissible disjunct?

[22] M, T, . . . , A, and U are the propositions that it rains on Monday, that it rains on Tuesday, . . . , that it rains on Saturday, and that it rains on Sunday.

report then leads her to qualify this claim: it might rain on Tuesday or Wednesday. By (UR_i), the sphere now expands to

$$\sim M\&\sim T\&\sim W\&\sim R\&\sim F\&\sim A\&\sim U + \Diamond(TvW)$$

$$= \sim M\&\sim T\&\sim W\&\sim R\&\sim F\&\sim A\&\sim U - \sim(TvW)$$

$$= \sim M\&\sim T\&\sim W\&\sim R\&\sim F\&\sim A\&\sim U - (\sim T\&\sim W).$$

Now, a conjunction minus the conjunction of *some* of its conjuncts is surely the conjunction of its *other* conjuncts.[23] So the remainder here is $\sim M\&\sim R\&\sim F\&\sim A\&\sim U$—which is the result we were hoping for. But let us follow the calculation through:

$$\sim M\&\sim T\&\sim W\&\ldots\&\sim U - \sim T\&\sim W.$$
$$= \sim M\&\sim T\&\sim W\ldots\&\sim U$$
$$U\{w: \sim M\&\sim T\&\sim W\&\ldots\&\sim U \text{ adds no falsity to } \sim T\&\sim W \text{ in } w\}^{24}$$
$$= \sim M\&\sim T\&\sim W\&\ldots\&\sim U$$
$$U\{w: \sim M\&\sim T\&\sim W\&\ldots\&\sim U \text{ lacks } \sim T\&\sim W\text{-compatible falsemakers in } w\}$$
$$= \sim M\&\sim T\&\sim W\&\ldots\&\sim U$$
$$U\{w: \text{all } \sim M\&\sim T\&\sim W\&\ldots\&\sim U\text{'s falsemakers in } w \text{ imply } TvW\}$$
$$= \text{the worlds where it's dry all week}$$
$$\text{plus the worlds where it isn't only because it rains Tuesday or Wednesday}$$
$$= \text{the worlds where it's dry Monday and Thursday-Sunday.}$$

Consider, for instance, a world x where it rains on Tuesday alone. x remains unbelievable iff among the reasons it *was* unbelievable are some that do not imply TvW. But the reasons x was unbelievable are one and all T-implying; they were entirely to do with its raining on Tuesday in x. Reasons that imply T are trivially reasons that imply TvW. So x is not unbelievable any longer. The same applies to worlds y where it rains just on Wednesday, and worlds z where it rains Tuesday and Wednesday; these worlds too *were* unbelievable only for (TvW)-implying reasons, and that kind of reason is irrelevant now that we've learned TvW might be true. Thus the effect of $\Diamond(TvW)$ is to cancel the ban on worlds where it rains on Tuesday and/or Wednesday. The effect of $\Diamond T$ followed by $\Diamond W$ is the same. This accounts for the feeling that "It might rain on Tuesday or Wednesday" implies both that it might rain on Tuesday and that it might rain on Wednesday.

The sixth problem we raised for SS was the Yalcin problem: it has trouble explaining the incoherence of "φ & it might be that $\sim\varphi$." The problem isn't unassertability, for unassertable hypotheses can still be hypothesized, say, in the antecedent of a conditional. And it makes no sense to say, "If it rained last night, but it might not have

---

[23] At least when the conjuncts are suitably independent, as the weather on one day is independent of the weather on another. I discuss content-parts and content-overlap elsewhere.

[24] I assume for simplicity that if $S + \Diamond(TvW)$ is not false in a world, it is true there.

rained, then the clothes we hung up will be wet." This is a problem, Yalcin contends, for any truth-conditional theory of "might." The following is an invalid argument: It might be the case that $\sim\varphi$, therefore $\sim\varphi$. A one-premise argument "X, therefore Y" is invalid, one would think, only if there is an intelligible scenario where Y is false even though X is true. But a scenario where it is false that $\sim\varphi$, but true that $\sim\varphi$ *might* be so, is a scenario where φ but maybe not—the very thing we have called unintelligible.

Recall that $\Diamond\sim\varphi$ on the cancelation view is not[25] a device for stating facts; it makes little sense, then, to ask whether it can happen that $\Diamond\sim\varphi$ is true to the facts without $\sim\varphi$'s being true to the facts. Instead of asking whether $\Diamond\sim\varphi$'s truth forces $\sim\varphi$ to be true, we should ask whether canceling the assertion that φ commits one to asserting that $\sim\varphi$. It obviously doesn't. No wonder the argument "$\Diamond\sim\varphi$, therefore $\sim\varphi$" strikes us as invalid; accepting the premise puts one under no rational pressure to accept the conclusion. One question remains: why does "$\varphi\&\Diamond\sim\varphi$" seems incoherent, even as a supposition? The problem is not that no *world* can answer both to the specification that φ and the specification that $\Diamond\sim\varphi$. It's that no world-*specification* can both demand that w be φ and fail to demand that w be φ. "$\varphi\&\Diamond\sim\varphi$" is supposition-ally incoherent because it gives the would-be supposer contradictory instructions: they are to suppose that φ while at the same time taking care *not* to suppose that φ.

Update semantics, we said, left it un- or under-explained why allowing that Ringo might not go to the party leaves intact the information that John, Paul, and George will be there. The present theory says that a world w remains unbelievable only if "John, Paul, and George will be there" adds falsity in that world to "Ringo will be there." "John, Paul, and George will be there" adds falsity to "Ringo will be there" in w iff it is false in w for a reason compatible with Ringo's presence at the party. "John, Paul, and George will be there" is false in w for a reason compatible with Ringo's presence at the party iff John, Paul, or George misses the party in w. But then worlds where any of John, Paul, or George misses the party are still unbelievable after we learn that Ringo might not attend—which was the desired result. This is an instance of the problem of clean cancelation. Assertive content that entails the falsity of what we learned might be true is canceled; the rest of what was asserted remains in place.

Our second worry about update semantics was this. It tells us that $\Diamond\varphi$ uttered in information state S has no effect unless S and φ are inconsistent. Suppose, for instance, that $S = \{\sim\chi\}$ and $\varphi = \chi \vee \psi$. $\chi \vee \psi$ is consistent with $\sim\chi$, so update semantics says that $S + \Diamond\varphi$ should be S again. But that seems wrong. For recall that $\Diamond(\chi$ or $\psi)$ has the same force as $\Diamond\chi$ followed by $\Diamond\psi$. To be told inter alia that $\Diamond\chi$ presumably cancels the information initially present in $S = \|\sim\chi\|$. Here, then, is a case where S $+ \Diamond\varphi$ is a proper subset of S, even though φ is fully consistent with S. What does the

---

[25] Not in the first instance, anyway.

cancelation theory say? When φ is consistent with S, we imagine it preceded by an assertion of $\sim\varphi$. $S + \diamondsuit\varphi$ is $(S\cap\|\sim\varphi\|)- \|\sim\varphi\|$. If the two-part operation of asserting and then withdrawing $\sim\varphi$ always left S unchanged, then this maneuver would not gain us much. But we have seen that $(S\cap\|\sim\varphi\|)-\|\sim\varphi\|$ is not always S. And in the present case $(S\cap\|\sim\varphi\|)- \|\sim\varphi\|$ would seem to be a much weaker proposition than S.[26]

That completes my explanation and defense of the cancelation theory. Many important topics have been left undiscussed. For instance,

(a) Master-Slave and Teacher-Student are highly unnatural games. How does the sphere evolve when deontic/epistemic authority does not rest with one person?[27]

(b) The focus has been on stand-alone "might"-statements. How should we understand "might"'s contribution in conditionals, or in complex predicates?

(c) If "might $\sim\varphi$" is a device for rejecting an imagined assertion of φ, what is "must φ"? A device for rejecting an imagined instance of "might $\sim\varphi$"—that is, for rejecting φ's rejection? Can I reject φ's rejection without going so far as to assert that φ?[28]

(d) How does the context-change function given in (UR$\diamondsuit$) relate to the contraction operators studied in the literature on belief revision?[29]

I would like to take the opportunity in closing to cancel any would-be assertions to the effect that these topics will not be discussed in future work.

Appendix: Proof of FACT

From (p3), which says that the right expansion should bring in at least one φ-world, we conclude that any package of commands all of whose members are consistent with φ is unreasonable; for such a package fails to enlarge the sphere of permissibility, as it has to be enlarged to make room for φ-worlds. From (p2), which says that the right expansion should bring in *only* φ-worlds, we conclude that any package of commands none of whose members is consistent with φ is unreasonable. For that kind of package expands the sphere of possibility to include *every* world, and we know by (p2) that permission to φ should bring in only φ-worlds. So, any reasonable package of commands $< \psi_i >$ has members consistent with φ and members inconsistent with φ. Let's use χ for the conjunction of all ψ_is *inconsistent* with φ, and ψ for the conjunction all ψ_is individually *consistent* with φ. Then

S = the set of $(\chi \wedge \psi)$-worlds

S^+ = the set of ψ-worlds

$S^+ - S$ = the set of $(\psi \wedge \sim\chi)$-worlds

[26] $(\|\sim\chi \| \cap \|\sim(\chi \vee \psi)\|)- \|\sim(\chi \vee \psi)\|=\|\sim(\chi \vee \psi)\|)- \|\sim(\chi \vee \psi)\|=\|\sim\varphi\| - \|\sim\varphi\|$.
[27] Thanks here to Sally Haslanger.
[28] This could bear on the puzzling weakness of "must φ" vis à vis φ.
[29] Fuhrmann (1996).

Again, $<\psi_i>$ is reasonable only if

(∃) $S^+ - S$ contains φ-worlds (from (p3))

(∀) $S^+ - S$ contains only φ-worlds (from (p2))

From (∃) we learn that ψ is consistent with φ. Proof: Suppose not. Then S^+ (= the set of ψ-worlds) does not contain any φ-worlds. But (∃) implies that S^+ does contain φ-worlds, since $S^+ - S$ contains them. A more interesting result follows from (∀): for all S^+-worlds w, χ holds in w iff φ does not hold in w. The "only if" direction is easy, since each of χ's conjuncts is by definition inconsistent with φ. For the "if" direction, suppose that χ does not hold in w. w cannot be an S-world because S-worlds have to satisfy all the ψ_is. But then w is in S^+- S. And according to (∀), every world in S^+- S satisfies φ. So, the implicit commands suitable to serve as backdrop to a permission to φ must be divisible into two parts: $\chi = \sim\varphi =$ the part that forbids φing, and $\psi =$ the part that allows φing.

References

DeRose, K. (1991). "Epistemic possibilities", *The Philosophical Review* 100 (4): 581–605.

Egan, A. (2007). "Epistemic modals, relativism and assertion", *Philosophical Studies* 133(1): 1–22.

——Hawthorne, J., and Weatherson, B. (2005). "Epistemic modals in context", in G. Preyer and G. Peter (eds.), *Contextualism in Philosophy: Knowledge, Meaning, and Truth* (Oxford: Oxford University Press) 131–68.

von Fintel, K., and Gillies, A. S. (2007). "An Opinionated Guide to Epistemic Modality", *Oxford Studies in Epistemology* 2 (Oxford: Oxford University Press) 32–62.

——   —— (2008). "CIA Leaks", *Philosophical Review* 117(1): 77–98.

Fox, D. (2006). Free Choice and the Theory of Scalar Implicatures (MS).

Fuhrmann, A. (1996). *An Essay on Contraction* (Chicago: University of Chicago Press).

—— (1999). "When hyperpropositions meet", *Journal of Philosophical Logic* 28: 559–74.

Gillies, A. S. (2004). "New foundations for epistemic change", *Synthese* 138 (1): 1–48.

Hacking, I. (1967). "Possibility", *Philosophical Review* 76: 143–68.

Hudson, J. L. (1975). "Logical subtraction" *Analysis* 35: 130–5.

Humberstone, L. (1981). Logical Subtraction: Problems and Prospects (MS).

—— (2000). "Parts and Partitions", *Theoria* 66 (1): 41–82.

Jaeger, R. A. (1973). "Action and subtraction", *Philosophical Review* 82: 320–9.

Kamp, H. (1973). "Free choice permission" *Proceedings of the Aristotelian Society* 74: 57–74.

Kratzer, A. (1981). "The notional category of modality", in H. Eikmeyer and H. Rieser (eds.), *Words, Worlds, and Contexts: New Approaches in Word Semantics* (Berlin: de Gruyter), 38–74.

Lewis, D. (1979). "A problem about permission", as repr. in Lewis (2000: 20–33).

—— (2000). *Papers in Ethics and Social Philosophy* (Cambridge Studies in Philosophy, Cambridge: Cambridge University Press).

MacFarlane, J. (2005). "Making Sense of Relative Truth", *Proceedings of the Aristotelian Society* 105 (1): 321–39.

—— (2011). "Epistemic Modals are Assessment-Sensitive", this volume.

Moore, G. E. (1962). *Commonplace Book* 1919–1953 (London: George, Allen, and Unwin).

Moss. S. (forthcoming). On the pragmatics of counterfactuals. *Noûs*.

Stanley, J. (2005). "Fallibilism and concessive knowledge attributions", *Analysis* 65 (2): 126–31.

Teller, P. (1972). "Epistemic possibility", *Philosophia: Philosophical Quarterly of Israel* 2: 303–20.

Thomson, J. J., and Byrne, A. (2006). *Content and Modality: Themes from the Philosophy of Robert Stalnaker* (Oxford: Clarendon Press).

Veltman, F. (1996). "Defaults in update semantics", *Journal of Philosophical Logic* 25 (3): 221–61.

Yablo, S. (2006). "Non-catastrophic presupposition failure", in Thomson and Byrne (2006), 164–90.

Yalcin, S. (2007). "Epistemic Modals", *Mind* 116 (464): 983–1026.

Zimmermann, T. E. (2000). "Free choice disjunction and epistemic possibility", *Natural Language Semantics* 8 (4): 255–90.

10

Nonfactualism about Epistemic Modality

Seth Yalcin

1. Introduction

When I tell you that it's raining, I describe a way the world is—viz., rainy. I say something factual, something whose truth turns on how things are with some aspect of the world. Likewise when I tell you that *the weatherman thinks* that it's raining. Here the truth of what I say turns on a different feature of the world, namely, the weatherman's state of mind. Likewise when I tell you that *I* think that it's raining. Here the truth of what I say turns on yet another feature of the world, namely, *my* state of mind.

Nothing like tedious platitudes to set the mood.[1] Okay—what about when I tell you that it *might* be raining? Or that it is *probably* raining? Or that it *must* be raining? In these cases, am I again to be understood as describing a way the world is?

An affirmative answer would be nice. For it seems like it would mean less work. It would let us take the view that sentences like these—sentences with epistemic modal operators taking wide scope—are not special. It would let us apply to these sentences whatever semantic and pragmatic explanatory strategies we already apply to other uncontroversially descriptive, fact-describing discourse. And, from a distance at least, an affirmative answer seems anyway not hard to pull off. Epistemic modals are so-called, after all, because they seem to serve to communicate information about some epistemic state or state of evidence. And states of evidence are, of course, aspects of the world. One could try, then, understanding epistemically modalized sentences— these sentences about what might or must be, or about what is probable—as telling

I am indebted to audiences at MIT, Berkeley, Princeton, NYU, and Arché for helpful feedback. Thanks especially to Andy Egan, John MacFarlane, Dilip Ninan, Robert Stalnaker, and Stephen Yablo for illuminating conversations on these matters. An earlier draft of this paper appeared in Yalcin (2008).

[1] Of course, one philosopher's tedious platitude is another's controversial thesis. An eliminativist about mental content would be uncomfortable with my opening, as would be a philosopher who takes content ascriptions to be normative, and who takes normative discourse not to be straightforwardly factual. I must set these views aside here.

how things are with some epistemic state or other, or with some body of evidence or other, in the world.

Since an affirmative answer means less work and looks not hard to pull off, little wonder that that answer is a popular one. Indeed, it has some title to being called the *standard view* about epistemic modality in philosophy. (Or at least, it had this title until recently.) One might spin the standard view either as a metaphysical thesis or as a linguistic thesis. We could call the linguistic thesis *descriptivism* about the content of epistemic modal discourse. To a rough first approximation, descriptivism is the idea that epistemic modal talk serves fundamentally to describe some feature of reality, to say how some aspect of the world is. (Compare the uncontroversial thesis of descriptivism about the content of weather talk.) The metaphysical thesis is *factualism* about epistemic modality. To a rough first approximation, factualism about epistemic modality is the view that there is a certain class of facts, the facts about what is (epistemically) possible, or probable, or necessary. For these facts to obtain is a matter of the world being one way rather than another. (Compare the uncontroversial thesis of factualism about the weather.) Descriptivism about the content of epistemic modal talk and factualism about epistemic modality are, I take it, really the same thesis in slightly different keys. I will use both terms for the view.

In this paper I am interested in developing an alternative to the factualist picture. With caveats to be provided in due course, the positive account I will set out could plausibly be called a kind of *expressivism* about epistemic modal discourse, and a kind of *nonfactualism* about epistemic modality. Before I begin developing this alternative, however, more should be said about the sort of view it is an alternative to. In the next section I say more about how I want to understand the descriptivist, factualist picture of epistemic modality. I then turn to some problems for the view, problems which recommend investigation into nondescriptivist alternatives.

2. Factualism

Descriptivism, I already said, is the view that epistemic modal talk serves to describe reality. Let me clarify 'epistemic modal talk' and 'serves to describe reality'.

By 'epistemic modal talk', I have in mind foremost sentences that are modalized with natural language epistemic modal operators. For instance, *It is possible that it is raining, It might be raining, It could be raining, It is probably raining, It is likely that it is raining*, and *It must be raining* all have readings on which the modals they contain are interpreted epistemically. (With *might, likely*, and *probably*, the epistemic reading is the preferred reading, if not the only reading; with *could, possible*, and *must*, other readings, such as a deontic reading, are often possible.) I don't attempt an operational definition of this class of modals now; the ultimate project is to provide a theory which delimits the class more precisely. Only let me be explicit that by 'epistemic modal operator', I don't have in mind complex operators such as 'for all I know, it might be that'—operators with simple epistemic modals scoped under epistemic attitude verbs. The importance of excluding these complex operators will become clear later. I will also avoid interactions with tense, restricting myself to the case where these modals take apparently present-tensed complements.

By 'serves to describe reality', I mean that epistemically modalized sentences serve to represent the world, or one's situation in the world, as being a certain way. Relative to context, the content of the sentence determines, and is understood as determining, a condition on metaphysically possible worlds or situations. It has the effect of dividing the space of possible ways things might be into those which conform, and those which fail to conform, with how things are represented as being; and moreover the fact that the sentence effects this division forms a crucial part of the explanation for its communicative import. Let me call a rule for dividing the space of possible worlds or situations *factualist truth conditions*. A descriptivist provides factualist truth conditions for epistemic modal talk.

This is close to what we want, but my characterization of descriptivism has so far blurred over an important distinction. This is the distinction between the *compositional semantic contribution* of a declarative sentence, and what we might call the *informational content* of the sentence when it is tokened in a context. Though often conflated in practice, these notions correspond to distinct theoretical roles. The former notion is for use in articulating our tacit semantic competence with the language—in particular, our in-principle ability to interpret, via a finitely specifiable competence, an infinitude of sentences. In contrast, the notion of informational content—what I have in mind here also sometimes gets called *the proposition expressed* or *what is said*—is best construed as a notion at the semantics-pragmatic interface. It comes into play when we ask:

> What information does a given sentence normally communicate in virtue of its compositional semantics, relevant features of the context of utterance, and the standing pragmatic norms which are common knowledge among speakers of the language?

To answer this kind of question, one needs some additional theory. Most obviously, one needs a general conception of what information or content is. One needs a theory of content. Such a theory might be influenced, or even largely driven by, considerations external to formal semantics *per se*.[2] One needs also some pragmatic theory—in particular, some view about what conventional rules govern the linguistic communication of information. The notion of informational content is constrained from these directions. While we can expect that knowledge of the semantic value of a sentence should be a fundamental part of the explanation of how a listener recovers the informational content of the sentence in context, it is not necessary to assume that the semantic value of a sentence is literally *identical* to the informational content of the sentence in context. As Lewis (1980) has noted, what we need is only the idea that the informational content of a sentence in context can be recovered in some

---

[2] Theories of content wherein the formal semantics of natural language plays no essential role are quite familiar in philosophy; Dretske (1981) and Stalnaker (1984) are two well-known examples.

systematic way from its semantic value (together with context and whatever standing, commonly known pragmatic principles there may be).

With the conceptual distinction between these two notions in mind, we can make it official that descriptivism, as I want to understand it here, is a view about the informational content of an unembedded, declarative epistemic modal sentence. It is the view that the informational content of these sentences has the effect of dividing the space of possible ways things might be into those which conform, and those which fail to conform, with how things are represented as being; and moreover it is the view that the fact these sentences effect such a division forms a crucial part of the explanation for their communicative import. And the thought is that in these respects, epistemic modal talk is just like ordinary, prosaically factual talk. So understood, the formal semantics of epistemic modals of course bears on the thesis of descriptivism, but its bearing is indirect. The question of whether descriptivism is true is not equivalent to the question of the compositional semantics of epistemic modal operators.

I hope descriptivism sounds like the straightforward view it is. Some examples of descriptivist views will help to round out the picture. Start with descriptivism about epistemic possibility talk. G. E. Moore writes:

People *in philosophy* say: The propositions that I'm not sitting down now, that I'm not male, that I'm dead, that I died before the murder of Julius Caesar, that I shall die before 12 tonight are 'logically possible'. But it's not English to say, with this meaning: It's possible that I'm not sitting down now etc.—*this* only means 'It is not certain that I am' or 'I don't know that I am'. (1962: 184)

Moore's view is descriptivist simply because according to it, epistemic possibility sentences in context are descriptions of the epistemic state of some agent in the world.

Most descriptivists agree with Moore's basic idea, that these sentences serve to describe the epistemic situation of some agent or agents. The internal debate among descriptivists concerns the detailed nature of the description—for instance, which agents matter, or what aspects of the agents' evidential situation are relevant. For example, three or four epicycles of analysis down from Moore, DeRose proposes that

S's assertion "It is possible that P" is true if and only if (1) no member of the relevant community knows that P is false, and (2) there is no relevant way by which members of the relevant community can come to know that P is false (1991: 593–4)

while Stanley seems to suggest that these sentences describe the epistemic state of some contextually given knower A:

It is possible$_A$ that p is true if and only if what A knows does not, in a manner that is obvious to A, entail not-p. (2005: 128)

The particular motivations for these departures from Moore's position needn't detain us. The point is just that, although Moore, DeRose, and Stanley all differ on exactly what facts epistemic possibility sentences describe, they all agree that these sentences serve to describe some facts or other, some feature of the world.

Those are examples of descriptivism about epistemic possibility. What about epistemic necessity? If, as is widely assumed, epistemic necessity modals (□) are the logical duals of epistemic possibility modals (◊) in the sense that

$$\Diamond \phi \leftrightarrow \neg \Box \neg \phi$$

then we can expect that each of the above accounts of epistemic possibility straightforwardly generates an account of epistemic necessity. So, given duality, Moore's view would be that 'It must raining', on the epistemic reading, is true just when 'I know it's raining' is; and so on for the other two views. It should be clear that the resulting positions on epistemic necessity are no less descriptivist than the positions on epistemic possibility they are constructed from. The duality of epistemic possibility and necessity is plausible; I will assume it throughout.

(But let me warn in advance: epistemic necessity will play second fiddle to epistemic possibility in this paper. What I say about it will be driven mostly by considerations about epistemic possibility, and the assumption of duality.)

Last, probability operators such as 'probably' and 'it is likely that', which I will abbreviate as '△'. Here, a simplistic example of a descriptivist position can be abstracted from the Bayesian paradigm: for one to say 'It's probably raining' is for one to say that one's credence in rain is above one-half, or above some contextually-determined value.[3] In calling something 'probable', one describes one's credal state. A second position, closer in form to the descriptivist accounts of (non-probabilistic) epistemic modality just described, adverts to some tacit body of knowledge or evidence. Suppose a body of evidence induces, or is representable by, a probability measure over a domain of propositions. Then instances of $\triangle \phi$ can be understood to say that the proposition that ϕ has some highish value according to the measure induced by the body of evidence determined by the context in which the sentence is uttered.[4] They would, in short, be factual claims about some contextually determined body of evidence.

The factualist, descriptivist view requires no fundamentally new assumptions. Epistemic modal sentences are taken to determine possible worlds truth conditions, so from a semantic point of view we can compositionally supply epistemic modal clauses with truth conditions in ordinary fashion. (The leading semantics is Kratzer's: see Kratzer (1977, 1981, 1991b); see also Lewis (1979).) Pragmatically, too, we needn't make waves. We can retain a familiar picture of communication, a picture that gives no special place to epistemic modal talk. Whether I say that it is raining or I say that it is probably raining, the story about what is happening, at least in straightforward cases, can be the usual Gricean one: I believe myself to have some information about the world, and wish to impart it to you; I say something whose truth turns on whether

---

[3] Jeffrey seems to have something like this in mind when he writes: "If you say the probability of rain is 70% you are reporting that, all things considered, you would bet on rain at odds of 7:3" (2004: 3). (For Jeffrey, one's credence just is a matter of one's disposition to bet.)

[4] To ease exposition, I will be loose about use and mention in this paper.

this information is true, presuming common knowledge of the language; in so doing I intend for you to come to accept that information, acting with the expectation that my intention to communicate that information is mutually recognized. More needs to be said to fill in the details, of course; but suffice to say that, for the descriptivist, the details will be filled in just the same ways for epistemic and non-epistemic modal talk alike.

Because descriptivism makes no semantic or pragmatic waves, there is a certain presumption in favor of it. In the next section I attempt to undermine this presumption.

3. Challenges for Factualism

3.1. Epistemic contradictions

Notice that the following sentences sound awful.[5]

    (1) # It's raining and it might not be raining.

    (2) # It's raining and it probably isn't raining.

Let us call sentences like these—sentences of the schematic form $(\phi \wedge E\neg\phi)$, where E is an epistemic modal—*epistemic contradictions*. Why do epistemic contradictions (1) and (2) sound awful?

At first glance, a descriptivist-friendly explanation seems easy enough. A descriptivist might try saying that these sentences sound terrible because, thanks to the semantics of the epistemic modals, these sentences both truth-conditionally entail

    (3) # It's raining and I don't know its raining.

relative to context. Obviously, (3) is Moore-paradoxical. Therefore, says the descriptivist, (1) and (2) should be pragmatically defective in whatever way (3) is defective. The defect in (1) and (2) is parasitic, as it were, on (3). Epistemic contradictions are not contradictions in any semantic sense. They are just Moore-paradoxical sentences in new guise.

The situation is not so simple, however. (1) and (2) are more than merely pragmatically defective. The conjuncts in these sentences are incompatible in a more robust sense. We can see this when we attempt to embed these conjunctions into larger constructions. Consider, for instance, the imperatives:

    (4) # Suppose it's raining and it might not be raining.

    (5) # Suppose it's raining and it probably isn't raining.

These imperatives sound incoherent and self-defeating. The fact that they do not make sense is not explained by the assumption that the conjunctions they each embed both truth-conditionally entail (3), because (3) is perfectly easy to embed under 'suppose':

---

[5] Here I review some points made in more detail in Yalcin (2007).

(6) Suppose it's raining and I don't know its raining.

(Indeed, the *intelligibility* of sentences like (6) is a popular motivation for denying that classically Moore-paradoxical sentences are contradictions in any semantically rich sense.) Or again, epistemic contradictions never sound acceptable in the antecedent position of an indicative conditional:

(7) # If it's raining and it might not be raining, then . . .

(8) # If it's raining and it probably isn't raining, then . . .

Conditionals that begin in this way seem beyond repair. But Moore-paradoxical sentences are acceptable in this environment:

(9) If it's raining and I don't know it, then I will get wet.

Compare that with the nonsensical

(10) # If it's raining and it might not be raining, then I will get wet.

The conditional (10) is particularly telling. If it really were the case that, relative to context, 'It might not be raining' entailed 'I don't know that it's raining', we would expect (10) to be about as acceptable as (9). But the difference in acceptability could hardly be greater.

The upshot is this. Epistemic contradictions 'project their unacceptability', as it were, in the embedded contexts described above. Moore-paradoxical sentences do not. The defect in sentences which embed epistemic contradictions is therefore not parasitic on Moore's paradox. It must be explained in some other way.

And the problem is that it is not clear how to explain it plausibly along descriptivist lines. Descriptivists want to tell us that epistemic contradictions such as (1) and (2) above have factualist truth conditions. In particular, they want to tell us that these sentences have *non-empty* factualist truth conditions, truth conditions that obtain in some possible situation.[6] If the truth conditions of (e.g.) 'It isn't raining and it might be raining' are non-empty, however, it seems there should be nothing at all preventing us from hypothetically entertaining the obtaining of these conditions. But we can't, evidently; there is no coherent way to entertain the thought that it isn't raining and it might be raining. This is quite unexpected from a descriptivist perspective.

Let me be clear about the extent to which these embedding facts do and do not tell against the descriptivist view. Considerations about where exactly epistemic modal clauses can felicitously embed most directly constrain the compositional semantics of epistemic modals. As we have noted, however, compositional semantics is one thing, and informational content another. The descriptivist therefore has a recourse: she could attempt to exploit the gap between these two notions in covering the above facts. She could do this if she can find semantic values for epistemic modals (and for attitude verbs like 'suppose', and for indicative conditionals) that will lead us to

---

[6] I assume the descriptivist does not wish to maintain that the conjuncts of an epistemic contradiction are truth-conditionally incompatible, hence that 'It might be raining' truth-conditionally entails 'It's raining'.

expect defectiveness in the case of the problematic embedded epistemic contradictions above, but which nevertheless contribute to determining a coherent (albeit Moore-paradoxical) informational content for the unembedded epistemic modal sentences (1) and (2).

As far as I can see, the descriptivist must take this sort of recourse in order to make sense of the embedding facts. That makes for a somewhat complicated wrinkle in the descriptivist view. But since a wrinkled view along these lines is certainly logically possible,[7] the embedding facts just described do not straightaway refute descriptivism. They do suggest, however, that descriptivism has the following surprising feature: when one says that it might be raining, the informational content one expresses is not the content one is related to when one supposes it might be raining. Moreover if, as seems plausible, the semantics of 'suppose' is taken to relevantly pattern with other attitude verbs such as 'believes', so that we can explain what is troubling about

(11) John believes it's raining and it might not be raining.

along structurally similar lines, the descriptivist view can be expected to have the result that to believe that it might be raining is not to believe the proposition (informational content) one would express when one says that it might be raining (that is, utters the unembedded declarative sentence 'It might be raining'). This result is surprising. Ultimately, I will offer a view that avoids this result.

3.2. Assertability and disagreement

We sometimes disagree, not merely about what is the case, but also about what might be the case, and about what is probably the case. The second concern about descriptivism is that it is hard to see how to deliver factualist truth conditions for epistemic modal talk which make sense of this kind of disagreement.

The trouble appears to have been first noted by Huw Price. Price considers the idea of assigning $\Delta\phi$ factualist truth conditions along the lines of 'Given the existing evidence, it is probable that ϕ'. He observes that the phrase 'the existing evidence' is ambiguous, admitting a spectrum of readings from the more subjective to the more objective. He first attempts a subjective reading of the phrase, along the lines of 'the evidence of which I [the speaker] am actually aware'. He objects that:

If I disagree with your claim that it is probably going to snow, I am not disagreeing that given *your* evidence it is likely that this is so

and contrariwise:

Indeed, I might *agree* [with your claim] that it is probably going to snow and yet think it false that this follows from your evidence. (Price 1983: 404)

Here the problem is that the proposed truth conditions for 'It is probably going to snow' are too weak to make sense of cases both of appropriate agreement and appropriate disagreement.

---

[7] The 'diagonal view' discussed in Yalcin (2007) is a precise version of such a view.

Next he tries an objective reading of 'the existing evidence', along the lines of 'the evidence accessible in principle'. He objects that this more objective reading wouldn't square with the facts about when $\triangle\phi$ is felicitous to assert:

consider the surgeon who says, 'Your operation has probably been successful. We could find out for sure, but since the tests are painful and expensive, it is best to avoid them.' The accessibility, in principle, of evidence which would override that on which the [probability] judgment is based, is here explicitly acknowledged. (Price 1983: 405)

Here the surgeon says $\triangle\phi$, but leaves open whether ϕ is probable given the evidence accessible in principle. No surprise he would leave *that* question open, after all; he simply does not have the evidence accessible in principle. Hence his statement of $\triangle\phi$ is not well understood as speaking to a question about the evidence accessible in principle.

This now provokes the question: what or whose evidence is relevant to settling the truth of a given claim of $\triangle\phi$? We appear to need something in between the evidence of the speaker and the evidence available in principle. It is hard to see, however, how something in between could ever really be assertable for the speaker. Something in between, after all, is by definition beyond the scope of the speaker's evidence. If we settled on something in between, our speaker would still be pictured as saying something whose truth turns on a body of evidence that she does not have. It seems she would be pictured as speaking, and knowingly speaking, from a position of ignorance, making a stronger claim than is warranted by her evidence alone. Her speech act looks in danger of being irrational.[8]

The objection to descriptivism, then, is that it faces a tension. Either descriptivist truth conditions systematically fail to capture the truth-value judgments that people actually make (by being too weak to capture the disagreement facts), or it captures these judgments but turns users of epistemic modal sentences into irrational asserters (by picturing them as making claims about/from a body of evidence they don't have). The difficulty here recurs exactly with epistemic possibility claims, as the reader may confirm by replacing 'probably' with 'possibly' in Price's examples.

3.3. Conflicting intuitions

Closely related, a third problem with descriptivism is that it leads us to expect clear intuitions in cases where intuitions are not clear. Consider the following case:[9]

---

[8] Couldn't her evidence include information about the state of some other, not-yet-possessed body of evidence? And in that case, couldn't her evidence provide her with the warrant to make claims about what is made probable by this not-yet-possessed evidence? But it is unclear whether one can have evidence that some other, larger body of evidence makes p probable without one's own evidence itself making p probable.

[9] These are usually called *eavesdropping cases*. See Egan et al. (2005), Egan (2007), von Fintel and Gillies (2008), and MacFarlane (this volume) for discussion. Some of these authors take the speaker judgments about eavesdropping cases to be less ambivalent than I do—on this matter we take different positions on what is ultimately an empirical question—and they use these cases to motivate different versions of *relativism* about epistemic modal talk. I will present a different view about how to respond to these cases.

Fat Tony secretly plants highly compelling evidence of his murder at the docks. The evidence is discovered by the authorities, and word gets out about his apparent death. The next evening, from his safehouse, Fat Tony watches a panel of experts on the news discussing the situation.

Expert A has had a good look at the evidence found at the scene. "Fat Tony is dead," he says.

Expert B has also had a good look at the evidence, but his assessment is more cautious. "Fat Tony might be dead," B says.

We can all agree that Expert A, however reasonable his speech act was in light of the information available to him, spoke falsely. Things are not as he says they are. Okay; what about Expert B? Is what he said true or false? Let me remind you that Fat Tony's planted evidence was highly compelling. Let me remind you also that Fat Tony is *definitely not dead*. And, before you settle on an answer, let me ask you also to ponder whether Fat Tony himself should agree with your answer.

Now, what do you say about what B said—true or false?

It appears that, as a matter of empirical fact, intuitions are unclear about cases such as this—cases where an epistemic modal claim is assessed for truth from outside the discourse context.[10] Some are inclined to say that B spoke truly; others are inclined to say that B spoke falsely; everyone else shrugs, or proposes to change the question to one with a clearer answer.

What needs explaining for eavesdropping cases such as this, I think, is not any univocal intuition we all have about the epistemic modal claim made in the case. In the absence of a systematic empirical study, there seems to be no single intuition there to explain. Rather, what needs explaining is the absence of agreement, by competent speakers of English, on what the right answer is. What needs explaining are the conflicting intuitions. My point for now is just that conflicting intuitions are not expected on descriptivist assumptions. If B's utterance is in the business of representing the world as being a certain way, as A's presumably is, then either the world is that way, or it isn't. Other things being equal, we'd expect intuition concerning the truth of B's utterance to be about as clear as it is with A's. Descriptivists have work to do, then, explaining why things are not equal.

A descriptivist might reply that this work is not really so hard. "Epistemic modals are, after all, highly context-sensitive on our view. Perhaps the lack of uniformity in judgments here is simply due to the fact that subjects considering this case resolve this context-sensitivity in different ways."

But this reply is unsatisfactory. If the interpretation of epistemic modals is as context-sensitive as suggested, presumably there is at least one reading of the modal according to which what B says above is both (a) true and (b) assertable for B. (Perhaps a reading along the lines of 'The evidence in the reach of B leaves open the possibility that Fat Tony is dead.') Where multiple interpretations of a speaker's utterance are

---

[10] I say this not from the armchair, but from having surveyed 128 subjects on the matter. For a brief discussion, and details on the data see Yalcin and Knobe (2010).

possible, subjects tend to gravitate towards true and assertable readings, for the simple reason that true and assertable readings tend to make most sense of what the speaker is doing—they tend to be easier to situate into a rational overall pattern of action. But this would lead us to expect a fairly robust judgment that what B says is true, the incorrect result.

It is striking, incidentally, that the body of evidence allegedly relevant to assessing the truth of an epistemic modal claim should be so obscure to speakers who actually use these sentences. If these sentences really do advert to some tacit body of evidence, as standard versions of factualism maintain, why are we competent speakers of the language not able to articulate what this body is? This opacity is puzzling. It is not a feature of context-sensitive language in general. For instance, when we use quantifiers in ordinary discourse, typically a restriction on the quantifier is provided tacitly by context. But with sufficient description of context, speakers can typically recover what the intended restriction is; and where context is insufficient, speakers can typically indicate what further information is needed to settle the question. In contrast, the interpretation of epistemic modals seems, from a contextualist perspective, to be far less constrained. Appeals to the context-sensitivity of epistemic modals seem to be of questionable explanatory power here, then.

Let me summarize. We have accumulated three desiderata for a theory of the content of epistemic modal claims. Such a theory should:

I. Be compatible with a plausible explanation of why **epistemic contradictions** are unembeddable.

II. Make sense of the **assertability and disagreement** facts concerning epistemic modal claims in context.

III. Make sense of the **conflicting intuitions** concerning epistemic modal claims in eavesdropping cases.

The first desideratum is plausibly understood as a constraint on the formal semantics of epistemic modals (together with the semantics of the relevant embedding environments). The second two desiderata are plausibly understood as constraining the pragmatics of epistemic modal claims—more precisely, their communicative content. The first of these pragmatic desiderata concerns the intra-contextual facts about how we assess epistemic modal claims *qua* participants in the discourse. The second concerns the extra-contextual facts about how we assess epistemic modal claims *qua* onlookers from outside the discourse.

Descriptivism is not well-positioned to satisfy these desiderata. It is time to take steps towards an alternative.

4. States of Mind

If we want to understand what is going on with epistemic modal talk, we may be better served by taking a less direct approach. Let us take a step back from the linguistic facts and from direct questions about the truth conditions of epistemic modal clauses. Let us ask instead:

What is it to be in a state of mind which accepts what an epistemic modal claim says?

I will suggest that descriptivism rests on a mistaken answer to this question, and that getting the answer right is the first step towards clarifying the meaning and role of epistemic modal discourse. The focus of this section will be on developing a model for what it is to believe that something might be so, or that something is possibly so.

In stepping back from direct questions about the truth conditions of epistemic modal clauses and asking instead about what it is to be in an epistemically modal state of mind, I make a move characteristic of meta-ethical expressivists like Gibbard (1990, 2003). Rather than asking after the truth conditions of normative sentences directly, Gibbard asks first what it is be normatively opinionated—that is, what it is to be in a state of mind with normative content. Once he develops a theory of this state of mind, he moves from that theory back to questions about the semantics of normative discourse and about the metaphysics of normativity. When direct inquiry into truth conditions does not seem to bear fruit, this kind of strategy—we could call it the method of *psychological ascent*, in contrast with the truth-conditions-focused method of semantic ascent—is, I think, sensible. I take this kind of strategy here.

We begin with epistemic possibility. I believe that it is possible that Bob is in his office; Frank believes that it might be raining in Topeka. What kind of states of mind are we each in? Doxastic states of mind, trivially. How to model a doxastic state of mind? For our purposes, we may represent a doxastic state by its informational content, abstracting for now from its functional role in cognition and action. How, then, to represent the informational content of a doxastic state of mind?

Start with a familiar picture of informational content in general. Information is foremost that which eliminates possibilities. To gain information is to transition to a state of mind which leaves fewer possibilities open as candidates for actuality. As a first approximation, then, let us represent a body of informational content as a set of possibilities, those possibilities left open by that informational content. So a state of belief is representable by a set of possibilities: intuitively, those not excluded by what is believed. The propositions true at each world in the set are the propositions believed by the agent. (Propositions, too, we will model via their truth-conditional content: a proposition is a set of possibilities, intuitively the possibilities with respect to which the proposition is true.)

As everyone knows, this classic possible worlds representation of belief faces acute problems.[11] Let me note now then that dialectically this classic picture will be serving as my point of departure, not arrival. Soon we will work this classic picture into

---

[11] For example, Frege's puzzle and the problem of logical omniscience (to name the two most commonly cited difficulties). The latter problem is discussed further below.

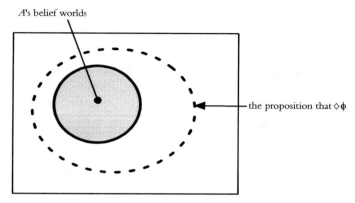

Fig. 10.1. $B_A \Diamond \phi$: The descriptivist model.

something more realistic. Meanwhile this model, idealized as it is, will supply us with a useful starting point.

Equipped with this representation, we can provide an abstract picture of the descriptivist model of epistemic possibility beliefs—of what, according to the descriptivist, it is to believe that it is possible that Bob is in his office, or that it might be raining in Topeka.[12] The picture is very simple (Fig. 10.1).

The rectangle is logical space, the space of maximally specific metaphysical possibilities. A subset of those possibilities is the proposition that $\Diamond \phi$, here the set of possibilities contained within the dashed ellipse. A believes that $\Diamond \phi$ just when A's belief worlds are a subset of the proposition that $\Diamond \phi$. Thus for me to believe that Bob might be in his office is for a certain proposition—whatever proposition it is the descriptivist says it is—to be true throughout my belief worlds. Again, standardly the descriptivist's truth conditions are propositions about some body of evidence, where this body of evidence includes the knowledge of the agent doing the believing. As a result, the typical descriptivist picture is one according to which states of $\Diamond \phi$-belief are *second-order* states of mind, states of belief about (perhaps *inter alia*) one's state of knowledge. And this prompts the question: when I believe Bob might be in his office, am I in a second-order state of mind?

We could try asking it like this. Is the question, "Why believe Bob might be in his office?" in part the question, "Why believe that I don't know that Bob isn't in his office?" Pre-theoretically, the idea seems to have little to recommend it. Our initial question seems to be about Bob's location, not about my views about Bob's location. The question "Why believe Bob might be in his office?" seems instead equivalent to the question, "Why fail to believe that Bob isn't in his office?" This latter question

---

[12] I have in mind here the 'unwrinkled' descriptivist, the descriptivist who holds that in saying that it might be raining, one expresses the proposition one believes when one believes that it might be raining.

is clearly not a question about what to believe about one's knowledge. It is just a question concerning what to believe about where Bob is.[13]

Other considerations lead in the same direction. Suppose we are eating dinner, and my dog Fido comes into the room and heels by my chair. Occasionally I toss Fido a bone at dinner, but usually I don't. You ask why Fido is sitting there staring at me. I say:

> (12) Fido thinks I might give him a bone.

What I say speaks to your question. Unless you have a particular theory of epistemic modals, I doubt you would flinch at this remark. But what exactly am I saying? Does my remark in part mean, as standard versions of descriptivism would recommend, that Fido believes that it is left open by what he knows that I will give him a bone? That is a bit much. The truth of (12) does not turn on recherché facts about canine self-awareness. Surely (12) may be true even if Fido is incapable of such second-order states of mind.

These considerations suggest that the question of whether $\Diamond\phi$ is 'transparent', as it were, to the question of whether ϕ. I think this is reflected in the kinds of reasons we understand to support epistemic possibility beliefs. Naively, correctly believing that $\Diamond\phi$ is a matter of there being an absence of conclusive reason to believe that $\neg\phi$. Correctly believing that ϕ is a matter of there being conclusive reason to believe that ϕ. Both kinds of reason concern how to settle one's doxastic state toward the proposition that ϕ. Believing that ϕ and believing that $\Diamond\phi$ are states of mind supported by reasons of the same category.

It seems, then, that we have found another desideratum for a theory of the content of epistemic modal claims. Such a theory should:

> IV. Avoid the assumption that to believe that something might be the case is to be in a **second-order state of mind** (i.e. a state of belief *inter alia* about one's own state of mind).

This is another desideratum that descriptivism is not well placed to capture. If one expresses a proposition one believes when one says (e.g.) 'It might be raining', and that proposition has the epistemic-state-describing truth conditions assigned to it by standard versions of descriptivism, it is a very short step to the thought that to believe it might be raining is to believe that very proposition.

Ask now: what minimal modification to the descriptivist model would be required to satisfy this new desideratum (IV)? I suggest that the modification is this one depicted in Fig. 10.2.

---

[13] While, I think, suggestive, these observations are perhaps not decisive. That is because it can be difficult to disentangle, from a first-person point of view, questions about what the world is like from questions about what one believes the world is like. As Evans observed, "If someone asks me 'Do you believe that there will be a third world war?', I must attend, in answering him, to precisely the same outward phenomena as I would attend to if I were answering the question 'Will there be a third world war?'" (1983: 225). (Though the point should not be overstated. The questions, "Why believe that ϕ?" and "Why believe that you believe that ϕ?" need not always have the same answer.)

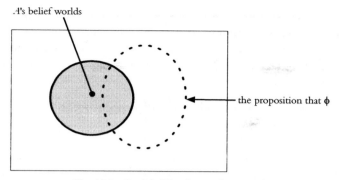

A's belief worlds

the proposition that ϕ

Fig. 10.2. $B_A \Diamond \phi$: The first-order model.

On this revised model, due essentially to Frank Veltman,[14] there is no proposition that $\Diamond \phi$ at work. There are no '$\Diamond \phi$-worlds'. The question of whether A believes that $\Diamond \phi$ is just the question whether A's belief worlds leave open possibilities wherein the proposition that ϕ is true. To believe Bob might be in his office is simply to be in a doxastic state which fails to rule out the possibility that Bob is in his office. It is a first-order state of mind. One might think of this as an 'adverbialist' model of epistemic possibility belief. Such beliefs do not correspond to a distinctive class of believed contents; rather, they correspond to a distinctive way of being doxastically related to a proposition. Note that on the first-order model, 'epistemic modal' is an unfortunate moniker, for there is no special role for a state of knowledge in this picture.

The first-order model is a considerable advance over the descriptivist model. It avoids the implausible idea that epistemic possibility beliefs are second-order states of mind, and in a way that lets us see why reasons that support belief that ϕ would be *ipso facto* reasons that support belief that $\Diamond \phi$. Besides satisfying our newly uncovered fourth desideratum, the first-order model helps also with our first three desiderata.

I. **Making sense of epistemic contradictions**. There is no difficulty at all giving a formal semantics for epistemic modals, indicative conditionals, and attitude verbs which can cover the embedding facts about epistemic contradictions in a manner consistent with the first-order model. (Indeed, as noted in footnote 14, the first clear occurrence of the idea was within a formal semantics.) Veltman's dynamic semantics for epistemic modals, when supplemented with appropriate semantics for conjunction, attitude verbs (e.g. Heim 1992) and indicative conditionals (e.g. Gillies 2004)

---

[14] See Veltman (1985, 1986, 1996), where this model is suggested by the dynamic semantics for epistemic modals developed in these works. (The first-order model is roughly what one would get as the truth conditions of epistemic possibility modal-embedding belief reports, were one to combine Veltman's semantics for epistemic modals with a straightforward dynamic possible worlds semantics for 'believes', such as Heim (1992).) Let me be clear that although what I am calling "the first-order model" is suggested by work in semantics, it is not itself a thesis in compositional semantics. Rather, it is a thesis about how to model a certain kind of state of mind.

will predict the defectiveness of epistemic contradictions in the relevant embedded contexts. (See Yalcin 2007 for more discussion, and for an example of a static semantics which can also accommodate the data.) Thus from a semantic point of view, the first-order model poses no special difficulties. On the contrary, it can be *motivated* by semantic considerations.

II. **Making sense of the assertability and disagreement facts.** We noted that the assertability and disagreement facts concerning unembedded epistemic modal claims are hard to explain under the assumption that there are some factual truth conditions which constitute their informational content. The first-order model suggests a different way of thinking about what we are up to when we say that something is possible, or might be the case. It recommends the idea that in modeling the communicative impact of an epistemic possibility claim, we construe the objective as one of coordination on a certain global property of one's state of mind—the property of being compatible with a certain proposition—not one of coordination concerning the way the world is.

First, this lets us avoid the demand, incumbent on the descriptivist, to say what or whose evidence is relevant to settling the truth of a given epistemic possibility claim. These claims do not have factualist truth conditions; *a fortiori* they do not have truth conditions turning on how things are with some body of evidence. Second, it lets us see the assertability and disagreement facts in a different light. To believe something might be the case, on the first-order view, is not really to embrace any positive thesis about how the world is. Rather, it is a way of lacking information; it is effectively a state of failing to believe something. And the relevant point to note here is that our intuitive notion of (dis)agreement is not really trained on such states of mind. If someone believes it's raining in Topeka right now, then you *agree* if you also think it's raining in Topeka right now, and you *disagree* if you think it's not raining in Topeka right now. If you neither agree nor disagree, you are agnostic on the matter. So understood, disagreement goes beyond mere failure of agreement. But what then is it to *agree with the agnostic* on this issue? The question feels ill-posed. This ill-posed question is, on the first-order view, similar to the question of what it is to agree or disagree with someone who believes it might be raining.[15]

If epistemic possibility claims do not have factualist truth conditions, what do they have? There are various ways one could build a formal model of the communicative impact of epistemic possibility claims—of their pragmatics—consistent with the first-order idea that the objective of such claims is to achieve coordination between states of mind on the openness of a possibility. One way is the one already standard in the

---

[15] One might try saying that to agree with the agnostic is to just also be agnostic, but this line is not promising. For what then would it be to disagree with the agnostic? Is it to take a definite stand on the relevant proposition? But it is not plausible to say that, merely in virtue of my lack of a positive stand on myriad propositions, I thereby disagree with anyone and everyone who takes a stand on these propositions. Suppose I don't have a view about where you parked your car, and you do. I do not thereby disagree with you, in any interesting sense.

dynamic semantics literature on epistemic modals stemming from Veltman's work (see e.g. Beaver 2001). Building on Stalnaker (1970), we associate with each conversation a *context set*, a set of possible worlds left open by what is mutually presupposed by the discourse participants. The communicative impact of an utterance is then formally modeled in terms of its characteristic tendency to change or update the context set. With ordinary factual discourse, the tendency is to eliminate worlds from the context set—to rule out ways the world might be. But with epistemic possibility claims, the tendency is only to ensure coordination on the leaving of a certain possibility open. The context set is just a representation of the speakers' presuppositions, and to presuppose something might be the case is exactly like believing something might be the case: it is a matter of the relevant proposition being compatible with the content of that state of mind.

III. **Making sense of conflicting intuitions about eavesdropping.** We observed above that we tend to have conflicting intuitions about the truth value of an epistemic modal claim when we are outside the discourse context and in a better epistemic position (with the respect to the epistemically modalized proposition) than those within the discourse. When Expert *B* says 'Fat Tony might be dead' in the scenario envisaged earlier, it is not clear what truth value the claim deserves.

The reason it is not clear, I suggest, is that Expert *B*'s speech act does not serve to describe the world. There is no way the world could be, or could fail to be, which would settle the question of the truth of the sentence. For this sentence there is no answering the question,

(T) Is the content of this speech act **true** in the sense that its factualist truth conditions characterize the actual world?

for it has a false presupposition. His utterance does not have factualist truth conditions.

The point of the speech act on the story I recommend is, again, to engender coordination among one's interlocutors with respect to the property of states of mind the sentence semantically expresses in context. Insofar as the claim has a content which is communicated, it is simply this property (and not a rule for eliminating possibilities—not a kind of factualist content). When assessing this kind of speech act for correctness, we cannot ask (T). At best it seems we ask one of two things:

(R) Is the speech act **rational** in the sense that someone equipped with the evidence of the speaker would be responding appropriately to the evidence by accepting the content of the speech act?

(A) Is the speech act **advisable** in the sense that a person equipped with full information about the relevant situation would be responding appropriately to that information by accepting the content of the speech act?[16]

---

[16] Gibbard makes an analogous distinction concerning questions about what it 'makes sense' to do (1990: 18–19).

Given this distinction, it is easy to see that Expert *B*'s speech act was *rational* but *inadvisable*. His state of mind responded appropriately (in one sense) to the evidence, but it is not the state of mind we would recommend to him given our superior epistemic position.

When we are asked about the truth value of claim in a given context, typically we understand the question to be (T). But where the claim is epistemically modalized, that question cannot arise. We therefore look for other criteria to assess the sentence for correctness; and the two kinds of features we check for instead, I suggest, are rationality and advisability. When ordinary speakers are asked, 'Is what Expert B said true?' some of them interpret the question as (R), and they answer 'yes'. Others interpret the question as (A), and they answer 'no'. Still others feel the intuitive pull of both interpretations. These enlightened subjects reject the question and say: "Look: Expert *B* was right to say what he did, given what he knows. But if he were to say that to me, I'd reject it, because I know the facts of the case." These speakers tacitly recognize that, as far as the correctness of the speech act goes, we can ask either of (R) or (A), but that no further question (T) arises.

We have now effectively wedded the first-order view to a kind of nonfactualism about epistemic possibility and a kind of expressivism about the associated discourse. To believe something is possible is not to take the world to be one way rather than another; it is not to think a certain sort of fact obtains. It is for one's state of mind to have a certain global property, one not reducible to a condition on worlds. We approach the question of the communicative impact of epistemic possibility claims from this perspective. To say that a proposition is possible, or that it might be the case, is to express the compatibility of the proposition with one's state of mind,[17] with the intention of engendering coordination on this property with one's interlocutor.

This expressivist, nonfactualist view about epistemic possibility is motivated by the facts—in particular, it is motivated by linguistic facts and by intuitive considerations about what it is to accept that something is possible. Unlike some versions of its meta-ethical cousin, this brand of nonfactualism is not driven by a metaphysical concern about the queerness of a certain class of properties. True, I deny that there is, or could be, any such thing as the fact that it might be raining, or the fact that it is possible that it is raining (where again facts are taken to correspond to ways the world might be). But this is not out of any metaphysical doubt that there are such things that might rightly be called epistemic possibilities. On the contrary, I embrace an ontology which includes metaphysically possible worlds,[18] and I embrace the coherence of the idea of a set of such worlds being compatible with a state of knowledge. In that sense, I fully embrace a metaphysics of epistemic possibilities; I am comfortable saying, in a factual tone of voice, that there are possibilities compatible with what I know. The view we

[17]   Expressing a state of mind is, remember, distinct from saying that one is in that state of mind.

[18]   Indeed my conception of factualism definitionally excludes the possibility of nonfactualism about metaphysical modality in general, for I deploy a 'robust' notion of metaphysical modality in saying what factualism is.

are developing is that, while there are such facts, the language of epistemic possibility does not serve to express them.[19]

What of epistemic necessity? Are we nonfactualist about these claims too? It is hard to make a direct case for that view, in the way we have for epistemic possibility. But an indirect case is easy, if we assume what looks plausible, that factual claims are closed under negation. (Factual claims are closed under negation just in case, if a claim ϕ has factualist truth conditions, so does $\neg\phi$.) Since by the duality of epistemic modality, the negation of an epistemic necessity claim is equivalent to an epistemic possibility claim, and epistemic possibility claims are nonfactual, epistemic necessity claims are nonfactual.

5. Question-Sensitivity

The first-order model is significant progress. Given the choice between it and a descriptivist approach, the choice seems to me clear. But I think there is room to improve on the model in an important way. We have one more desideratum to uncover. It arises in connection with a certain problem facing the model.[20]

Recall Frank, who believes it might be raining in Topeka. Why does he believe this? We could imagine various accounts of how it happened. For instance: He left Topeka this morning and it looked cloudy then. Or the weatherman just now said the chance of rain was 30%. Alternatively, perhaps his evidential situation is more impoverished. Perhaps he has no noteworthy reasons in favor of believing that it's raining in Topeka; rather he merely notices his lack of sufficient reason to believe it isn't raining in Topeka. Perhaps on the way out the door, en route to Topeka, he glances by chance at his umbrella, and the question of rain in Topeka then occurs to him. He realizes he doesn't know whether to expect rain in Topeka. He then comes to think that, well, it might be raining in Topeka.

This last kind of case raises a basic question. What is the difference between Frank's state of mind before the question of rain in Topeka occurs to him and his state of mind after? The question is an uneasy one for the dynamic model. We know, on the model, that Frank's posterior state of belief must be one compatible with the proposition that it's raining in Topeka. But what, we ask, was his prior state of mind? The same: he had no prior beliefs one way or the other as concerns rain in Topeka, so what he believed was compatible with either circumstance. So he has transitioned

---

[19] At least, not without the help of operators besides epistemic modals. To say *It might be raining* is to say something nonfactual; but to say *For all I know, it might be raining* is to say something factual—it is to describe one's state of knowledge. This is consistent with the view I advocate. (Compare the normative case: *You ought to go to confession* is a normative claim, while *According to Scripture, you ought to go to confession* is not. The meta-ethical expressivist denies the former claim is factual, but makes no such claim about the latter.)

[20] A problem along the lines of the one I will describe was noted by Frank Veltman at the University of Michigan Philosophy and Linguistics Workshop of 2006, though I do not know if he would agree with my statement of it. Swanson (2006) also raises a version of this problem.

from its being compatible with his doxastic state that it's raining in Topeka to . . . its being compatible with his doxastic state that it's raining in Topeka. No change. This is wrong: clearly some aspect of Frank's state of mind has changed, and our model ought to capture this change.

We could just as well make the point synchronically, by considering two states of mind at a single time rather than one across time. Compare Frank (in his posterior state) to Hank, a man living across the globe in Rotterdam. Hank has heard of Topeka, and he even knows roughly where it is on the map. But Topeka has no place in his life, and thoughts of Topeka simply have not crossed his mind in years. Like myriad other questions, the question of rain in Topeka today has just not occurred to Hank; and indeed, we stipulate it never will. Does Hank believe it might be raining in Topeka? It seems bizarre to answer affirmatively. It is true, we may stipulate, that for all Hank believes, it is raining in Topeka. For nothing he believes rules that possibility out. But this is just to observe that 'Hank believes it might be raining in Topeka' and 'For all Hank believes, it is raining in Topeka' do not have the same truth conditions. The states of mind of Frank and of Hank, we might say, are alike in as much as for all they each believe, it is raining in Topeka. But they differ in that Frank believes it might be raining in Topeka, whereas that is not so for Hank.[21]

We should like to model the difference. This gives us our last desideratum.

v. Capture the difference between a proposition's merely being compatible with a state of mind and its being epistemically possible according to that state—that is, possible in the thicker sense connoted by epistemic possibility modals.

But what exactly is that thicker sense? What extra does Frank have over Hank?

It is not easy to say. Should we say that if one believes $\Diamond\phi$, one has to be entertaining the proposition ϕ, or to be "seeing the possibility" that this proposition is true? No: we are after a kind of state, not a kind of activity. One does not lose one's beliefs about what might be the case by shifting one's attention to a new topic, or by going to sleep. Should we say instead the requirement is that one has to have entertained the proposition ϕ? This is a state at least, but it is too demanding. Suppose Jones is looking for his cell phone. He suddenly thinks to himself, *the cell phone might be in the glove compartment of the car*. Thereby a flood of epistemic possibility attributions normally become appropriate for him. For instance:

Jones thinks the cell phone might be in the car.
Jones thinks the cell phone might be in a vehicle.
Jones thinks the cell phone might not be in the living room.

---

[21] A third way to put the worry: on the model as so far described, there is no difference between not believing (failing to believe) that a proposition is possible ($\neg B\varphi$), and believing that the proposition is not possible ($B\neg\varphi$). For believing that a proposition is not possible is just believing its negation ($B\neg\varphi$), and this is the only way, on the current model, to fail to believe a proposition is possible. But that is intuitively wrong: my suggestion here is that one can fail to believe a proposition is possible without believing its negation. (This way of stating the problem makes it look analogous to a problem which allegedly afflicts expressivist accounts of normative talk, the so-called "negation problem.")

Jones thinks it might be that one has to go to the car to find the cell phone.
Jones thinks it might be that if one looks in the glove box of the car, one will find the cell phone.

And so on. But clearly we should not say that each of the corresponding propositions here must have been entertained by Jones.

Perhaps we should say this: an agent believes $\Diamond\phi$ just in case ϕ is compatible with his belief state, and moreover ϕ is a nearby consequence of a proposition one has entertained, or recently entertained. Even supposing we can make the idea of a nearby consequence precise, however, we now must worry about amnesiacs who have recently entertained ϕ, but have no recall of that event. If Frank gets hit with a shovel and reverts back to his prior state, he is no longer appropriately described as believing that it might be raining in Topeka, though it is true that he has recently entertained ϕ, and ϕ is compatible with what he believes. This last point suggests the state of believing that something might be the case is not, or not merely, a backward-looking state depending on a history of considered propositions. It has a forward-looking character.

Rather than focusing on states of entertainment or events of seeing possibilities, I want to approach the issue from a different direction. My thermostat is awfully imprecise—it only indicates that the room temperature falls somewhere within a ten degree range. Today it indicates that the temperature in the room is somewhere between 65 and 75 degrees. Thus if you were to ask me if the temperature in the room was 70 degrees (imagine, if you like, you are confirming the accuracy of your newfangled temperature-sensing watch), I could reply: *Well, according to my awfully imprecise thermostat, it might be.* That is to say, my awful thermostat indicates that the temperature in the room might be 70 degrees.

Now like most thermostats, mine does not carry information about the weather in Topeka. The thermostat's occupying any of its information-bearing states in normal conditions is compatible with any state of weather in Topeka. Rain in Topeka, for instance. Thus: for all my thermostat indicates, it's raining in Topeka. Nevertheless it is off to say: *According to my thermostat, it might be raining in Topeka.* (Still worse does it sound to say, in one breath: *According to my thermostat, the temperature in the room might be 70 degrees, and it might be raining in Topeka.*) We have here an asymmetry rather like the one observed between Frank and Hank, but in this case there is little temptation to appeal to what my thermostat may have recently entertained. Rather, in this case it is tempting to press the point that the thermostat is sensitive to some questions, or some subject matters, or a certain class of distinctions, and not others, and that this fact affects the felicity of the relevant uses of the epistemic possibility modal.

Following this line, I suggest that the extra thing that Frank has, and that Hank lacks, is some kind of sensitivity to a question. My thermostat is sensitive to some questions, or some issues, or some distinctions, and not others; so too with Frank and Hank. To count as believing $\Diamond\phi$, ϕ should be compatible with one's beliefs; but in addition, one's state of belief should also be sensitive to a question for which ϕ is an answer, or partial answer.[22] This will be our way of satisfying the fifth desideratum.

What is it to be sensitive to a question in the relevant sense? I think this is the right question to be asking, but I am less sure how to answer it. It seems to be at least this: it is to be equipped with possible states that distinguish possible answers to the question, and it is to be receptive to information which speaks to the question. My thermostat is equipped with possible states that distinguish possible answers to the question, *within what range is the temperature in this room?*, and it is receptive to information which speaks to that question. It is not equipped with possible states that distinguish possible answers to the question, *how is the weather in Topeka?*, and (a fortiori) is not receptive to information which speaks to the question.

This gives us a foothold, but just that. Moving from simple devices back to human beings and their states of belief, matters are less easy to describe. Perhaps if Hank had never heard of Topeka, had no concept of Topeka, and had none of the relations of acquaintance which are prerequisites to having Topeka thoughts, we might comfortably deny that Hank is equipped with possible states that distinguish possible answers to the question. We could say he lacks the resources to frame that question. And surely were that the case, it would indeed be off to say that Hank believes that it might be raining in Topeka. But in our original story, Hank is not so cognitively impoverished. He knows of Topeka. (And about weather.) He is not lacking in conceptual resources. Thus in some sense, he is equipped with possible states that distinguish possible answers to the question of weather in Topeka. Yet our judgment was that the relevant ascription is not correct. Perhaps this is because he is not appropriately equipped in some *other* sense; but I myself can't make this sense out. So I would prefer to press instead the thought that Hank's trouble is that he is not appropriately receptive to information which speaks the question. The question has not arisen for him, and he would have no interest in it if it did: that itself is sufficient to make an agent insufficiently receptive to information which speaks to the question.

It is sufficient, but let us add that it is not necessary. We can imagine agents who are keenly interested in questions for which they are insufficiently attuned to information about, and so who still may not count as having the relevant epistemic possibility beliefs. Whether something is attuned or receptive to a kind of information is a comparative matter, and judgments about this are sensitive to context. If we are anxiously awaiting learning the result of a cancer test whose result is in a sealed envelope, the salience of the test, whose states are far more sensitive to the relevant question than ours, might trump our claim to be receptive to such information. In that case, although our state of belief is compatible with John's having cancer and we have keen

[22] The notion of sensitivity I am trying to make precise is distinct from the notion of sensitivity developed by Nozick (1981) pursuant to an analysis of knowledge. On Nozick's use, one's state of belief is sensitive, not to questions, but to propositions: to be sensitive to a proposition in his sense is to be such that one would not believe it, were it not true. (But the two notions are related in at least the following way: if one is sensitive to a proposition in Nozick's sense, this is sufficient, though not necessary, for being sensitive to the question whether the proposition is true in my sense.)

interest in the question, we may prefer to say that we are really not sure whether John might have cancer. (See DeRose 1991.) Likewise, I may hesitate to say that the temperature in my room might be 70 degrees before checking my thermostat. The salience of a test, or device, or a relevant expert may change what counts as being appropriately sensitive to information which speaks to a question.

6. Modeling Question-Sensitivity

Turning from these intuitive considerations back to the modeling question, the plan is to run with the idea that belief is a question-sensitive state. We want to implement this idea formally, in a way that will yield a technical distinction between a proposition's merely being compatible with a state of belief and its being epistemically possible in the more robust sense.

To begin, we need a formal conception of what questions are. I will embrace the conception of questions which goes back to Hamblin (1958), according to which the meaning of a question is taken to be the set of its possible complete answers, where the complete answers to a question are taken to form a set of mutually exclusive propositions.[23] On this conception, a question determines a partition of logical space (or if it is based on some presupposition, a partition of a particular subregion of logical space). The partition gives all the alternative complete answers to the question. The true answer corresponds to the cell of the partition which contains the actual world. Any union of a set of more than one complete answer is an incomplete or partial answer.

Lewis has offered a parallel analysis of *subject matter*. A subject matter is partition of logical space, one that forms equivalence classes of worlds depending on whether the worlds yield the same verdict concerning the subject matter. It divides up logical space, but only so far as concerns those distinctions native to the subject matter. If, for instance, the subject matter is demography, then two worlds demographically alike in all respects will fall into the same cell within the partition determined by the subject matter, though they may differ in any other respect. We can say that a proposition is *about* a subject matter just in case the truth value of the proposition supervenes on the subject matter; equivalently, if the proposition is identical to some unions of cells from the partition. See Lewis (1988a, b) for further details and applications.

---

[23] In the semantics literature, Hamblin's idea—questions as partitions of a space of options—was developed into its best known form by Groenendijk and Stokhof (1984); see also Groenendijk and Stokhof (1997), Belnap and Steel (1976), Higginbotham (1993, 1996). It is perhaps the leading alternative to the most influential account of questions, namely Karttunen (1977). A central difference between the partition account and Karttunen's account is that on Karttunen's account, it is not assumed that the complete answers to a question must be mutually exclusive. As a result a question might have several true answers. This feature makes Karttunen's treatment of certain phenomena—for instance, so-called 'mention some' questions (e.g. *Where can I find a good sandwich?*) more elegant. The story I am about to tell can, I think, be adjusted to comport with a Karttunenian conception of questions, but I will not be able to go through the exercise here.

As Lewis notes, these two ways of thinking about a partition of logical space—as a question, or as a subject matter—are complementary and come to much the same. I will help myself to both ways of thinking of partitions of logical space. And, at the risk of mixing too many metaphors, I will help myself to a third: I will sometimes call a partition of logical space a *resolution* for logical space. We can think of a resolution as foregrounding some distinctions, bringing them into focus, and backgrounding others. Some propositions will be *visible* at a resolution—that is, about the corresponding subject matter—while the rest will be invisible and off-topic. The cells of a resolution are sets of possible worlds, but we may equally think of the cells themselves as 'coarse' possible worlds, worlds that settle some, but not all, questions. I restrict attention to finite resolutions.

The modeling proposal is then this: states of belief are resolution-sensitive. (Or question-sensitive, or subject matter-sensitive.) They are states which are partly relations to some way of resolving logical space, to some way of dividing up the alternatives. Relative to a resolution, a doxastic state will select a set of cells at that resolution as candidates for actuality.[24] Formally a doxastic state is, not simply a set of possible worlds, but rather a partial function taking a resolution to a subpartition of that resolution—that is, to a set of coarse possible worlds which is a subset of the resolution, what we may call the *view* of the agent at that resolution. A view gives the doxastically open 'coarse' possibilities for the agent at that resolution.

Equivalently, the proposal is that a belief state is a function from questions to answers. The answers may only be partial, eliminating some but not all alternatives. (Or indeed it may eliminate no alternatives. A question is one of its own partial answers—the least helpful one.) And the question reflected by a resolution needn't be one particular easy to express in language. Depending on how fine it is, it may be preferable to understand it as a capturing a family of topically related questions on which the doxastic state takes a stance—as capturing a relatively detailed project of inquiry. We can say a belief state is *sensitive* to a question just in case it is defined on the question (or is defined on a strictly finer question). We take it belief states are not, or at any rate need not be, sensitive to every possible question. A belief state is a partial function, so it may not be total. In realistic cases we may assume it is partial (indeed, defined only on finitely many questions). If a belief state is undefined on a question, say it is *insensitive* to the question. Let us assume that if a belief state is defined on a question, it is defined on any coarsening of the question (where Π' is a *coarsening* of Π just in case every cell of Π' is a union of cells of Π).

A view about a subject matter or question supplies the agent with *commitments* concerning that subject matter or question: these are the propositions true throughout the worlds left open by the agent's view.[25] Within the set of propositions which form the agent's commitments concerning a subject matter, we can distinguish the visible

---

[24] In the sense that a cell is the *actual cell* just in case it contains the actual world.

[25] By which I mean the worlds in the union of the agent's view.

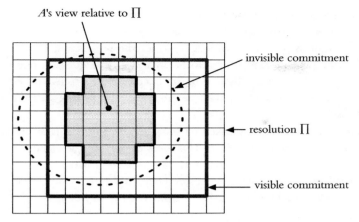

Fig. 10.3. Resolution-sensitive belief.

commitments from the invisible ones. The visible commitments are the ones about the subject matter, in the sense defined above; the invisible ones are the rest. Fig. 10.3 illustrates the distinction between the two sorts of commitments.

Say a proposition is *compatible* with an agent's view (with respect to a resolution his belief state is defined on) just in case it is true at one of the worlds left open by that view. Within the set of propositions which are compatible with an agent's view concerning a subject matter, we can distinguish the visible propositions from the invisible ones. I want to suggest that we use this distinction between ways that

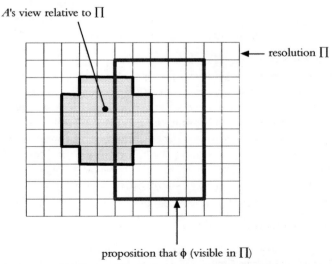

proposition that ϕ (visible in Π)

Fig. 10.4. $B_A^\Pi \Diamond \phi$: Resolution-sensitive model.

a proposition might be compatible with one's view to model what extra is required to believe that something is possible, in the epistemic sense we are after. To believe that a proposition is possible, or might be, is for the proposition to be compatible with one's view, and moreover for it to be an answer to a question one is sensitive to. (Equivalently, for it to be about a subject matter one is sensitive to; equivalently, for it to be visible at a resolution one is sensitive to.) This kind of state is depicted in Fig. 10.4 below.

We could think of this as a 'pixelated', low-resolution version of the first-order model of epistemic possibility belief. This gives us our fifth desideratum. Our suggestion is that Frank's head looks like this. Hank's state of belief, by contrast, is not defined on a question making the proposition that it's raining in Topeka visible—even though the resolutions his state of belief is defined on yield views entirely compatible with this proposition.

7. Fragmented Inquiry

The question-sensitive model enriches the classic possible worlds model in two ways. First, one has a view of things only relative to a resolution. Second, one has views relative to many distinct resolutions.[26]

In the latter respect, the resolution-sensitive model can be seen as a more articulated version of the idea of 'fragmented' or 'compartmentalized' belief (Lewis 1982; Stalnaker 1984). On the fragmentation upgrade to the classic possible worlds model, a belief state is still a set of possible worlds, but an agent's total doxastic state is modeled as a set of belief states. One has a belief only relative to a state within this set. Thus belief becomes a three-place relation between a person, a belief state, and a proposition. The key motivation for this upgrade is to avoid the closure of belief under believed material implication and under conjunction. Lewis illustrates the idea nicely:

> I used to think that Nassau Street ran roughly east–west; that the railroad nearby ran roughly north–south; and that the two were roughly parallel. . . . Now, what about the blatantly inconsistent conjunction of the three sentences? I say that it was not true according to my beliefs. My system of beliefs was broken into (overlapping) fragments. Different fragments came into action in different situations, and the whole system of beliefs never manifested itself all at once. The first and second sentences in the inconsistent triple belonged to—were true according to—different fragments; the third belonged to both. The inconsistent conjunction of all three did not belong to, was in no way implied by, and was not true according to, any one fragment. That is why it was not true according to my system of beliefs taken as a whole. Once the fragmentation was healed, straightaway my beliefs changed: now I think that Nassau Street and the railroad both run roughly northeast–southwest. (Lewis 1982: 436)

---

[26] Thus the two most recent figures are actually quite incomplete representations of our agent's state of belief: they depict only one resolution, and so just one of the plurality of inquiries that the agent presumably takes a view on.

The basic idea of fragmentation is, I think, right. That is why the resolution-sensitive model encodes a version of the idea: understand the 'fragments' to correspond to the various distinct views associated with the various distinct questions one's state of belief is defined on. If situations for action can be associated with different questions or subject matters, we can say that the aspect of an agent's state of belief relevant to explaining their behavior in a particular situation is determined by the question they associate with that situation—with the way in which they carve up the options. Since the views of an agent relative to one way of carving up the options may not line up with his views relative to another way of carving up the options, an agent may have inconsistent views—but without thereby counting as believing everything (as is the case on the classic possible worlds model when one has inconsistent beliefs).

In general, we want our views concerning our disparate inquiries to cohere and be compatible. When we see incompatibilities, we shift our views so that they cohere. Fragmentation occurs because it is a non-trivial matter to bring our inquiries together into a single state of mind.

Why is this a non-trivial matter? If we want, we can use the resolution-sensitive model to formulate an answer to this question. Wherever you have a finite space of alternatives of the sort presented by a resolution, you can give a measure of how much information, in bits, would be needed to reduce those alternatives to one. This is just the logarithm, to the base 2, of the number of alternatives. Call this number in bits the *information potential* of a resolution. Now although the idea of resolution-sensitivity does not come with any specific commitments about the detailed form by which the content of belief is represented, we might wish to construe it so that it does at least demand that the representational vehicle of belief at least have the complexity to encode, in bits, the information potentials of the various resolutions the agent is sensitive to. Resolutions impose what we could call an *encoding cost*. This is a way, albeit a highly abstract way, that this framework for representing belief imposes a constraint on a model of the mechanism of representation. Then we can say that fragmentation happens because bringing out disparate inquiries together into a single state of mind carries an encoding cost we cannot afford. It would require a state of mind at a higher resolution than we are capable of.

So the resolution-sensitive model has the advantage of the fragmentation model, *vis-à-vis* the closure properties that motivate fragmentation. One's commitments are not generally closed under conjunction, because we cannot speak of "one's commitments" full stop. Rather, various questions give rise to various views, which give rise to various packages of commitments. Relative to a particular question, an agent's commitments will be closed under conjunction; but not necessarily so, for commitments stemming from different questions.

And the resolution-sensitive model arguably has a further advantage. The problem of the closure of belief under conjunction, the problem eased by fragmentation, is not the most problematic closure property afflicting the classic possible worlds account. The heart of the problem of logical omniscience results from the closure of belief under truth-conditional entailment. The simple fragmentation model does nothing to ease this problem. But the resolution-sensitive model has resources here. Relative to a subject matter, one's commitments are indeed closed under entailment; but one's visible commitments are not. This affords us the option, then, of using the distinction between visible and invisible commitments to articulate a sense in which realistic agents are not logically omniscient.

Let me illustrate a simple application in this connection, using an example from Stalnaker (1984). Suppose the following is true:

(13) William III of England believed, in 1700, that England could avoid war with France.

The proposition that England could avoid war with France truth-conditionally entails the proposition that England could avoid nuclear war with France. Thus it appears that on the classic possible worlds model, it follows from (13) that

(14) William III of England believed, in 1700, that England could avoid nuclear war with France.

But this seems absurd. Perhaps in some sense William III believed something which committed him to the truth of a proposition concerning nuclear war, but the belief ascription (14) sounds wrong. We can offer the following explanation on the resolution-sensitive upgrade: William III's state of belief is not sensitive to questions concerning nuclear war. Equivalently, it is not sensitive to subject matters about nuclear war. The proposition that England could avoid nuclear war with France was nowhere among his visible commitments. The belief ascription suggests otherwise, and this is why it is defective.

8. Subject Matters in Language

Except, we need to explain in virtue of what the belief ascription 'suggests otherwise'. When we fragment belief, whether in the style of Lewis and Stalnaker or in the resolution-sensitive manner I have advocated, we incur a semantic obligation. Belief ascriptions appear to relate to individuals and propositions, but advocates of fragmentation are committed to the idea that the underlying reality involves a further relativity to a belief state (Lewis, Stalnaker) or to a question (Yalcin). To my knowledge, neither Lewis nor Stalnaker has attempted to pay this debt. But to fully vindicate our treatment of (14), we require a semantics for belief reports in the resolution-sensitive setting. In this section I mainly wish to acknowledge this debt, and make a small down payment.

There are various ways one might attempt to connect the technical model we have described to a semantics for belief reports, and in paular reports embedding possibility modals. Without being able to motivate it fully, let me briefly sketch one approach. It uses the resources of alternative semantics, an approach developed in connection with the semantics of questions and of focus (Hamblin (1973), Rooth (1985, 1992), among others).

An alternative semantics recursively defines two functions. First there is the usual *semantic value function* $[\![\ ]\!]$, which takes expressions to extensions (relative perhaps to some points of evaluation). Second there is what I will call the *alternative semantic value function* $[\ ]$, which maps an expression to a set of alternatives appropriate to the type of the expression. It is easiest to illustrate the concept with an example from the focus literature. If our sentence is:

(15) Mary likes *Sue*.

with 'Sue' focused, then the alternative semantic value of the sentence is a certain set of propositions:

$$\{\text{Likes}(\text{Mary}, y) : y \in E\}$$

(Where E is the domain of individuals). Intuitively, these propositions constitute the alternatives to Mary liking *Sue*. Roughly speaking, they are the various propositions which would be determined by the replacement of 'Sue' in the sentence with a name for another individual.[27] This set includes (e.g.) the proposition that Mary likes Alice and the proposition that Mary likes John, but it does not include (e.g.) the proposition that Sue likes Mary. Note this set also includes the proposition that Mary likes Sue: we assume the proposition determined by the ordinary semantic value of the sentence is an element of its alternative semantic value. The alternative semantic value of a sentence is compositionally determined from the alternative semantic values (and regular semantic values) of its components, but we remain agnostic on those details. (See Rooth (1985), Kratzer (1991a) for proposals and further references.)

The alternative semantic value of a sentence is a partition of logical space. So it is a resolution, or subject matter, or question. I wish to exploit this fact in the semantics of 'believes'. The alternative semantic value of the complement of 'believes' supplies a question. By the resolution-sensitive model, the subject of a belief ascription, together with the world of evaluation, determines a belief function—a function from questions to answers, or from subject matters to views. Semantically then, we can say that in evaluating belief ascriptions, we evaluate the agent's belief function relative to the question or subject matter equivalent to the alternative semantic value of the complement clause.

So consider an agent A, whose belief function is B relative to w. If Π is a partition this function is defined on, then $B(\Pi)$ delivers the agent's view relative to Π. On the model we have developed $B(\Pi)$ is a subpartition of Π—a set of cells from Π—but within the semantics, it will be simpler to use a function that directly gives the union of the relevant subpartition. So take it B is a function from a partition of logical space

---

[27] This is rough because an individual x does not need to have a name in the language in order for the proposition that Mary likes x to be among the alternatives to (15).

to a set of worlds, a set equivalent to a union of cells from that partition. Then we can give a possible worlds semantics for the belief operator as follows:

$$[\![B_A\phi]\!]^w = 1 \text{ iff } \forall w' \in B_A^w([\phi]) : [\![\phi]\!]^{w'} = 1$$

In respect of its universal quantification over worlds, this parallels the classic account going back to Hintikka (1962). Note this semantics encodes the requirement that the proposition expressed by ϕ be relevantly visible for the agent, because B_A^w must be defined as a question for which ϕ is an answer in order for the ascription to be true. The ascription (14) would fail this requirement, because William III's belief state is not defined on any partition that could correspond to [**England can avoid nuclear war with France**].

An immediate problem with this semantics is that it does not easily mesh with the first-order picture of epistemic possibility belief we have been defending. It is wedded to the notion that the belief operator must combine with something determining a condition on possible worlds, but we have seen reason to doubt that idea. Fortunately, it is not hard to adapt the semantics so that it expresses what we want. The following style of adjustment is motivated by Yalcin (2007) (see also MacFarlane (this volume); Kolodny and MacFarlane (2010)). Let semantic values be defined relative, not just to worlds, but also to *states of information s*, which we will take to be sets of possibilities (construing possibilities now as partition cells). For most sentences this new parameter will be idle, but it comes into action in connection with the semantics of attitudes and epistemic modals. Let epistemic possibility clauses existentially quantify over the possibilities open according to the information state parameter, as follows:

$$[\![\Diamond\phi]\!]^{w,s} = 1 \text{ iff } \exists w' \in s : [\![\phi]\!]^{w',s} = 1$$

Next, adjust the semantics for belief operators so that, in addition to effecting universal quantification over a certain view as above, these operators shift the value of the information parameter to that view. As follows:

$$[\![B_A\phi]\!]^{w,s} = 1 \text{ iff } \forall w' \in B_A^w([\phi]) : [\![\phi]\!]^{w',B_A^w([\phi])} = 1$$

Last, take it that the alternatives to $\Diamond\phi$ reduce to the alternatives to ϕ:

$$[\Diamond\phi] = [\phi]$$

With all this, it follows that:

$$[\![B_A\Diamond\phi]\!]^{w,s} = 1 \text{ iff } \exists w' \in B_A^w([\phi]) : [\![\phi]\!]^{w',B_A^w([\phi])} = 1$$

which is just what we want. Epistemic possibility beliefs come out as first-order states of mind, and one is in this state of mind only if one is sensitive to a question for which the relevant proposition is an answer.[28]

---

[28] It may strike some readers as questionable to assume that the alternatives to $\Diamond\phi$ reduce to the alternatives to ϕ. Perhaps the facts about focus, for instance, will teach us otherwise. That is certainly possible. But, first, theoretically we can take [ ] to be a *sui generis* function for use in modeling the question-sensitivity of thought, a function related, but not identical to, the alternative semantic values relevant to focus interpretation. Second, we really only need the weaker assumption that $\{w : [\![\phi]\!]^{w,\emptyset} = 1\} \in [\Diamond\phi]$ to get what

A second, rather different approach to giving resolution-sensitive semantics for belief reports would be to treat 'believes' as expressing a three-place relation between a person, a proposition, and a resolution, but where the latter component is not supplied by any secondary kind of semantic value. Since (focus structure aside) there is no obvious linguistic constituent corresponding to a resolution in an ordinary belief report, this view would take the value of resolution variable to be either indexically supplied by context, or (more plausibly) to be tacitly existentially quantified over. So the relevant logical form would be something like:

$$\exists \Pi : B(A, \Pi, p)$$

So-called 'hidden-indexical' analyses of belief reports give semantics in a structurally parallel fashion. Traditionally that approach has been motivated by a desire to reconcile a Russellian view of propositions with Fregean intuitions about belief reports. Belief is taken to be a three-place relation, but the third argument place is occupied by a mode of presentation (concept, Fregean sense), not a question or subject matter. There is an extensive literature on this approach, as it has played a non-trivial role both in debates about Frege's puzzle and in debates about the extent to which syntax constrains semantics. (For relevant discussion see Schiffer (1977, 1992, 2003), Crimmins and Perry (1989), Crimmins (1992), Ludlow (1996), Stanley (2000), Recanati (2002), Hall (2008).)

I see some room for the hidden-indexical and resolution-sensitive approaches to dovetail. There is a perfectly intelligible sense in which a resolution supplies a mode of presentation of a proposition in the possible worlds setting. A proposition is a rule for dividing maximally specific possibilities, but a resolution reflects what features of those possibilities are at issue, foregrounding the distinctions that matter and backgrounding the distinctions that do not. A single proposition may be 'presented' relative to various partitions of logical space, and these will highlight different features of the kinds of possibilities the proposition rules in and rules out.

But if you enjoy thinking of subject matters as senses, realize you can do this already on the alternative semantics given above. Second, I doubt resolutions alone would be of great use in solving Frege's puzzle, the chief motivation for classical hidden-indexical theories. (I myself would prefer a solution to Frege's puzzle that adverts to unstructured sets of certain finer-grained possibilities—trading in possible worlds for possible world, sequence-of-individual pairs—but that is another story. See Ninan (2008) and Cumming (2008) for views in the spirit of the approach I favor.) Third, if the relevant alternative semantic values are independently motivated by the semantics of questions and of focus, as I suspect, an alternative semantics is more elegant. It uses structure already needed elsewhere, and does not posit any tacit quantifiers whose scoping possibilities we would have to artificially restrict. Only if

we want. And indeed, it seems not implausible that one of the alternatives to 'Bob *might* be in his office' is 'Bob *is* in his office'.

an alternative semantics for belief reports cannot be made out should we turn, then, to a hidden-indexical analysis.

9. Credal Expressivism

I advertised a defense of nonfactualism about, not just pure claims of epistemic modality—*might* and *must* claims—but also graded claims of epistemic modality—of *probably* claims. But my theory-building so far has been obsessed with epistemic possibility.

Probability operators give rise to epistemic contradictions; they give rise to puzzles of agreement and disagreement; they give rise to the tensions of eavesdropping; and they bear straightforward logical relations to the epistemic modals *might* and *must*. It is also not at all hard to motivate the idea that believing something is probable is a first-order state of mind. Indeed, that is arguably the default view in the Bayesian literature. If you ask a Bayesian to tell you what sort of constraint a credence function C has to satisfy in order for an agent to count as believing a proposition p is probable, I wager she will say the constraint is this: $C(p) > .5$. (Or at any rate, she will say $C(p)$ must take some highish value.) This would be to say that to believe a proposition is probable is to be in a doxastic state of mind modelable by a probability space, one whose measure assigns that proposition a relevantly high value. And that is already to say that this state of mind is not fundamentally second-order in character. It is not a matter of one's credence in a proposition *about* one's credence; neither is it a matter of one's credence in some proposition about one's evidence, as the descriptivist proposals discussed above would most naturally recommend. It is simply a matter of how one is credally related to p.[29]

So the signs point to an expressivist, nonfactualist view about probability claims, at least if we have been right so far about epistemic possibility. How exactly to extend the resolution-sensitive model to make room for probabilities is a subtle matter, and I regret I must save detailed discussion for elsewhere.[30] For now at least, we can briefly mention some of the obvious moves to make, and some obvious contours of the view to be spelled out. Lay down probability measures over the resolutions the agent's state of mind is defined on, measures which place all the probability mass within the boundaries of the relevant views. Just as an agent's acceptance of an epistemic possibility claim is a function of whether a visible proposition is compatible with the relevant view of the agent, his acceptance of an epistemic probability claim will be a function of whether a visible proposition gets a high enough probability according to the probability measure of the relevant view. One expresses one's highish credence in a proposition when one says something is likely. But thereby, one does not say that one

---

[29] Thus the Bayesian picture itself needn't be tied to anything like a descriptivist account of probability talk, as is sometimes informally assumed (e.g. by Jeffrey (2004); see n. 3 above).

[30] See Yalcin (2007, 2010) for some relevant discussion, and Swanson (2006) for a related approach.

is in a state of high credence. One does not describe oneself, or one's evidence. One expresses a property of one's state of mind—not a proposition, but a condition on a probability space—with the intention of coordinating one's interlocutors' states on the satisfaction of that property. In a given context, there may be intelligible questions of rationality or advisability to be raised about such claims. But the question of truth as it arises for ordinary factual informational content does not arise here, any more than it would for epistemic possibility claims.

10. Nonfactual Parameters

In meta-ethics, the name 'expressivism' is sometimes attached to a cluster of theses to the effect that normative claims are fancy riffs on 'Boo!' and 'Yay!'—that they are essentially yelps in linguistic dress, primarily 'expressing' some non-contentful attitudes pro and con and having no compositional semantics. I find that view—perhaps better called *emotivism*—totally unbelievable, and I hope it is clear that the theory I have defended has hardly anything in common with it. On the contrary, the view I have defend is partly *motivated* by considerations from compositional semantics.

But some readers will find my position puzzling. I have said that epistemic possibility claims are nonfactual, and yet I offer a semantics for the epistemic possibility modal which looks like this:

$$\llbracket \Diamond \phi \rrbracket^{w,s} = 1 \ \text{ iff } \ \exists w' \in s : \llbracket \phi \rrbracket^{w',s} = 1$$

And this seems awfully like truth-conditional semantics. Isn't '1' just another name for The True, after all? Am I then not really a factualist, albeit one with some overblown expressivist rhetoric? Or worse—since the recursive definition of '1' above involves relativity to a state of information—am I not really a *relativist* about epistemic modality?

The distinction between relativism and expressivism has been questioned (Field 2009) but there is, I think, a way to make it out. The crucial point is to recognize a distinction between a view about compositional semantic value and a view about informational content. The notion of *truth at a point of evaluation* is a technical notion from semantics. We use it to articulate our tacit semantic competence, a competence usefully characterized, at the level of sentences, by an ability to effect a distinction between a certain space of points. The structure of these points depends on the contingencies of human language—for instance, on what operators the language contains. Separate from this technical notion of truth is the notion of truth as it applies to propositions, or items of informational content. Insofar as there is a concept of truth relevant to whether a claim or state of mind is factual in character, it is the latter notion we should be concerned with.

I said above that I follow Lewis (1980) in taking it that where semantics meets pragmatics, we need not assume that the semantic value of a declarative sentence is its informational content. We need only assume that the informational content of a sentence is recoverable from its semantic value, together with features of context and whatever standing pragmatic knowledge there may be. Now on one familiar way of interpreting the two-dimensional semantics of Kaplan (1989), there is a simple recipe for recovering the informational content of a sentence from its semantic value. If the semantics of ϕ is the two-dimensional intension $[\![\phi]\!]^{c,i}$, where c is a context and i is index (a tuple of features of context shiftable by operators in the language), then (on one view) the informational content of the sentence in context is:

$$\lambda c. [\![\phi]\!]^{c,i_c} = 1$$

(where i_c is the index determined by the context). This is the *diagonal proposition* determined by the sentence. This notion of informational content is naturally paired with a notion of truth distinct from, but definable in terms of, truth at a point of evaluation:

$$\phi \text{ is } \textit{true at a context } c \text{ iff } [\![\phi]\!]^{c,i_c} = 1$$

Whether a sentence is *true at a context* tracks exactly when the diagonal proposition it expresses is true. Diagonal content is a kind of factual content: it discriminates between metaphysically possible ways a context might be.

Now the point to be clear about is that if one holds that the diagonal corresponds to the informational content of the sentence, then one must already acknowledge a gap between truth at a point of evaluation, the notion appropriate to compositional semantics, and the notion of truth appropriate to content. And indeed, it should be clear that the same is true if one holds that the informational content of the sentence is the horizontal proposition of the sentence in context. Thus the idea that there is a gap between truth at a point of evaluation and truth as it applies to the objects playing the role of content is not a new idea. It is built into the usual ways of interpreting Kaplan's framework.

Expressivism about a domain of discourse is sometimes characterized as the view that the claims of the discourse are not truth-apt. But once we recognize this distinction between two notions of truth—the notion of truth belonging to formal semantics and the notion of truth belonging to the theory of content, or as we might have it in a two-dimensional setting, *truth at a point of evaluation* and *truth at a context*—the expressivist position can be more subtle than this. The expressivist can give a recursive definition of truth at a point of evaluation in the usual way for his discourse, thereby preserving compositionality, but he can reject the demand to give truth conditions in the more robust sense, the one appropriate to ordinary factual informational content. To illustrate more precisely: if our starting point is two-dimensional semantics, and the informational content of a sentence is taken to characteristically be its diagonal, what the expressivist can deny is that the notion of truth at a context is well-defined for the sentences of his target discourse. This is to say that the claims of the discourse do not have informational content—or at least, that they do not have it in the ordinary, factual sense, the sense which a well-defined diagonal makes out.

Bringing this to bear on the above semantics for epistemic possibility, the claim would be that according to the expressivist,

$$\lambda c.[\![\lozenge\phi]\!]^{c,w_c,s_c} = 1$$

is not well-defined, because there is no such thing as s_c—no such thing as 'the information state of the context'. While of course there presumably are information states in the context (the states of the interlocutors, for instance), we stipulate as theorists that the role of this parameter is not to represent any of them. Rather, it is a *nonfactual parameter*. Unlike the world coordinate or time coordinate (if such there be), this parameter does not correspond to any possible feature of context. There is no 'initializing' it; rather, what is communicated is variable with respect to its value. The expressivist can make this move, compatible with telling a story that makes communication employing the claims of the discourse intelligible. As we have said: relative to context, an epistemic possibility claim determines a condition, or property, on states of information—on states of mind. It is the satisfaction of this property that the speaker aims to coordinate his listeners on. The speaker thereby expresses a feature of his state of mind, and does so without describing himself, or the world.

This approach is, I think, relevantly analogous to that of Gibbard (1986; 1990; 2003; see especially 2003: ch. 6). Gibbard has his own nonfactual parameter—a parameter for a system of norms, or in more recent work, for a maximally complete plan for action, or *hyperplan*. One's state of belief is plan-laden, representable as a set of possibility-hyperplan pairs. Normative sentences serve chiefly to divide the space of hyperplans. Crucially for Gibbard, when hyperplans appear in the formal semantics, they are not taken to correspond to any feature of context. The truth of a normative claim is not, for instance, a matter of what norms the participants in the conversation accept. If it were, such claims would then merely describe the norms endorsed by the interlocutors, and that is not the idea. Rather, the parameter is nonfactual. The question of which hyperplan is the *right* one to use in evaluating a sentence is not one determined by the facts of the context. Rather, on Gibbard's view, it is a practical question, a question about what to do. Gibbard uses hyperplan parameter to say what it is we are up to in communicating with normative sentences:

Plan-laden conviction, though, pertains not to the diagonal of the character matrix, but to the diagonal with a hyperplan dimension added. It is given by a diagonal plane in the extended character matrix. We can talk now of the *extended import* of a thought or other concept. When I accept what someone says on his authority, it is the extended import of what he says that gets communicated; I come to accept it. (Gibbard 2003: 132)

On Gibbard's picture, purely factual content (purely factual import) corresponds essentially to diagonal content of the sort already described. Even if, for the sake of uniformity, all content is represented in terms of sets of possibility-hyperplan pairs—*extended imports* in Gibbard's terminology—we can distinguish factual from nonfactual content, for content which is purely factual does not vary with the choice of hyperplan. That means there is a perfectly interesting, factually-oriented, well-defined notion of *truth at a context* applicable to all factual discourse in Gibbard's setting—basically, the Kaplanian notion.[31] This is just as we would want, I presume.

But we have no such definition available for normative thought and talk, if Gibbard is right. If the extension of a sentence varies with choice of hyperplan, it is normative. Since context does not determine a choice of hyperplan, we cannot define a diagonal from the semantics of the sentence without fundamentally distorting the import of the claim. Instead of the factualist truth conditions that a diagonal would supply, what we have is an object—a non-trivial extended import—which is variable with respect to hyperplan. It is this object Gibbard uses to say what agents engaging in normative talk are communicating and coordinating on.

Expressivists have felt cornered on the question of truth. If they deny that normative discourse is truth-apt, they fall prey to the Frege-Geach problem; if they affirm it is, it becomes hard to see how their from that of the factualist. If they go minimalist about truth, their position applies to all of language, not just a fragment of it. I am suggesting that the expressivist—or one attractive brand of expressivist, anyway—can say what is distinctive about his position by exploiting the independently motivated distinction between compositional semantic value and informational content. And I have suggested that one concrete way of doing this begins from the perspective of two-dimensional semantics. Like the factualist, the expressivist defines a notion of truth at a point of evaluation. Thereby he vindicates the undeniable compositionality of natural language. But unlike the factualist, he rejects the view that the sentences of the relevant discourse are apt for truth in a richer sense, the sense of truth which applies to factual information content—the kind of content whose main business is to rule out ways things might be.

References

Beaver, David (2001). *Presupposition and Assertion in Dynamic Semantics*. Studies in Logic, Language and Information. CSLI Publications.

Belnap, Nuel, and Steel, Thomas (1976). *The Logic of Questions and Answers* (New Haven: Yale University Press).

Crimmins, Mark (1992). *Talk about Beliefs* (Cambridge, Mass.: MIT Press).

——and Perry, John (1989). "The prince and the phone booth: Reporting puzzling beliefs", *Journal of Philosophy* 86(12): 685–711.

Cumming, Samuel (2008). "Variabilism", *Philosophical Review* 117(4): 525–54.

DeRose, Keith (1991). "Epistemic possibilities", *Philosophical Review* 100(4): 581–605.

Dretske, Fred (1981). *Knowledge and the Flow of Information* (Cambridge, Mass.: MIT Press).

Egan, Andy (2007). "Epistemic modals, relativism and assertion", *Philosophical Studies* 133(1): 1–22.

---

[31] One precise version of such a definition: ϕ is *true at c* just in case $[\![\phi]\!]^{c,i_c,h} = 1$, for any h (where h is a variable over hyperplans).

—— Hawthorne, John, and Weatherson, Brian (2005). "Epistemic modals in context", in G. Preyer and G. Peter (eds.) *Contextualism in Philosophy* (Oxford: Oxford University Press) 131–68.

Evans, Gareth (1983). *The Varieties of Reference* (Oxford: Oxford University Press).

Field, Hartry (2009). "Epistemology without metaphysics", *Philosophical Studies* 143(2): 249–90.

von Fintel, Kai, and Gillies, Anthony S. (2008). "CIA leaks", *Philosophical Review* 117(1): 77–98.

Gibbard, Allan (1986). "An expressivistic theory of normative discourse", *Ethics* 96(3):472–85.

—— (1990). *Wise Choices, Apt Feelings* (Cambridge, Mass.: Harvard University Press).

—— (2003). *Thinking How to Live* (Cambridge, Mass.: Harvard University Press).

Gillies, Anthony (2004). "Epistemic conditionals and conditional epistemics", *Noûs* 38: 585–616.

Groenendijk, Jeroen, and Stokhof, Martin, (1984). *Studies on the Semantics of Questions and the Pragmatics of Answers*. PhD thesis, University of Amsterdam.

—— —— (1997). "Questions", in J. van Benthem and A. ter Meulen (eds.), *Handbook of Logic and Language* (Amsterdam: Elsevier Science), 1055–124.

Hall, Alison (2008). "Free enrichment or hidden indexicals", *Mind and Language* 23(4): 426–56.

Hamblin, Charles L. (1958). "Questions", *Australasian Journal of Philosophy* 36(3): 159–68.

—— (1973). "Questions in Montague English", *Foundations of Language* 10(1): 41–53.

Heim, Irene (1992). "Presupposition projection and the semantics of attitude verbs", *Journal of Semantics* 9: 183–221.

Higginbotham, James (1993). "Interrogatives", in K. Hale and S. J. Keyser (eds.), *The View from Building 20* (Cambridge, Mass.: MIT Press), 195–227.

—— (1996). "The semantics of questions", *The Handbook of Contemporary Semantic Theory* (Oxford: Blackwell), 361–83.

Hintikka, Jaakko (1962). *Knowledge and Belief: An Introduction to the Logic of The Two Notions* (Ithaca, NY: Cornell University Press).

Jeffrey, Richard (2004). *Subjective Probability: The Real Thing* (Cambridge: Cambridge University Press).

Kaplan, David (1989). "Demonstratives", in J. Almog, J. Perry, and H. Wettstein (eds.), *Themes from Kaplan* (Oxford: Oxford University Press), 481–563.

Karttunen, Lauri (1977). "Syntax and semantics of questions", *Linguistics and Philosophy* 1: 607–53.

Kolodny, Niko, and MacFarlane, John (2010). "Ifs and oughts", *Journal of Philosophy* 107(3): 115–43.

Kratzer, Angelika (1977). "What 'must' and 'can' must and can mean", *Linguistics and Philosophy* 1: 337–55.

—— (1981). "The notional category of modality", in H.-J. Eikmeyer and H. Rieser (eds.), *Words, Worlds, and Contexts: New Approaches to Word Semantics* (Berlin: de Gruyter), 38–74.

—— (1991a). "The representation of focus", *Semantics: An International Handbook of Contemporary Research* (Berlin: de Gruyter), 825–34.

—— (1991b). "Modality", in A. von Stechow and D. Wunderlich (eds.), *Semantics: An International Handbook of Contemporary Research* (Berlin: de Gruyter), 639–50.

Lewis, David K. (1979). "Scorekeeping in a language game", *Journal of Philosophical Logic* 8: 339–59.

Lewis, David K. (1980). "Index, context, and content", in S. Kanger and S. Ohman (eds.), *Philosophy and Grammar* (Reidel), 79–100.

—— (1982). "Logic for equivocators", *Noûs* 16(3): 431–41.

—— (1988a). "Statements partly about observation", *Philosophical Papers* 17(1): 1–31.

—— (1988b). "Relevant implication", *Theoria* 54: 161–74.

Ludlow, Peter (1996). "The adicity of 'believes' and the hidden indexical theory", *Analysis* 56 (2): 97–101.

MacFarlane, John (this volume) "Epistemic modals are assessment-sensitive", Ch. 5.

Moore, G. E. (1962). *Commonplace Book 1919–1953* (London: George Allen, and Unwin).

Ninan, Dilip (2008). *Imagination, Content, and the Self*, PhD thesis, Massachusetts Institute of Technology.

Nozick, Robert (1981). *Philosophical Explanations* (Cambridge, Mass.: Belknap Press).

Price, Huw (1983). "Does 'probably' modify sense?", *Australasian Journal of Philosophy* 61(4): 396–408.

Recanati, Francois (2002). "Unarticulated constituents", *Linguistics and Philosophy* 25(3): 299–345.

Rooth, Mats E. (1985). *Association with focus* (Cambridge, Mass.: University of Massachusetts).

—— (1992). "A theory of focus interpretation", *Natural language semantics* 1(1):75–116.

Schiffer, Stephen (1977). "Naming and knowing", *Midwest Studies in Philosophy* 2(1): 28–41.

—— (1992). "Belief ascription", *Journal of Philosophy* 89(10): 499–521.

—— (2003). *The Things We Mean* (Oxford: Oxford University Press).

Stalnaker, Robert (1984). *Inquiry* (Cambridge: MIT Press).

—— (1970). "Pragmatics", *Synthese* 22: 272–89.

Stanley, Jason (2000). "Context and logical form", *Linguistics and Philosophy* 23(4): 391–434.

—— (2005). "Fallibilism and concessive knowledge attributions", *Analysis* 65(2): 126–31.

Swanson, Eric (2006). *Interactions with Context*, PhD thesis, Massachusetts Institute of Technology.

Veltman, Frank (1985). *Logics for Conditionals*, PhD thesis, University of Amsterdam.

—— (1986). "Data semantics and the pragmatics of indicative conditionals", in E. Traugott, A. ter Meulen, J. Reilly, and C. Ferguson (eds.), *On Conditionals* (Cambridge: Cambridge University Press), 147–68.

—— (1996). "Defaults in update semantics", *Journal of Philosophical Logic* 25(3): 221–61.

Yalcin, Seth (2007). "Epistemic modals", *Mind* 116 (464): 983–1026.

—— (2008). *Modality and Inquiry*, PhD thesis, Massachusetts Institute of Technology.

—— (2010). "Probability operators", *Philosophy Compass* 5(11): 916–37.

—— and Joshua Knobe. (2010). "Fat Tony Might Be Dead. An Experimental Note On Epistemic Modals." Unpublished, http://www.semanticsarchive.net/Archive/TdiZjA3N/

Index